CliffsNotes® AP
Environmental Science

CliffsNotes® AP

Environmental Science

by
Jennifer L. Sutton, M.S., and Kevin Bryan, M.S.

Contributing Authors

James R. Centorino, M.S.

Garth Sundem, M.S.

Houghton Mifflin Harcourt
Boston   New York

About the Authors

Jennifer L. Sutton holds a Master of Science degree in Environmental Studies. She currently teaches AP Environmental Science and biology, and has previously taught chemistry, earth science, ecology, and evolution. Kevin Bryan has been a reader and consultant for AP Environmental Science and the College Board since 2002. He holds advanced degrees in biochemistry, science, business admisinistration, and German. He has been working in scientific research and education since 1994 and is currently teaching AP Environmental Science, Chemistry, and Biology.

Editorial

Acquisitions Editor: Greg Tubach
Project Editor: Elizabeth Kuball
Copy Editor: Elizabeth Kuball
Technical Editors: Scott McDougall, Scott Ryan

Composition

Proofreaders: John Greenough, Betty Kish
Wiley Publishing, Inc. Composition Services

CliffsNotes® AP Environmental Science

Copyright © 2011 Kevin Bryan and Jennifer L. Sutton

Library of Congress Control Number: 2011928442
ISBN: 978-0-470-88975-6 (pbk)
ISBN: 978-1-118-09610-9 (ebk)

Printed in the United States of America
DOH 10 9 8 7   4500705327

For information about permission to reproduce selections from this book, write to trade.permissions@hmhco.com or to Permissions, Houghton Mifflin Harcourt Publishing Company, 3 Park Avenue, 19th Floor, New York, New York 10016.

www.hmhco.com

Table of Contents

Introduction 1
  Format and Scoring 1
  Underlying Themes and Topics 2
    Themes 2
    Topics. 2
  Multiple-Choice Questions 3
    Question Types 3
    Strategies 7
  Free-Response Questions 8
    Question Types. 9
    Strategies 10

PART I: SUBJECT REVIEWS

Chapter 1: Earth's Systems and Resources. 15
  Earth 15
    Geologic Time Scale 15
    Earth's Structure 15
    Plate Tectonics. 17
    Earthquakes. 20
    Volcanoes 21
    Solar Radiation, Intensity, and Seasons. 23
  The Atmosphere 24
    Composition 24
    The Structure of the Atmosphere. 25
    Weather and Climate 26
    Atmospheric Circulations 26
    El Niño and La Niña 28
  Water Dynamics. 28
    Water Cycle. 28
    Freshwater. 29
    Oceans/Saltwater. 30
    Ocean Currents. 30
  Soil Dynamics. 30
    Rock Cycle. 31
    Soil Formation 31
    Soil Profile 32
    Soil Properties 33
  Practice. 35
  Answers 37

Chapter 2: The Living World 39
  Ecosystem Structure. 39
    Biological Populations and Communities. 39
    Ecological Niches. 39
    Species Interactions. 39
    Biomes: Terrestrial and Aquatic 41
  Energy Flow 43
    Photosynthesis and Cellular Respiration. .43
    Food Webs and Trophic Levels 43
    Ecological Pyramids. 45

Ecosystem Diversity 46
   Biodiversity 46
   Evolution and Natural Selection 47
   Ecosystem Services 49
   Biodiversity Loss, Conservation, and Extinction 49
Natural Ecosystem Changes 51
   Climate Shift 51
   Species Movement 51
   Ecological Succession 51
Biogeochemical Cycles. 52
   Carbon Cycle. 52
   Oxygen Cycle 53
   Nitrogen Cycle 55
   Phosphorus Cycle 56
   Sulfur Cycle 57
Practice 59
Answers 61

Chapter 3: Population 63
Population Biology Concepts. 63
   Population Ecology 63
   Carrying Capacity 64
   Reproductive Strategies. 65
   Survivorship. 65
Human Population. 66
   Human Population Dynamics. 66
   Population Size 70
   Impacts of Population 73
Practice 76
Answers 79

Chapter 4: Land and Water Use 81
Agriculture 81
   Feeding a Growing Population. 81
   Genetic Engineering and Crop Production 82
   Crop Diversity 83
   Deforestation. 83
   Irrigation 84
   Sustainable Agriculture 84
   Controlling Pests 85
   Livestock and Feedlots 86
Forestry. 86
   Tree Plantations. 86
   Old Growth, Secondary Growth 86
   Forest Fires. 87
   Forest Management 87
   National Forests. 87
Rangelands. 87
   Overgrazing 88
   Deforestation 88
   Desertification 88
   Rangeland Management 89
Other Land Use 89
   Urban Land Development 89
   Transportation Infrastructure. 90
   U.S. Federal Highway System. 91

Canals and Channels 91
Public and Federal Lands 91
Management. 91
Wetlands 92
Land Conservation Options 92
Sustainable Land-Use Strategies. .93
Mining 93
Mineral Formation. 94
Mineral Extraction. 94
Mining Oceans 95
Mining Reclamation 95
Mining Laws and Treaties. 95
Fishing 96
Fishing Techniques 96
Overfishing 96
Coral reefs 96
Aquaculture. 97
Fishing Management 97
Global Economies 98
Globalization 98
World Bank 99
Tragedy of the Commons. 99
Global Economics Laws and Treaties 99
Practice. 100
Answers 102

Chapter 5: Energy Resources and Consumption. 103
Energy Concepts 103
APES Math Problems 106
Laws of Thermodynamics. 109
Energy Consumption. 110
The History of Energy Consumption 110
Present Global Energy Use. 112
Future Energy Use 112
Fossil Fuel Resources and Use. 113
Coal, Oil, and Natural Gas 113
World Reserves and Global Demand. 117
Environmental Advantages and Disadvantages of Fossil Fuels 117
Nuclear Energy 119
Nuclear Power. 119
Nuclear Fission Process. 120
Nuclear Fuel 120
Nuclear Reactors 121
Nuclear reactor types 122
Safety Issues 123
Radiation and Human Health. .123
Understanding Half-Life 124
Hydroelectric Power. 125
Case Study: The Colorado River 126
Case Study: Salmon 127
Energy Conservation 127
Energy Efficiency. 128
Energy Star 128
Corporate Average Fuel Economy 129
Hybrid Electric Vehicles. 130
Mass Transit 132

Renewable Energy 133
   Solar 133
   Hydrogen Fuel Cells 135
   Biomass 136
   Wind 137
   Geothermal 137
   Ocean and Tidal Waves 138
Practice 140
Answers 142

Chapter 6: Pollution 145
Pollution Types 145
   Air Pollution 145
   Noise Pollution 151
   Light Pollution 151
   Genetic Pollution 152
   Water Pollution 152
   Solid Waste 154
Impacts on the Environment and Human Health 156
   Hazards to Human Health 156
   Acute and Chronic Effects 157
   Hazardous Chemicals in the Environment 161
Economic Impacts 162
   Cost-Benefit Analysis 162
   Marginal Costs 163
   Cost of Pollution Control 164
   Sustainability 164
Practice 165
Answers 168

Chapter 7: Global Change 169
Stratospheric Ozone 169
   Formation of Stratospheric Ozone 169
   Ultraviolet (UV) Radiation 170
   Ozone Depletion 171
   Relevant Laws and Treaties 175
Global Warming and Climate Change 176
   Impacts and Consequences of Global Warming 179
   Reducing Climate Change 182
   Laws and Treaties 182
Loss of Biodiversity 183
   Massive Extinctions from Human Activity 183
   Issues Related to Loss of Biodiversity 183
   Maintenance through Conservation 186
Practice 188
Answers 190

PART II: PRACTICE EXAMS

Chapter 8: Practice Exam 1 193
Answer Sheet 193
   Section I 193
   Section II 194
Section I: Multiple-Choice Questions 199
Section II: Free-Response Questions 213

Answer Key 215
   Section I: Multiple-Choice Questions 215
Answer Explanations 216
   Section I: Multiple-Choice Questions 216
   Section II: Free-Response Explanations 224

Chapter 9: Practice Exam 2 . . . . **229**
Answer Sheet 229
   Section I 229
   Section II 230
Section I: Multiple-Choice Questions 235
Section II: Free-Response Questions 247
Answer Key 249
   Section I: Multiple-Choice Questions 249
Answer Explanations 250
   Section I: Multiple-Choice Questions 250
   Section II: Free-Response Explanations 256

Chapter 10: Practice Exam 3 . . . . **261**

Answer Sheet
   Section I 261
   Section II 262
Section I: Multiple-Choice Questions 267
Section II: Free-Response Questions 281
Answer Key 283
   Section I: Multiple-Choice Questions 283
Answer Explanations 284
   Section I: Multiple-Choice Questions 284
   Section II: Free-Response Questions 290

PART III: RESOURCES

Appendix A: Glossary **297**

Appendix B: Case Studies **315**
Species 315
   Loss of Amphibians 315
   Zebra Mussels: Invasive Species 315
   Extinction of the Passenger Pigeon 316
   DDT 316
   Kudzu Invasion 316
   Reintroduction of Gray Wolves to Yellowstone National Park 317
   California Condor 317
Water 318
   Lake Erie Waste Dumping 318
   St. James Bay Hydroelectric Dams 318
   Gulf of Mexico's Dead Zone 318
   Aral Sea 319
   Three Gorges Dam 319
   California Water Project 320
Human 320
   China: One-Child Policy 320
   Easter Island: Tragedy of the Commons 321
   Biosphere 2 321

    Events 322
        Bhopal Chemical Disaster 322
        Chernobyl Nuclear Disaster 322
        Cuyahoga River Fire 322
        Deepwater Horizon Oil Spill 322
        Exxon Valdez Oil Spill 323
        Fukushimi Daiichi Nuclear Disaster 323
        Hurricane Katrina 323
        Kissimmee River Dredging 324
        London Fog Air Pollution 324
        Love Canal Waste Dumping 324
        Santa Barbara Oil Spill 325
        Three-Mile Island Nuclear Disaster 325

Appendix C: Labs 327
    Common Labs 327
        Acid Deposition 327
        Air Quality 327
        Biodiesel from Vegetable Oil 327
        Biodiversity of Invertebrates (Shannon-Wiener Diversity Index) 328
        Composting with Worms 328
        Coriolis Effect 328
        Eco-Columns 329
        Ecological Footprint 330
        Ecosystem Ecology 331
        Energy Audits 331
        Field Studies 331
        Food Webs 331
        Mining 331
        LD_{50}: Bioassay 331
        Oil Spill Cleanup 331
        Predator-Prey Simulation 332
        Productivity 332
        Population Growth in *Lemna minor* 332
        Porosity 332
        Salinization 332
        Soil Analysis Labs 332
        Solar Cooker/Solar House 334
        Specific Heat: Solar Absorption 334
        Tragedy of the Commons 334
        Transects 334
        Water Quality 334
        Weathering 335
    Analysis of Past Exams 336
        Free-Response Questions 336
        Experimental-Design Questions 336

Appendix D: Laws and Treaties 337
    United States Federal Laws 337
    International Treaties 340

Study Guide Checklist

❑ 1. Read AP Environmental Science information available on the College Board website (www.collegeboard.com).

❑ 2. Read the Introduction and familiarize yourself with the test format and questions types. Make sure that you understand the different types of multiple-choice questions.

❑ 3. Review the scoring scales on page 1 for multiple-choice and free-response questions.

❑ 4. Read the chapters of this book to refresh your understanding of the material covered.

❑ 5. Practice multiple-choice questions at the end of each chapter, and review the answers and explanations to determine areas in which you need improvement.

❑ 6. Review the appendices.

❑ 7. Take each Practice Test, strictly observing the time allotments.

❑ 8. Review the answer explanations for each test. Analyze your strengths and weaknesses after each test. Before you proceed to the next Practice Test, go back over any information you missed by rereading specific chapter material as necessary.

Introduction

The study of environmental science is increasing in popularity and global relevance. The Advanced Placement Environmental Science examination focuses on your ability to identify and analyze environmental issues and scientific concepts within the natural world. The exam requires you to recall and utilize basic facts and concepts to answer and critically evaluate problems related to physical geography, ecosystems, cultural geography, land and water use, energy, pollution, and global change. These can be natural and/or human-made problems. The risks connected to these problems also are studied.

The AP Environmental Science exam is offered by the nonprofit College Board and administered by the Educational Testing Service (ETS) to those students interested in testing in environmental and natural sciences. The exam is recognized by over 3,800 colleges and universities (approximately 90 percent). Students who score successfully on the exam may qualify to receive college credit for a comparable college-level course.

Format and Scoring

The following table outlines the format of the AP Environmental Science exam.

Section	Number of Questions	Time
Section I: Multiple choice	100 questions	90 minutes
Section II: Free response	4 essays	90 minutes

In the multiple-choice section, you earn one point for each correct answer. In 2011, a quarter-point deduction from the total for each wrong answer was discontinued. Because there is no longer a penalty, it is in your best interest to take an educated guess. Unanswered questions do not count for or against your score. The multiple-choice section is 60 percent of your total exam score.

In the free-response essay section, each of the four essays is scored holistically, and scores range from zero to ten (or zero for a blank paper). These scores are then calculated to equal 40 percent of the total exam score. The essays may have different point values depending upon their complexity, but all essays carry the same weight value. This means that each will count for one-quarter of your score in the free-response section of the test.

The free-response questions are scored by college professors and highly qualified high school AP teachers using standards developed by a committee of the College Board. Students are notified by mail of their test results. In addition, students, teachers, and administrators can see the scores online at the College Board website (www. collegeboard.com). Each year the free-response questions, scoring guides, student samples, and other information are posted online.

The multiple-choice section score is added to the free-response section score to produce a composite total score. This composite is translated into a five-point scale that is reported to the student, the student's high school, and any college designated by the student.

The College Board scores the exam on a five-point scale:

   5 = Extremely well qualified

   4 = Well qualified

   3 = Qualified

   2 = Possibly qualified

   1 = No recommendation

A score of 3 is considered passing, but most colleges and universities require a score of 4 or 5 to receive credit or placement. A score of 1 or 2 is not accepted for credit. On previous exams, the mean score was approximately 2.6 and 50 percent of the students scored 3 or higher. Colleges and universities establish their own policies regarding what scores qualify. Updated scoring information is available through the College Board at http://collegesearch.collegeboard.com/search/index.jsp. Enter the name of the university in the College QuickFinder section and go to the Tests section when you get to the profile. Here you can see what scores are acceptable for placement, credit, or both. Because colleges and universities frequently change their policies and regulations, it is always a good idea to double-check with colleges directly when in doubt about acceptable credits.

Underlying Themes and Topics

Themes

The study of environmental science incorporates many aspects of both physical and biological sciences and focuses on how humans and the environment are intertwined and impact one another. In the AP Environmental Science course, the basic principles of science underscore the material.

Earth is a system with many interconnected components, both living and nonliving. Because humans are part of this system, people can alter and impact the Earth's cycles and processes. Both population growth and technological advancements have increased the rate at which humans have modified the natural environment. The implications of human actions not only have a physical effect but also impact social, economic, and political structures. The management and responsible use of the Earth's resources is, therefore, essential to the continued success of humans and the planet.

Topics

The College Board Development Committee has established seven major topics that provide the content standards for the AP Environmental Science exam. Each topic is further divided to provide the basics to understanding the course material.

Topics on the AP Environmental Science Exam		
Topic	**Description**	**Portion of Exam**
Earth Systems and Resources	Includes key geologic processes such as plate tectonics, the rock cycle, and soil formation. Also includes seasons, atmospheric properties, weather and climate, solar radiation, the relationship between the atmosphere and oceans, freshwater, and saltwater.	10% to 15%
The Living World	Involves ecosystem interactions and structure in both aquatic and terrestrial biomes, including components of populations and communities, flow of energy and nutrients, natural selection and evolution, and changes in ecosystems.	10% to 15%
Population	Focuses on components of a population including reproductive strategies, interactions, characteristics, growth, transition, and carrying capacity. The human population is also addressed and includes implications of population growth and sustainable practices.	10% to 15%
Land and Water Use	Addresses human use of land and water resources, including agriculture, forestry, development, fishing, and mineral resource use. Conversation and preservation are also included.	10% to 15%

Topic	Description	Portion of Exam
Energy Resources and Consumption	Involves assessments of nonrenewable fossil fuels as energy sources and alternative and renewable sources, such as nuclear, hydropower, solar, wind, biomass, hydrogen, tidal, and geothermal sources. Human use and approaches to efficiency are also addressed.	10% to 15%
Pollution	Addresses types of pollution, including air, soil, water, and noise pollution, as well as the impacts on humans physically and economically.	25% to 30%
Global Change	Includes issues relating to the earth as a whole, such as atmospheric change, climate alteration, and biodiversity loss.	10% to 15%

Multiple-Choice Questions

The multiple-choice questions cover a broad range of topics while considering a variety of themes and scientific constructs. To be successful on the exam, you need to have a solid depth and breadth of knowledge about these important areas of study in environmental science. This section provides you with valuable information detailing the underlying themes and topics relevant to the basics of the AP Environmental Science exam. The information provided will also help you to identify and analyze areas that are foundational to your success on the exam.

We recommend that you budget your time wisely to be sure that you have enough time to finish all sections. Because you have 90 minutes to complete the multiple-choice section, you should spend less than 1 minute per question to answer 100 questions. Multiple-choice scores are based on the number of questions answered correctly and no points are deducted for incorrect answers. Eliminate as many incorrect answer choices as possible and make an educated guess from the remaining answer choices. Multiple-choice questions are scored by computer soon after the exam in mid-May.

Question Types

Multiple-choice questions are designed to test your knowledge and understanding of environmental science. Questions cover the topics noted in the preceding section and require you to recall basic facts and major concepts. They may appear as different question types:

- Matching
- Problem solving
- Multiple-multiple choice
- Cause and effect
- Tables, graphs, and charts
- Basic math

We cover each of these question types in the following sections.

Matching

Matching problems require you to match a word with a statement. Match the correct word from the five-lettered choices A through E to the statements. Note that, in the following examples, choices A through E may be used more than once or not at all.

EXAMPLES:

A. Coal
B. Sun
C. Aluminum
D. Trees
E. Clay

> **1.** A resource that is a fossil fuel.

The correct answer is **A.** Coal is the only fossil fuel listed. It is one of three types of fossil fuels; the others are natural gas and crude oil. Fossil fuels come from organic material that has undergone a chemical change due to pressure and heat. Fossil fuels take millions of years to form.

> **2.** A resource that is a metallic mineral.

The correct answer is **C.** Aluminum is a metallic ore. Aluminum ore is mined and processed to obtain the aluminum for human use.

> **3.** A resource used in the storage of foods and drinks.

The correct answer is **C.** Aluminum is used to store drinks for a long shelf life such as soda, noncarbonated drinks (such as fruit juice), teas, and other drinks. Aluminum also is rolled into thin sheets to produce aluminum foil, which is used to wrap foods for cooking and storing.

Remember: In matching problems, the same answer may be used more than once. Therefore, choice C is the correct answer for both questions 2 and 3.

> **4.** A resource that is considered renewable and is a primary source of energy in many parts of the world.

The correct answer is **D.** Trees are considered a renewable resource and can be replanted to grow within a normal human life span. Trees also are biomass, which is a major form of energy in many developing countries.

Problem Solving

Problem-solving questions are framed as standard questions, reverse-type questions identified with the words *except* or *not,* or short quotations followed by five possible answer choices. Many problem-solving questions are straightforward and require you to remember facts and significant developments in environmental science. The goal is to determine the best possible answer to the question.

EXAMPLE:

> During the last 50 years, meat consumption worldwide has nearly doubled. Which is NOT a disadvantage of an associated increase in meat production?
>
> A. Increase of greenhouse gases due to increased use of fossil fuel in meat production
> B. Concentration of animal waste in a small area
> C. Increased use of antibiotics, which has led to an increased resistance to microbes
> D. Increased protein in the diet of humans
> E. Increased inputs of grain, water, and fossil fuels

The correct answer is **D.** The increased consumption of protein is considered part of the reason why the average human height has increased. The other four answer choices are all disadvantages to the current method we use to produce meat for human consumption. Increased meat production, especially cattle, has seen an increase in feed and water for meat production. As more fossil fuels are used, more greenhouse gases are released. The animals are often housed in small pens, which concentrates their waste in a small area. Finally, to help prevent the spread of disease, antibiotics are routinely given to the animals.

Multiple-Multiple Choice

In multiple-multiple-choice questions, you are given three statements numbered I through III. You must determine which of these three statements is correct and choose the corresponding answer choice. The correct choice may be one of the statements, two of the statements, or all three of the statements.

EXAMPLE:

> Which of these is an environmental impact of mining for ore?
>
> I. Increased air pollution from dust and particles in the air
> II. Increased availability of fossil fuels
> III. Increased soil degradation from mining activities
>
> A. I only
> B. II only
> C. III only
> D. I and II only
> E. I and III only

The correct answer is **E**. When ore is mined, there are many possible outcomes. The land is altered and disturbed, causing dust particles to pollute the air. In addition, there can be runoff into water systems, causing increased erosion, a destruction of habitat, and a loss of biodiversity. Coal, iron, and aluminum are a few examples of mined ores.

Cause and Effect

A cause-and-effect problem describes a relationship between one event (cause) and another event (effect). Because this is a test of your knowledge of environmental science, a common cause-and-effect problem will focus on the effect that an event had upon the environment.

EXAMPLE:

> Love Canal is both an environmental disaster and a human health disaster. Which of the following is NOT a consequence of Love Canal?
>
> A. There has been an increase in birth defects.
> B. A river flowing through the area has spread chemicals beyond Love Canal.
> C. Vegetation has died and, in most places, only small shrubs grow.
> D. There has been an increase in miscarriages.
> E. Metal drums filled with chemicals showed visible signs of deteriorating in some areas of the dumping zone.

The correct answer is **B**. A river did not flow through the area and spread chemicals downriver. In this example, notice that all the choices except B describe environmental health concerns. Therefore, B is not a consequence of Love Canal.

Tables, Graphs, and Charts

Some questions on the exam present you with a table, graph, or chart and ask you to answer one or more questions based on it.

EXAMPLE:

Biome Characteristics	
Trait	Description
Precipitation	Moderate precipitation; two prolonged dry seasons with abundant rain the rest of the year
Temperature	Warm year-round
Location	Africa
Fauna	Herds of grazing and browsing hoofed animals, including zebras, giraffes, and antelopes
Flora	Grasses, scattered shrubs, and occasional deciduous trees

The information in the table is characteristic of which of the following biomes?
A. Temperate grassland
B. Tropical rain forest
C. Polar grassland
D. Savanna
E. Deciduous forest

The correct answer is **D.** The biome described is a savanna. Because the table lists the location as Africa, you can eliminate polar grassland (choice C). Animals such as zebras and giraffes are not found in temperate grasslands, eliminating choice A. The flora (plant life) is primarily grass, which indicates that the biome is not a tropical rain forest (choice B) or a deciduous forest (choice E). That leaves the correct answer, choice D.

Notice that by using the process of elimination, you can narrow the choices. This elimination strategy is useful when you are not sure which answer choice is correct but you know which choices are incorrect.

Basic Math

Basic math questions require simple computation and may require more time to answer than the other question types. Unless math is your strength and you think you can easily answer the problem in less than a minute, mark the question and move on. You can go back and answer the questions you marked at the end. (For more on this strategy, see the next section.)

EXAMPLE:

A nation currently has a population of 200 million and an annual growth rate of 3.5 percent. If the growth rate remains constant, what will be the population of this nation in 40 years?

A. 250 million
B. 400 million
C. 600 million
D. 800 million
E. 1 billion

The correct answer is **D.** This calculation question requires that you apply your knowledge of the Rule of 70, which says that the approximate time it would take a population to double (known as the doubling time, or dt) is expressed by the following formula:

$$dt = \frac{70}{\text{growth rate}}$$

Use the Rule of 70 to obtain the doubling time (dt):

$$dt = \frac{70}{3.5} = 20 \text{ years}$$

So, the population will double in 20 years. However, the question asks for what the population will be in 40 years, so there are two doubling times. You start with 200 million people. After the first 20 years, the population is 200 million × 2 = 400 million. Then, after another 20 years, the population is 400 million × 2 = 800 million.

Keep in mind that the dynamics of population growth rates are complex. The Rule of 70 tells you what the doubling time would be if the population were growing exponentially at a constant rate.

Strategies

Many students who take the AP Environmental Science exam do not get their best possible score on the multiple-choice questions because they spend too much time on difficult questions and fail to leave enough time to answer the easy questions. Do not let this happen to you. Keep in mind that there is no right or wrong way to answer questions, but there are general strategies that can help you get your best possible score.

Because every multiple-choice question is given the same point value, consider the following guidelines when taking the exam:

- **Manage your time wisely.** When you begin the exam, make a note of the starting time in your test booklet (not your answer booklet). Keep in mind that you will have an average of less than a minute for each multiple-choice question (there are 100 questions and you have 90 minutes).
- **Read each question carefully.** Do not make a hasty assumption that you know the correct answer without reading the whole question and all the possible answers.
- **Mark the correct answer on your answer sheet.** Be very careful that your responses on the answer sheet match the question number. When answering questions quickly, it is common to fill in the wrong number on the answer sheet (especially if you have skipped a question), which may throw off all the subsequent questions.
- **Answer all the questions.** To guarantee the highest number of correct answers, you must answer every question in the multiple-choice section.

Use the plus-minus strategy to help you answer questions that are solvable first (those that require minimal thought). Try to work all the way through the entire set of 100 questions, even though you will probably be skipping quite a few questions. Some of the questions at the end of the test might be very easy for you to answer. If you try to answer an early question that takes a long time to reason out, you may not have time to read the questions at the end of the exam. Time saved by using the plus-minus strategy will also allow you more time later to tackle the questions that are more difficult.

The Plus-Minus Strategy

❑ Answer the easy questions immediately. If a question is not easy, mark it with either a plus (+) or a minus (–). Mark a plus (+) next to the questions that you think will be easy to answer but are too time-consuming during the first round. Mark a minus (–) next to the questions that seem difficult to answer. Continue this process until you have either answered or marked all 100 questions. Then go back through and answer all the questions you marked with a plus (+). Finally, go back and answer all the questions you marked with a minus (–). If you find that a question is impossible to answer, try to eliminate incorrect answers to increase your odds of guessing the right answer; fill in your answer sheet and move on.

❑ You will notice that as you are working through the exam, a later question may trigger your memory of how to solve an earlier question that you marked with a minus (–). If this happens, write a quick note to yourself in the test booklet so you can remember how to answer the minus (–) question later. Do not try to hunt for the question when your memory is triggered or you will lose valuable time. You can always go back to the original question later, after you have finished the entire multiple-choice section.

❑ If you run out of time, and you still have questions unanswered, choose one letter (A, B, C, D, or E) and use it for the remainder of the questions. Statistically, your odds of guessing the correct answer are greater when you choose one letter for all the unanswered questions instead of filling in different letters for different questions.

Free-Response Questions

There are four essay questions on the AP Environmental Science exam. You will be given 90 minutes for this part of the exam to write all four essays. You will have approximately 22 minutes to write each essay. *Remember:* The score on the free-response questions is 40 percent of your total overall grade.

What Not to Do

❑ Do not waste time on background information or a long introduction unless the question calls for historical development or historical significance. Answer the question.

❑ Do not ramble. Get to the point. Say what you know and go on to the next question.

❑ Do not worry about spelling every word correctly or using perfect grammar. Incorrect spelling, grammar, and sentence structure are not a part of the criteria for grading standards, but you need to minimize your errors.

❑ Do not write about multiple topics if given a choice of two or three topics to write about. Only the first one(s) you write about will count. If you decide that your first choice was a bad one, then cross out that part of the answer so the reader clearly knows which part you want to be considered for credit.

❑ Do not leave questions blank. There is no penalty for a wrong guess.

❑ Do not list items in an outline form. Always use complete sentences.

❑ Do not use a calculator. For questions involving calculations, calculators are not allowed. You can receive credit for setting up a problem correctly and showing all work including correct units. You will not receive credit for only providing the correct answer.

❑ Do not quit!

Question Types

There are three types of free-response questions on the exam:

- Data analysis
- Document-based
- Synthesis and evaluation

We cover each of these question types in the following sections.

Data Analysis

In data-analysis questions, information is provided in the form of a map, table, chart, graph, or written, and you will be asked to analyze and interpret the information in your essay. The data provided requires some calculations you must solve before writing your essay. Although the use of calculators is not permitted on the exam, complex calculations are not required.

Graphing

There are two basic graphs on the free-response section of the AP Environmental Science exam: those that you draw and those that are provided for you. Graphs that you draw also may require an interpretation.

Here are some steps to follow when including a graph on the free-response portion of the exam:

1. **Set up the graph with the independent variable along the *x*-axis and the dependent variable along the *y*-axis.**

2. **Mark off the axes in equal (proportional) increments and label with proper units of measure.**

   You may be provided with grids to help you decide the scale of the graph. However, you may be given only the *x*- and *y*-axes, so you must demonstrate accuracy in your graphing skills. If the latter is the case, set a desired length and draw small marks on the *x*- and *y*-axes and lightly trace a grid to achieve accuracy.

3. **Plot the points and attempt to draw in the curve or line.**

4. **If more than one curve or line is plotted, write a label on each curve.**

   Labels are better than legends.

5. **Label each axis.**

6. **Give your graph an appropriate title denoting what the graph is showing.**

Document-Based

Document-based questions require you to read a real-life document (for example, a magazine or newspaper article) and respond to the questions provided based on that information from the document. You should draw on your knowledge of environmental science to respond.

Synthesis and Evaluation

There are two synthesis and evaluation questions on the exam. These question types may ask you to draw conclusions in relationships between two or more environmental science concepts.

Experimental Design

In 1999, 2001, and 2003, an experimental design question appeared on the AP Environmental Science exam. Although the type of question may not appear again, it is important to be familiar with this question type in the event that one appears on your exam. In 1999, there was a synthesis and evaluation question. In 2001 and 2003, there were document-based questions.

If you are asked to design or describe an experiment, be sure to include the following:

- A hypothesis and/or predictions

- The independent variable (what treatments you will apply)

- The dependent variable (what you will measure)

- Several variables to be controlled (very important)

- The organism, materials, and apparatus to be used

- What you will do

- How you will take and record data

- How the data will be graphed and analyzed

- How you will draw a conclusion (compare results to hypothesis and predictions)

Your experimental design needs to be at least theoretically possible. It is very important that your conclusions or predictions be consistent with the principles involved and with the way you set up the experiment. When designing the experiment, plan it backward—work from the expected result to the hypothesis. This is a great place to use the note-taking booklet that is returned to ETS. Write it backward (expected result → hypothesis); then write it in the typical experimental-design method (hypothesis → results):

1. **Expected results:** What is your conclusion? Compare it to your hypothesis.

2. **Analysis:** How are you going to analyze the results (graph, calculations, and so on)?

3. **Procedure:** A brief outline of how you are going to conduct the test. This is a great place to discuss your control group and experimental group and dependent and independent variables. Explain what data you will collect and how you will collect the data.

4. **Hypothesis:** This is a testable outcome to the problem. It is a prediction of what you think will happen. You may use the null hypothesis if you expect nothing to happen. If using a null hypothesis, then an alternate hypothesis must be provided as well.

Strategies

During the administration of the exam, you will be given a separate answer booklet to write your essay responses. After the exam, your answer booklet with your written essays will be sent to ETS to be graded. The question booklet, however, will be returned to you within 48 hours after the exam. During the exam, the question booklet is a great place to organize your notes, outline your answers and write down calculations. Only essays written in the answer booklet will be graded, so be sure that you transfer any notes you want to be graded to your answer booklet. Each essay will probably be no longer than two pages.

- **Read and mark the questions.** Read all four questions before you attempt to answer them. Before you begin to answer any question, carefully reread the question and restate the question to yourself before attempting to answer it. Circle or underline key words or phrases in the prompt, and be sure that you clearly understand what is being asked. A common mistake is misreading the question. Be sure to answer the question asked and *only* that question, and be sure to respond to *all* parts of the question. As you read the accompanying passage analytically, always keep the essay question in mind.

- **Identify key words and phrases.** Pay close attention to words used in the directions such as: *analyze, assess, calculate, compare, contrast, define, describe, discuss, evaluate, explain, graph, identify, provide evidence for,* and *support.* Be sure to follow the directions.

- **Start with the question you find the easiest to answer.** Many times while answering one question, you will recall answers to other questions. If this happens, write down this information as a reminder to help you later. If you are given a choice of parts to answer, choose carefully. It is best if you can answer the question parts in the order presented, but you don't have to. It's a great idea to label the parts "A," "B," "C," and so on, as they are labeled in the question. You can always answer the earlier parts later, and you don't need to save space—just label the section.

- **Prewrite.** The purpose of prewriting is to organize your thoughts and plan your essay. Use the space in the test booklet. Twenty-two minutes is not a great deal of time to develop and write a coherent essay, but by writing down your thoughts and ideas, you should be able to clearly organize your written response. It should take only a few minutes to outline your thoughts and ideas in the test booklet. It is important to write an essay that clearly supports scientific facts, concepts, and principles. Thinking and planning ahead helps avoid scratch-outs, asterisks, skipping around, and rambling on your written response.

- **Answer each question.** If you cannot answer all the parts of the question, answer what you can. Try to write a complete response to the question when possible, but you may earn points if your essay fits the scoring rubric specifications.

- **Remember that outlines and diagrams, no matter how elaborate and accurate, are not essays.** Outlines will not earn you much, if any, credit by themselves. Write the essay! There is one exception: If you are asked to calculate a number as a part of an essay, be sure to show how you arrived at your answer. Show the formulas you used and the values inserted into those formulas. Many times, points are awarded for setting up the problem. If you provide only the answer and do not show how you obtained the answer, you will receive no points. In addition, be sure to show all units. If you are asked to include a diagram, be sure to label the components carefully and correctly.

- **Remember that only the answer booklet is turned in for a score.** If the question asks for two responses and you provide three responses, then only the first two are scored. If the first response is incorrect, you will not get any credit for that response. Extra points may be available for elaboration, but only when they are requested.

- **A well-written essay:**
  - Presents a clear thesis statement on the topic and stays focused on the main idea throughout the essay
  - Develops the essay in an organized, logical sequence—introduction, body, and conclusion
  - Uses smooth transitions that flow from one paragraph to another
  - Supports the main idea with relevant and specific supporting evidence, details, technical terms, and examples
  - Responds to all parts of the essay question

Helpful Hints

❏ Define and/or explain any scientific technical terms you use. Write an example or provide a description of each of the important terms that you use to prove to the grader that you understand the terms. Rarely would the exam ask for a list of scientific buzzwords, and one- or two-word answers do not demonstrate a depth of knowledge about the topic.

❏ Write clearly and neatly. If the grader cannot read your answer because of poor penmanship, you may receive a zero for your response.

❏ Provide details about the subject, and be sure to stay focused on the topic. Provide supporting evidence that is relevant to the topic (for example, "light is necessary for photosynthesis"). Points will be given if you show your basic knowledge of the topic.

❏ If you cannot remember the definition of a term, take a shot at it with an educated guess. You may surprise yourself with information stored in your long-term memory. After writing a few words, your memory may be triggered to remember facts that will help you describe the term. Even if you cannot remember the name of a concept or term, by providing a description you may at least be able to receive partial credit.

❏ Be concise and precise. This is a science test, not an English test.

❏ Manage your time wisely. Do not waste time adding any unnecessary information. Avoid restating the question—doing so will only use up valuable time. Stay on task. Credit is only given for information requested.

PART I

SUBJECT REVIEWS

Chapter 1

Earth's Systems and Resources

Earth is a spectacular and ever-changing place, with constant activity and incredible transformations. The changes include everything from earthquakes and volcanoes to the formation of life and extinction of it. This chapter covers Earth's geologic changes and time scale, along with its atmosphere, water, and soil.

Earth

To prepare for the AP Environmental Science exam and to fully understand the concepts and workings of Earth's systems, you need to understand how the planet functions and its composition.

With a unique set of characteristics and features, Earth is the only planet in our solar system that is known to support life. It is the third planet from the sun, with the order of the planets being Mercury, Venus, Earth, Mars, Jupiter, Saturn, Uranus, and Neptune. Although Pluto used to be considered a planet, it is now classified as a dwarf planet.

Geologic Time Scale

At an age of approximately 4.6 billion years, Earth has seen many radical changes throughout its eons, eras, periods, and epochs. This span of time, and the changes that have taken place in it, are grouped into the **geologic time scale.** On the geologic time scale, eons are the largest spans of time; they include the Archean, Proterozoic, Hadean, and Phanerozoic. The eons Archean and Proterozoic are referred to as Precambrian time with seven eras. Eons are divided into eras, which are divided into periods.

Earth's Structure

With its varying composition and dense core, Earth is layered, and each layer has its own properties. From the interior outward, Earth is composed of a core, a mantle, and a crust.

The **crust,** the outermost layer of the Earth and the surface on which we live, can be either continental crust or oceanic crust, depending on where it's found. **Oceanic crust** is denser than continental crust because it is, in large part, made up of basalt, which contains the heavier elements iron and magnesium. The **continental crust** has a high amount of granite, which is rich in the lighter element aluminum. Because of its brittle nature, the crust can fracture and lead to earthquakes. Continental crust is 22 to 44 miles thick, and oceanic crust is 3 to 6 miles thick.

Below the crust is the **mantle,** which makes up approximately 80 percent of Earth's volume. It contains the upper mantle and lower mantle. The crust and upper mantle are grouped together in a structure called the **lithosphere,** which is the rigid outer layer of the Earth. Below the lithosphere but still above the lower mantle is a layer called the **asthenosphere,** which is made up of a plastic-like substance that tends to flow. The lower mantle is semi-rigid and flows very slowly. Combined, the upper and lower mantle are 1,802 miles thick.

The dense **core** at the center of the Earth is similarly subdivided into an inner and outer core. The inner core is mainly made up of iron and nickel and is solid because of the extreme pressure from the other layers above it. The liquid outer core is composed mainly of iron and nickel; it is molten because of its extreme heat, which is at least 10,832°F. The outer core is about 1,429 miles thick, and the inner core is 746 miles thick.

GEOLOGIC TIME SCALE

EON	ERA	PERIOD		EPOCH	Age in millions of years before present
Phanerozoic	Cenozoic	Quaternary		Holocene	Present
					0.01
				Pleistocene	
					1.6
		Tertiary	Neogene	Pliocene	
					5.3
				Miocene	
					23.7
			Paleogene	Oligocene	
					36.6
				Eocene	
					57.8
				Paleocene	
					66.4
	Mesozoic	Cretaceous			
					144
		Jurassic			
					208
		Triassic			
					245
	Paleozoic	Permian			
					286
		Pennsylvanian	Carboniferous		
					320
		Mississippian			
					360
		Devonian			
					408
		Silurian			
					438
		Ordovician			
					505
		Cambrian			
					570
Precambrian		Proterozoic			
					2500
		Archean			
					3800
		Hadean			
					4550

Source: U.S. Geological Survey

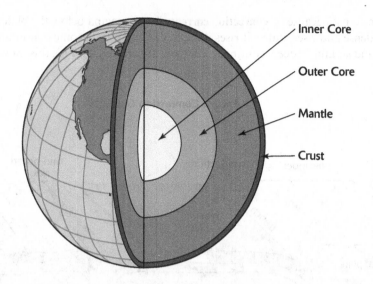

- Inner Core
- Outer Core
- Mantle
- Crust

Plate Tectonics

The Earth's lithosphere (the crust and upper mantle) is broken into **tectonic plates** (also known as lithospheric plates). These plates are in constant motion atop the **asthenosphere,** which is the Earth's molten mantle layer that keeps the continents slowly moving. This movement of the continents is called **continental drift.**

The reason that tectonic plates are in constant motion is a process called **seafloor spreading,** which is the movement of the seafloor at the **mid-ocean ridge.** A mid-ocean ridge is the location from which **magma** (molten rock within the Earth) rises to the surface from the asthenosphere. It looks like a scar across the ocean floor. As the magma pushes through the crust and hardens, new seafloor is created. As new magma surfaces, it pushes away the existing seafloor, causing it to spread and move apart.

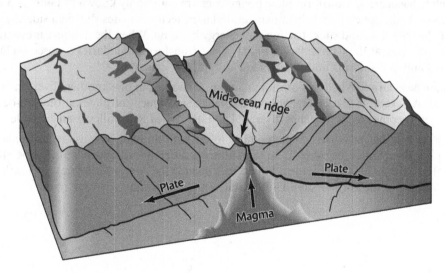

Magma rises through the crust because of **convection currents** in the magma below the plates. When magma is heated, it becomes less dense and rises, but as it rises it cools, causing it to become denser and sink. As the heating and cooling, rising and sinking process continues, currents are created, and it's this movement that drives the plate motion.

Earth's Convection Currents

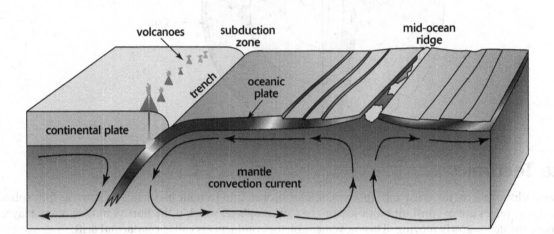

Plate boundaries

At plate boundaries, major geologic activity occurs, including earthquakes, volcanoes, and the formation of mountain ranges. The type of activity depends on the type of plate movement. The three types of plate boundaries are

- **Transform plate boundaries:** Transform plate boundaries are commonly known as **faults** and are found on the ocean floor. At the zone of transform plate boundaries, tectonic plates slide in a sideways motion past one another. As they slide and stick, friction and energy build up. When the pressure is eventually relieved, earthquakes can occur at these boundaries. Examples of transform boundaries exposed on land include the San Andreas Fault in California and the Alpine Fault in New Zealand.

- **Divergent plate boundaries:** When two or more plates pull away from one another, divergent plate boundaries are created. An example of a divergent boundary is the movement of plates at the mid-ocean ridge, where the ocean becomes wider as plates diverge. The East Africa Rift Valley is an example.

- **Convergent plate boundaries:** When two plates move toward one another, a convergent plate boundary is created as one plate dives under the other. With this collision, different events can follow, depending on the type of crust involved. Examples of convergent boundaries include the Andes Mountains in South America, the Cascade Mountains in the northwestern United States, and the Marianas Trench in the Pacific Ocean.

Earth's Plates and Plate Boundaries

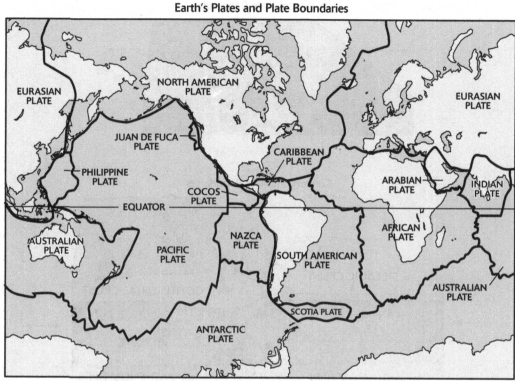

Oceanic and continental plates

Oceanic and continental plates in collision lead to **subduction.** Subduction of oceanic plates at plate boundaries is the cause of continental crust being older than oceanic crust. The denser oceanic plate is pushed below the lighter continental plate. When the crust is compacted and pushed up during the collision of two continental plates, mountain ranges are formed. This motion created the Himalaya Mountains, which are still growing today. When two oceanic plates collide, one plate may be pushed below the other, forming a trench or producing a volcano and allowing magma to rise. Formations created from convergent boundaries include the Andes Mountains in South America, the Cascade Mountains in the northwestern United States, and the Marianas Trench in the Pacific Ocean. Earthquakes also can occur as a result of movement at plate boundaries.

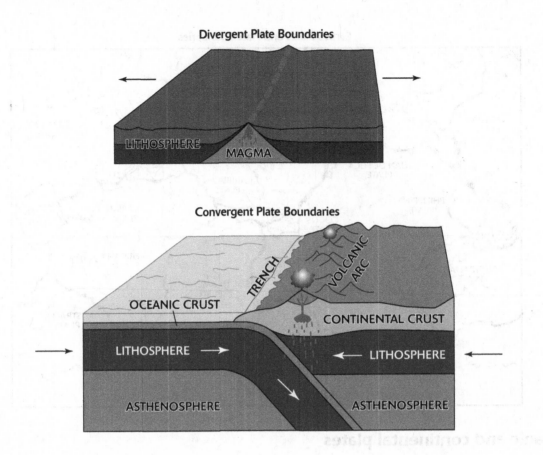

Divergent Plate Boundaries

LITHOSPHERE   MAGMA

Convergent Plate Boundaries

OCEANIC CRUST   TRENCH   VOLCANIC ARC   CONTINENTAL CRUST

LITHOSPHERE   LITHOSPHERE

ASTHENOSPHERE   ASTHENOSPHERE

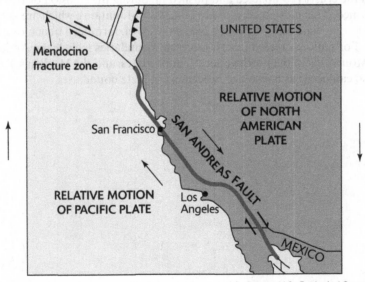

Transform Plate Boundaries

Mendocino fracture zone

UNITED STATES

San Francisco

RELATIVE MOTION OF NORTH AMERICAN PLATE

SAN ANDREAS FAULT

RELATIVE MOTION OF PACIFIC PLATE

Los Angeles

MEXICO

Source: U.S. Geological Survey

Earthquakes

At times, pressure builds up at plate boundaries because of friction from plate movement, and stress is created. When this stress is ultimately discharged, energy is released throughout the Earth's crust, causing vibrations, or

earthquakes. Often, earthquakes are caused by movement of the lithospheric plates and occur at plate boundaries. The focus of an earthquake is the location at which the earthquake originates within the Earth. Above the focus is the **epicenter,** which is the first place on the Earth's surface affected by the earthquake.

The types of faults from which earthquakes can occur include strike-slip, normal, and reverse. **Strike-slip faults** occur where the plates slide past one another horizontally. **Normal faults** are caused by tension from a pulling-apart motion. **Reverse faults** are caused from compression.

Earthquakes themselves do not generally kill people, but their effects on human-built structures do. Because an earthquake is a vibration of the Earth caused by a sudden release of energy, this movement transfers into buildings, roadways, and other infrastructures. The consequences of structural failure in constructed facilities ultimately cause harm. **Tsunamis** are seismic sea waves generated from undersea earthquakes or volcanic eruptions and are an exception to this statement, though. They are not dangerous while traveling through the ocean, but they can cause massive destruction once they reach a coastline, which can be thousands of miles from the location of the earthquake or volcano.

Volcanoes

Volcanoes are openings in the Earth's surface that allow magma, gases, ash, cinder, and other volcanic material to escape from the mantle. A volcano's structure includes a magma chamber, which contains a pool of magma deep within the earth; a pipe (conduit) that brings lava, gases, and other materials from the magma chamber to the surface; and a vent, which is the opening through which lava and other material escapes. Some volcanoes also have a crater, or depression, at the mouth,

Because of the ever-changing interior of the Earth, volcanoes have various stages and remain active for a period of time. An **active volcano** is either presently erupting or will eventually erupt because of a large amount of seismic and thermal activity occurring within it. A **dormant volcano** is inactive but could potentially erupt again. An **extinct volcano** is not erupting and most likely will never erupt again.

Types of volcanoes

Three main types of volcanoes have been identified:

- **Shield volcanoes** are large with broad sides, gradual slopes, and usually a crater at the top. They typically erupt slowly, with lava oozing from the vent or multiple vents. Examples include Mauna Loa in Hawaii, Mount Wrangell in Alaska, and Skjaldbreiður in Iceland.
- **Composite volcanoes** (strato volcanoes) are tall, symmetrical, and steep. They're built of alternating layers of ash, lava, and cinders. Examples include Mount Hood in Oregon, Mount Lassen and Mount Shasta in California, Mount Fuji in Japan, Arenal in Costa Rica, Mount Cotopaxi in Ecuador, Mount Etna in Italy, and Mount Rainier and Mount St. Helens in Washington. Eruptions of composite volcanoes can be either explosive or lava extruding; therefore, predicting the type of eruption and its severity is difficult.
- **Cinder cone volcanoes** are usually made of lava that erupts in the form of cinders, which are blown into the air and then settle around the opening of the volcano, ultimately forming a small, steep-sided mountain. This is the most common type of volcano. Examples include Mount Mazama in Oregon (a destroyed volcano that is now the location of Crater Lake), Paricutin in Mexico, Mount Shasta in California, and Cerro Negro in Nicaragua.

Locations where magma emerges from within the Earth but not at plate boundaries are called **hot spots.** Hot spots form in the middle of tectonic plates. The magma's extreme heat burns through thin crust, and then cools and forms new crust. Over time, this new land can build up to form volcanoes in the middle of plates or islands in the ocean. Examples of places where hot spots have occurred include the Hawaiian Islands, the Galapagos Islands, Iceland, and Yellowstone National Park.

Earthquakes, Active Volcanoes, and Plate Tectonics

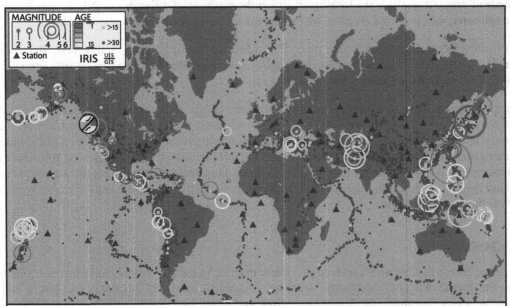

TOP: World-wide earthquakes on July 7, 1999, and past 5 years, demonstrating how earthquakes define boundaries of tectonic plates. Data from NEIC. Chart from IRIS Consortium, USGS, U. Colorado, Reel Illusions, Inc., and U. Washington. Chart modified for web use. Purple triangles are seismic stations, green/yellow "ball" is 5.1 event of July 3, 1999. **BOTTOM:** World-wide active volcanoes (red circles), tectonic plates, and the "Ring of Fire". Chart modified from Tilling, Heliker, and Wright, 1987, and Hamilton, 1976. — *Topinka, USGSICVO, 1999*

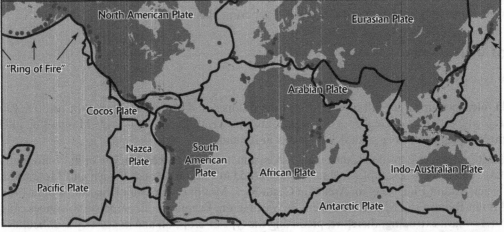

Source: U.S. Geological Survey

Effects of Volcanoes

Although volcanoes are natural events, they still have an impact on people's health, the environment, and other organisms. A variety of gases are released into the atmosphere during a volcanic eruption, and the effects vary, depending on the amount released, the location, the wind pattern, the height of discharge, and other factors. The most abundant gases released during an eruption include water vapor (H_2O), carbon dioxide (CO_2), and sulfur dioxide (SO_2). Other gases released include carbon monoxide (CO), helium (He), hydrogen (H_2), hydrogen chloride (HCl), hydrogen sulfide (H_2S), and hydrogen fluoride (HF).

Posing the potentially most harmful effects on organisms and the environment are

- **Hydrogen fluoride (HF),** also called sewer gas, which can cause respiratory tract irritation, bone degeneration, and pulmonary edema in high concentrations. At lower concentrations, exposure can cause eye irritation, diarrhea, dizziness, excitement, and staggering. When HF coats grass and animals then ingest it, poisoning can occur, as can bone degeneration and even death. HF also contributes to acid rain.
- **Carbon dioxide (CO_2)** has a density greater than that of air, so it sinks and can kill animals, people, and plants. The CO_2 replaces the air, so asphyxiation can occur in areas with abundant CO_2. This gas can also collect in soils, which can affect the microbial population in the soil and nutrient intake by plants.
- **Sulfur dioxide (SO_2)** can lead to acid rain, air pollution, and smog at a local level. On a global level, it can lower surface temperatures and exacerbate depletion of the ozone layer. SO_2 also can harm human health mainly by affecting the respiratory system and also irritating skin, eyes, nose, and throat.
- **Hydrogen chloride (HCl)** causes irritation of the eyes, throat, and respiratory system. It can lead to acid rain because of its solubility in water, as well as to loss of ozone.

Atmospheric Effects of Volcanoes

Because these volcanic gases are released into the atmosphere, the effects can be dramatic:

- Ozone can be broken down when reactions occur with HCl or SO_2. Fortunately, the ozone depletion diminishes once the gases are reduced in the atmosphere.
- Volcanic gases can contribute to global warming because CO_2 and water vapor trap and absorb solar energy, raising the temperature of the planet over time.
- The gases can contribute to the haze effect (smog), in which particulate matter in the atmosphere blocks out solar radiation and ultimately can lower the mean global temperature.

These effects usually are not long-term when they occur because of volcanic activity, but they're exacerbated by human activities that also release these gases into the atmosphere.

Solar Radiation, Intensity, and Seasons

Solar energy affects the entire dynamic of the planet, including climate, weather, biodiversity, and life's productivity. The amount of solar energy the Earth receives depends on the tilt of Earth's axis, its rotation around that axis, and its revolution around the Sun. One rotation equals one day, and a revolution equals a year.

Throughout the year, Earth has two **equinoxes,** times when day and night are equal. Toward the end of March, the **vernal equinox** occurs, signifying the start of spring in the Northern Hemisphere and fall in the Southern Hemisphere. The **autumnal equinox,** marking the beginning of fall in the Northern Hemisphere and spring in the Southern Hemisphere, occurs at the end of September.

Solstices occur when the sun is most north or south of the celestial equator. In the Northern Hemisphere, the summer solstice, when the sun is northernmost, occurs on June 21 over the Tropic of Cancer. The winter solstice occurs on December 21 over the Tropic of Capricorn and is when the sun is southernmost. In the Northern Hemisphere, the summer solstice is the longest day of the year, and the winter solstice is the shortest.

Seasons

Earth's seasons are created by the tilt of Earth's axis to its orbital plane and its rotation around the sun, which is 23.5 degrees. At different times throughout the year, different parts of the Earth are facing the sun. **Summer** occurs when the sun's rays hit Earth's surface at the most direct angles, also giving summer the longest daylight hours. During **winter** the angle of the sun's rays are more oblique, giving that portion of the Earth shorter days and less solar energy. The seasons are not related to Earth's distance from the sun. The Earth is actually closest to the sun in January (**perihelion**) and farthest away in July (**aphelion**).

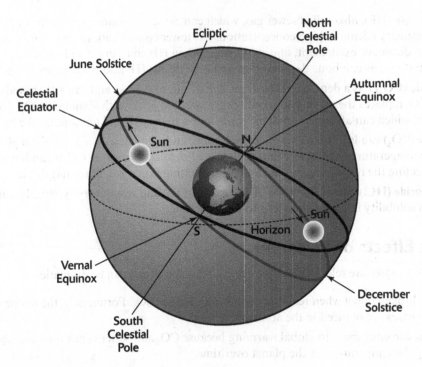

Celestial Coordinate System

The Atmosphere

As a protector of Earth, the atmosphere deflects many harmful UV rays from the sun and helps to maintain a stable temperature by helping to retain heat with a natural greenhouse effect. Without the atmosphere, life as we know it would not be able to exist on this planet. It is also a dynamic aspect of Earth, changing over the 4.6 billion years of the planet's existence.

Composition

Earth's atmosphere is composed of 16 dry gases and water, usually in the form of water vapor.

Atmospheric Gases	
Nitrogen (N_2)	Nitrogen makes up approximately 78 percent of the total composition of the atmosphere. It is in equilibrium with Earth's abiotic and biotic systems. Nitrogen enters the biotic system either through nitrogen fixation or lightning, which turns nitrogen gas into usable forms of nitrogen for plants. In order to be converted back to atmospheric nitrogen, nitrogen in the lithosphere undergoes denitrification. The combustion of biomass can also release nitrogen into the atmosphere.
Oxygen (O_2)	Oxygen represents approximately 21 percent of the total composition of the atmosphere. Oxygen is released to the atmosphere during photosynthesis and is used by plants and animals during cellular respiration.

Natural Greenhouse Gases	
Water vapor (H_2O)	The concentration of water vapor in the atmosphere varies greatly depending on location, but it is about trace to 4 percent of the total composition of the atmosphere. Above the world's oceans, near the equator, and in the tropical regions, the water vapor percentage is higher than it is in the atmosphere over the poles and the world's deserts, where it can be very low.

Carbon dioxide (CO_2)	Since the beginning of the last ice age and prior to the Industrial Revolution, carbon dioxide has been in equilibrium between the atmosphere and living organisms. CO_2 is important for photosynthesis and for helping to maintain the natural greenhouse effect on Earth. However, since the beginning of the Industrial Revolution, the volume of CO_2 has increased approximately 25 percent (though it is still less than 1 percent of the atmosphere). Chapter 7 will discuss how humans are altering the concentration of CO_2 in the atmosphere.
Methane (CH_4)	Methane is a naturally occurring component of the atmosphere, making up less than 1 percent of the total gases. Methane is a principal component (approximately 87 percent) of natural gas and is used for heating and cooking in many countries. It is one of the fossil fuels that is tapped by drilling into the Earth. Natural gas may seep from the Earth's crust, contributing to methane in the atmosphere, but it's more likely to be leaking from the gas pipes used to transport it or from equipment that burns it. Humans have increased the concentration of methane in the atmosphere approximately 150 percent since the beginning of the Industrial Revolution, which will be discussed further in Chapter 7.
Nitrous oxide (N_2O)	Naturally occurring nitrous oxide is a greenhouse gas that is produced by bacteria in solids and from the oceans. It has the ability to remain in the atmosphere for over 100 years and makes up less than 1 percent of the atmosphere. The major sources of nitrous oxide are agricultural practices, industrial activities, burning of solid waste, and fossil fuels. This is further explored in Chapter 7.
Ozone (O_3)	Ozone, which is less than 1 percent of the total atmosphere, is very important for life on Earth. The majority (over 90 percent) of ozone is found in the stratosphere 8 to 30 miles above the Earth. The ozone layer absorbs UV radiation from the sun, thereby protecting life on Earth from harmful rays. Ozone (O_3) is formed by a naturally occurring reaction in the atmosphere. The chemical reaction for the formation of ozone is: $$O_2 + UV \rightarrow O + O$$ $$O + O_2 \rightarrow O_3$$ Troposphere ozone is considered a pollutant. Ozone in the stratosphere was once in equilibrium. These issues are further discussed in Chapter 7.

The Structure of the Atmosphere

Temperature is the criterion for determining the different layers in Earth's atmosphere. In the troposphere and mesosphere, the temperature decreases with increased altitude. In the stratosphere and thermosphere, the temperature increases with increased altitude. Between these four major layers are small layers where the temperature stays roughly the same. These are the pauses between the layers: the tropopause, stratopause, and mesopause.

Layer Name	Height (miles)	Temperature	Comments
Troposphere	0–9	Decreases with increasing altitude; coldest reaching −70°F	Life exists in this layer and weather occurs here. Holds most of atmospheric water vapor. Significantly thinner at the poles than at the equator. Contains 75 percent of the atmosphere's mass due to higher air density near Earth's surface.
Stratosphere	9–31	−60°F to 5°F	Contains ozone layer. Temperature increases with distance from Earth. Heat is produced as part of the process of ozone being created. Aircraft usually fly within this layer. Warmer air is located above cooler air, so little vertical mixing occurs.
Mesosphere	31–50	Can drop to −130°F	Contains coldest temperatures in atmosphere, with temperatures decreasing as distance from Earth increases. Low air pressure due to thinning of gas particles. Least explored part of atmosphere.
Thermosphere	50+ (no well-defined upper limit)	Up to 2,192°F	Known as the upper atmosphere and contains very thin air. Little mixing of air particles, which are moving fast but are very far apart. High temperatures due to absorption of high energy wavelengths from solar radiation.

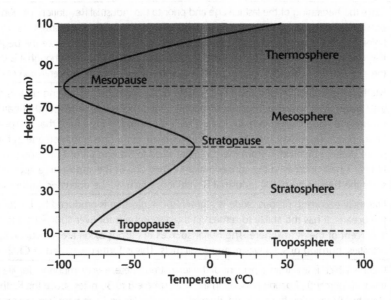

Weather and Climate

Weather is the name given to the short-term events of temperature, wind, and precipitation. The constant patterns developed from averaging the daily weather for an extended period of time is **climate.** Climate is typically the weather averages for at least 30 years. Many areas have recorded data for more than 100 years now, though the more recent data is more accurate as instruments have become more standardized and computerized.

The transfer of heat energy causes weather, and the source of heat energy is solar energy heating the Earth. This solar energy heats the Earth unevenly because of the distribution of water and land on the Earth and the specific heat of each. This heating of the Earth is reflected in the temperature, movement of air masses, and availability of sunshine. The rotation of the Earth also plays a role in the weather patterns.

Latitude and altitude have an effect on the climate of a region. The farther from the equator, the less solar radiation and the cooler the climate. There is also a greater seasonal variation throughout the year when farther from the equator. Altitude, the distance above the Earth's surface (sea level), is also a determining factor on the climate of a region. Each 1,000-foot gain in altitude reflects a 4°F decline in air temperature. For example, at 10,000 feet, an alpine tundra climate zone air temperature might average 35°F. Changes in latitude and altitude influence plant and animal distribution.

Atmospheric Circulations

The circulation of air in the atmosphere is the result of solar heating, the rotation of the Earth, and the properties of air, land, and water. Earth is heated unevenly for three reasons:

- **More solar energy hits the Earth at the equator than the poles, and the per unit of energy by per surface square area varies.**
- **The tilt of the Earth on its axis points some regions toward the sun and others away from the sun.** Areas angled toward the sun receive more direct energy than areas angled away from the sun. The various seasons on Earth are caused by the tilt of the planet's axis and the rotation of Earth around the sun over the course of a year.
- **Earth's surface is moving faster at the equator than the poles.** This is the reason for the phenomenon known as the Coriolis effect (the apparent deflection of a moving object in a rotating reference frame).

As solar energy heats the Earth's surface, some heat is transferred to the atmosphere by radiational heating. This energy warms the gases, the gases expand, they become less dense and then rise, whereupon they cool and fall back to the Earth's surface to be reheated again, thus creating a continuous cycle. This constant heating and cooling creates vertical currents called convection currents. On a global scale, these convection currents are called the Hadley, Ferrel, and Polar cells:

- **Hadley air circulation cells** occur close to the equator. The surface air in this region is warmed from the strong solar radiation, causing the air to rise and expand. This process releases moisture and provides high amounts of rain, a major contributing factor for the tropical rainforests in the equatorial region. The air, now holding less water, heads north and south, ultimately cooling and sinking back towards the surface. Now containing very little water, the arid air helps to produce deserts. The Hadley cell is the strongest of the three air circulation cells.

- **The Ferrel air circulation cells** generally occur at mid-latitudes between the Polar and Hadley cells. Because of the sinking air coming from the Hadley cells and the rising air brought in by the Polar cells, westerly surface winds are produced in these regions.

- **The Polar air circulation cells** are the northernmost of the three types of cells and contain dense, cold air moving towards the poles. As the air reaches the poles, it sinks and then moves south back towards the mid-latitudes. In this process, air starts to warm and rise again, creating low pressure areas.

Another component of atmospheric circulation is the **Coriolis effect.** This occurrence creates the deflection of objects from otherwise moving in a straight line. This is due to the rotation of Earth. For example, if you spin a disk and try to draw a line from the center to the edge, the result will be a curved line. This is caused by the Coriolis effect. This effect causes winds in the Northern Hemisphere to deflect to the right and in the Southern Hemisphere to deflect to the left. The Coriolis effect contributes to the creation of the three air circulation cells and has effects on weather patterns and ocean circulation.

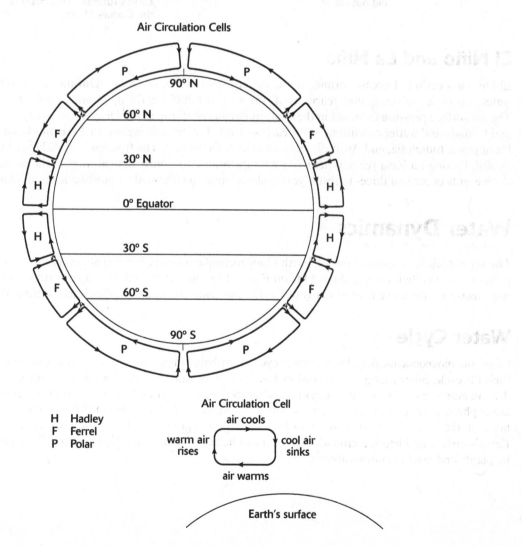

Air Circulation Cells

H Hadley
F Ferrel
P Polar

Air Circulation Cell

air cools

warm air rises — cool air sinks

air warms

Earth's surface

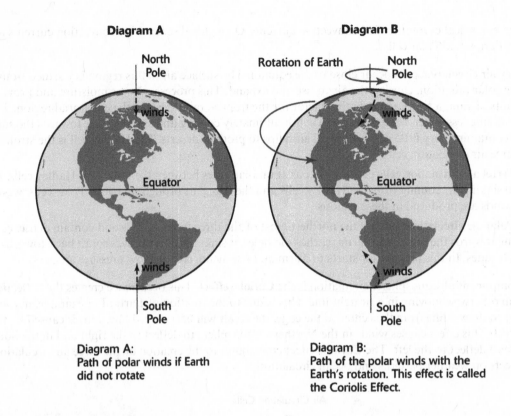

Diagram A   Diagram B

Diagram A:
Path of polar winds if Earth
did not rotate

Diagram B:
Path of the polar winds with the
Earth's rotation. This effect is called
the Coriolis Effect.

El Niño and La Niña

El Niño is a period of ocean warming in the eastern tropical Pacific Ocean. During the El Niño, the surface waters warm due to strong undercurrents of warm water inhibiting the upwelling of colder, nutrient-rich waters. The air surface pressure increases in the western Pacific, resulting in milder climates in the northern United States and Canada and wetter conditions in the eastern United States and regions of Peru and Ecuador, while the Philippines, Indonesia, and Australia become drier than normal. The frequency of Atlantic hurricanes is reduced as well. During La Niña years, water surface temperatures are colder than average in the eastern Pacific Ocean. Both events occur in a three- to seven-year cycle, relating to large-scale atmospheric circulation.

Water Dynamics

The water cycle is considered one of Earth's biogeochemical cycles, but it is also very important to weather patterns, ocean circulation, and most life on Earth. The water cycle is the most important cycle because it's responsible for the movement of many of Earth's nutrients and impacts other biogeochemical cycles.

Water Cycle

Of all the biogeochemical cycles, the water cycle is probably most familiar. Energy provided by solar radiation fuels the cycle. Solar energy is absorbed by Earth's surfaces and bodies of water, increasing the heat content and driving evaporation. Water evaporates from these bodies of water and transpires from vegetation. Once in the atmosphere, water condenses and forms clouds. When the clouds contain enough water, the water falls as precipitation in the form of rain, snow, sleet, or hail. Once on the ground, water can run off as surface water, infiltrate Earth's surface and become groundwater, or it can be evaporated again. Water near soil's surface can be absorbed by plants and used in photosynthesis.

The following is a list of terms related to the water cycle:

- **Condensation:** The transformation of water vapor from gaseous to liquid phase, with water droplets condensing onto atmospheric particles and producing clouds and fog.
- **Evaporation:** The transformation of water from liquid to gas phase due to heating of the water, usually from solar radiation.
- **Groundwater:** Water that is located beneath the Earth's surface in the pore spaces of soil, the fractures in rock formations, or held in aquifers.
- **Infiltration:** The process by which surface water seeps into the soil.
- **Percolation:** The movement of water down through the soil.
- **Precipitation:** Condensed water vapor in the atmosphere that falls to Earth's surface in the form of rain, snow, hail, and sleet.
- **Runoff:** Water that flows along the Earth's surface but does not infiltrate the surface, ultimately percolating into the ground, evaporating into the atmosphere, or running into other bodies of water such as rivers, lakes, streams, or oceans.
- **Transpiration:** The loss of water vapor from plants, mainly from leaves.

Water can be stored in three main areas: the atmosphere, on Earth's surface, or within the ground. There are a variety of sinks (where water is stored), including polar ice and glaciers, bodies of water such as oceans and rivers, below the surface of the Earth in aquifers, and as water vapor in the atmosphere. In some of these sinks, water may be trapped for millions of years.

The oceans hold 97 percent of Earth's water. Approximately 78 percent of the global precipitation falls over the surface of the oceans. Evaporation from ocean waters accounts for 86 percent of all evaporation. This constant precipitation and evaporation helps keep the Earth from overheating.

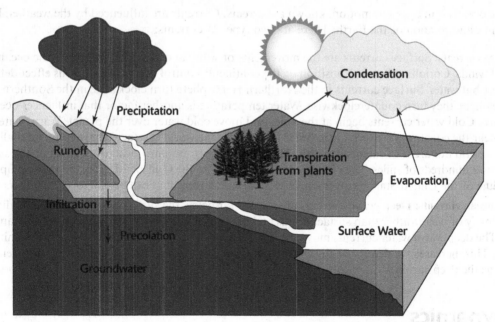

Source: National Oceanic and Atmospheric Administration

Freshwater

Only 2.5 percent of Earth's water is freshwater, most of which is locked in polar ice caps and glaciers. Therefore, only about 21 percent of the 2.5 percent is available in the form of groundwater, lakes and rivers, and water vapor in the atmosphere. Freshwater is critical for life on Earth because most life forms need water on a daily basis in order to survive, and freshwater ecosystems support an abundance of life.

Oceans/Saltwater

Most saltwater is found in Earth's oceans, with a small amount in terminal lakes such as the Great Salt Lake in Utah. On average the salt content in the oceans is 3.5 percent. Ocean water is a mixture of salts, with sodium chloride (NaCl), magnesium chloride (MgCl), and calcium chloride (CaCl) being the three primary salts. The salts are transported mainly in runoff and wind as sediment from continental land. There are many unique and diverse ecosystems that depend on the saltwater environment.

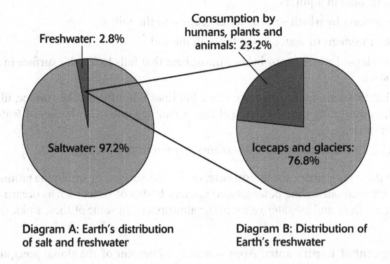

Diagram A: Earth's distribution of salt and freshwater

Diagram B: Distribution of Earth's freshwater

Ocean Currents

Water in the oceans is in constant motion, known as **currents.** Currents are influenced by the weather, location of the continents, and rotation of the Earth. There are two types of currents:

- **Surface currents:** Surface currents are the movements of water at or near the surface of the ocean. The global winds, Coriolis effect, and position of the continents control them. The Coriolis effect deflects not only air but water. Surface currents in the Northern Hemisphere turn clockwise; in the Southern Hemisphere, they turn counterclockwise. Water temperature is another factor that influences ocean surface currents. Cold water currents begin at the poles and move cold water over the planet. Warm water currents start near the equator and move warm water throughout the world. Surface currents can be shallow or reach several hundreds of meters in depth. They can be short movements across the top of the surface or can travel hundreds of miles. The Gulf Steam coming out of the Gulf of Mexico and moving up the eastern coastline of the United States is an example of a surface current that can be 800 to 1,200 meters deep.

- **Deep ocean currents:** Deep ocean currents are located far below the surface and are created by differences in the density of water rather than surface winds and other effects. Density is a factor of salinity and temperature. The deep warm water currents move toward the poles where ice forms, increasing the salinity of the water. This increases the density of the water, and it sinks to the ocean floor, where this cold, dense water flows as the deep currents.

Soil Dynamics

Soil is more than simply dirt. It is a complex system that includes eroded rock material, organic matter, nutrients, air, water, and living organisms. The air and water are held within pore spaces throughout the soil. Because soil is largely composed of weathered rock, soil types depend on which type of rock is the parent material in a given location. Ultimately, this basic rock material is one of the factors that affects the type of vegetation that grows in specific locations.

Rock Cycle

Before studying soil formation, it is important to understand how rocks are created and broken down on Earth. The rock cycle is a continual process that breaks down, alters, and re-forms rock into one of three types. The three types of rock are:

- **Igneous rock:** Igneous rock is formed from cooling magma. When magma cools slowly below Earth's surface, it forms intrusive igneous rock, and when it cools quickly, as when ejected from a volcano, it forms extrusive igneous rock. Examples of igneous rock include granite (intrusive) and basalt (extrusive).
- **Sedimentary rock:** Sedimentary rock is the result of sediments derived from erosion and weathering being compressed and cemented together. Clastic sedimentary rock is formed after rock is physically eroded, and chemical sedimentary rock is formed when dissolved minerals precipitate from water. Examples of sedimentary rock include sandstone (clastic) and limestone (chemical).
- **Metamorphic rock:** Metamorphic rock is formed under extreme heat and pressure, usually deep underground. When heat and pressure force minerals to align and create a layered formation, this is called foliated rock. Unfoliated rock is not layered. Examples of metamorphic rock include marble (unfoliated) and slate (foliated).

One type of rock can be converted into another type through Earth's continual geologic processes.

The Rock Cycle

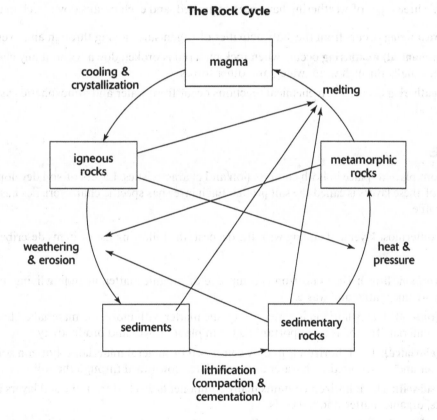

Soil Formation

Rocks are continually being altered by the rock cycle, and this parent material is the basis of soil formation, but other factors also have an effect on the formation of soil.

Soil formation is based on five factors, each of which plays a role in how and what type of soil is formed in an area. The five factors include parent material, living organisms, topography, climate, and time.

- **Parent material:** The core component of soil is the parent material, which is eroded and weathered from the existing geologic material in a given area.
- **Living organisms:** Living organisms play a role in turning and aerating soil while also aiding in the decomposition and addition of organic matter. Worms, insects, snails, spiders, fungi, bacteria, gophers, squirrels, and many other organisms contribute to this process.
- **Topography:** Earth's shapes and features, called topography, aid in soil formation by the angles of hills, valleys, mountains, and other structures. Factors relating to topography include slope, wind exposure, sun exposure, and water.
- **Climate:** Another factor in soil formation is climate because precipitation and temperature affect climate, and both have an impact on the erosion and weathering of parent material.
- **Time:** It takes time for weathering and erosion to occur, so the amount of time an area has been exposed to various elements affects the makeup of the soil and size of the soil particles.

Weathering

Parent material is broken down by water, wind, temperature fluctuations, and living organisms through a process called **weathering.** Three types of weathering have been identified, and each breaks down rock in a different way:

- **Biological weathering** occurs from the daily activities of organisms moving through and over soil.
- **Physical (mechanical) weathering** occurs when rock material is broken down without any chemical change taking place, usually through wind, water, and other forces.
- **Chemical weathering** occurs when chemical reactions occur from water and atmospheric gases reacting with parent material.

Soil Profile

Soil types vary from place to place in both composition and characteristics. Layers of soil develop over time, and the cross-section of these layers is called the **soil profile.** Each layer has specific characteristics based on its location in the soil profile.

Starting with the outermost layer and ending with the deepest, the following list of items describes a cross-section of a soil profile:

- **O Horizon (organic litter):** The O horizon is composed of organic matter, including living organisms, as well as decaying organic matter and waste.
- **A Horizon (topsoil):** The A horizon is a mix of organic matter with inorganic materials. This includes weathered parent material. Topsoil is an important factor in plant growth and productivity.
- **E Horizon (eluviated):** The E horizon is mainly composed of mineral material. E horizon soil is leached from this layer and transported with water as it percolates downward through the soil.
- **B Horizon (subsoil):** The B horizon contains many components leached from the soil layers above it, including nutrients, organic matter, and minerals.
- **C Horizon (minimally weathered):** The C horizon is weathered from parent material, but the weathering and erosion it has experienced is minimal, so it contains mainly larger fragments.
- **R Horizon (bedrock):** The R horizon is the parent material and is called bedrock.

The O and A horizons are where most soil organisms live, while the A horizon contains the most nutrients for plant growth. The concentrations of organic matter and the extensiveness of weathering decrease with depth. Minerals are transported through each horizon by **leaching.**

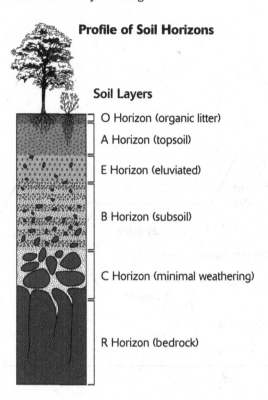

Profile of Soil Horizons

Soil Layers

O Horizon (organic litter)

A Horizon (topsoil)

E Horizon (eluviated)

B Horizon (subsoil)

C Horizon (minimal weathering)

R Horizon (bedrock)

Soil Properties

Soil is classified based on the properties of pH, texture, color, and structure. Soil texture affects the other properties, including porosity and permeability. **Soil porosity** is the amount of open space between each soil particle, the ratio of void space to total volume. Water, air, or other gases fill these pore spaces. More pore space means a high water-holding capacity and, therefore, a higher porosity. Conversely, lower porosity means a lower water-holding capacity. **Soil permeability** is the ability of a liquid to flow through the soil. Larger particles have large pore spaces, allowing water to pass through more easily. Clay is considered to have low permeability because it's hard for water to flow through easily. Sand has a higher permeability.

Soil Texture

Soil texture is used to describe grain sizes in soils. It is divided into three main groups:

- **Clay** is classified as having very fine particles and low permeability (water does not pass through easily). Particle diameter is less than 0.002 mm.
- **Silt** has fine particles, but they are larger than those of clay. Particle diameter is 0.002 to 0.05 mm.
- **Sand** particles are larger than those of silt, so water passes through relatively easily. Particle diameter is 0.05 to 2 mm. Sand is not conducive to plant growth or crop growth unless the plants' requirements for water are low.

Loam is an even mixture of sand, silt, and clay particles. Generally, loamy soils with a pH close to neutral are ideal for agricultural plant growth because of their ability to retain water and nutrients.

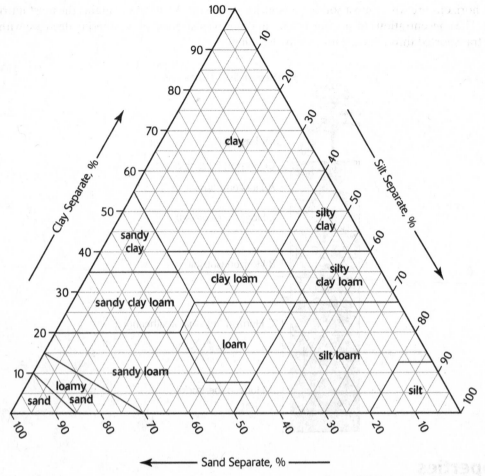

Source: U.S. Department of Agriculture

pH

The pH scale measures hydrogen ion concentrations on a scale of 1 to 14. Acidic substances range from 1 to 6.9, and alkaline (or basic) substances range from 7.1 to 14; a pH of 7 is neutral. Soils that are acidic lack nutrients, and alkaline soils can contain an excess of sodium. In general, agricultural soils are best in the range of 3 to 7.

Soil characteristics and properties vary from place to place depending on temperature and precipitation. Human activities are having a profound impact on soils globally because of deforestation, nutrient depletion, overgrazing, overuse, and ultimately erosion. Human effects on soil are reviewed in Chapter 4.

Practice

1. Tectonic plate boundaries are an important component of geologic activity because:

   A. Plate movement affects wave motion and tides.
   B. Minerals form at the boundaries.
   C. Earthquakes, volcanoes, and formation of mountain ranges occur here.
   D. Gases are released here.
   E. Weather is affected by the activity at the plate boundaries.

Questions 2–4 refer to the following answer choices.

   A. Sulfur dioxide
   B. Carbon dioxide
   C. Hydrogen fluoride
   D. Carbon monoxide
   E. Hydrogen chloride

2. An atmospheric gas that can cause acid rain and increase the rate of ozone depletion.

3. An atmospheric gas that may cause bone deterioration, poisoning of animals, and acid rain.

4. An atmospheric gas that replaces breathable air and can lead to asphyxiation.

5. On Earth, summer occurs when:

   A. The Earth is closest to the sun.
   B. The sun's rays are at the steepest angle on the Earth.
   C. The sun's rays are at their most direct angle to Earth.
   D. The Earth is farthest from the sun.
   E. The vernal equinox occurs.

6. Which is NOT a component of the water cycle?

   A. Water is stored in sinks, including ice caps, oceans, rivers, and lakes.
   B. The sun is a key component and acts as a power source for the water cycle.
   C. The movement of nutrients is largely dependent upon the water cycle.
   D. Water vapor is considered an atmospheric gas.
   E. Most water is held in freshwater sources, such as rivers and lakes.

7. Which of the following has an effect on surface currents?

   I. Water temperature
   II. Coriolis effect
   III. Winds
   IV. Dissolved oxygen
   V. Location of continents

   A. I and II only
   B. I, II, and III only
   C. I, II, III, and IV only
   D. IV and V only
   E. None of the above

Questions 8–10 refer to the following figure and answer choices.

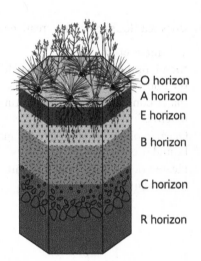

   A. O horizon layer
   B. A horizon layer
   C. E horizon layer
   D. B horizon layer
   E. R horizon layer

8. Which soil profile horizon contains most nutrients for plant growth?

9. Which soil profile horizon is considered subsoil?

10. Which soil profile horizon is the parent material?

11. Which of the following is NOT an effect of El Niño?

    A. A loss of nutrients in the affected ocean waters
    B. A warming of the waters off the western coast of South America
    C. Dryer conditions in the eastern United States, Peru, and Ecuador
    D. A cooling cycle known as La Niña
    E. Dryer conditions in the Philippines, Indonesia, and Australia

12. Which layer of the atmosphere has most of the mass and is the layer where weather occurs?

    A. Troposphere
    B. Stratosphere
    C. Mesosphere
    D. Thermosphere
    E. Exosphere

13. How does sea floor spreading create new land?

    A. Volcanoes erupt.
    B. Magma pushes through the Earth's crust at the mid-ocean ridge and hardens.
    C. Plates continually move, disrupting the magma.
    D. Oceanic plates are subducted at plate boundaries.
    E. Heated ocean water rises and sinks at the mid-ocean ridge.

14. In which way do volcanic gases NOT temporarily affect the atmosphere?

    A. Ozone is broken down when reactions occur with HCl or SO_2.
    B. Gases ultimately lower the mean global temperature.
    C. Acid rain is reduced.
    D. The temperature of the planet increases over time.
    E. Smog is created regionally.

15. Three convection currents impact atmospheric circulation: the Ferrel, Hadley, and polar air circulation cells. Which of the following is NOT true of these convection cells?

    A. The polar air circulation cells are characterized by two major biomes, tundra and taiga.
    B. Both the Hadley and polar circulation cells influence the Ferrel air circulation cells.
    C. Two distinct regions—the equatorial region of high humidity and heavy rain and the subtropical region of low humidity, few clouds, and high water evaporation—characterize the Hadley air circulation cells.
    D. The three types of convection cells occur only in the northern hemisphere.
    E. Ferrel circulation cells are defined by the four traditional seasons—spring, summer, fall, and winter.

Answers

1. **C** Earthquakes, volcanoes, and the formation of mountain ranges take place at plate boundaries and occur due to the continual movement of the tectonic plates. Plates can converge, diverge, or slide past one another, leading to geologic activity and the creation of geologic structures.

2. **A** Sulfur dioxide chemically reacts with hydrogen and oxygen to form H_2SO_4, which forms acid and increases the rate of ozone depletion.

3. **C** Hydrogen fluoride can cause bone deterioration, poisoning of animals, and acid rain. Excess fluorine in animals can poison animals and can lead to fluorosis, which deteriorates bones and may lead to death.

4. **B** Carbon dioxide is denser than air, so excess amounts can create pockets of CO_2 close to the ground in low-lying areas. Ultimately, this could lead to asphyxiation and death.

5. **C** Summer occurs when the sun's rays hit the Earth's surface at the most direct angles. Summer is also marked by the longest daylight hours.

6. **E** Of the Earth's water, 97.5 percent is held in oceans, while 2.5 percent is freshwater.

7. **B** Ocean currents are impacted by the movement of wind, the heating of the ocean's surface by the sun, the Coriolis effect, and density differences in the water.

8. **B** The A horizon is considered the topsoil and is an organic and inorganic mix of materials.

9. **D** The B horizon contains many components leached from overlying layers, including nutrients, organic matter, and minerals.

10. **E** The R horizon is bedrock, the parent material that erodes through time, and is the main component from which soil is made.

11. **C** The other four answers are effects of El Niño. El Niño causes wetter conditions in the eastern United States, Peru, and Ecuador.

12. **A** The layers of the atmosphere are listed in order from the innermost layer to the outermost layer. As you move away from the Earth's surface, the mass decreases; thus, the inner layer, the troposphere, has the greatest mass. In addition, weather is caused by the transfer of heat from solar energy hitting the Earth's surface, where the lower layer of Earth's atmosphere, the troposphere, is located.

13. **B** At the mid-ocean ridge, magma pushes through the crust and hardens, creating new seafloor. As new magma surfaces, it pushes away the existing seafloor, causing it to spread and move apart. Magma rises through the crust because of convection currents in the magma in the asthenosphere below the plates.

14. **C** Acid rain increases with larger amounts of certain gases in the air, such as HCl and SO_2.

15. **D** The three types of convection currents occur in both the Northern and Southern hemispheres.

Chapter 2

The Living World

For an ecosystem to function properly and remain healthy, countless organisms and the environment have interactions that affect one another. To understand how an ecosystem functions, it is necessary to understand the living components, how they work together, and how they are affected by other biotic and abiotic factors. This chapter reviews the structure of ecosystems, the relationships between organisms and their environment, energy flow and nutrient cycling, and ecosystem changes.

Ecosystem Structure

Ecosystems are made up of all their living and nonliving components interacting in a specific area at the same time. The parameters of an ecosystem can vary, but all ecosystems are made up of the same components. Every ecosystem contains communities and populations of organisms, which are made up of a variety of species and individual organisms, all interacting with the abiotic factors including rocks, water, and climate. Lifting up a rock in a forest can expose a mini-ecosystem. A forest functions as an ecosystem, while Earth's entire biosphere can also be considered an ecosystem.

Biological Populations and Communities

A group of individuals (organisms) of the same species living in the same area at the same time is considered to be a **population.** For example, all the black bears currently living in eastern Oregon would be a population. A **community** is made up of multiple populations of different species in a given area. As an example, in eastern Oregon, the American badger, bullfrog, painted turtle, deer mouse, elk, mountain lion, black bear, and Douglas squirrel populations are all part of the animal community within this region, along with many other species. Population ecology examines how the individuals within a species interact, while community ecology examines how a variety of species interact. (For additional information on population ecology, refer to Chapter 3.)

Ecosystems are made up of not only the living organisms in an area but the nonliving components as well. When studying populations and communities, the habitats are also important for understanding interactions and ultimately species' survival and reproduction. An organism's **habitat** is the location in which it lives, and it includes the soil, vegetation, water supply, and many other factors.

Within most ecosystem communities are **keystone species,** which are species that have an important and dramatic affect on the ecosystem in which they live. This is not to say that other organisms are not important—a keystone species has an effect on a wide range of other organisms, impacting both the ecosystem's structure and functioning. Examples of keystone species include sea otters, elephants, beavers, and wolves.

Ecological Niches

An organism's **niche** is both how the organism uses its resources and its role in the community. Niche components include habitat use, food consumption, interactions with other species, and shelter, among many other aspects. Organisms that have the ability to survive in a variety of environments and can adjust to different situations and niches are considered to be **generalists.** They can handle changing conditions and temperatures and do not especially thrive in any specific type of environment. **Specialists,** on the other hand, have adapted to a specific environment and are very good at their role within that niche, but this makes the species more vulnerable to any type of change.

Species Interactions

In ecosystems, organisms interact with other organisms in a variety of ways. Interactions can lead to positive or negative effects on the organisms involved. These interactions include competition, mutualism, predation, parasitism, herbivory, commensalism, and amensalism.

Competition is the process by which organisms vie for the same resources, resulting in one outperforming the other. Resources over which competition occurs include food, water, shelter, mates, and sunlight. When two or more different species compete, it is called **interspecific competition.** When individuals of the same species compete, the situation is called **intraspecific competition.** When organisms are in competition, generally each has a negative impact on the other, since one will outcompete the other for the resource. In some situations, though, species adapt to competition over time through evolution. The result is that each species reduces competition with others by sharing a resource but using it differently or by using somewhat different resources to fulfill its needs. This is called **resource partitioning.**

In **mutualistic interactions,** two or more species benefit from one another, each helping the other. For example, bees and flowers help one another. The bees take nectar and pollen from the flowers for food while also assisting with the spreading of pollen from one flower to another. Neither organism is harmed during their interactions. Another example is lichens, which are made up of fungi and algae living together in a symbiotic relationship. The fungi provide shelter for the algae, and the algae provide food for the fungi through their photosynthetic abilities. Lichens are also an important pioneer species.

During **predation,** one species hunts, captures, kills, and consumes another species, resulting in the second species' instant demise. One species benefits and the other is harmed. This is a predator/prey relationship. Because this relationship is how energy is transferred throughout the trophic levels of ecosystems, most predators are also prey at some point. This relationship contributes to the dynamics of a population. The more prey there are, the greater number of predators that can be supported. More prey supports an increase in the number of predators, but at some point the population of predators will meet its carrying capacity and will start to decline. The prey population will eventually begin to increase again once the predators decline, keeping the predator/prey cycle in motion.

With **parasitism,** one organism uses another for food and nutrients while also harming the other individual. The **parasite** is the organism that benefits, and the **host** is the organism that is harmed. The damage usually is not immediate but occurs over a period of time. Parasites can live in a variety of places relative to their hosts. Some live inside their hosts, others live on their exterior, and still others live on their own and meet their hosts only sporadically. Often, parasites and hosts will evolve relative to each other in a process called **co-evolution.**

When plants are consumed by animals, the process is termed **herbivory.** In this interaction, the plants' growth and reproduction are affected, while the animals benefit from the nutrients the plants provide. The most common herbivores are insects. In many cases, plants produce defenses—such as toxins, thorns, or hairs—to discourage herbivorous consumers.

Commensalism is the process by which one species benefits from their relationship and the other species is neither positively nor negatively affected. For example, cattle egrets are often seen around cattle, standing on their backs and on the ground around them. The egrets benefit because the cattle's movements stir up insects on which the birds feed, while the cattle are not affected in either a positive or negative way by the egrets' presence.

In **amensalistic relationships,** one organism harms or inhibits another while remaining unaffected itself. Only limited examples of amensalism are understood because of the difficulty in proving that one species does not in some way benefit from the harm it has caused to another. A common example, though, is the fungus *Penicillium notatum,* which produces the antibiotic penicillin. Penicillin inhibits the growth of certain types of bacteria, but it appears that the *Penicillium* is unaffected.

Summary of Effects of Species Interactions			
Interaction	**Species A**	**Species B**	**Description**
Competition	Harmed	Harmed	Organisms vie for the same resource.
Predation	Benefits	Harmed	One organism hunts, captures, kills, and consumes another.
Parasitism	Benefits	Harmed	One organism benefits from another organism while at the same time doing it harm.
Herbivory	Benefits	Harmed	Animals consume plant tissues.

Interaction	Species A	Species B	Description
Mutualism	Benefits	Benefits	Two organisms both benefit from one another.
Commensalism	Benefits	Unaffected	One organism benefits while the other is unaffected.
Amensalism	Unaffected	Harmed	One organism is unaffected while harming another.

Biomes: Terrestrial and Aquatic

Throughout the planet are a variety of **biomes,** large ecological areas dominated by a particular plant type. The location of biomes is based on many factors, including temperature, precipitation, soil type and characteristics, and oceanic and atmospheric circulation. Precipitation and temperature are the main influence on vegetation type and, therefore, on biomes.

Aquatic biomes are slightly more complicated to define and are not grouped the same way as terrestrial biomes. Salinity, temperature, nutrients, currents, depth, wave action, and bottom substrate, as well as animal life, all help to define an aquatic biome. Aquatic biomes include lakes, rivers, streams, ponds, wetlands (freshwater and marine), estuaries, and coral reefs.

The Earth has ten major terrestrial biomes: tropical rain forest, tropical dry forest, temperate rain forest, temperate deciduous forest, boreal forest (taiga), savanna, chaparral, temperate grassland, tundra, and desert. The following chart summarizes the main characteristics of each biome.

Characteristics of Earth's Terrestrial Biomes					
Biome	**Precipitation**	**Temperatures**	**Biotic Forms**	**Locations**	**Other**
Tropical rain forest	High year-round	Warm throughout the year	Lush; high biodiversity	Central America, South America, Southeast Asia, West Africa	Soils are acidic and lack nutrients because most nutrients are within the vegetation; near equator
Tropical dry forest	Low overall, but seasonal; rainy half the year, dry half the year	Warm year-round	Adapted for seasonal fluctuations; deciduous plants	India, Africa, South America, northern Australia	
Temperate rain forest	High year-round	Moderate	Coniferous trees (firs, cedars, spruces), mosses, moisture-loving species	Pacific Northwest of the United States, Japan	
Temperate deciduous forest	Spread evenly throughout year	Varied seasonally	Deciduous broadleaf trees	Europe, eastern China, eastern North America, southern Great Lakes in the United States	Fertile soils
Boreal forest	Long cold winters, short cool summers	Moderate	Evergreen forests; mainly feed and breed in warm, wet months; includes wolves, moose bear, lynx, and many migratory birds	Canada, Alaska, Russia, Scandinavia	Has many bogs and lakes; poor nutrients in the soil, which is also somewhat acidic; also known as taiga

(continued)

(continued)

Biome	Precipitation	Temperatures	Biotic Forms	Locations	Other
Savanna	Short rainy season with increased rainfall	Warm; slight seasonal variation	Grasslands with groups of acacias and other trees; includes zebras, gazelles, lions, hyenas, and giraffes	Africa, South America, Australia, India	Animals gather near watering holes
Chaparral	Very seasonal with wet winters and dry summers	Mild winters, warm summers	Evergreen shrubs	California coast in the United States, Chile, Southern Australia, land surrounding the Mediterranean Sea	Has frequent fires, which helps some seeds germinate; sometimes called a Mediterranean climate
Temperate grassland	Low	Extreme differences between summer and winter	Mainly grasses due to low rainfall; includes bison, prairie dogs, antelope, and prairie chickens	North America, South America, central Asia	Much has been cleared for agriculture; also known as steppe or prairie
Tundra	Very low	Cold winters and cool summers	Lichens, low vegetation; most animals cannot survive all year and migrate, such as caribou and birds; polar bears and musk oxen live here year-round	Arctic Russia, Canada, Scandinavia, Alpine, High Mountain Alps, Rockies, and Andes	Short winter days and long summer days; located in high latitudes; soil remains frozen permanently (permafrost)
Desert	Extremely low; the driest biome	Dramatic variation between day and night; limited vegetation and humidity to hold heat at night	Some deserts are mostly bare and some have limited vegetation such as cacti; kangaroo, mice, and rattlesnakes live here; organisms develop adaptations to survive the extreme environment, including plants with green trunks to conduct photosynthesis without leaves, and animals that are nocturnal	Africa, Arizona in the United States, northwest Mexico	Soils are usually saline with a high mineral content and low organic matter

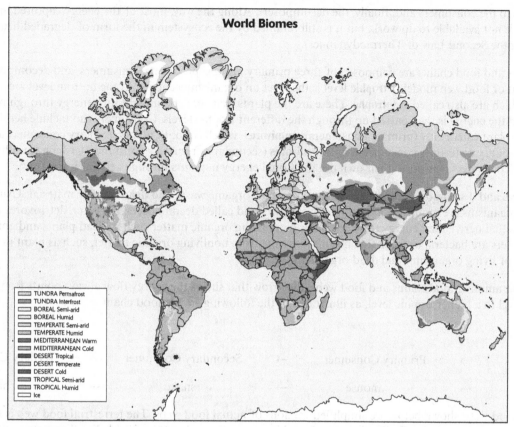

World Biomes

TUNDRA Permafrost
TUNDRA Interfrost
BOREAL Semi-arid
BOREAL Humid
TEMPERATE Semi-arid
TEMPERATE Humid
MEDITERRANEAN Warm
MEDITERRANEAN Cold
DESERT Tropical
DESERT Temperate
DESERT Cold
TROPICAL Semi-arid
TROPICAL Humid
Ice

Source: U.S. Department of Agriculture

Energy Flow

Photosynthesis and Cellular Respiration

Photosynthesis is one of the most important biological processes for living organisms because. Through photosynthesis, most life on Earth obtains energy from the sun, directly or indirectly. The only exceptions are the chemosynthetic organisms that live at heat vents in the oceans and geysers in terrestrial systems.

Photosynthesis occurs when plants take in carbon dioxide (CO_2) and water (H_2O) while absorbing energy from the sun. The absorption takes place in their chloroplasts and produces glucose (a carbohydrate, $C_6H_{12}O_6$) and oxygen (O_2). **Cellular respiration** (or just respiration) is the process of "burning" the carbohydrate glucose in the presence of oxygen to release the stored energy for use by the organism.

The balanced chemical reaction for photosynthesis is $6\ CO_2 + 6\ H_2O + \text{light energy} \rightarrow C_6H_{12}O_6 + 6\ O_2$, where glucose ($C_6H_{12}O_6$) is the initial storage of energy in plants. This energy is then released by cellular respiration in the balanced reaction $C_6H_{12}O_6 + 6\ O_2 \rightarrow 6\ CO_2 + 6\ H_2O + \text{energy}$. This released energy is usable by the plant or animal for a variety of other internal chemical and energy transfer reactions.

Food Webs and Trophic Levels

Food webs are models made up of multiple overlapping food chains. A **food chain** is a simple layer of energy flow from the producer to various consumers. A food web represents more realistic and complex flow of energy from the producers to the consumers and, finally, the decomposers. Along the way, most of the energy captured in the food web is not available to do work, but it is still retained by the ecosystem in the form of degraded heat energy (following the Second Law of Thermodynamics).

Food webs and food chains are composed of three primary groups: producers, consumers, and decomposers. In a food chain or food web model, a **trophic level** is the layer an organism occupies. At the bottom level are the producers, which are also called **autotrophs**. These are the plants that convert sunlight into energy through photosynthesis, and the energy is then passed up through the different trophic levels. Consumers can include **herbivores,** which are plant eaters only (primary consumers); **omnivores**, which eat both plants (primary consumer) and animals (secondary or tertiary consumers); and **carnivores** (secondary or tertiary consumers), which eat other animals. The consumers convert to their own use the stored energy in plants through cellular respiration.

Detritivores and decomposers complete the breakdown of organic waste and dead organic material. Usually both types of organisms are grouped together in one category and called decomposers. However, detritivores are organisms that derive their energy from consuming nonliving organic matter such as dead plants and animals. Decomposers are bacteria or fungi that absorb nutrients from nonliving organic matter, such as plant material, the waste of living organisms, and dead organisms.

When diagramming food chains and food webs, the arrow that shows the energy flow always points from a lower trophic level to a higher trophic level, as illustrated in the following simple food chain.

Food Chain

Producer	→	Primary Consumer	→	Secondary Consumer	→	Tertiary Consumer
grass	→	mouse	→	snake	→	hawk

The two food webs shown below are simplified versions of actual food webs. The terrestrial food web is from the Arctic, and the marine water food web can be found in oceans throughout the world. The direction of the arrows shows the flow of energy. Energy flows from the lower trophic level to the higher level.

Terrestrial Food Web

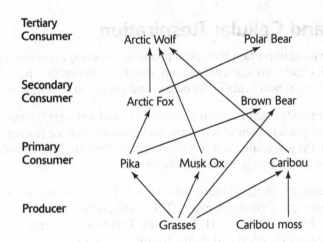

Marine Water Food Web

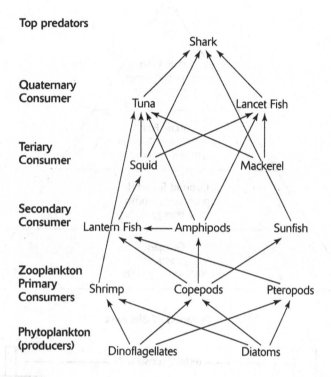

Top predators

Quaternary Consumer

Teriary Consumer

Secondary Consumer

Zooplankton Primary Consumers

Phytoplankton (producers)

Ecological Pyramids

An **ecological pyramid,** also called an energy pyramid, is a diagram that shows the loss of available energy at each trophic level. Some energy is transformed into heat, which enters the environment and cannot be used. Losses may be caused by the incomplete digestion of food, incomplete capture of energy released during cellular respiration, or degradation of energy into heat energy.

An average energy loss of 90 percent occurs from one trophic level to the next, from the bottom of the pyramid to the top. That means that of 100 percent of the energy captured in the producers, only 10 percent of it moves to the primary consumer, and 90 percent is lost. Energy transfer from primary consumer to secondary consumer accounts for another 90 percent loss; thus, the net energy gain to the secondary consumer from the system is 1 percent. Transfer from secondary to tertiary consumer results in a 0.1 percent net gain to the tertiary consumer. This energy is usually measured in kilocalories (kcals). The passing of only 10 percent of energy from one trophic level to the next is sometimes referred to as the 10 percent rule.

The Pyramid of Energy diagram below shows the trophic levels of an arctic food pyramid which indicates an organism's energy level of consumption. The numbers indicate the amount of energy available to consumers at that level. The energy decreases moving up the pyramid due to energy lost. The Pyramid of Biomass represents the biomass at each trophic level in both a grassland ecosystem and an aquatic saltwater ecosystem. In the ocean pyramid, the mass of producers in the open ocean may be relatively small compared to consumers. This is because they grow and reproduce rapidly and are able to produce enough energy to support the species in higher trophic levels.

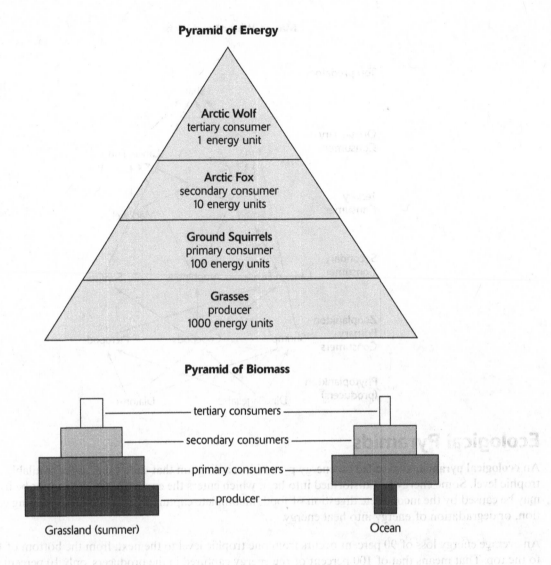

Pyramid of Energy

Arctic Wolf
tertiary consumer
1 energy unit

Arctic Fox
secondary consumer
10 energy units

Ground Squirrels
primary consumer
100 energy units

Grasses
producer
1000 energy units

Pyramid of Biomass

tertiary consumers

secondary consumers

primary consumers

producer

Grassland (summer)

Ocean

Ecosystem Diversity

Biodiversity

The total of all species in a given area at a specific time encompasses biological diversity, or **biodiversity.**
Biodiversity can be viewed in terms of ecosystems, species, or genetics.

- **Ecosystem diversity** is the variety of ecosystems within a specific area, including communities and habitats.
  An ecosystem includes all living organisms in an area. A large section of prairie land will have lower biodiversity than a forested area with many different varieties of trees supporting many types of species.

- **Species diversity** is the number (or variety) of a species within a particular community. A **species** is classified
  as a group of organisms that share particular sets of characteristics and can breed and reproduce to create
  fertile offspring. The higher number of different species in an area means there is high biodiversity. In evaluating species diversity, there are two key components: species richness and relative abundance. **Species richness** is the number of species in an area, while **relative abundance** is the number of each species in relation to
  one another, or how equal the numbers are of each species.

- **Genetic diversity** is the variation of heritable DNA among individuals of a species or population. All organisms have different DNA makeup, so a population of organisms with a large number of individuals will

have more genetic diversity than a population with a few individuals. Populations with low genetic diversity are at higher risk for extinction because fewer genetic variations are available to allow for adaptation to environmental change. As an example, if the climate in a region is altered dramatically and becomes warmer, the organisms with thicker fur may not survive, thus leaving those with thinner coats to survive and reproduce. Also, if only a few individuals have this variation, the whole population could suffer. In addition, low genetic diversity can lead to inbreeding issues when organisms with a very similar genetic makeup breed and produce offspring with physical problems.

Biodiversity is not evenly distributed because factors such as climate, altitude, and topography affect what species live in particular locations. Species richness is greater closer to the equator. This difference in richness from poles to equator is called the **latitudinal gradient** and is supported by the consistent amount of solar radiation, humidity, and precipitation near the equator. The result is increased plant life near the equator, which, in turn, supports numerous animal populations.

Evolution and Natural Selection

Biodiversity on Earth has been created through the process of **evolution,** the variation in genetic makeup of a population of organisms through generations. Genetic changes take place in organisms within a population over many generations, occurring randomly or through the process of natural selection. **Natural selection** results when genetic traits that strengthen an organism's chance of survival and reproduction are passed on from generation to generation, ultimately altering the genetic makeup of a population, creating a new species. In the process of natural selection, some organisms in a population are better suited to survive than others; therefore, the organisms that survive are those that have a reproductive advantage and are more likely to pass on their genes. Across time, entire populations contain traits that increase the likelihood to adapt, survive and reproduce.

The traits that lead to success are **adaptive traits,** or **adaptations.** For these traits to be passed on to offspring, genes in an organism's DNA must code for that trait. During DNA replication, which occurs in an organism's cells millions of times throughout its life, errors can arise. These errors lead to accidental alterations in DNA, called **mutations.** Most mutations don't have an effect, but some can be favorable and some can be fatal. The positive mutations can lead to a better ability to survive and reproduce in an environment, leading to natural selection. These mutations also can occur through mating, when genetic material combines during sexual reproduction.

If not enough individuals in a population have traits that help them survive and reproduce in a changing environment, then the chance is higher that the species will dwindle in numbers and possibly go extinct. The Monteverde golden toads are one example. (See the Case Studies in Appendix B for additional information about the Monteverde golden toad.)

The environment plays a key role in determining which traits are beneficial; thus, an organism's environment as well as genetic makeup affect natural selection and ultimately the evolution of a species.

Artificial selection occurs when humans have an impact on which traits are selected during breeding. Examples of species that have been artificially selected include dogs, cats, horses, cows, and many types of flowers.

Types of Selection

Three models of natural selection have been described:

- **Stabilizing selection** occurs when a population's characteristics stay within a moderate range and neither extreme is dominant. If individuals fall away in either extreme, their chances of survival are reduced. This structure reduces evolutionary change and diversity. For example, birds are important to flower pollination. If a bird's beak is too short or too long, it will not effectively reach and transfer pollen between flowers; therefore, a medium-length bill is most effective and most common.

- **Disruptive selection** discriminates individuals with characteristics at the extremes, so fewer individuals fall within the average. With this model structure, evolution does occur, as individuals fall to either extreme in the population. As a general example, in an area that has small and large seeds for the bird population to eat, but no medium seeds, birds with small and large beaks will dominate while birds with medium-sized beaks will be present in low numbers.

- **Directional selection** favors one extreme of the population, so the opposite extreme and the average in the model are not where the majority of a population falls. As with disruptive selection, evolution does occur. An example is the peppered moth. At one time, most of these moths were light in color, but following increases in pollution from the Industrial Revolution, the species shifted and darker moths became more abundant than lighter individuals.

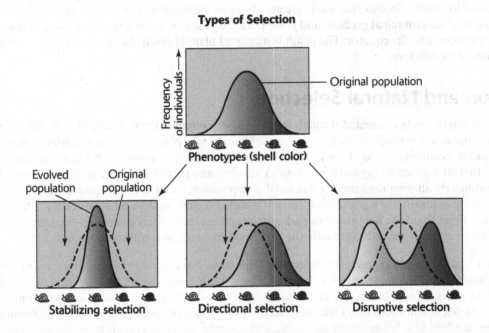

Types of Selection

Frequency of individuals

Phenotypes (shell color)

Original population

Evolved population   Original population

Stabilizing selection   Directional selection   Disruptive selection

Speciation

Speciation is the process by which new species are created. This process can occur in many ways but two are common: allopatric and sympatric. **Sympatric speciation** occurs when similar organisms live within the same location but fulfill different niches; therefore, they do not mate and reproduce. The most common way speciation occurs is through **allopatric speciation**, when a new species is created over time because of a physical separation of a population. Separation can result from physical changes such as:

- Formation of mountain ranges
- Rivers changing course
- Habitat fragmentation
- Advancement of glacial ice sheets
- Alteration of climate in a region
- Shift of ocean currents
- Formation of islands from volcanism

When a physical division takes place parts of a population are separated. As a result, the divided population can no longer reproduce with each other because of geographic distance. Over time each population develops and passes on new and different mutations. Given enough time, a new species may form because of the genetic variations in the populations. If at some point in time these different populations would reunite, they would no longer be able to interbreed. Speciation has occurred.

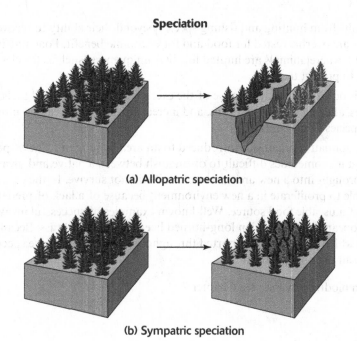

Speciation

(a) Allopatric speciation

(b) Sympatric speciation

Ecosystem Services

Benefits provided by ecosystems that help support life on Earth, and in many cases the human economy, are known as **ecosystem services.** A few examples of such services include the cycling of nutrients, purification of air and water, creation of soil, and the supplying of raw materials.

Without these services offered by the environment, life would not be able to flourish and survive. For humans, our economic structure would not exist without its raw materials for industry, beauty to support tourism, or the natural cleaning and recycling it enables. Major benefits afforded to humans include food security, tourism and recreation, drugs and medicine, and a connection to nature and other life (referred to as **biophilia**).

Biodiversity is the key to ecosystem services. Because of the diversity of species in an area, an ecosystem is better able to remain stable or recover quickly after a disturbance.

Biodiversity Loss, Conservation, and Extinction

Biodiversity Loss

Species and biodiversity are being lost at an extremely rapid rate, largely because of human activities. Such activities include habitat alteration, pollution, overharvesting, climate alteration, and introduction of invasive species, each of which can harm a particular population of a species and potentially put the entire species at risk. **Extinction** occurs when all populations of a species are lost and no individuals remain. On a smaller scale, **extirpation** is the point at which a population vanishes from a particular area but remaining populations are still in other locations on the planet.

- **Habitat alteration** results from any human activity that changes an ecosystem. Deforestation, farming, mining, development, and dams are examples of activities that affect habitats. Habitat alteration is the largest contributor to biodiversity loss and population declines.
- **Pollution** can affect the water, air, and soil, all of which have an impact on not only the local ecosystem and its organisms but also those in distant areas as well because pollution can be transported far from its source. Pollution also has a detrimental effect on human health (see Chapter 6).

- **Overharvesting** results from hunting and fishing species beyond their ability to recover the numbers of their population. Species are overharvested for food and for economic benefit. Poaching is still an issue in some regions of the world, where animals are hunted for their uniqueness (such as for elephant tusks and tiger claws) despite laws to protect them.

- **Climate alteration** is occurring partly because of the excessive burning of fossil fuels, which is increasing global temperatures, altering weather patterns, and increasing dramatic weather, ultimately changing the climate globally for species of all kinds.

- **Invasive species** are nonnative organisms introduced to an area by humans. These species are so numerous and widespread that it's sometimes difficult to distinguish between a native and invasive species in an area. When a species is brought into a new area, most often it will not survive. In the case of invasive species though, they are able to proliferate in a new environment because of a lack of predators and disease as well as the availability of a useable food source. Well-known examples of successful invasive species include zebra mussels, European starlings, Asian long-horned beetles, and cheatgrass. Because of the global economy and ease with which goods are transported throughout the world, invasive species are continually being introduced and are an ongoing problem.

For more information on biodiversity loss, see Chapter 7.

Conservation

Conservation biology studies the environment and biodiversity in an effort to protect species and their habitats. Through these studies, solutions are developed to address habitat loss and species loss.

People are trying to protect and conserve our natural world in many ways. Nonprofit organizations, communities, and individuals bring awareness and take initiative to protect habitats and wildlife, and laws and policies are put in place to support conservation efforts.

Many laws and initiatives have been established to support conservation efforts on local, regional, national, and global scales. For example, in the United States the **Endangered Species Act** (ESA) does not allow governments or private citizens to perform actions that would affect endangered species and their habitats. Internationally, the **Convention on International Trade in Endangered Species of Wild Fauna and Flora** (CITES) bans the transporting of body parts of endangered species internationally.

Extinction

Without human efforts to conserve and protect the environment, the reality of extinction can come to fruition. Throughout Earth's history, most species have disappeared over time and gone **extinct.** On average, species spend between 1 million and 10 million years on this planet, depending on a variety of factors. Because the process of natural selection doesn't happen rapidly—it takes a multitude of generations to occur—if an environmental change occurs abruptly, species do not have time to adapt and may go extinct. Environmental change can take place for many reasons, such as a rise in sea level, climate fluctuations, arrival of invasive species, and natural disasters.

Extinction is a natural process, although in many cases it has been accelerated by humans. Species that are **endemic** to an area, or occur in only one location on the planet, are more susceptible to these changes, as are species that are considered **specialists,** filling a narrow niche in their ecosystems.

When extinctions happen gradually over time, the rate at which they occur is considered to be the **background extinction rate.** When extinction occurs relatively quickly and on a large scale, affecting many species, it is considered a **mass extinction event.** So far, there have been five known mass extinction events and each has killed between 50 percent and 95 percent of all species on Earth. Because of the brisk rate at which species are presently being lost, some say that the sixth mass extinction event is underway, this time at the hands of humans.

Natural Ecosystem Changes

Climate Shift

Over geologic time, the Earth's climate naturally shifts as the planet changes and evolves. In the past one billion years, the Earth has experienced six glacial periods. Currently, the Earth is in a period of glacial retreat called the Holocene epoch, which started about 14,000 years ago. Within this epoch, though, is a brief time period that is an exception to this retreat. The 1500s to the 1800s were a time of cooling, and because it was the coldest climate since the Holocene began, it has been termed the "Little Ice Age." From the mid-1800s to present times, there has been a period of general warming. Some of this is natural, but many people think it is a result of human activities.

Natural climate shifts can be caused by many changes on Earth. The following are events that can alter the Earth's climate:

- Volcanoes block solar radiation from reaching the Earth's surface, creating a cooling effect.
- Continental drift alters oceanic currents and atmospheric winds, both of which impact the distribution of heat on the planet and the altering of water evaporation into the atmosphere.
- Earth's tilt can change, which affects seasons and the amount of sunlight reaching various parts of the planet.
- Comets and meteorites can have a catastrophic impact on Earth, sending debris and clouds into the atmosphere and blocking solar radiation.
- Geomagnetic reversals may cause localized climate shifts and are currently being researched.

Human activities that can alter the climate include the extensive combustion of fossil fuels and deforestation. For more information on human-induced climate change, see Chapter 7.

Species Movement

As climates have shifted and changed during the coming and going of the ice ages, species have either adjusted or died out. Plant species, which can't physically move, must adjust where they grow or face extinction. Plants can spread by a variety of methods: seeds can blow in the wind, attach to animals and drop a great distance away from the original plant, or pass through the digestive systems of animals and be spread as the animals migrate. Plants may spread slowly along the edge of their ranges to extend their territory. Since most ice ages take long periods of time to form and retreat, plants can adjust their territory as the climate shifts.

Still, animals may have an easier time adjusting to a changing climate because many have the ability to move. As the climate shifts, animals can more easily change their territory as long as suitable habitat is within reach. Even the smallest of animals have shown evidence of moving as climate changes.

Ecological Succession

Communities are not static but are constantly changing. Species of plants and animals come and go, evolve and die out. Change is constant, although often slow by human standards. Change in a given geographical area that is predictable is described as **ecological succession.**

Two types of ecological succession have been identified:

- **Primary succession** is the process that starts with bare rock where no soil or life are present, such as a new volcanic island, an area emerging from beneath a retreating glacier, or the Earth when it was very young.
- **Secondary succession** is the re-growth of an area after an event has wiped out an existing community, but soil and some life remain. The "event" might be a fire, tornado, volcanic eruption, or human activity. Examples of human activities are abandoning an agricultural field to regrow on its own, clear-cutting a forest, or setting a fire.

The organisms that start succession in both types are called **pioneer species.** These species typically have a wide range of environmental tolerances and generally include lichens, mosses, algae, and bacteria. The pioneer species lay the foundation of nutrients on which succeeding species come and settle. Grasses are typically second; they add organic material to the developing soil and hold the new soil in place with their root systems. Small herbaceous plant species appear next, and they continue to add organic matter to the soil. Small bushes join the mix, adding still more organic matter but, more important, adding shelter and shade to the area for other plants yet to come. Conifers appear and add to the growing habitat. Short-lived hardwoods move in (such as the maples), and finally the climax community of long-lived hardwoods (such as the oaks) is reached. The succession of animals follows a similar pattern: insects are the first to arrive, and then small rodents and lizards. Birds come and bring with them the seeds of new plants for the community. As the community becomes more complex, larger mammals join the changing ecosystem.

How long this process takes depends on whether the area is undergoing primary or secondary succession. Another driving force is the climate; areas in dry climates take longer to develop than those in moist climates. Areas that receive large amounts of precipitation may also take longer to develop because the newly accumulating nutrients can be washed away by flowing water. Obviously an area undergoing primary succession will take much longer to fully develop than one in secondary succession. Secondary succession is also driven by the proximity of returning organisms. The size of the disturbed area and how close the former members of the community are to the area will play a determining factor in the succession of the area.

Biogeochemical Cycles

Biogeochemical cycles (nutrient cycles) describe the movement of nutrients throughout ecosystems (movement between Earth's abiotic and biotic systems). The word *biogeochemical* is a combination of *bio* (meaning "life"), *geo* (meaning "earth"), and *chemical* (meaning "elements or compounds that cycle through the living and nonliving world"). While many nutrients are essential for life and health on our planet, five nutrient cycles are vital for ecosystem function and survival: carbon, oxygen, nitrogen, phosphorus, and sulfur. These five nutrient cycles are being altered by human activity.

Key components of each cycle include where the nutrients are stored, how long they remain in the storage areas, and the process of movement between the living and nonliving parts of each cycle. Nutrient storage is commonly referred to as **reservoirs** or **sinks.** These reservoirs may be different for each nutrient or they may be common, depending on the nutrient. How long they remain depends on whether the nutrients are in living organisms or nonliving components. In living organisms, a reservoir may exist for only a few hours (in some bacteria) or as long as several thousand years (in a redwood or bristlecone pine). In the nonliving components, nutrients could be locked up for millions or even billions of years, either in the atmosphere or Earth's crust. The movement of each nutrient between the living and nonliving is described in each nutrient cycle.

Carbon Cycle

As a major part of life, carbon exists on Earth in living organisms, decomposing components of ecosystems, and in abiotic factors of the environment. Also, it is found in gaseous and solid states. Carbon enters living organisms through plants when CO_2 is converted to carbohydrates during photosynthesis. Carbon moves through animals when they consume plants and other animals. Carbon is released into the atmosphere in the form of CO_2 during cellular respiration and when decomposers break down the remains of dead plants and animals.

The major reservoirs of the carbon cycle include plants, oceans, and sedimentary deposits. Plant matter, while a small sink, is one that humans must consider as we grow more plants and animals for human food consumption. Some of this carbon is stored for a short time, such as in the annual plants we grow for food, while other carbon is stored for thousands of years in giant sequoias, for example. Because plants are constantly releasing and capturing CO_2, they are considered to cause zero change in the atmosphere.

Carbon dioxide is soluble in water, so the world's oceans are a major sink for carbon. It is dissolved in the world's oceans just as oxygen is dissolved. This dissolved CO_2 is important for aquatic plant photosynthesis. Carbon is also found in the shells and skeletons of marine organisms. An exchange of CO_2 occurs between the atmosphere and marine waters. Because of the net increase in CO_2 in the atmosphere from the combustion of fossil fuels, it is believed that the world's oceans are becoming more acidic.

Earth's rocks contain some carbon, although silicon and oxygen are their primary components. Rocks that contain carbon are called carbonate rocks, and the form of carbon is calcium carbonate.

A final sink and the form that is the primary focus of human interventions in the carbon cycle is the carbon in coal, gas, and crude oil, what we refer to as fossil fuels. This carbon—originally from living organisms that have undergone a chemical change over time, with pressure and heat, to be converted into coal and oil—has been sequestered for millions of years. Thus, the combustion of fossil fuels has contributed to a shift from carbon stored in the lithosphere to the atmosphere, creating a net gain of CO_2 in the atmosphere.

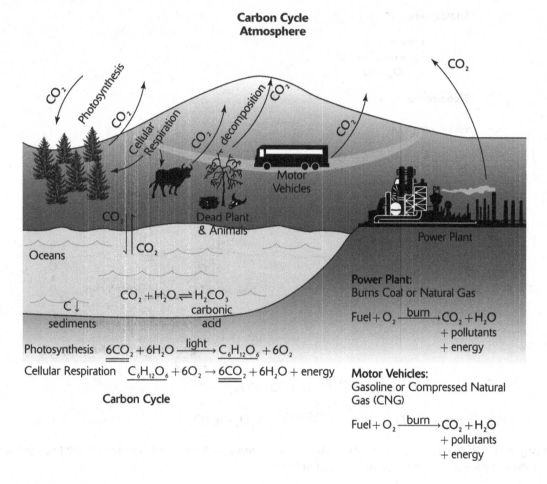

Carbon Cycle
Atmosphere

Photosynthesis $6CO_2 + 6H_2O \xrightarrow{\text{light}} C_6H_{12}O_6 + 6O_2$

Cellular Respiration $C_6H_{12}O_6 + 6O_2 \rightarrow 6CO_2 + 6H_2O + \text{energy}$

Carbon Cycle

Power Plant:
Burns Coal or Natural Gas

$Fuel + O_2 \xrightarrow{\text{burn}} CO_2 + H_2O$
$+ \text{pollutants}$
$+ \text{energy}$

Motor Vehicles:
Gasoline or Compressed Natural Gas (CNG)

$Fuel + O_2 \xrightarrow{\text{burn}} CO_2 + H_2O$
$+ \text{pollutants}$
$+ \text{energy}$

$CO_2 + H_2O \rightleftharpoons H_2CO_3$
carbonic acid

Oxygen Cycle

The oxygen cycle is not described in most textbooks but is nevertheless very important for the living world. Oxygen (O_2) is the byproduct of photosynthesis in plants and a reactant in the cellular respiration of plants and animals. Oxygen is the second major component of the atmosphere after nitrogen gas (N_2) and composes approximately 21 percent of the atmosphere.

Oxygen is a reactive molecule. Besides involvement in the photosynthetic and cellular respiration reactions, oxygen is removed from the atmosphere during the weathering process of rock and minerals. As new rock and minerals are exposed to the atmosphere during weathering, oxygen combines with them in a process called oxidation and is, thus, removed from the atmosphere.

Oxygen is also important in the formation of atmospheric ozone. Sunlight breaks water (H_2O) vapor into hydrogen gas and oxygen, and the hydrogen escapes Earth's atmosphere and travels into outer space. Ozone (O_3) is a naturally occurring reaction product in the atmosphere, where it forms a layer. The ozone layer is important for filtering out much of the harmful ultraviolet (UV) radiation from the sun and keeping it from hitting the Earth. The chemical reaction for the formation of ozone is:

$$O_2 + UV \rightarrow O + O$$
$$O + O_2 \rightarrow O_3$$

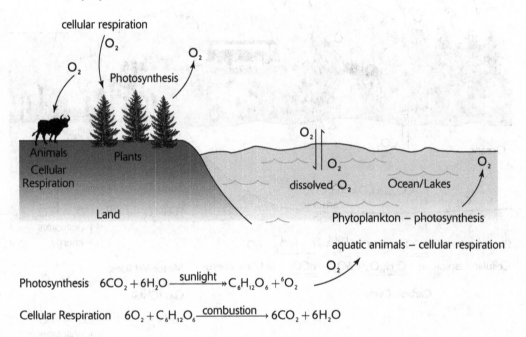

Oxygen Cycle

Atmosphere

Stratosphere

Ozone
$O_2 + UV \rightarrow O + O$
$O + O_2 \rightarrow O_3$

Troposphere

cellular respiration
O_2
O_2
Photosynthesis
O_2

Animals
Cellular
Respiration
Plants
Land

O_2
O_2
dissolved O_2 Ocean/Lakes
O_2
Phytoplankton – photosynthesis

aquatic animals – cellular respiration
O_2

Photosynthesis $6CO_2 + 6H_2O \xrightarrow{\text{sunlight}} C_6H_{12}O_6 + 6O_2$

Cellular Respiration $6O_2 + C_6H_{12}O_6 \xrightarrow{\text{combustion}} 6CO_2 + 6H_2O$

As you can see from the carbon and oxygen cycles, both carbon and oxygen are common in the two cycles. Photosynthesis produces O_2 and cellular respiration burns O_2.

Nitrogen Cycle

Our atmosphere is composed of 78 percent nitrogen and 21 percent oxygen. However, this atmospheric nitrogen cannot be used by organisms without some assistance. The nitrogen cycle is unique because it has stages during which bacteria help convert the nitrogen into useable forms. Nitrogen is essential for life because it helps to develop proteins, DNA, and RNA, and provide for plant growth. It can also be a limiting factor in plant growth.

The nitrogen cycle begins in the atmosphere as a gas (N_2). It then goes through many steps throughout its cycle.

- For it to be made useable by organisms, N_2 needs to be "fixed." This can occur by lightning or with the help of nitrogen-fixing bacteria. Nitrogen-fixing bacteria live in the soil and in nodules on the roots of legumes.
- When N_2 is fixed, it's combined with hydrogen to form ammonia (NH_3). This fixing process is called ammonification.
- The water-soluble ion of NH_3 is ammonium (NH_4^+), which can be taken in by plants through their roots.
- NH_4^+ then goes through a process known as nitrification, in which it is converted into nitrite ions (NO_2^-) and then nitrate ions (NO_3^-). This process is conducted by specialized bacteria called nitrifying bacteria. These ions can also be taken in by plants since they, too, are water soluble.
- The ammonium, nitrite, and nitrate ions can be assimilated and taken in by plants. Animals then receive nitrogen through consuming plants. Decomposers receive nitrogen through the decomposition of waste and decaying plants and animals.
- Decomposers process the nitrogen substances they take in and return the nitrogen to the soil as ammonium ions. Decomposition makes the nitrogen available to go through nitrification again.
- For nitrogen to return to the atmosphere in its gaseous N_2 form, it must be denitrified. Denitrifying bacteria convert nitrates into N_2.

Humans have intervened in the nitrogen cycle by developing a way to fix nitrogen artificially, creating fertilizer. This fixation process, called the **Haber-Bosch process,** conducted on an enormous scale, has negatively altered the nitrogen cycle by nearly doubling the amount of nitrogen fixation occurring on the Earth. Excess nitrogen in an aquatic environment can lead to the eutrophication of the ecosystem.

Nodules on Plant Roots

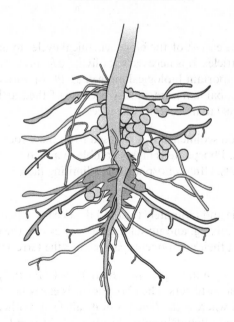

Nitrogen Cycle

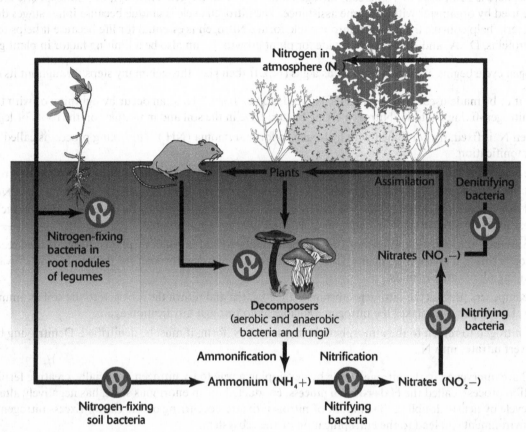

Source: Environmental Protection Agency

Phosphorus Cycle

The phosphorus cycle is probably the easiest of the biogeochemical cycles to describe. Phosphorus does not exist in the atmosphere except in dust particles. It is necessary for living organisms, as it is the backbone of nucleic acids (DNA and RNA) and other important biological molecules. Phosphorus tends to move through a local cycle, whereas the other cycles are global in nature, mostly because of the Earth's weather. Since phosphorus is limited in the atmosphere, it is unlikely to move great distances.

Phosphorus is found in soil, rock, and sediments. It is released from these rock forms through chemical weathering in the form of phosphate (PO_4^{3-}). Phosphate is highly soluble in aqueous solutions and can be absorbed from the soil into plants through their roots. Often phosphorus is a limiting factor for plant growth, as little of it is released into the environment.

Phosphorus can enter the water table and ultimately travel to the oceans, where it settles on the ocean floor. Later, through geological processes, ocean mixing, and upwelling, these rocks on the ocean floor may rise and become new land surface, with the result that their components can reenter the terrestrial cycles.

Humans affect the phosphorus cycle by mining phosphorus-rich rocks for the purpose of processing them and adding them to commercial inorganic fertilizers. The phosphorus is easily leached into the groundwater and can find its way into aquatic ecosystems, where it can help promote algae and other aquatic plant growth that can lead to overgrowth of these plants and ultimately eutrophication of the pond or lake. Phosphorus also can be added to ecosystems by humans through the release of untreated sewage, agricultural runoff, and detergents.

Phosphorus Cycle

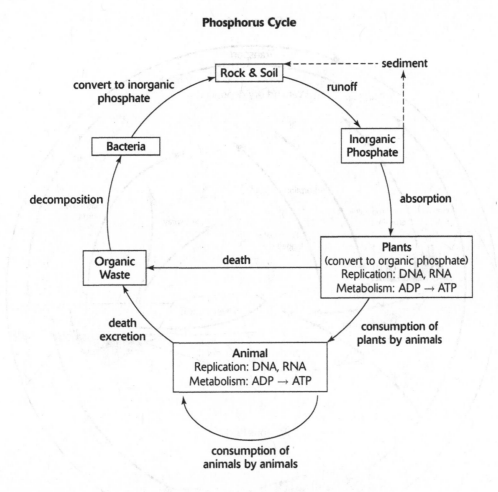

Sulfur Cycle

An important component of protein and vitamins, sulfur is essential for plant and animal health. Naturally, most sulfur is located in rocks and ocean sediments, but some is also found in the atmosphere.

The natural sulfur cycle is described by the following path:

- Sulfur is naturally released into the atmosphere from rocks and sediment in the forms of hydrogen sulfide (H_2S) and sulfur dioxide (SO_2) through weathering, volcanic eruptions, and the decay of dead organisms.
- Once in the atmosphere, SO_2 reacts with oxygen to form sulfur trioxide (SO_3) and with water to form sulfuric acid (H_2SO_4).
- Sulfur particles are deposited back into the soil and water, or they combine with water and fall in the form of acid precipitation.
- Plants absorb sulfate ions (SO_4^{2-}) through their roots, and animals receive sulfur by consuming plants.

Humans have also affected the sulfur cycle through industrial processes and coal burning, from which sulfur is emitted into the atmosphere in the forms of SO_2 and H_2SO_4.

In each biogeochemical cycle, matter is being cycled throughout ecosystems. This movement of nutrients throughout various parts of an ecosystem—both biotic and abiotic—exemplifies the conservation of matter, which states that matter cannot be created or destroyed.

Sulfur Cycle

Source: U.S. Geological Survey

Practice

1. How is solar energy used on Earth?

   I. Air circulation is partly a result of the heating of the Earth by solar energy.

   II. Solar energy is absorbed by chloroplast and used to convert carbon dioxide and water into glucose and oxygen.

   III. The water cycle is powered by solar energy.

   A. I only
   B. II only
   C. III only
   D. I and II
   E. I, II, and III

2. Which of the following is NOT true of food webs?

   A. Food webs are composed of multiple food chains.
   B. A food web shows the flow of energy from producers to consumers and, finally, to decomposers.
   C. In food webs, decomposers break down organic waste to return nutrients to the ecosystem.
   D. When diagramming food chains and food webs, the arrows should be drawn from the lower trophic levels to the higher levels to show the flow of energy.
   E. As energy is moved up the food web, most of it is conserved by the species in the next trophic levels.

3. Secondary succession is the regrowth of a disturbed area, and primary succession is the development from the beginning. Which of the following is primary succession?

   A. Changing soil to rock
   B. Changing ice to water
   C. Changing rock to soil
   D. Growth after a forest fire
   E. Formation of an island by volcanic action

4. The cycle most responsible for linking biogeochemical cycles is the:

   A. Carbon cycle
   B. Hydrologic cycle
   C. Nitrogen cycle
   D. Phosphorus cycle
   E. Sulfur cycle

5. Humans are disrupting the carbon cycle in ways that have resulted in increased levels of carbon dioxide in our atmosphere. Which of the following human activities are most directly responsible for this increase?

   A. Deforestation and the clearing of plants that absorb CO_2 through photosynthesis
   B. The addition of large amounts of CO_2 to the atmosphere by burning fossil fuels and wood
   C. The use of fertilizers and pesticides for agriculture
   D. A and B only
   E. All of the above

6. Which of the following is NOT true regarding oxygen?

   A. O_2 is a natural occurring gas in the atmosphere.
   B. O_2 is a byproduct of photosynthesis.
   C. O_2 is a reactant in cellular respiration.
   D. O_2 is the largest component of the atmosphere.
   E. O_2 is a very reactive molecule.

7. Which of the following is NOT true of phosphorus and the phosphorus cycle?

   A. Living organisms do not need phosphorus.
   B. Phosphorus tends to be more localized compared with other biogeochemical cycles that can move more freely in the global system.
   C. Phosphorus is generally found in rocks, sediments, and soil.
   D. Phosphorus does not exist in the atmosphere as a gas.
   E. Phosphorus is mined from phosphorus-rich rock, which is processed and then added to commercial inorganic fertilizers.

8. Which of the following examples would NOT be considered an adaptive trait?

    A. Thicker fur coats on wolves in northern Canada
    B. Echolocation in bats
    C. Longer claws on rodents that dig in the soil for food
    D. The ability for hummingbirds to maneuver in the air quickly
    E. High water requirements of plants in the desert

9. Due to a major flood, a dam broke, altering the course of a river. A population of ground squirrels became separated due to the river's change of course. Over time, the divided population developed new adaptations and eventually created separate species. This is an example of

    A. Sympatric speciation
    B. Stabilizing selection
    C. Allopatric speciation
    D. Directional selection
    E. Disruptive selection

10. All of the following are ways in which humans are contributing to extirpation and extinction of organisms EXCEPT through:

    A. Introducing invasive species
    B. Polluting land, water, and soil
    C. Creating wildlife refuges
    D. Altering the climate
    E. Overharvesting resources

11. If a species is endemic to an area, it is:

    A. Only found in one location on the planet
    B. A generalist species
    C. Less prone to extinction
    D. Considered an invasive species
    E. Almost always protected under the Endangered Species Act

Questions 12–14 refer to the following answer choices.

    A. Predation
    B. Mutualism
    C. Competition
    D. Herbivory
    E. Parasitism

12. Organisms feed on another organism for nutrients, which also harms the organism being fed upon.

13. The algae and fungi working together in lichen, where neither organism is harmed and both benefit.

14. During a period of drought, various species are competing for the same water source.

15. The nitrogen cycle is unique in that atmospheric nitrogen cannot be converted directly by organisms into usable nitrogen. What is necessary in order for atmospheric nitrogen to be converted to usable nitrogen by organisms?

    A. Ammonification
    B. Denitrifying bacteria
    C. Nitrifying bacteria
    D. Decomposition
    E. Nitrogen fixation

Answers

1. **E** All three statements are true. Solar energy is responsible for heating the Earth and for the formation of glucose and oxygen; it also powers the water cycle.

2. **E** Most energy is converted into a non-useable heat form that escapes into the environment.

3. **C** Choices A and D are both secondary succession. Changing rock to soil is accomplished by water, by weathering, and by lichen; this is a long process.

4. **B** The hydrologic cycle, also called the water cycle, moves components of the carbon, nitrogen, and sulfur cycles. Phosphorus usually is not found in the atmosphere unless it is in dust particles. Nitrogen- and sulfur-containing compounds combine with water to form acids, which fall to the Earth's surface as acid deposition. Carbon dioxide moves between the atmosphere and bodies of water such as lakes and oceans, where the dissolved carbon dioxide reacts with water to form carbonic acid.

5. **D** Cutting down trees and clearing other plants that absorb CO_2 for photosynthesis increases the amount of CO_2 in the atmosphere. In addition, the combustion of fossil fuels and wood also increases the amount of CO_2 in the atmosphere. The use of fertilizers and pesticides may have the opposite effect, reducing CO_2 in the atmosphere, by increasing plant growth.

6. **D** The other answers are all true. Oxygen is the second major component of the Earth's atmosphere (21 percent), far behind nitrogen (78 percent).

7. **A** The other answers are all true regarding the phosphorus cycle. Living organisms need phosphorus in their DNA and RNA molecules, as well as in the ADP-to-ATP reaction.

8. **E** Requiring large amounts of water in a desert environment would not benefit the plants. It would actually dramatically lower their chance of survival in an environment where water is scarce.

9. **C** Allopatric speciation occurs when a new species is created over time due to a physical separation of a population, including the changing of a river's course.

10. **C** Wildlife refuges serve as a safe haven for species, while also occasionally allowing hunting and fishing in order to regulate populations; species benefit from wildlife refuges.

11. **B** Endemic species are usually specialists, which fill a small, specific niche.

12. **E** Parasitism occurs when one organism uses another for food and nutrients, while also harming the other organism.

13. **B** In lichen the algae provides food for fungi through photosynthesis, while the fungi provide a safe environment in which algae can grow. In a mutualistic relationship, two or more species benefit one another, each helping the other.

14. **C** When different species compete for the same resource, it is considered interspecific competition.

15. **E** In order for nitrogen to be useable by organisms, it goes through the process of fixation, which can occur from lightning strikes or from nitrogen-fixing bacteria found on the roots of legumes or in soil.

Chapter 3

Population

An ecosystem is made up of many components and their interactions. When examining at the species in a given location, assessing the populations of that species gives important information about the structure, growth, and potential decline of that species. Many of these characteristics and structures can apply to the human population as well, but humans are unique and, therefore, also have distinctive population dynamics. In this chapter, the basic concepts of population dynamics are reviewed, followed by a more detailed look at the human population.

Population Biology Concepts

A **population** is a group of individuals of the same species living in a particular area at the same time. The size of a population is dependent upon four factors:

- Birth rates in a population (also called **natality**)
- Death rates in a population (also called **mortality**)
- Immigration of organisms into one population from another population
- Emigration of organisms leaving a population

Population Ecology

Population ecology is the study of how individuals within a population interact with one another. Populations of organisms are described based on characteristics that help to better understand that population and to predict what might happen in the future. Characteristics include:

- **Population size:** The number of individuals in a population at a given time. Over time, the size of a population of organisms can change, remain the same, or go through cycles of increasing and decreasing numbers.
- **Population distribution:** The spatial arrangement of organisms in an area. This can be explained as:
  - **Random distribution:** With random distribution, organisms are spaced arbitrarily, with no organization or intention, as with free-floating larvae in the ocean. This is the least common arrangement in nature.
  - **Uniform distribution:** Uniform distribution occurs when organisms are spaced evenly from one another. This occurs due to necessity, such as limited resources making distance necessary for survival of organisms that are territorial. Wolves are one example of a species with uniform distribution because they are territorial animals.
  - **Clumped distribution:** The most common in nature, clumped distribution occurs because organisms often gather around a necessary resource. Animals that live in herds demonstrate clumped distribution, such as buffalo.
- **Population density:** The number of individuals in a population per unit area. Usually more resources and a larger area are necessary for species that are larger in size, whereas smaller organisms don't need as much space or as many resources. With any organism, high population density could lead to increased competition for resources and an increased chance of the transfer of disease, but it also betters the chances of mating. Lower population densities decrease the chance of competition and the spread of disease but may also make it more difficult to find a mate.
- **Age structure:** Examines the number of organisms in each age range within a population. This distribution will affect whether a population grows, declines, or remains stable over time. If most individuals are younger, the population will most likely increase in number. When a population is comprised mostly of older individuals past reproductive age, the population will probably decline. Even age distribution reflects a stable population. The age structure of a population is shown in age-structure diagrams or age pyramids.
- **Sex ratio:** The number of males to females in a population. This can affect whether a population of organisms will increase or decrease over time because it affects the chances of mating.

Carrying Capacity

Given the right situation and enough resources, a population can grow. In **exponential growth,** a population increases by a fixed percentage per unit of time. Exponential growth is represented on an exponential growth curve (see the following figure). A population can grow exponentially when it's using an unused resource or colonizing a new environment. Exponential growth cannot last indefinitely, though, because resources are finite. Humans are an example of a population that has experienced exponential growth. The question is, when will our resources run out?

Exponential Growth Curve

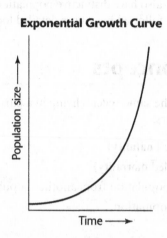

Because resource availability will eventually decrease, exponential growth will be halted when a population reaches **carrying capacity (K).** This is the maximum number of organisms in a species that an environment can support indefinitely. Carrying capacity is not a set number and can vary depending on the environment, populations, and limiting factors.

A population reaches its carrying capacity based on **limiting factors,** which are the factors that control a population's growth. Limiting factors can be the availability of food, shelter, water, mates, or anything else an organism depends upon for survival. A population can also be limited by disease, predators, natural disasters, sunlight, moisture, temperature, or nutrients. And in an aquatic ecosystem, salinity, sunlight, pollutants, dissolved oxygen, or temperature can play a role in restricting population growth. All limiting factors acting on a population together are called **environmental resistance.** Sometimes a species can alter its environment, thus increasing its carrying capacity and decreasing its environmental resistance. Humans are an example of a species that has created ways of bettering survival through alteration of the environment and through invention.

Some limiting factors are related to the density of a population. These factors are considered **density-dependent factors** and include disease, availability of mates, and predation. A population that is denser is at an increased risk of predation or the transmission of disease, yet it has a higher probability of finding mates. On the other hand, **density-independent factors** do not depend on the density of a population. For example, natural disasters, extreme temperature fluctuations, or lack of sunlight can affect the numbers of a species, regardless of whether the organisms are in a crowded population.

In order to represent a population that grows exponentially and then reaches its carrying capacity, a **logistic growth curve** (see the following figure) is used. Initially, a population increases quickly; then it levels off due to limiting factors. The logistic growth curve is generally a theoretical model because actual populations of organisms don't behave as the curve suggests. Different populations act in a variety of ways depending on the environment, the species, and limiting factors. More realistic logistic growth curves show populations that:

- Fluctuate above and below carrying capacity for an indefinite amount of time
- Rise quickly and then decrease abruptly
- Fluctuate for a period of time, and then start to experience less dramatic changes and stabilize to an extent
- Exhibits a pattern similar to the theoretical model

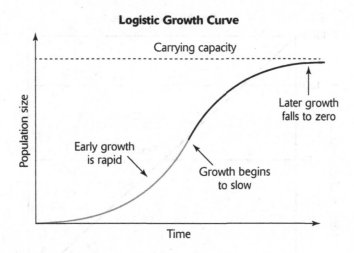

Logistic Growth Curve

Reproductive Strategies

Limiting factors affect a population's growth and decline, along with an organism's **biotic potential,** the ability of an organism to produce offspring. There are two types of reproductive strategies:

- **K-selected:** K-selected species are species that have relatively few offspring and devote a large amount of time, energy, and resources toward nurturing and raising their young. These organisms usually are larger, have long gestation periods, and live longer. Because only a few offspring are produced, k-selected species have low biotic potential. Overall, these populations also remain close to carrying capacity and have a relatively constant population size. Examples include humans, elephants, horses, and cows.

- **R-selected:** R-selected species are small organisms that have short gestation periods and produce thousands of offspring at one time; therefore, they have high biotic potential. Energy and resources are put into producing many offspring and not into raising the young. This strategy means that the young are left to their own survival, and survival depends on chance. R-selected species are short-lived and have population sizes that vary, usually not remaining near carrying capacity but well below it. Examples include spiders, fish, and frogs.

Not all species fit into one of these two strategies. Some organisms fall in between.

Survivorship

Survivorship curves (like the one shown on the next page) represent the number of individuals surviving at each age for a given species. The y-axis shows the number of individuals and the x-axis reflects time or age. The three types of survivorship curves are

- **Type I:** Organisms that reproduce at a relatively young age, have a small number of deaths at young ages, have a long lifespan, and experience mortality mostly at an older age. Examples include humans and most large mammals.

- **Type II:** Organisms that mature quickly and have even mortality rates at all ages. Examples include rodents, many reptiles, and most birds.

- **Type III:** Organisms that have many offspring, and reproduce often. Many individuals die at an early age, and there is less mortality later in life. Examples include sea turtles, parasites, and most insects.

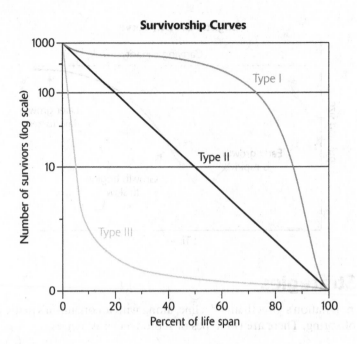

Survivorship Curves

Human Population

The human population is unique compared to other species due to our ability to alter our environment effectively and efficiently with the use of technology and invention. Although population growth has begun to stabilize or decline in some countries, it continues to soar in others. Overall, the human population continues to grow exponentially, and since we can alter our environment to suit our needs, we have extended the carrying capacity of our planet for ourselves, while reducing the carrying capacity for other species.

Human Population Dynamics

Historical Considerations

Through most of human history, the Earth was not overpopulated and held only a few million people at any given time. As humans became more advanced and began to invent more efficient ways of doing day-to-day tasks and a safer way of life evolved, the population gradually and steadily increased. Two key events are responsible for this change:

- The **Agricultural Revolution** began about 10,000 years ago, and people started to grow crops and raise livestock. This meant that a nomadic lifestyle was no longer necessary, and it was easier to get essential nutrients to survive. People began to have more children and live longer lives.

- In the 1700s, the **Industrial Revolution** began. Life started to become more urban. Most people lived in and near cities, sanitation and medical care improved, and manufacturing became prevalent. The use of fossil fuels as an energy source sparked this new way of life and made it possible for manufacturing, production, and transportation to be more efficient. Improvements in sanitation and healthcare increased longevity, so people were living longer as well.

Currently, there are more than 6.9 billion people living on Earth, and the number is still growing exponentially. Since 1967, the human population has doubled, with over 80 million people being added every year.

Distribution

Population growth is not the same in every country or every region. Currently, growth is slowing in developed nations, while many developing countries are still growing at an astounding rate.

Studying the statistical change in human populations and applying the concepts of population ecology to this is called **demography.** By studying the size, density, distribution, sex ratios, age structure, birth and death rates, and movement of people, a demographer can help to predict shifts in populations and potential environmental consequences throughout the world.

The distribution of the human population is considered to be clumped, with more people living in regions with climates that are tropical, subtropical, or temperate. Such locations include China, India, Europe, and Mexico. Populations are also the densest near water, whether freshwater or saltwater. More people living in a particular area means there is more of an impact on the environment from use and pollution in that area.

Today, China has the world's largest population, with about 1.3 billion people; India is close behind, with 1.15 billion people; and the United States comes in third with about 300 million people. China and India still are considered developing nations but are quickly catching up to developed countries due to increased job growth and opportunities. The environmental impact of both countries is already large, but with more and more people having the means to consume and the desire to live lifestyles based on consumerism, the effect on the environment will be even more dramatic and humans will move even closer to reaching carrying capacity on the planet.

The IPAT Model

As a way to look at the human impact on the environment, in 1974 Paul Ehrlich and John Holdren developed the **IPAT model,** which examines how technology, affluence, and population all work together to impact the environment. It's shown as $I = P \times A \times T$, where

- I stands for the impact on the environment.
- P stands for population. Population can affect the environment because more people mean more land and resources are used and more waste is produced.
- A stands for affluence. Greater affluence means larger resource consumption per person due to increased wealth.
- T stands for technology. Technology can act positively or negatively either by creating ways to exploit resources faster and more easily, or by developing better ways to reduce our impact, such as better pollution controls or renewable energy.

Sensitivity can also be added to the IPAT model, taking into account the sensitivity of an environment when being used by humans. For example, deserts and grasslands are more susceptible to degradation if they are not managed properly.

The Rule of 70

Overall, a population's net change in size, per 1,000 individuals, is measured by its **growth rate**, which is calculated as follows:

$$\text{Growth Rate} = (\text{Birth Rate} + \text{Immigration}) - (\text{Death Rate} + \text{Emigration})$$

For example, if the birth rate is 10 individuals, immigration is 20 individuals, the death rate is 15 individuals, and emigration is 5 individuals, it would be calculated as follows:

$$(10 + 20) - (15 + 5) = 30 - 20 = 10 \text{ per 1,000 individuals}$$

This means that the population will grow by 10, so in one year the population will add 10 individuals per 1,000 individuals. Expressed as a percentage, the growth rate is

$$10 \text{ per } 1,000 \times 100 \text{ percent} = 1 \text{ percent annually}$$

As mentioned earlier, with exponential growth, a population grows by a fixed percentage each year. Therefore, although the population of 1,000 individuals grew by 10 in one year, if that same 1 percent growth rate continues each year, the population grows by 1 percent each year. For example, a population of 1,000 mice that grows at a rate of 1 percent each year will end up at 1,010 mice after one year. Although this doesn't sound like a large increase in population, due to exponential growth, the population will grow to 1,100 after ten years if it remains at a 1 percent growth rate. Look at this on a larger scale, such as with a population of 1 million individuals, and it is evident how quickly a population can multiply and grow.

The human growth rate was at its highest in the 1960s at 2.1 percent. Since then, it has dropped to 1.2 percent, but this rate still reflects growth, so the human population continues to grow exponentially. In the early 1800s, the human population was close to 1 billion people; in 1950 the human population was approximately 2.5 billion; and in 2005 humans totaled about 6.5 billion. By 2050, the human population could reach over 9 billion.

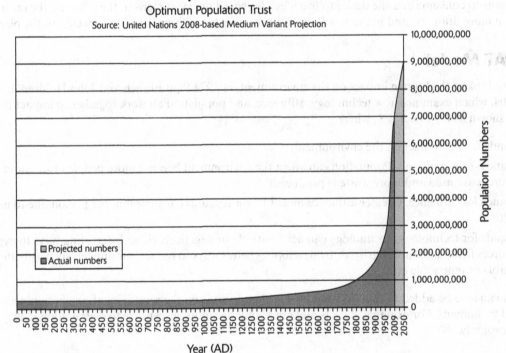

World Population Growth
Optimum Population Trust
Source: United Nations 2008-based Medium Variant Projection

Year (AD)

Source: Population Matters

Doubling time is the amount of time it takes for a population to double. It is also called the Rule of 70, because to find doubling time, 70 is divided by the annual percentage growth rate of a population. For example, a population with a 3 percent growth rate will double in a little over 23 years ($70 \div 3 = 23.3$).

Demographic Transition

As the Western world has become more and more industrialized, there have been many shifts in birth and death rates. In order to explain this, a model was developed by Frank Notestein in the 1940s and 1950s called **demographic transition.** Demographic transition moves from a pre-industrial stage, to a transitional stage, to an industrial stage, and ends in a post-industrial stage. Not all nations have or will pass through this demographic transition; it's dependent on cultural and economic structures of each nation.

- **Pre-industrial stage:** Death and birth rates are high due to poor medical care, extensive disease, difficulty in acquiring food, and people having many children because of high infant mortality. The population of people is relatively stable.

- **Transitional stage:** Death rates start declining because of medical advancements and better food production. Birth rates remain high, leading to large population growth.

- **Industrial stage:** Birth rates stabilize because more people are working outside the home as opposed to farming, and there are increased work opportunities for women. Birth control becomes more commonly used. Death rates remain stable at their low levels from the transitional stage. Population growth slows.

- **Post-industrial stage:** Both birth and death rates are low and stable, leading to a stabilization or small decline in population.

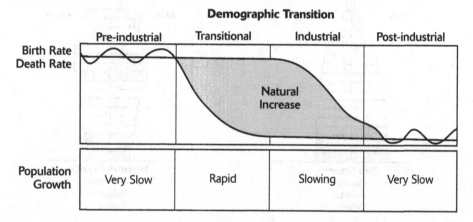

Age structure diagrams, also called age pyramids, are used to show the distribution of ages throughout a population and can help to forecast what might happen to a population over time. There are three general structures with some variation depending on the changes within a population:

- A balanced age structure generally has the same number of individuals throughout each age group and represents a stable population and no growth. Examples include Denmark, Austria, and Spain.

- A pyramid-shaped diagram reflects a population with a large number of young people. This is a growing population, and in the long term this population will increase assuming no major changes to any particular group. A pyramid can represent either rapid growth or slow growth. Examples of rapid growth (a steep-sided pyramid) include Afghanistan, Angola, Kenya, Nigeria, and Guatemala. Examples of slow growth (a gently sloping pyramid) include the United States and Canada.

- An inverted pyramid structure, or diamond-shaped structure, shows an aging population with fewer young. This population will decline over time, but it may put pressure on the young to take care of the elderly. Also, there could be a decline in the economy and in the strength of that nation's military, with fewer young entering the workforce. Examples include China and Germany.

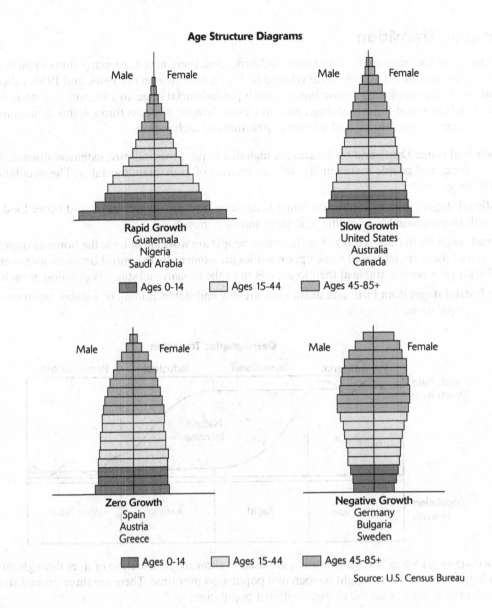

Age Structure Diagrams

Male   Female

Rapid Growth
Guatemala
Nigeria
Saudi Arabia

■ Ages 0-14   □ Ages 15-44   ■ Ages 45-85+

Male   Female

Slow Growth
United States
Australia
Canada

Male   Female

Zero Growth
Spain
Austria
Greece

Male   Female

Negative Growth
Germany
Bulgaria
Sweden

■ Ages 0-14   □ Ages 15-44   ■ Ages 45-85+

Source: U.S. Census Bureau

Population Size

For most of human history, the total population has been relatively small. In 1804, the human population was 1 billion; today, it's more than 6.9 billion. Many changes in human society worked together to create the dramatic increase in world population in just over 200 years.

The initial human population is thought to have been stable at approximately 1 million because, at that time, humans were mainly hunters and gatherers, a lifestyle that ensured a low population. With the agricultural revolution about 10,000 years ago, humans began to transition from hunting and gathering food to growing their own food. Studies have shown that in seven or eight locations around the world, agriculture developed independently. The nomadic human society of hunters and gatherers was changed into a sedentary society, which led to the development of villages and small towns. As societies grew and developed, they altered the lands they used to grow their crops, and they selected crops that would increase production, longevity, and other beneficial features. The availability of more food and access to it year-round helped push the population to nearly a billion at the beginning of the Industrial Revolution. By far, the larger populations were in agriculturally developed countries compared to societies that continued to hunt and gather.

As harvests began to supply a surplus, fewer people had to grow crops, which led to specialization of tasks, such as the development of the blacksmith, baker, shoemaker, and many more trades. The development of the arts and music as we know them today can be credited to the specialization brought about by the changes in society during the agricultural revolution.

A look through human history shows many periods of dramatic decline in human population. These declines can be attributed to more densely populated societies living in villages and towns. Diseases spread easily and were more difficult to isolate with higher numbers of people living closely together. One notable period in world and European history was the Black Death pandemic of the 14th century, when the estimated world population of 450 million was reduced to between 350 million and 375 million. Approximately 200 years passed before Europe regained its 1300 population level.

At the beginning of the Industrial Revolution, the human population began to climb. One cause was a drop in infant mortality rates from roughly 75 percent in the 1730s to 32 percent in the 1820s. Then, in the later 1800s, with the development of an understanding of the transmission of diseases and improvements in medical practices, dental care, and food pasteurization, a dramatic reduction in death rates affected all age levels. The population of the world began to grow rapidly. The following table shows the historic human population from 1804 to the present with estimates for the future as well.

Population									
	1 billion	2 billion	3 billion	4 billion	5 billion	6 billion	7 billion (estimated)	8 billion (estimated)	9 billion (estimated)
Year	1804	1927	1960	1974	1987	1999	2011	2025	2050
Years elapsed		123	33	14	13	12	12	14	25

Based on a 2010 list maintained by the United Nations (UN), the world has 230 countries, 38 of which are identified as developed. The remaining countries are considered to be developing. The ten most populated countries include China, with the greatest population; India, close behind at number two; and the United States, a distant third. Of the ten countries with the largest populations, only three—the United States, Russia, and Japan—are completely developed. China is fast becoming a developed country.

The world growth rate is 1.17 percent, but many of the poorest countries have rates higher than 2 percent. Fifty-two countries have a growth rate higher than 2 percent. Seventy-five countries are experiencing a growth rate between 0 percent and 1 percent. A 0 percent growth rate means the particular population is not growing, and a 1 percent rate means the population will double in 70 years, based on the Rule of 70. A growth rate of less than zero means the population is declining. The world has 25 countries with a negative growth rate.

The Ten World's Largest Human Populations				
Rank	Country	Population	Year	Growth Rate (Percent)
1	China*	1,338,820,000	2010	0.58
2	India	1,183,600,000	2010	1.46
3	United States	309,810,000	2010	0.97
4	Indonesia	231,369,500	2010	1.16
5	Brazil	193,243,000	2010	1.26
6	Pakistan	170,090,000	2010	1.84
7	Bangladesh	162,221,000	2009	1.67
8	Nigeria	154,729,000	2009	2.27
9	Russia	141,927,297	2010	−0.47
10	Japan	127,530,000	2009	−0.19
	World	6,901,490.881	2010	1.17

* China is the People's Republic of China and excludes the special administrative regions of Hong Kong and Macau as well as the islands of Taiwan.

Source: United Nations 2005–2010

Exactly what defines *developed* and *developing* countries depends greatly on the listing organization. No set criteria exist for listing a country as developed or developing; they vary from one organization to the next. One former UN Secretary General describes developed countries as nations that allow their citizens to enjoy a free and healthy life in a safe environment. Other organizations focus on income levels, access to safe drinking water, medical care, and jobs. The following list of developed countries is based on the United Nations list.

Middle East

1. Israel
2. Kuwait
3. Qatar
4. United Arab Emirates

Asia

5. Brunei
6. Hong Kong
7. Japan
8. Singapore
9. South Korea

Australia

10. Australia

Europe

11. Andorra
12. Austria
13. Belgium
14. Czech Republic
15. Denmark
16. Finland
17. France
18. Germany
19. Greece
20. Iceland
21. Ireland
22. Italy
23. Liechtenstein
24. Luxembourg
25. Malta
26. Netherlands
27. Norway
28. Portugal
29. Slovenia
30. Spain
31. Sweden

32. Switzerland
33. United Kingdom

North America

34. Canada
35. United States

Other

36. Barbados (Caribbean island)
37. Cyprus (Eurasian)
38. New Zealand (South Pacific island)

Population Sustainability

Exactly what is meant by population sustainability? Does it mean that the population will remain the same (zero growth rate), grow rapidly, grow slowly or decline? Will the world's population exceed the carrying capacity of Earth, or has it already exceeded the carrying capacity?

Population sustainability refers to these types of questions; scientists and their governing institutions continue to seek answers for them. Understanding the complex interactions between Earth's population and the amount of its resources used is a difficult task. There are organizations that believe that humankind has exceeded the carrying capacity of Earth and that the number of existing human organisms in the world cannot be supported by the given sustainability on Earth. In addition, there is a growing concern among ecologists who suggest that the total population must be lowered to support sustainability.

The continued research and study of population sustainability recognizes the importance of the preservation of human-valued natural resources (land, air, and water) to sustain the population and preserve quality of life for future generations. There is no way to measure whether global population has reached the carrying capacity of Earth, or if there are sufficient renewable resources to support the number of living organisms for future generations. What we do know is that over 6 million children die every year from preventable or treatable diseases, nearly 1 billion people do not have access to clean water, nearly 1 billion people are malnourished, and 96 percent of the population growth between 2005 and 2050 will occur in the developing countries. In addition, sub-Saharan Africa has high levels of HIV/AIDS—as high as 50 percent in some regions. Other issues that affect population growth include religion, the availability of family planning, education, income, attitudes toward birth control, the role of women, and cultural norms.

Population Policies

In order to slow population growth, many countries have established policies and programs to educate people and promote family-planning programs. The efforts to institute programs with the goal of lowering the growth rate, in both developed and developing nations, have been successful. For example, Iran has successfully lowered growth based on a campaign for contraception. Many nations, including Thailand, Brazil, and Bangladesh, have some form of family planning programs, public awareness, and policies in place to focus on reducing population growth. China's one-child policy, where limitations have been established for the number of children a couple can have, is the only one of its kind, though. Countries sometimes address immigration as opposed to birth rates as a way to reduce population growth.

Impacts of Population

There are two distinct population-related impacts on the environment. The populations of developing countries have one impact, while the populations of industrialized countries have a different impact. In developing countries, populations are continually occupied with acquiring and sustaining basic needs (food, water, and shelter). In comparison, industrialized countries have the basic needs and are more concerned about their desires (cellphones, cars) than basic needs.

Poverty

In countries in which a large percentage of the population lives in severe economic hardship, people are generally more concerned about food, water, and shelter than they are about environmental impact. Many of these impoverished countries have large populations that rely on biomass (wood fuel) for their energy needs. Denuding the landscape depletes the habitat needed for native plants and animal species to flourish and erodes the soil. As farming becomes less productive, it necessitates hunting for game, with the possibility that some species of animals may be hunted to extinction.

Economics

Populations, economics, and the environment are interrelated. A wealthy population requires a wealthy economy and, in an industrialized society, is supported by natural resources. Conversely, an abundance of natural resources will infuse wealth into an economy and has the possibility of creating wealth for the population. As a wealthy population's natural resources are depleted, it has the economic wealth to expand and/or locate new resources. This often occurs at the expense of poor populations and their natural resources. Wealthier nations (the United States, many European countries, and Japan) generally have strong economies that provide medical, educational, and social services for most members of their societies. Poorer nations provide uneven services for their populations. Education in the poor nations may be limited, restricted to males, or based on ethnicity. The wealthy in poor nations can usually obtain medical and educational services.

Culture

Culture is the patterns of human knowledge, belief, and behaviors that are considered the norm for a society. This is based on shared attitudes, values, goals, and practices that characterize the society and can be based on a set of religious beliefs, a common history, or a common goal. The way in which a society treats the environment is impacted by cultural values. These human actions can pertain to agricultural use of the land, fishing practices, land development, resource extraction, or by-products from use including pollution. Cultural influence combined with personal experiences affects how an individual views and treats the environment.

Disease

Disease affects population growth. Death rates, especially infant mortality rates, are lower in industrialized societies than in developing nations. Industrialized societies have better access to medicines, hospitals or clinics, and doctors. Developing countries may have difficulty providing inoculations against diseases commonly considered eliminated in developed countries, such as polio, measles, and tuberculosis. Education, medicines, and preventive measures for HIV infections, available in developed nations, are seriously lacking in the developing countries. Africa has severe issues with HIV and AIDS infections. Malaria, which is almost nonexistent in the industrialized nations, is common in African countries.

Resource Use

By far, industrialized societies use more resources and a larger variety of resources than developing societies. The developing society is primarily concerned about the basic needs of obtaining or providing food, water, and shelter. Food tends to be locally grown, found, or even hunted. Water often comes from a local stream, river, or well. It is usually used without purification and is often carried in containers, instead of being piped into homes. Homes are small, often lacking electricity or indoor plumbing, and often in disrepair. Industrial societies have larger homes, appliances, cars, recreational vehicles, and personal articles. They have indoor plumbing and don't get their water from a local stream. Many industrialized countries utilize dams and aqueducts to acquire their purified water supplies and provide hydroelectric power. They use their own resources and then buy additional resources from other countries. Japan has virtually no resources and must import all its resources. As the population uses more and more finite resources without recycling or discovering new resources, fewer resources are left for the flora and fauna of Earth.

Habitat Destruction

Large populations have a direct impact on the land necessary to support the human population. More land is necessary to grow food, provide space for living requirements, dispose of waste, and harvest and extract resources. These actions all have an impact on the environment and, therefore, on the habitats of other organisms. Loss of habitats for species will continue to grow as the human population continues to grow, further imposing on these habitats.

Populations in both industrialized and developing nations have environmental impacts, although the differences in land use affect habitats differently. Also, industrialized countries tend to have smaller populations but have a larger amount of land destruction than developing countries. Populations in industrialized countries not only use local, regional, or national resources when available, but also use resources from other countries, often from developing countries. The developing countries need the money from their own resources to help them develop. Per capita, the industrialized countries have higher energy usage, greater land use (for their homes, businesses, schools, and recreational activities), and consume more calories (thus, they have a larger land and energy requirement for food production). Due to an industrialized nation's high consumption of food and great use of energy and resources, accompanied by the production of waste, their environmental footprints become quite large. The footprint can reach beyond the industrialized nation and quite often leaves a greater footprint in the developing countries than their own country.

Practice

Human Population Growth		
Human Population (in billions)	Year	Years Elapsed
1	1804	
2	1927	123
3	1960	33
4	1974	14
5	1987	13
6	1999	12

1. Which of the following is NOT a reason that helps explain the change in population?

    A. Surplus in the availability of food for human consumption
    B. Availability of food year-round
    C. The ability to transport food over great distances
    D. Higher infant mortality in developed countries
    E. Improvements in medical practices

2. During the past 100 years, human population growth is primarily due to a/an _____ in the _____.

    A. decrease; death rate
    B. increase; death rate
    C. decrease; birth rate
    D. increase; infant mortality rate
    E. increase; birth rate

3. If a nation has a growth rate of 2 percent, how many years will it take for the population to double in size?

    A. 2
    B. 10
    C. 20
    D. 35
    E. 350

4. A nation currently has a population of 100 million and an annual growth rate of 3.5 percent. If the growth rate remains constant, what will be the population of the nation in 40 years?

    A. 150 million
    B. 200 million
    C. 300 million
    D. 400 million
    E. 500 million

5. On which continent are most of the developed countries located?

    A. Africa
    B. Asia
    C. Europe
    D. North America
    E. South America

6. Which of the following issues does NOT directly affect human population size?

    A. Poverty
    B. Culture
    C. Disease
    D. Habitat destruction
    E. Government policy

7. Which are the four main factors that affect population size?

    A. Birth rate, death rate, poverty, culture
    B. Birth rate, death rate, immigration, emigration
    C. Poverty, culture, immigration, emigration
    D. Poverty, female empowerment, ethnicity, disease
    E. Birth rate, death rate, disease, culture

8. Territorial animals display which type of distribution?

    A. Clumped
    B. Random
    C. K-selected
    D. Uniform
    E. R-selected

9. The following logistic growth curve best describes a population as:

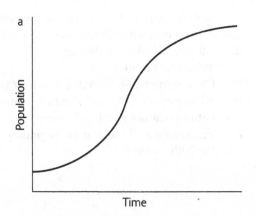

A. Increasing quickly and then leveling off
B. Fluctuating above and below carrying capacity for an indefinite amount of time
C. Rising quickly and then decreasing abruptly
D. Growing indefinitely without reaching carrying capacity
E. Fluctuating for a period of time and stabilizing

10. Of the following limiting factors of a population, which is NOT a density-dependent factor?

A. Temperature fluctuations
B. Disease
C. Soil nutrients
D. Availability of mates
E. Predation

11. Which of the following describes an R-selected species?

A. Very few offspring are produced at once.
B. The gestation period is long and parents dedicate large amounts of energy to nurturing their young.
C. Thousands of offspring are produced at once.
D. They have low biotic potential.
E. They have long life spans.

12. Which of the following organisms shows a Type III survivorship curve?

A. Lizard
B. Oak tree
C. Elephant
D. Mosquito
E. Panda

13. The following age-structure diagram best shows the age structure in which type of population?

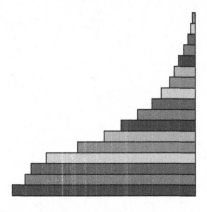 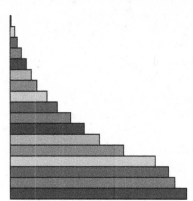

A. A growing population with many young
B. A stable population with no growth
C. A population harshly impacted by disease during early-adult years
D. An aging population with few young
E. A population with few individuals entering the workforce

14. Which three components are used as a way to analyze how the environment is impacted by human use?

    A. Culture, poverty, death rates
    B. Technology, affluence, population
    C. Pollution, chemicals, water use
    D. Pollution, affluence, technology
    E. Time, population, affluence

15. The demographic transition model was created to help explain the:

    A. Shift in birth and death rates as Western nations became industrialized
    B. Change in affluence throughout industrialization
    C. Change in male-to-female ratios over time
    D. Variation in immigration and emigration patterns during industrialization
    E. Increase in birth rates at the beginning of the 20th century

Answers

1. **D** The other four answers played a role in the increase seen in the population after 1804. Infant mortality is lower in developed countries. A high infant mortality rate may result in lower population growth.

2. **A** Death rates declined at a fast rate and were the primary reason for the population increase. Birth rates declined later and at a slower rate than death rates.

3. **D** The Rule of 70 is used to determine the doubling time. The formula is $dt = \frac{70}{r}$, where dt = doubling time and r = growth rate. So, $dt = \frac{70}{2} = 35$ years.

4. **D** Again, use the Rule of 70 to determine the number of years and then find the answer:

   $dt = \frac{70}{r} = \frac{70}{3.5} = 20$ years.

   The question asks "What will the population be in 40 years?" If the doubling time is 20 years, that means there are two doubling times. The starting population is 100 million. At the end of 20 years, the population will be 200 million; this is the first doubling time. The population at the end of 40 years (the second doubling time) will be 400 million.

5. **C** The list in this chapter identifies Europe as having the most developed countries.

6. **D** Although habitat destruction is an effect of population size, it does not directly affect the size of the human population. Over time, destroyed habitat may not be able to support a certain population size.

7. **B** The size of a population depends on its birth and death rates combined with immigration and emigration. Basically, it is the number entering into a population and the number leaving a population at the same point in time.

8. **D** When organisms' territories are spaced evenly from one another, it is considered to be uniform distribution. Organisms that are territorial (such as wolves, lions, and other large predators) require large amounts of space for their territory. Generally, they're evenly distributed.

9. **A** This curve shows a rapid increase, then a leveling off of the population as it reaches carrying capacity. This is the theoretical model, as populations in nature may not act this way.

10. **A** Temperature fluctuations are a density-independent factor because this limiting factor doesn't depend on the density of a population. Temperature changes can affect a species regardless of whether they're densely populated.

11. **C** Because R-selected species put their energy into producing many young that are not nurtured after they're born, they produce thousands of offspring at one time. These organisms are also small, with short gestation periods.

12. **D** Mosquitoes and other insects frequently produce many offspring, and they have a short life span.

13. **A** The large bulge on the bottom indicates a large number of young in this population, with a decline in numbers as the population gets older.

14. **B** The IPAT model was created by Paul Ehrlich and John Holdren in 1974 to examine how technology, affluence, and population work together to impact the environment. Sometimes sensitivity (S) is also incorporated to take into account the sensitivity of an environment when being used by humans.

15. **A** During industrialization, there have been shifts in birth rates and death rates that were hard to explain. In the 1940s and 1950s, Frank Notestein developed a demographic transition model to better explain this phenomenon. The model moves from a pre-industrial stage to a transitional stage to an industrial stage and ends in a post-industrial stage.

Chapter 4

Land and Water Use

The Earth is comprised of continents and water resources, which are interrelated dynamic and complex systems. Humans depend on both systems for food, shelter, and resources that sustain our lives and economic structure. Land is used by people for agriculture, forestry, rangeland, and minerals, as well as for development, infrastructure, and recreation. Through fishing and aquaculture, water resources provide food, while minerals can be attained from the oceans. The resources provided from both land and water provide the basis of the global economic structure and its use is regulated through many laws and treaties.

Agriculture

One of the great challenges of humanity's transition from hunter-gatherer societies to cities was feeding a densely packed population. Now with the Earth's population pushing toward 7 billion, the challenge is greater than ever, requiring the development of efficient farming and livestock techniques. These techniques have so far allowed the food supply to keep pace with the population (though problems in markets and distribution leave many hungry millions). Still, agricultural science is not without its drawbacks including the potential for environmental damage. *Note:* The term *agriculture* applies to both crops and livestock, but this section focuses on farming of crops.

Feeding a Growing Population

Earth's human population is growing exponentially, from 1 billion people in 1800 to almost 2 billion in 1900 to 6 billion in 2000. More people require more food, and more food requires the use of more land, water, and fossil fuels, all of which impacts the environment.

Human Nutritional Requirements

Globally, the amount of food being produced per person has increased in modern times, and the ability to farm food has become faster and less work-intensive due to current technologies. Still, approximately 1.2 billion people do not get enough to eat on a daily basis and are considered undernourished according to the Food and Agriculture Organization of the United Nations. **Malnutrition** (in which people do not consume enough daily nutrients) and **undernourishment** (in which people do not receive enough calories) are worldwide issues, even with the modern abundance of food and reliability of food sources. The United Nations Commission on Human Rights estimates that every second, one person dies of starvation or hunger-related diseases. At the same time, others struggle with **over-nutrition** (receiving too many calories), which can lead to obesity and many related health issues.

Types of Agriculture

The practice of **agriculture** includes growing crops and raising livestock. The human practice of agriculture began about 10,000 years ago, following the period of the nomadic hunters and gatherers. At that time, humans began to cultivate crops, which required settling in one area to plant, tend, and harvest them. Along with this newly settled lifestyle, humans began raising livestock (and keeping domesticated animals including dogs). Crop agriculture that used human power, animal power, and simple tools is considered **traditional agriculture.** In its simplest form, traditional agriculture is conducted by a family for its own consumption and use. This is considered **subsistence agriculture,** in which enough food is created for the family but not for others. In contrast, agriculture on a large scale, with crop production for many people, and including the use of fertilizer, pesticides, irrigation, seeds, fossil fuels, monoculture (growing one single crop), and human power is considered **industrialized agriculture,** also called **conventional agriculture.** (For more information about industrialized agriculture, see the upcoming section "The Green Revolution.")

The Dust Bowl

Soil erosion, in which soil is transported from a location via wind or water, has an impact both at the site from which it was taken and the site at which it is deposited. Erosion is a natural process, but human intervention has led to its rapid increase to the point that we are losing nutrient-rich topsoil faster than it is created. One source of this erosion is the removal of trees and undergrowth to clear land for crops, rangeland, construction, and roadways. The roots of plants and trees are especially important as they trap soil and prevent wind and water from carrying it away. This erosion or other factors including overgrazing, drought, soil compaction, can lead to **desertification,** which is loss of soil productivity. In extreme cases, desertification can, as its name implies, lead to expansion of deserts and giant dust storms. Today, dust storms are common in areas of China and Africa, where the land has been overworked, but desertification also led to a dust storm in the United States that dated several years and devastated many states.

Due to the food needs of human expansion into the western United States in the late 1920s and early 1930s, natural land was cleared and replaced with crops and rangeland. The removal of vegetation, including grasses, trees, shrubs, and plants, exposed the soil to wind and water. To this newly overworked land, nature added a drought. This combination in the southern Great Plains, along with the stock market crash of 1929, led to the environmental, agricultural, and economic catastrophe known as the **Dust Bowl.** In hopes of averting another Dust Bowl, the United States created the Soil Conservation Act of 1935, the Soil Conservation Service (now the Natural Resources Conservation Service), and new guidelines for better farming practices.

The Green Revolution

The advent of industrialized agriculture in the mid- and late 20th century became known as the **Green Revolution.** This revolution included combining more effective farming techniques with the science of newly created crops to increase yields and efficiency. Developments during the Green Revolution included the following:

- High-yield crop varieties (mainly wheat, maize, and rice) created through breeding and crossbreeding techniques (selective breeding)
- Increased irrigation infrastructure
- Wide use of pesticides and fertilizers

The enormous benefit of the Green Revolution was the ability to produce more food on less land. Instead of feeding only the local population, crop excesses led to international markets in which food is exported and imported.

That said, more output requires more input. In the case of industrialized agriculture, inputs include fossil fuels for machinery and transportation, water, fertilizers, and pesticides. The environmental impacts of industrial agriculture can include pollution, contaminated waterways and drinking water, decreased available freshwater, reduced soil quality, and increased erosion, desertification, and salinization.

Another technique that became frequently used during the Green Revolution is **monoculture,** in which a field is planted with only one crop. Generally, monoculture makes planting and harvesting more efficient and, thus, more cost-effective. However, since a monoculture crop shares genetic makeup, the crop is at increased risk of decimation by one type of pathogen or pest. Also, monoculture allows fewer ecological niches, decreasing the potential for biodiversity. Without increased use of fertilizers, monoculture can deplete the soil of nutrients. Monoculture also is used in the livestock and aquaculture industries.

Genetic Engineering and Crop Production

Changing segments of an organism's DNA is called **genetic engineering** or **genetic modification,** and organisms that are altered are called **genetically modified organisms.** In the process of genetic modification, genes from an organism with a desired trait are harvested and spliced into the DNA of an existing organism. Ultimately, the combination creates the desired traits (for example, increased growth rate, disease resistance, or size). The result of artificially transferring genetic material is known as a **transgenic organism.** Historically, the technique used to introduce desired traits in existing crops or livestock was selective breeding, but genetic modification differs in its altering of an organism's DNA; it might mix genes from different species with little or no similarities.

Here are some examples of genetically modified crops:

- **Golden rice:** Contains vitamin A, a missing nutrient in many developing countries
- **Ice-minus strawberries:** Frost resistant
- **Bt corn and cotton:** Contain insecticide, removing the need to spray chemicals
- **Long-lasting tomatoes:** Remain fresh longer

Generally, both sides of the genetic modification admit that genetically modified foods are entrenched in our food supply, for better or worse. Still, genetic engineering is a much-debated and highly emotional topic, with the basic points on both sides as follows.

Advantages and Disadvantages of Genetic Modification	
Pros of Genetic Modification	**Cons of Genetic Modification**
The ability to feed more people with less energy, making farming more efficient	Unknown long-term effects on human health
The capability for foods to stay fresh longer, allowing them to be transported farther and have a longer shelf life	The ability for pests and weeds to grow resistance to the seeds containing built-in pesticides and herbicides, ultimately creating the need for more powerful products
The possibility to create foods resistant to weather extremes, which reduces the loss to the farmer and creates more consistent products and markets	The destruction of native, non-genetically-modified crops
The potential to develop foods containing nutrients missing in a local culture	The possibility of exacerbating allergies in people by creating either more products with the same allergen or a new allergen
The potential for improvements in medicine through development of new products	The unknowns of a new technology
The potential for seeds with built-in resistance to pests and weeds	The belief that, ethically, altering the food supply is not right
The potential to build crops that use less fertilizer and water	The fact that genetically modified seeds are patented, forcing farmers to purchase these seeds on an ongoing basis, which could lead to only a few companies having power over the entire global food supply

Crop Diversity

Our current food supply uses only a small sampling of existing crop types. Critics contend that this could make the agricultural industry susceptible to widespread devastation by an unforeseen event targeting one type of essential crop. One way to lessen this danger is by preserving diverse seed types, including wild varieties. For this purpose, **seed banks** exist throughout the world. Housing and preserving many seed types is a way to protect seed genetic diversity along with safeguarding our food supply in case of disaster.

Deforestation

Historically, in order to create land for agriculture, people have cleared forests and other land. While **deforestation** may have short-term benefits on food production, it has a negative and potentially disastrous effect on wildlife, ecosystems, and long-term human sustainability. Forests provide food, shelter, and habitat for an enormous variety of organisms; hold soil in place and reduce erosion; act as "carbon sinks," trapping carbon dioxide; and provide resources for human use. Deforestation devastates ecosystems, reduces biodiversity, can destroy human populations, and has long-term global ramifications.

Irrigation

Supplying water for agricultural purposes is called irrigation. **Irrigation** allows areas that would otherwise be dry and unusable for agriculture to become fertile and productive. However, if land is over-watered, it can become **waterlogged,** a condition in which soil becomes saturated or oversaturated and the water table rises. This can ultimately suffocate plant roots, compact soil, and lead to salinization. **Salinization** occurs when salts accumulate on the soil's surface. When water evaporates from the soil's surface, it leaves behind the salts that were once dissolved in it. This salinization can reduce crop productivity. Salinization is more common in arid regions where there is limited precipitation, but it also can occur from over-irrigation and water logging.

Ways to reduce salinization include the following:

- Ensuring proper drainage
- Using only the necessary amount of water for irrigation
- Planting crops according to water need (not planting crops that require large amounts of water in areas with minimal natural water sources)
- Using low-salt irrigation water

Many modern irrigation systems use **drip irrigation,** which allows water to drip directly onto plants, as opposed to mass spraying of water onto an entire field. This increases water efficiency while reducing salinization.

Sustainable Agriculture

Some modern farmers use a variety of methods to reduce the environmental impact of growing crops, including conservation of soil, land, and water. Ironically, many of these methods were common in traditional agriculture, including the following:

- **No-till farming:** When farmland is only minimally disturbed while it is being prepared for crops. With conventional tillage, soil is plowed and turned, which can ultimately lead to soil erosion and soil compaction in the deeper layers. With no-till farming, more crop residue is turned back into the soil, reducing erosion and compaction.
- **Crop rotation:** The alternation of the types of crops grown on a piece of land from year to year or season to season. This regular change in crops allows nutrients to be returned to the soil and minimizes depletion of certain nutrients, such as nitrogen. It also helps to reduce the impact of insects and disease.
- **Intercropping:** Planting alternating crops throughout a field. Such diversifying reduces the impact of any single disease or crop-specific insects and can reduce erosion and nutrient depletion. This strategy also increases the diversity of crop yield on a single piece of land. In planning intercropping, it is important to use crops that do not compete with one another for nutrients, space, water, or sunlight.
- **Shelterbelts:** Created when tall plants or trees are planted along the edges of fields or farms to reduce the wind that creates soil erosion.
- **Contour farming:** Plowing rows across a hill, following the hill's contour lines. These rows of uniform elevation better trap water and reduce erosion.
- **Terracing:** Used on steep slopes of mountainous terrain. Often looking like steps, terraces are used to minimize erosion and retain water in areas otherwise unsuitable for planting crops. A well-known historic example is the terraces of the Inca ruins of Peru.

Only by using land sustainably can we ensure that land can be used indefinitely to provide a consistent and stable food supply. This includes conditions in which soils are not depleted of nutrients, water is used efficiently, crop diversity does not diminish, and rangeland is not overgrazed.

Sustainable agriculture tends to use resources in a more targeted, specific way. For example, drip irrigation directly waters where necessary and minimizes excess runoff. Fertilizer and pesticide use is replaced by natural, nonchemical products, or fertilizer and pesticides are used in efficient amounts instead of excessively. When no chemicals and only biological approaches are used, this is referred to as **organic farming.**

Controlling Pests

Humans consider many things to be "pests" (such as flies and bees), yet many insects are important to crop productivity. The difficulty for farmers has been fending off crop invaders while keeping the insects necessary for pollination and ecosystem balance.

Pesticides

The agricultural definition of the term *pest* includes insects, fungi, weeds, viruses, rodents, and other organisms that harm crops. Humans have developed synthetic chemicals and natural substances to control pests. As a whole, these substances are called **pesticides** but can be further categorized according to the organisms they are meant to kill. *Fungicides* are used to kill fungi, *herbicides* kill plants and weeds, and *insecticides* target insects.

Pesticides increase crop yields, decrease crop loss and failure due to pests, and can reduce the spread of disease (such as malaria) when they are used to kill certain types of insects (such as mosquitoes).

In addition to their intended use, however, pesticides can have detrimental effects:

- Pests evolve and develop resistance to pesticides over time (see below for additional information).
- Pesticides kill insects necessary for pollination.
- Many pesticides are toxic, especially in large amounts, and can harm humans and wildlife (see Chapter 6).
- Runoff from sites where pesticides are used contaminates water sources.
- Pesticides are expensive to use.
- Many pesticides are nonspecific and kill more than just the targeted organisms.
- Organism loss can alter entire ecosystems.

Pests evolve and develop genetic resistance to pesticides over time. When a pesticide is applied, most of the targeted organisms die, but some survive. The ones that survive then reproduce, passing on the genes that allowed them to survive. Over several generations, a population develops increasing resistance to the pesticide, forcing the use of more powerful pesticides to target these organisms. This creates a perpetual cycle of organisms developing resistance to pesticides and humans increasing our use of different and more powerful chemicals to control the pests.

Some pesticides have proven extremely harmful to the environment and to humans. For example, DDT (dichlorodiphenyltrichloroethane) was used as a pesticide in the United States until 1973, when it was banned due to its detrimental effects on the nervous systems of humans and wildlife. Some countries still use it, though, to control mosquitos and prevent the transmission of malaria.

Increasingly, farmers are exploring alternatives to synthetic pesticides, including oils from trees and plants, such as mint, clove, and rosemary. Also, farmers are using certain pesticides in a more targeted way for specific pests, resulting in less overall ecosystem destruction.

Integrated Pest Management

Another way to address the issue of pest control involves using more than one technique in a process known as **integrated pest management.** This process uses knowledge about the pest's life cycle and environmental interactions, with other control methods such as biological control, crop rotation, and chemicals when necessary. The goal of IPM is to reduce pest impact while also reducing pesticide use.

Livestock and Feedlots

Raising livestock is widely considered to be another essential part of feeding the human population. **Livestock** includes cows, chickens, pigs, goats, sheep, and other domesticated animals raised for profit. Commonly, animals such as cows are kept on large expanses of land to graze for a period of time until they are sold to feedlots. **Feedlots,** also called factory farms or concentrated animal feeding operations, are areas where livestock are fed foods high in energy to fatten them up before market. Feedlots require less land per cow and are a more efficient way of meeting the meat consumption needs of a large population. Also, the manure produced by feedlot animals is frequently used as fertilizer for farms.

Negative aspects of feedlots include potential contamination of water sources from runoff containing waste products and the increased potential for the spread of disease among animals in close contact, which necessitates use of antibiotics. This industry is monitored by states and federally by the Environmental Protection Agency, to help minimize the environmental impact.

The "Rangelands" section of this chapter discusses the environmental impacts of livestock agriculture on rangelands.

Forestry

The challenge of forestry is to balance humans' use of wood products with the importance of forests as ecosystems. Wood is used as fuel and provides the chief material for many products, including furniture, paper, packaging, and homes. Additionally, the timber industry is a major global resource, and many people depend on the jobs and income it creates. This necessitates finding a balance between human needs and ecological preservation.

Tree Plantations

Many timber companies are now planting fast growth species to most efficiently produce timber on land and maximize economic gain. These **timber plantations** are monocultural, with only one species being planted at a time. Since the trees are all planted and then harvested at the same time, they are all the same age, or **even-aged.** Once the trees are harvested, new seedlings are planted. Plantation forests have minimal diversity since the trees are all the same species, which limits the habitat they can provide for other organisms. However, timber plantations can potentially be used as a restoration strategy for previously degraded land, stimulating secondary growth.

Old Growth, Secondary Growth

Because of the extensive deforestation that has occurred globally and throughout the United States, many remaining forests are considered to be secondary growth. **Secondary growth** occurs when an original, **old-growth** forest is cut down and new growth emerges. Much of the original deforestation in the United States occurred soon after European colonization and subsequent westward movement, during which wood was used for building and fuel and land was cleared to make room for agriculture and development of homes and towns. Many of the forests have since been reforested with secondary-growth forests.

Currently deforestation continues on a grand scale in developing countries. The reason for extensive deforestation in these countries is the resulting economic gain—directly from the timber, from selling the rights for timber harvesting, or from the use of the land once it is cleared.

The negative consequences of deforestation include the following:

- Loss of species and biodiversity
- Release of excess carbon into the atmosphere, contributing to climate change
- Reduced conversion of carbon dioxide into oxygen in the process of photosynthesis
- Erosion of unprotected soils

- Depletion of soil nutrients
- Increased desertification
- Flow of effects through an ecosystem

Forest Fires

Forest fires are certainly destructive and can be dangerous, but they are also a necessary part of the forest ecosystem. Many ecosystems depend on fires to help seeds germinate and to return nutrients to the soil. For example, in a chaparral ecosystem, fire's extreme heat causes some species' seeds to open. Periodic fires also help to thin the underbrush in an ecosystem. Small fires that burn branches, twigs, and dead trees help to reduce a future fire's fuel, making a future fire less intense. However, if underbrush accumulates over a long period of time, as it did under the former Forest Service policy of fire suppression, the forest can be more prone to a larger, more devastating fire. Now, rather than suppressing fire, many areas use **prescribed burns** or **controlled burns** to help maintain forests.

Forest Management

Timber harvesting methods have improved their ability to keep ecosystems stable. Previously, timber was harvested only through **clear-cutting,** or taking all trees in an area and leaving nothing standing. This process destroys habitat and can lead to the issues of deforestation previously noted. When secondary growth does begin, if unmanaged, the new developing ecosystem can still be very different from the initial, native habitat. While clear-cutting is still used, other harvesting methods are gaining popularity.

Shelterwood systems leave a low number of full-grown trees in order to create shelter for emergent seedlings. Cutting is done on a regular basis with select tress taken each time. The mix of large and small trees provides continual coverage. In contrast, the **seed-tree** method leaves only mature and seed-producing trees standing, providing the seeds necessary for the regrowth of harvested trees. Both the shelterwood and seed-tree approaches are similar to clear-cutting in that many trees are taken and much of the land is left bare. With the **selection system,** though, most trees are left standing while only a few are harvested from an area at a time. This allows for uneven-aged stands of trees and reduces the impact on habitats and ecosystems.

National Forests

In the United States, the government has taken many actions to protect and preserve forest ecosystems. In 1905, the **U.S. Forest Service** was established to manage and conserve the nation's forests, with the goal of managing the timber resources for both use and ecosystem preservation. In response to the declining timber resources throughout the country, the **U.S. National Forest System** was created and is managed by the U.S. Forest Service. Also, the National Forest Management Act was passed in 1976 by the U.S. Congress, directing every national forest to have a resource management plan.

Australia, Canada, Brazil, India, Japan, the Philippines, and many other nations are working toward reducing deforestation as well. Also, in May 2010, at the Oslo Climate and Forest Conference in Norway, approximately 50 countries signed the REDD+ Partnership, aimed at reducing emissions from deforestation and forest degradation.

Rangelands

Rangelands are large expanses of undeveloped land containing primarily low vegetation such as grasses and shrubs, and are suitable for grazing of livestock. Throughout the world, cattle, goats, and sheep are necessary for the survival of many people and cultures, both for food and for the economic value of the animals. Commonly, these animals are grazed on rangeland. If not managed properly, though, these lands can become overused and degraded, ultimately negatively impacting the local environment along with the people and animals that depend on the land.

Overgrazing

When vegetation on rangelands is over-consumed, it hinders plant regrowth. If the plants that are being eaten are not being replaced over time, the land becomes degraded and unusable. Consequences of overgrazing include the following:

- Soil erosion
- Soil compaction
- Desertification
- Proliferation of invasive species
- Reduction in biodiversity and native vegetation
- Economic loss to those who depend on the land, such as ranchers

When excessive vegetation is removed from the soil, the land is exposed to wind and water. Once soil starts to erode, it is more difficult for plant cover to regrow. The vegetation that does get a toehold in degraded rangeland consists mainly of invasive, weed-type plants, which livestock do not eat. The livestock also compact the soils with their weight and hooves; over time, the soil can become compacted enough that it is more difficult for water to seep through, blocking air from filling pore spaces, which roots need to grow. Once the consequences of overgrazing become visible, the cycle is hard to break, and each step creates more degradation of the land.

This cycle of degradation creating more degradation is called a *positive feedback loop,* in which, once the system starts moving in a direction, it accelerates in that direction unless an intervention stops the progression. This ultimately drives a system to an extreme. In this case, the extreme is degraded, unusable land.

Deforestation

Not all livestock is grazed on natural grassland. In some cases, forests are destroyed so local people can raise cattle and other livestock on the cleared land. The methods used to clear the land include slash and burn, in which entire sections of forest are cut down and burned. Sometimes grasses are then planted for livestock. In some countries, such as Brazil, the leading cause of deforestation is cattle ranching. For decades, governments, activists, businesses, and citizens have discussed deforestation due to its rapid rate of destruction and devastating effects such as biodiversity loss and ecosystem alteration. Forests, including rain forests, are cleared not solely for livestock use but also for crop production, timber, land rights, and tax incentives.

Luckily, people are increasingly learning the consequences of deforestation, so new and sustainable methods are being introduced and implemented in many places with the hope of saving natural forests and regenerating degraded land, while also continuing to raise livestock.

Desertification

The loss of vegetation and available water can lead to land degradation and, ultimately, desertification. Overgrazing is a major contributor to desertification, more so even than crop production. Contrary to popular opinion, land does not move toward desertification from drought only. Drought can exacerbate the problem, but overuse, deforestation, and climate change are the catalysts that create an area of land prone to desertification. Erosion born of deforestation and excessive use degrade the land, making it more difficult for the land to recover. Eventually, the land loses its ability to recuperate, especially in circumstances that are exacerbated by drought. Under these conditions, the land can become a desert. This is more common in arid or semiarid areas that do not receive large amounts of water on an annual basis. However, due to the large-scale deforestation of rain forests, even these water-rich, tropical regions have seen the desertification of the land that was once covered by lush vegetation and leaf litter. When a rain forest loses its trees, the soil is exposed to direct sunlight and dries out. With vegetation gone, roots and leaf litter are not available to hold the soil in place. This starts the process of desertification.

Rangeland Management

Grazing of cattle on rangeland can be sustainable when managed properly. Historically, in the United States, public lands have been open to grazing, and ranchers have been paid subsidies for their cattle to graze lands, so there has been little motivation to conserve. Now range managers control the use of rangeland by rotating use and continually monitoring carrying capacity of the land. This, combined with the creation of overgrazing laws and the efforts of ranchers to compromise with concerned parties, has led to more sustainable use of rangeland.

Internationally, the issue of overgrazing is even more dramatic, due to issues such as lack of available land. A variety of initiatives are used to support better land-use practices globally. For example, the Farmer-Centered Agricultural Resource Management Program (FARM) run by the United Nations helps farmers in eight Asian countries use proven sustainable farming practices. Also, in China the Farmland Protection Law (1994) mandates that businesses building on farmland create equal farmland in another area.

Conservation-Related Laws

Because of the serious soil depletion and erosion issues the United States has faced, laws have been enacted to protect this precious resource. In 1935, in response to the Dust Bowl, Congress enacted the Soil Conservation Act, which established the Soil Conservation Service to monitor soil erosion. Now called the Natural Resources Conservation Service, the agency has expanded to include water quality and pollution control.

Other conservation-related acts include the Food Security Act (1985), the Conservation Reserve Program (1985), the Taylor Grazing Act (1934), the National Environmental Policy Act (1969), the Endangered Species Act (1973), the Federal Land Policy and Management Act (1976), the Public Rangelands Improvement Act (1978), and the Federal Agriculture Improvement and Reform Act (1996). For more information about U.S. laws, please refer to Appendix D.

Other Land Use

While much human land use involves extracting resources, ecosystems are impacted by other human actions as well. The resources we harvest are used to develop and build products in a process that uses space, consumes resources, and creates waste. Increasingly, modern humans are exploring ways to do so sustainably.

Urban Land Development

As human society has shifted from a rural, agricultural society to an urban, industrialized society, land use has changed. Industrialization centralized many new jobs in urban areas, and since technological advancements also made agricultural processes more efficient, fewer people were needed to produce the needed food. This movement of people from rural to urban lifestyles is termed **urbanization.**

Increased manufacturing and the associated developments in technology, along with increasing population density in urban centers, have had both positive and negative consequences for the environment.

Advantages and Disadvantages of Urbanization	
Benefits of Urbanization	Disadvantages of Urbanization
Increased sanitation	Increased air, water, and land pollution
Improved access to healthcare	Habitat destruction

(continued)

(continued)

Benefits of Urbanization	Disadvantages of Urbanization
Easier access to a variety of resources and choices	Increased land use in urban areas
Increased job opportunities	Potential for "urban sprawl"
Use of public transportation and decreased use of individual transportation	More people per area of land
Ability to fulfill daily needs without traveling a great distance	Health issues
Centralized land use (less land use for a large number of people)	Reduced recreational space

Transportation Infrastructure

Increasing populations and the globalization of our society necessitate the need for a larger **transportation infrastructure,** which encompasses the roads, rails, docks, gas stations, and additional framework that makes our transportation system possible. Common modes of modern transportation include automobiles, boats, trains, subways, and airplanes, all of which require a unique structure. All of our goods and resources are transported at some point in time, whether locally or internationally. Food must be transported from farms to processing centers to grocery stores and restaurants. Raw resources must be extracted and transported prior to manufacturing. After a product has been manufactured and packaged, it must be transported to a distribution warehouse and then finally to the store for purchase. And, of course, many people must travel to work, to school, to run errands, to see family and friends, and to enjoy recreational activities. In essence, almost every aspect of our modern world depends on transportation and, therefore, on transportation infrastructure.

Transportation and transportation infrastructure impact the environment, increasing air pollution by burning fossil fuels, destroying and fragmenting habitats, creating noise and light pollution, and increasing animal deaths due to collisions. However, since infrastructure is essential in today's world, instead of depending on decreasing infrastructure to lessen environmental impact, many point to thoughtful design and implementation of these systems as key to sustainable transportation.

A properly designed transportation system can effectively reduce the environmental impact of its use. For example, efficient highway systems can reduce the amount of time necessary for travel and can help to eliminate congestion. Reducing congestion reduces the amount of fuel needed and, thus, automobile emissions. Also reducing fuel consumption are urban transportation systems, such as subways and buses.

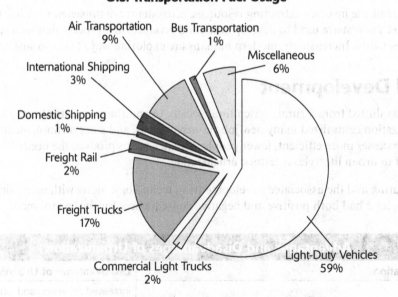

U.S. Transportation Fuel Usage

Air Transportation 9%
Bus Transportation 1%
International Shipping 3%
Miscellaneous 6%
Domestic Shipping 1%
Freight Rail 2%
Freight Trucks 17%
Commercial Light Trucks 2%
Light-Duty Vehicles 59%

Source: EIA, Annual Energy Outlook 2008, Supplemental Table 36
(http://www.eia.doe.gov/oiaf/aeo/supplement/suptap_36.xls).

Source: U.S. Energy Information Administration

U.S. Federal Highway System

The U.S. highway system began in 1944 with the Federal-Aid Highway Act, which approved the national system of highways. Then, in 1952, the Federal Highway Systems Act was passed, designating federal monies to help with the development of an interstate highway system. After years of debate over how the funds should be divided among the states, the Federal-Aid Highway Act of 1956 was passed, mandating, among other things, uniform highway design taking into account future traffic levels. These acts, combined with the efforts of Franklin D. Roosevelt and many others, gave rise to the existing interstate highway system.

Although this highway system drastically increased the ease of interstate travel, the environmental impact has been equally drastic, in large part due to the fragmentation of habitats. In hopes of lessening this fragmentation, today, before a highway can be constructed, an environmental impact statement (EIS) must be created to assess potential environmental impacts from the development.

Canals and Channels

Although less common than roadways, artificial waterways such as canals and naturally occurring waterways called channels still play an important part in the transportation of goods and services. A canal can be used to transport water for irrigation and human use, for recreation, and to control floods, as well as to transport people and goods.

A canal can be created by further digging and expanding an existing stream, creating a canal from dry land where no water source existed, or by developing a canal parallel to a stream or river. Canal size can vary from a small irrigation ditch in the Midwestern Unites States to the immense Panama Canal in Central America, to the series of canals in Venice, Italy. When canals are created, other waterways are affected, since the canal must be fed by a natural source of water. In some cases, canals are also dug into wetlands. This process alters the flow of natural waterways, removes vegetation, increases chances for erosion, and can lead to habitat fragmentation. Canals also can become contaminated from waste and runoff, leading to increased environmental degradation and threats to wildlife and human health. The modification of channels can lead to impacts similar to those of canal development. With increasing awareness of these issues and impacts, more effort is being made to keep canals healthy, minimize environmental impact, and properly plan the construction and use of canals and channels.

Public and Federal Lands

In the United States, land usage and the goals of land usage have changed, in part, due to human immigration and migration. During westward expansion, people explored and settled new areas, largely in the hopes of extracting and profiting from natural resources such as gold, silver, and timber. Laws created during these times including the Homestead Act of 1862 and the General Mining Act of 1872, focused on promoting the expansion and settlement of the country.

The federal government now manages about 29 percent of the land in the United States, which is overseen by four federal agencies: the Bureau of Land Management, the National Park Service and the Fish and Wildlife Service in the U.S. Department of the Interior, and the Forest Service in the U.S. Department of Agriculture.

Management

Created in 1905, the U.S. Forest Service manages public lands within national forests and grasslands. Originally it was established to provide water and timber for the nation, but its role eventually expanded to include the responsibility of managing all renewable resources found in national forests, including water, wildlife, wood, and recreation. The National Park Service, established in 1916, manages the nation's 394 national parks, preserving the wildlife, ecosystems, and historical value of the lands. In 1940, the Fish and Wildlife Service was created as a result of the merging of the Bureau of Fisheries and the Bureau of Biological Survey. This agency works to protect and conserve fish, wildlife, plants, and their habitats. The Bureau of Land Management was created in 1946, combining the General Land Office and the U.S. Grazing Service. Its mission is to protect resources and monitor resource use on public lands.

Gradually, the government's focus has shifted toward managing the increasing populations and establishing infrastructure and laws to support higher population densities while also protecting ecosystems and resources. In 1969, the National Environmental Policy Act was passed, and the law went into effect in 1970, mandating that environmental impacts be taken into account with any federal decision. The act also established the Council on Environmental Quality, requiring that an environmental impact statement be prepared for any action taken by a federal agency. Also established in 1970 was the Environmental Protection Agency (EPA), with the mission of establishing and enforcing environmental protection standards, gathering and using information pertaining to pollution, helping others through grants and other means to reduce pollution, and working with the Council on Environmental Quality to establish new environmental policies. Basically, the EPA writes and enforces regulations based on established laws pertaining to the environment.

Wetlands

Wetlands are terrestrial areas with water-saturated soils; they include marshes, swamps, and bogs. Found all over the world and in a wide variety of biomes, wetlands vary in vegetation, wildlife, water levels, nutrients, and many other factors, depending on the local environment. As one of the most productive ecosystems in the world (along with coral reefs and tropical rain forests), wetlands are an important component of our ecosystems, providing habitats for wildlife, recharging subsurface water supplies such as aquifers, filtering pollutants, preventing erosion of coastlines, and acting as flood control. A major human threat facing these important ecosystems is their destruction as a result of being filled in for agricultural use or for the development of buildings, roads, and other human uses. They are also threatened by high pollution levels, loss of vegetation, and alteration of water supplies. In the United States, many laws have been enacted to help prevent the destruction and loss of wetlands. These include the Clean Water Act, the Rivers and Harbors Act, and the Swampbuster provision in the Food Securities Act. Internationally, the Ramsar Convention on Wetlands of International Importance serves to protect wetlands and their resources. Extensive efforts are also being made to restore previously affected wetlands where possible.

Land Conservation Options

Numerous conservation efforts are being conducted at the local, regional, national, and global levels. **Conservation** focuses on managing land though sustainable use. In contrast, **preservation** takes the approach of no usage, attempting to completely eliminate human impact and to protect the valuable biodiversity and habitats of ecosystems. The choice of approach depends on individual circumstances, with most organizations and program managers taking the conservation approach.

U.S. Federal Programs

In the United States, various federal programs have been established to conserve and protect wildlife and ecosystems, including U.S. National Forests, U.S. National Grasslands, National Wildlife Refuges, and wilderness areas. Laws have also been created to help protect biodiversity; they are often amended to protect endangered species. Such laws include the Wilderness Act and the Endangered Species Act.

National Forests are United States federal lands, comprised mainly of forests and woodlands, which can be used by the public and for commercial use, including timber. This dual use has created much conflict, because the interests of the recreational and commercial uses are frequently at odds.

Similar to National Forests, **National Grasslands** have been established to conserve prairie grasslands. Grasslands are also used commercially for grazing and resource extraction, as well as recreationally for hunting and other recreation. National Grasslands are managed by the Department of Agriculture.

National wildlife refuges protect wildlife, fish, and vegetation, and seek to maintain ecosystem balance. Still, in many refuges, hunting and fishing are allowed, frequently to cull overpopulation, and for the revenue from hunting and fishing licenses, which helps to fund the protection and conservation of wildlife and the maintenance of the wildlife refuge system. The first national wildlife refuge was Pelican Island in Florida, designated as such in 1903 by President Theodore Roosevelt. There are now over 550 wildlife refuges and 38 wetland management areas, which are managed by the U.S. Fish and Wildlife Service.

As a result of the Wilderness Act of 1964 some federal lands were designated as **wilderness areas,** in which the land is relatively undisturbed and undeveloped by humans. These areas are considered part of the National Wilderness Preservation System and are managed by the Bureau of Land Management.

International Programs

Most international conservation efforts are overseen by the United Nations Environment Programme (UNEP), which promotes biodiversity and natural resource conservation on a global level. For example, the UNEP created the Convention on International Trade in Endangered Species of Wild Fauna and Flora to regulate international wildlife trade, helping to protect endangered and threatened species. The United Nations Convention on Biological Diversity was established to conserve biodiversity and to promote sustainability. The Convention on the Conservation of Migratory Species of Wild Animals (also known as the Bonn Convention) regulates migratory species, including avian, marine, and terrestrial organisms that cross national boundaries, conserving them throughout their migratory range.

Under the supervision of the International Union for Conservation of Nature, the World Commission on Protected Areas works toward the selection, establishment, and management of national parks and protected areas internationally, for the protection of plant and animal species. The organization works with governments and other key parties to plan and finance protected areas, including marine and terrestrial ecosystems.

Another approach to international preservation of terrestrial and coastal marine ecosystems is through the use of **biosphere reserves.** Operating under the World Network of Biosphere Reserves, these reserves combine the protection of biodiversity with sustainable land use, education, and scientific research. Each reserve is split into three, standardized zones: a central core area where there is almost no human activity, a buffer zone where there is limited human activity, and the transition zone in which a wide variety of sustainable human activities are allowed. Currently there are over 530 biosphere reserves globally.

Nongovernmental Programs

Nongovernmental organizations (NGOs) also play a large role in land conservation efforts. The Nature Conservancy is one of the world's largest NGOs working toward ecosystem conservation. The Sierra Club was founded in 1892 by John Muir to protect communities and wild places; it is the oldest and largest such organization in the United States.

Sustainable Land-Use Strategies

Advancements in sustainable building techniques help balance the needs of human society with environmental impact. Much of the policy governing sustainable building is designed at the city and regional levels. Effective city planning takes into account the location and types of parks and green areas, transportation infrastructure, recreation, commerce areas, housing options, hospitals, schools, energy usage, waste removal, and many other components. One way cities manage these diverse needs is through zoning (meaning that only certain types of building are allowed in certain areas). Zoning helps to control how a city grows and includes restrictions on what can be done with land, separating commercial, industrial, and residential areas.

Partly in response to congestion and high population density in cities, some people now choose to move out of large urban areas to surrounding suburban and rural areas, broadening the continued environmental issues associated with urbanization.

Mining

Humans use many minerals—such as copper, silver, cobalt, aluminum, nickel, tungsten, magnesium, lead, uranium, manganese, potassium, and many others—to manufacture the products necessary for everyday life. In order to obtain these minerals, the raw materials are mined from the layer of the Earth's crust called the lithosphere. People also extract resources such as limestone, gypsum, gravel, salt, and gemstones. Extraction processes can be very destructive to the environment and can have far-reaching impacts, especially due to the market-driven need for companies to extract as much as possible as fast as possible and as cheaply as possible. However regulations exist to reduce environmental impact and help to conserve resources.

While the concept of mining applies to minerals and fossil fuels, this section addresses the mining of minerals. Fossil fuel formation and extraction are addressed in Chapter 5.

Mineral Formation

Minerals are nonrenewable resources formed through geologic processes. Most minerals are found not in their pure form but as an ore. An **ore** is a mixture of mineral elements packed together into naturally occurring molecular compounds. For example, galena is lead combined with sulfur (PbS) and is the most common form of lead found in nature.

Minerals can be formed through a variety of processes. Some minerals are formed when molten magma cools and the minerals it contains crystallize into deposits. Crystallization and, thus, mineral formation also can occur as water evaporates. Bodies of water contain dissolved minerals. When mineral-rich water evaporates, the minerals are left behind. Since oceans are high in salt content, much of the minerals left behind by evaporating water are salts. Minerals also can be formed as hot water cools. Minerals dissolve in hot water, but as water cools it can hold fewer minerals in solution. The excess crystallizes into mineral deposits. This crystallization due to cooling often occurs deep within the Earth and near hydrothermal vents in the ocean.

Mineral Extraction

The extraction of minerals is an invasive process that commonly has detrimental environmental impacts, such as the following:

- Habitat destruction due to the removal of vegetation
- Soil erosion
- Acid runoff from extraction processes, contaminating soil and water
- Air pollution as a result of fossil fuel combustion from machinery operations and smelting processes

Minerals and resources are extracted from the Earth in the following ways:

- **Surface mining:** Removes the soil and rock covering mineral deposits. This technique is used when deposits are located relatively close to the surface. Once the mineral deposit is completely extracted, the hole is commonly refilled with the original soil and rock.
- **Mountaintop removal:** When the tops of mountains are blasted off to access the resource. This technique is common in the coal mines of the Appalachian Mountains.
- **Placer mining:** Uses water to separate the heavier minerals from lighter mud and debris. This technique is commonly used to extract deposits found in riverbeds.
- **Open-pit mining:** Involves digging in order to reach the desired resource. Some pits are so large that the sides are terraced so that trucks can get in and out. Open pits are usually called quarries.
- **Subsurface mining:** Creates shafts deep underground to extract resources from pockets or seams of minerals. Dynamite blasts, drilling, and manual labor are used to remove rock and access the resource.

Impacts of Mining		
	Impact	**Common Use**
Surface mining	Soil erosion, acid drainage*	Gravel, sand, coal, oil sands
Mountaintop removal	Deforestation, soil erosion, complete modification of local communities	Coal

	Impact	Common Use
Placer mining	Excessive debris in streams inhibiting biotic community, erosion of stream banks, loss of riparian habitat	Gems, gold
Open-pit mining	Complete ecosystem destruction, acid drainage*	Copper, iron, diamonds, gold, coal
Subsurface mining	Health hazards to miners, acid drainage*	Gold, copper, uranium, zinc, lead, nickel, coal, other metals

Acid drainage occurs when sulfuric acid is created by the exposure of oxygen and water to sulfide compounds, which causes a reaction. This natural process is accelerated by the increased exposure of rock surfaces during mining processes. In some situations, the leakage from acid drainage could continue for hundreds of years and has the potential to filter into groundwater.

While the specific negative impacts of mining techniques are noted in the table above, all mining processes cause habitat alteration and degrade ecosystems for the short term and potentially the long term. Ecosystem changes due to mining can include deforestation, soil removal, soil erosion, stream alteration, and the displacement of many organisms.

Mining Oceans

The ocean floor provides many resources, and the extraction of these resources is a relatively recent human endeavor. Sand, gravel, calcium carbonate, sulfur, phosphorites, silica, and valuable ores are all mined from the ocean bottom. **Manganese nodules,** a unique creation in the benthic environment, are ball-like structures created on the ocean floor. They contain manganese, along with many other minerals in smaller amounts, such as copper, zinc, and nickel. Mining of manganese nodules can be very destructive, as it disrupts and relocates large amounts of sediment. Also, the mining processes remove benthic organisms and can destroy structures on the ocean floor.

Mining Reclamation

Mining operations are destructive to the land, so the **reclamation,** or restoration, of the land after mining activities are completed can be a difficult and costly process. The process of reclamation varies depending on the type of mine, type of operations, location, and extent of environmental destruction. Metal mining can produce heavy metal and acid contamination, which can affect surface water and groundwater as well as potentially being toxic to humans and wildlife. With mining practices that disturb the surface of the land, it is not always possible to return the land back to its original state. One technique to restore land disturbed by mining is to replace lost topsoil with new topsoil reclaimed from agriculture.

Some mining sites are contaminated with hazardous wastes that require specialized cleaning techniques, as specified by the Comprehensive Environmental Response, Compensation, and Liability Act (CERCLA), or Superfund. The cleanup of **Superfund** sites is the job of the federal government and paid for by a tax on the chemical and petroleum industries.

Mining Laws and Treaties

The General Mining Act of 1872 gives people the right to prospect on public lands, serving as the basis for further mining regulations. Mining operations also must comply with federal laws such as the Surface Mining Control and Reclamation Act (SMCRA); the Clean Water Act (CWA); the Clean Air Act (CAA); the Safe Drinking Water Act (SDWA); the Resource Conservation and Recovery Act (RCRA); CERCLA; and many others.

Since minerals are nonrenewable resources, sustainable use is an important aspect of managing them. This can be accomplished through recycling and reuse of products, as well as by thoughtful purchasing of products with the goal of reducing consumption.

Fishing

Throughout history people have fished Earth's oceans and freshwater sources. In modern times, however, these waters are being over-fished and depleted, mainly due to the use of techniques capable of harvesting large numbers of fish to meet the demand of our increasing global population. The excessive consumption of fish, combined with the destruction of aquatic habitats and ecosystems, has brought some fish populations close to extinction, with other populations declining rapidly, and many species are considered to be endangered or threatened. Ultimately, the balance of entire ecosystems and food webs can be dramatically altered by overfishing, with the potential for devastating ecosystem collapse.

Fishing Techniques

Modern fishing practices are designed to catch the most fish as quickly as possible and as cheaply as possible. As a result, these techniques tend to be both efficient and destructive. The three main industrial fishing techniques include bottom trawling, long-lining, and drift netting.

- **Bottom trawling** includes dragging a large net along the bottom to capture organisms. This can crush coral reefs and other organisms. It also can stir up sediment and decrease the amount of sunlight that reaches the deeper parts of the ocean. Other types of trawling target species that are either just above the benthic zone or in the pelagic zone (mid-ocean). Many nations have placed restrictions on when, where, or how trawling can be conducted.

- **Long-lining** involves dragging a long fishing line with baited hooks along its length behind a boat or attaching it to an anchor. Long-lining is used to catch surface fish such as swordfish or can be deployed closer to the ocean floor to catch benthic fish such as cod. One side effect of this fishing method is the high rate of bycatch, or fish and other organisms caught unintentionally while trying to catch a particular species of fish. Organisms commonly caught as bycatch include sea turtles and a variety of birds. Recently, the fishing industry has started making modifications to the lines in order to reduce bycatch.

- **Drift netting** is the practice of dragging large nets through the water to catch fish. The primary negative environmental impact of this technique is the large amount of bycatch, including sharks, dolphins, sea turtles, and whales. In some regions, the use of drift nets is regulated, with limits set on the size of the net. In other regions, this practice has been banned, either for particular species or altogether.

Overfishing

The extensive fishing of the oceans and freshwater sources allowed by large-scale commercial fishing methods has caused a dramatic decline in fishery numbers. Many fisheries are now collapsing, meaning the numbers are very low and continue to decrease. Because of the decline in populations of the larger, more desirable fish, fleets have started fishing the smaller, less desirable, less valuable fish. This process has been termed "fishing down the food chain," reflecting the literal change from harvesting larger fish, to medium-size fish, to smaller fish, similar to the progression down the aquatic food chain.

For years, fish harvest numbers remained stable, so many people assumed that the fisheries themselves were stable. But the fact is that population declines were simply balanced by developments in fishing techniques and technologies, including fishing in deeper waters, setting out more nets and lines, fishing for a longer period of time, traveling farther for the harvest, and using better technologies to locate the target. Not only does over-harvesting affect fishery populations, but it has economic impact on the individual, local, regional, and national scale.

Coral reefs

Very sensitive yet important aquatic ecosystems are coral reefs. Within the past half-century, though, these areas have been dramatically harmed by human activities, including pollution, harvesting of corals, acidification of the oceans, and water temperature changes. The changing aquatic environment around coral reefs has lead to a process called coral bleaching, in which the microorganisms (called zooxanthalae) that live in a symbiotic relationship with coral leave the coral. The microorganisms provide food for the coral through photosynthesis, and the coral provides shelter for them. When the zooxanthalae leave, the coral loses its source of food and dies. It is considered "bleaching" because the microorganisms are the color in the coral, so when they leave, the color goes as well.

Aquaculture

As an alternative to fishing, humans have developed aquaculture to raise both freshwater and marine aquatic species in enclosed, monitored environments similar to farms on land. This helps to ensure continued and consistent fish products for consumption. Whether the farm is in a large, open-water floating pen or in ponds and tanks, there are environmental pros and cons to this newer form of agriculture. As with other human activities, if conducted on a responsible and regulated level, aquaculture can be sustainable.

Advantages and Disadvantages of Aquaculture	
Advantages	**Disadvantages**
Reduces bycatch	Increases risk of disease due to close proximity (monoculture)
Is energy efficient	Is associated with increased antibiotic use
Reduces consumption of wild populations	The fish may escape into the wild and could become invasive
Provides more reliable sources of food and protein	Results in excessive waste in a small area
	Some transgenic farmed fish are larger and faster than wild, so they outcompete them for resources.

Fishing Management

Historically, fishery conservation efforts were focused on individual species like salmon or swordfish, but this approach has proven to be largely unsuccessful. More recent management practices take an ecosystem-based approach, creating areas in the ocean that have limited or no human activity in hopes that the species will use these areas to restore themselves.

Fishing Laws and Treaties

There are numerous ways in which restrictions are made on fisheries at the state, federal, and international levels, including limits on the number of fish taken and pollution controls. Fishing regulations detail the species, amount allowed for harvesting per day, closed seasons, and other information specific to each type of fishery. Pollution regulations include the establishment of effluent limitation guidelines (ELGs), created to reduce pollutants from aquaculture wastewater released into open waters.

Major federal laws governing fisheries include the Marine Protection, Research, and Sanctuaries Act (MPRSA, also known as the Ocean Dumping Act); the Oil Pollution Act (OPA); the Clean Water Act; and the Endangered Species Act. International treaties include the United Nations Convention on the Law of the Sea (UNCLOS); the United Nations Fish Stocks Agreement; and the Agreement on Port State Measures to Prevent, Deter and Eliminate Illegal, Unreported, and Unregulated Fishing.

With heightened conservation efforts and awareness, the use of more sustainable fishing methods and the enactment of laws, treaties, and regulations have helped to reduce bycatch and to reestablish some of the fishery populations that were previously in decline. However, there is still a long way to go in creating a sustainable fishing industry.

Marine-protected areas (MPAs) have been created to reduce fishing demands on marine organisms living within their boundaries. Still, most MPAs allow for some fishing and harvesting of marine life. Restrictions vary but can include bans on mining, extraction of resources, and the use of sonar. The size of the area included in an MPA also varies, from small to very large. Currently there are about 400 MPAs worldwide, in more than 65 countries. There is still a debate as to how useful MPAs are in protecting ecosystems and fisheries, but an increasing body of evidence demonstrates some progress in local fishery populations and ecosystem improvements due to MPAs.

A more restrictive type of MPA is a **marine reserve**, which does not allow human interference within the ecosystem and prohibits any activity that would remove or damage life in that area. This designation can help decimated fishery populations and ecosystems recover and/or remain stable. However, many people oppose the establishment of marine reserves, some citing the prevalence of locations in the oceans that are already off-limits to fishing and recreation.

Marine reserves demonstrate an increase in the following:

- Density of populations of organisms
- Biodiversity
- Biomass
- Organism size
- Larval supply

In both MPAs and marine reserves, there can be various levels of protection within the area, with some parts having to follow more stringent rules than others. There might also be seasonal restrictions. This multiple-use approach has the potential to meet the needs of fisheries and ecosystems, as well as humans who use the areas for economic and recreational purposes.

Global Economies

Globalization

The economy and the environment are interdependent. Not only do humans extract Earth's resources for use in making goods sold throughout the world, but this extraction and the services that support it provides jobs. The Earth's resources are the basis for the economy. Additionally, some have argued that without the economic need for Earth's resources, there would be reduced cause to preserve and protect them.

As human societies become more global, so does the economy and the use of resources. For example, a Japanese multinational company can buy rights to harvest timber in Canada and then export it for sale throughout the world. However, this globalization of resources can increase environmental damage because countries may not feel as much incentive to protect the ecosystems that house resources on the other side of the world.

Three ways in which the United States and other countries address the relationship between the environment and the economy are through the use of subsidies, green taxes, and permit trading:

- A **subsidy** is financial assistance given by the government to a business, a person, or an economic sector in an effort to support an activity that is thought to be beneficial to the public. Subsidies can be used to encourage sustainable activities such as energy conservation, research and development of new technologies, farming practices, and the production of fossil fuels. Unfortunately, there are often unintended negative consequences arising from the use of subsidies.
- **Green taxes** are placed on activities that are considered to be harmful to the environment. For example, the federal government has placed a tax on eight chemicals considered damaging to the ozone. Ultimately, this tax is frequently passed on to consumers, as companies increase the cost of their product to cover the cost of the tax.

- In **permit trading,** a maximum or "cap" is placed on the amount of pollution that an industry can emit, and individual companies are given permits for the amount they are allowed to pollute. If a company emits less pollution and, thus, does not need all its permits, it can sell the excess permits to another company that goes over its allotted amount of pollution. For example, a cap-and-trade system for carbon may help control the amount of carbon dioxide being released into the atmosphere.

World Bank

The World Bank was created in 1944 to help developing nations in need of financial and technical assistance in an effort to eliminate poverty. It provides loans, grants, and credits for activities deemed important to help a country reduce poverty and develop sustainable actions for working toward a more secure future. These activities frequently include agricultural, environmental, and natural resource management, education, health, infrastructure, finance, and public administration. The World Bank is made up of two separate institutions: the International Bank for Reconstruction and Development and the International Development Association. Examples of projects include the improvement and maintenance of roads in Argentina, the restoration of irrigation systems in Afghanistan, efforts to address India's energy shortage by laying power lines, and programs to treat and prevent malaria in Zambia.

In keeping with the mission to eradicate poverty and move toward more sustainable practices, the United Nations created the Millennium Declaration in 2000. One hundred and eighty-nine U.N. member states adopted it, making a pledge to eliminate poverty, increase development projects, and protect the environment.

Tragedy of the Commons

"The Tragedy of the Commons" is an essay written by Garrett Hardin in 1968. The essay's central point is that unregulated resources will eventually be overused and depleted, because although it is in the communal good to protect shared areas, it is in no individual's best interest to do so. To use economic terms, this "maximization of personal utility" means that each person's self-serving actions decreases the "utility" of the group in the long run.

Examples of these tragedies of the commons include the overharvesting of our fisheries in international waters, pollution of the air, and excessive use of underground water supplies. A well-known case study demonstrating a tragedy of the commons is the demise of Easter Island and its inhabitants. The native Polynesians overused the trees of the island, ultimately leaving their land devoid of timber, which had far-reaching impacts on their society and survival. (For additional discussion, see Appendix B.) Another common example is the overgrazing of cattle on public, unmonitored lands. Although it is in any one rancher's individual interest to exploit these lands to their fullest, with every rancher making this decision, the benefit of the shared resource is removed for all, as ultimately this practice does not allow for the regrowth of the grasses, leaving the land barren and ungrazable.

Global Economics Laws and Treaties

Making and enforcing international environmental laws and treaties can be difficult since many environmental issues cross national boundaries. There are over 1,000 treaties that pertain to the environment. Following are a few examples:

- The **Convention on Long-Range Transboundary Air Pollution** aims to gradually reduce air pollution, including trans-boundary pollution that travels over great distances.
- The **Convention for the Conservation of Antarctic Marine Living Resources** was established to protect marine life and ecosystems in and close to Antarctica. It is part of the Antarctic Treaty System.
- The **Basel Convention on the Control of Transboundary Movements of Hazardous Wastes and Their Disposal** controls the transport of hazardous waste between nations, especially the transfer of waste from developed to less-developed countries. It also focuses on exemplary management practices and the reduction of toxicity of waste.

Practice

1. Which of the following is NOT a result of the Green Revolution?

   A. Increased food production
   B. High-yield crop varieties due to selective breeding
   C. Decreased use of monoculture
   D. More land being converted for use in agriculture
   E. Use of pesticides and fertilizers

2. Deforestation, overgrazing, and the overworking of soil for crop production can lead to which of the following?

   A. Salinization
   B. Monoculture
   C. Desertification
   D. Increased crop rotation
   E. Depletion of aquifers

3. Which of the following is an example of a project that would be supported by the World Bank?

   A. Building commercial skyscrapers
   B. Expansion of a shipping fleet
   C. Development of military weapons
   D. Purchase of land to be used as a hazardous waste site
   E. Improvements in healthcare

4. What is the result of the suppression of forest fires?

   A. Increase in succession in forest ecosystems
   B. Severe fires when wildfires do occur
   C. Increase in biodiversity in forest ecosystems
   D. Abundance of soil nutrients
   E. Strengthening of overall ecosystem health

5. Which of the following are issues that need to be addressed when planning for the reclamation of a mining site?

   A. Acid drainage into water sources, loss of wildlife, erosion
   B. Overpopulation of wildlife and over-accumulation of biomass
   C. Desertification and salinization
   D. Increase in eutrophication in local freshwater sources
   E. Invasive species

6. Which of the following is associated with fishing down the food chain?

   A. Harvesting of all fish species
   B. The extinction of small fisheries
   C. Harvesting of benthic organisms
   D. Fishing for smaller and smaller fish due to the decline of larger fisheries
   E. Selective breeding of fish species

7. Which of the following was the main driving force behind urbanization in the United States?

   A. Better healthcare and education
   B. Industrialization and technological advancements
   C. Decline of the agricultural sector
   D. Increased disease transmission
   E. High levels of pollution in rural areas

8. Which of the following organizations is responsible for the management of public lands?

   A. U.S. Forest Service
   B. National Park Service
   C. Congress
   D. Bureau of Land Management
   E. Environmental Protection Agency

9. Aquaculture has many benefits and many drawbacks. Which of the following is considered a positive aspect of aquaculture?

    A. Decrease in disease among species of fish
    B. Less waste in benthic environments
    C. Reduction in fossil fuel use
    D. Increased consumption of wild populations
    E. Elimination of long-line fishing

10. Which of the following is one way to encourage businesses and people to use sustainable practices through monetary support?

    A. A green tax
    B. Marketable emissions permits
    C. Subsidies
    D. Laws and regulations
    E. Imports and exports

11. Which of the following factors did NOT contribute to the Dust Bowl in the United States?

    A. No-till agriculture
    B. Removal of vegetation cover
    C. Soil erosion
    D. Desertification
    E. Drought

12. The genetically engineered golden rice has been developed to do which of the following?

    A. Resist the harm caused by frost
    B. Provide vitamin A
    C. Resist pests
    D. Have long-lasting freshness
    E. Produce more seeds

13. What is the role of the Comprehensive Environmental Response, Compensation, and Liability Act in relation to mining sites?

    A. It mandates that mining activities must not change the contour of the land.
    B. It states that mined land must be restored after the closing of the mine.
    C. It sets limits on the amount of resources that can be harvested at any given time.
    D. It established a tax-and-response process for hazardous waste.
    E. It gives mining companies full control over the land on which they mine.

14. What is the goal of marine-protected areas?

    A. Create areas where fishermen can fish without regulation
    B. Establish a protected area in the ocean where resources are allowed to be extracted
    C. Reduce stresses on fisheries by restricting some activities
    D. Create zones for use in aquaculture
    E. Eliminate fishing in the ocean altogether

15. Which of the following is a way city planning can reduce human impact on the environment?

    A. Build efficient highway infrastructure
    B. Create a downtown area that is spread out
    C. Build zoos
    D. Build directly on wetland areas to be close to the ocean
    E. Eliminate recycling programs to reduce cost

Answers

1. **C** The use of monoculture increased during the Green Revolution. Large areas of land were converted for agricultural use, and new high-yield seed varieties became widely used. Monoculture is generally more efficient in planting and harvesting. The technological advancements during this time enabled new agricultural processes.

2. **C** Desertification is the loss of soil productivity due to erosion, overgrazing, drought, soil compaction, and any other factors that deplete the soil.

3. **E** The purpose of the World Bank is to help developing nations in need of financial and technical assistance in an effort to eliminate poverty. Therefore, an initiative to improve healthcare would be an initiative that the World Bank would undertake.

4. **B** Extended periods of fire suppression lead to increased fuel, mostly in the form of underbrush, causing the wildfires that inevitably occur to burn hotter and potentially consume more land. Forest fires naturally clear out dead brush, trees, and leaves, helping to keep the ecosystem clear of debris while returning nutrients to the soil. Also, many types of vegetation germinate after a fire because the seeds open from the extreme heat.

5. **A** Mining is a destructive process. Acid drainage can run off and contaminate freshwater and groundwater sources. Habitat alteration occurs to varying degrees in mining processes, with some techniques resulting in complete habitat destruction and others being less dramatic. This leads to loss of wildlife and biodiversity in the area of the mine. Also, the removal of vegetation leaves soil exposed and prone to erosion.

6. **D** Humans harvested the largest, most desirable fish to the point of drastically decreasing populations, forcing humans to then hunt for smaller fish, further down the food chain. As this process continues, smaller and less desirable fish are targeted. Basically, humans are "fishing down the food chain."

7. **B** As the country became industrialized, people started moving to city centers for jobs, healthcare, and education. The cities offered more opportunities and options.

8. **D** The Bureau of Land Management is responsible for the management of public lands.

9. **C** Because aquaculture farms are located close to shore and fishing fleets are not required to harvest the fish, fossil fuel use is reduced. In traditional fishing, boats may travel hundreds of miles for long periods of time to achieve their harvest goal. This consumes large amounts of fossil fuels and emits pollution.

10. **C** Subsidies are monies given by the government to people and companies in order to encourage certain desired practices.

11. **A** No-till agriculture does not cause soil disturbances like tillage agriculture does and can, thus, reduce soil loss due to erosion. A variety of factors contributed to the devastating impact of the Dust Bowl, including the clearing of land, overusing and overtilling for agricultural use, and drought.

12. **B** Golden rice was engineered to contain vitamin A, an important vitamin that some food supplies in developing or impoverished countries lack. This rice was developed as an aid toward addressing worldwide hunger.

13. **D** The Comprehensive Environmental Response, Compensation, and Liability Act (CERCLA) established a tax on the chemical and petroleum industries and gave the federal government the authority to handle released hazardous substances or ones that have the potential to be released. Mining processes can use and produce acid, and heavy metals can contaminate water sources. These products are considered hazardous waste and must be dealt with in accordance with CERCLA regulations.

14. **C** Marine-protected areas (MPAs) have been created to conserve fisheries through the restriction of some activities such as mining and resource extraction. MPAs also have restrictions and limits on fishing and harvesting of various species.

15. **A** An efficient highway infrastructure can reduce the use of fossil fuels and emissions from vehicles because it will reduce the amount of time spent commuting from one location to another. If less time is spent driving, less fossil fuel is used and less emissions are produced.

Chapter 5

Energy Resources and Consumption

A variety of sources provide the energy necessary to power developing and industrialized societies. Fossil fuels, which included coal, oil, and natural gas, are the result of millions of years of decay of organic material deep within the Earth. Humans now extract these resources in order to harness the stored energy through combustion processes. Alternative fuel sources, such as hydroelectric power and nuclear power, have been used for many generations. New advancements in energy production have led to new types of energy sources, such as solar, wind, biomass, hydrogen, geothermal, tidal, and wave energy. Now more than ever, the importance of addressing both energy production and consumption on a global scale is at the forefront of modern society. Conservation initiatives and sustainable sources are becoming the focus of the energy industry and societies as a whole.

Energy Concepts

Energy comes in many forms, both natural and man-made. Forms of energy include mechanical, thermal, chemical, nuclear, electrical, and electromagnetic. Energy measures the ability of an object to perform work and to move objects. Energy can be transferred or converted from one form to another. There are two forms of mechanical energy: potential energy and kinetic energy. Energy possessed by a moving object is called **kinetic energy.** A stationary object has **potential energy** if its position can be converted into movement. If you suspend a coin from your fingers as if you are going to drop it, but you don't let it fall, the coin has potential energy, or energy stored in a system or an object. If you drop the coin, as it falls through the air it has kinetic energy, or energy due to its motion.

Forms of Potential and Kinetic Energy	
Potential Energy	**Kinetic Energy**
Chemical energy is the most practical form of energy. It is a chemical reaction between bonds of atoms to form molecules. Chemical energy is converted to thermal energy when we burn wood in a fireplace.	**Thermal energy,** or heat energy, is the energy created by the movement of molecules within a substance. As a substance gets warmer, the vibrations of the molecules within that substance increase. When boiling water, for example, thermal energy is added to the bottom of a pot. This thermal energy is transferred across the pot, into the water, and the water molecules move faster. Eventually, enough heat is added to boil the water, and as the water boils, it quickly turns to steam.
There are two types of chemical reactions: endothermic and exothermic. Endothermic reactions take in heat energy; thus, providing no usable energy. Exothermic reactions release energy during the reaction. For example, when we burn coal in the presence of oxygen, we get carbon dioxide, water, pollutants, and energy. The chemical reaction is $coal + O_2 \xrightarrow{burn} CO_2 + H_2O + pollutants + energy$	

(continued)

Potential Energy	Kinetic Energy
Mechanical potential energy is energy stored in objects by tension or position. A stretched rubber band is an example of stored mechanical energy, as are objects held above the ground. Gravitational energy is also classified as a type of mechanical energy.	**Kinetic (electromagnetic) energy** is energy of motion, which can be transformed into electrical energy. One way to generate electrical energy is to turn a generator, which consists of coiled copper wire and magnets. As the wire coil spins, it cuts through the magnetic field, resulting in a flow of electrons through the wire. (Moving electrical charges possess both an electric and a magnetic field.) This process generates an alternating current that passes into electrical transmission lines. This is the form of electrical energy we use in our houses. Anything that turns the copper coil through the magnetic field possesses kinetic energy that can create electromagnetic energy, including wind or water turning a turbine, or coal or nuclear fusion boiling water, whose steam powers similar turbines.
Nuclear energy is stored in the nuclei (core) of an atom and is released when an atom splits apart or two atoms join together. The process of splitting an atom is called **fission,** and the process of joining atoms is called **fusion.** For example, fission occurs in nuclear power plants when huge amounts of heat are created by splitting the nuclei of uranium atoms. The process of fusion occurs when the sun combines the nuclei of hydrogen atoms.	
Gravitational energy is energy stored in an object's height. The higher and heavier the object, the more gravitational energy is stored. When you ride a bicycle down a steep hill and pick up speed, your gravitational energy is converted to motion, or kinetic energy. Hydropower generation converts the gravitational energy of water in reservoirs to kinetic energy of moving water, which drives turbines that create electricity.	
Electrical energy is created from the motion of electrons. Electrical energy is transferred by tiny charged particles called **electrons,** typically moving through a wire. Just as gravitational energy is stored in stationary water in reservoirs, electrical energy is stored in batteries. When electrical energy is allowed to convert itself into the kinetic energy of electrical current, it can be used to power a cellphone or start a car. During a storm, electrical energy may be generated and released as lightning. Walk across the carpet on a dry day and you store electrical energy in your body, which you release with a small zap when you touch a conductive object. This is static electricity.	

The following table contains some of the most common energy terms used in AP Environmental Science.

Common Terms Used in AP Environmental Science	
Term	**Definition**
British Thermal Unit (BTU or Btu)	The amount of heat it takes to raise the temperature of 1 pound of water by 1°F
Calorie (c)	The amount of heat it takes to raise the temperature of 1 gram of water by 1°C (1.8°F)
Kilocalorie (C)	The amount of heat it takes to raise the temperature of 1 kilogram of water by 1°C (1.8°F)
Horsepower (hp)	Primarily used in the combustion engine market, such as in autos, trucks, boats, and backup generators; 1 horsepower = 746 watts
Joule (J)	The force of 1 Newton applied through 1 meter of displacement
Watt (electrical) (W)	Measures the rate of energy conversion and is defined as 1 joule per second; commonly used in terms of kilowatt-hour (kWh) energy consumption; used by power plants to describe how much energy they generate (megawatt-hours) and on home energy bills (kWh)
Watt (thermal)	Used in nuclear power plants to measure the amount of thermal energy generated

Common SI (International System of Units) Prefixes Used in Energy	
Term	**Definition**
Kilo– (k)	1,000 or 10^3; common metric term that is used in the power industry
Mega– (M)	1,000,000 or 10^6; common metric term that is used in the power industry
Giga– (G)	1,000,000,000 or 10^9; commonly used in the computer industry and in talking about energy needs and energy produced in regions and smaller countries.
Tera– (T)	1,000,000,000,000 or 10^{12}; new term used in the computer industry and is becoming more common in talking about the total energy needs and energy produced in a country

Following is a table of conversion factors useful in environmental science. On the AP Environmental Science exam, the conversion factors are provided, and conversions are rounded. For example, 1 kWh is equal to 3,413 BTU, but the AP Environmental Science exam rounds this number to 3,400 BTU, which makes multiplication easier. Despite the fact that conversions are given on the exam, it is useful to familiarize yourself with the conversions below to build intuitive understanding of relationships between units.

Conversions		
Symbol	**Unit**	**Conversion**
1 c.	Calorie	3.968 BTU or 4,186 J
1 BTU	British Thermal Unit	0.254 c or 1,055 J
1 W	Watt	1 W for 1 hour is 3.413 BTU
1 kWh	Kilowatt hour	1 kW for 1 hour is 3,413 BTU **Note:** 3,400 BTU is commonly used on the AP exam to simplify calculations.
1 MW	Megawatt	1,000,000 W or 1,000 kW
1 GW	Gigawatt	1,000,000,000 W, 1,000,000 kW, or 1,000 MW
1 hp	Horsepower	0.7457 kW or 2,545 BTU
1 gallon gas	Gallon of gasoline	125,000 BTU
1 barrel oil	Barrel of crude oil	25,000,000 BTU or 42 gallons of crude oil
1 CF natural gas	Cubic foot of natural gas	1,031 BTU

APES Math Problems

Every set of free-response questions on the AP Environmental Science exam includes at least one math-based problem. Recently, including more than one math problem has become the norm. For the most part, the math consists of algebraic word problems, including determining a percentage change to using dimensional analysis for unit conversion problems, and problems of straightforward arithmetic.

Math Problems on Prior AP Environmental Science Exams

The following is a review of the math problems for previous AP Environmental Science exams, with energy calculation problems in bold:

- 1998: **Energy calculation (BTU) of a dishwasher**, dimensional analysis
- 1999: Percentage change, air pollutants
- 2000: **Energy calculation (BTU) of a power plant**, pollutant calculation (pounds of sulfur), dimensional analysis
- 2001: **Energy calculation (BTU) of a house**, dimensional analysis
- 2002: **Gasoline consumption vs. electric vehicles**, dimensional analysis; Graphing of LD_{50}
- 2003: Graphing, population growth rate calculation
- 2004: **Energy calculation in kWh of wind power, conversion between kilo and mega**, comparison, dimensional analysis
- 2005: Percentage change, meat consumption; **Usage calculation of barrels of crude oil**, ANWR, simple dimensional analysis
- 2006: Net change, ratio, CO_2 and temperature; Change over time, graph provided, decline of fish population
- 2007: Water usage and cost, dimensional analysis
- 2008: Cross-multiplication, how many acres; Calculation of volume for a landfill, dimensional analysis; Graph total fertility, no grid lines provided
- 2009: **Energy calculation for methane digesters** (number was a decimal but had to round to the whole number; number was not nice and neat, dimensional analysis); Percentage of land use change, graph provided, GM crops
- 2010: Cost to capture CO_2 emissions, simple dimensional analysis; methane emissions from termites, dimensional analysis; rising sea level, simple dimensional analysis

Dimensional Analysis

A dimensional analysis uses conversion factors to transform data represented in one type of units to data represented in other units.

Here's how to solve a math problem using dimensional analysis:

1. **Read the question to determine the final units.**
2. **Set the final units at the end of a dimensional analysis equation.**

    These desired final units are the only units that will not "cancel." All other units will be used to convert from starting units toward the desired ending units.

3. **Check that the problem is set up so that starting units are converted into ending units.**

    To cancel units, you need the unit on one top numerator and one bottom denominator of the dimensional analysis equation. Units should cancel the same way numbers would cancel.

4. **Simplify the math, cancel out zeros, and simplify the numbers.**
5. **Solve the math.**
6. **Rewrite the answer including the units.**

    Indicate that this is the final answer.

EXAMPLE:

Several AP Environmental Science teachers were sitting around a table discussing the full coal cars heading east to several big cities and the empty coal cars returning to the mines in the west. The teachers were wondering how much energy was in each coal car and how long the coal would last. In addition, they discussed the environmental impact of mining and transporting the coal across these distances.

A large, coal-fired power plant produces 48 million kWh of electricity each day. Assume the following: 10,000 BTUs are required to produce 1 kWh of electricity; 1 pound of coal produces 5,000 BTUs of heat; each coal car can hold 120 tons; 1 ton is 2,000 pounds.

A. How much heat in BTUs is needed to operate the coal plant for one day?
B. How many coal cars will be needed to operate the power plant for the day?
C. How many trains will be needed to power the plant for a day if the train pulls 100 coal cars?

Follow the steps listed earlier:

1. **Read the question to determine the final units.**

    The first question asks how much heat in *BTUs* is needed to produce the power for one day.

2. **Set the final units at the end of a dimensional analysis equation.**

    Using the information provided, days should be on the bottom and BTUs on the top (BTUs/day). kWh/day, is included in the statement "48 million kWh are produced in one day." Write this first. Next, it states that 10,000 BTUs are used to produce 1 kWh of electricity, so place BTUs/kWh second in the analysis. Now, with kWh on the top and kWh on the bottom, the units cancel.

$$\frac{48 \text{ million kWh}}{\text{day}} \left| \frac{10,000 \text{ BTUs}}{1 \text{ kWh}} \right. =$$

3. **Check that the problem is set up so that starting units are converted into ending units.**

4. **Simplify the math, cancel out zeros, and simplify the numbers.**

$$\frac{48 \text{ million } \cancel{kWh}}{\text{day}} \Bigg| \frac{10,000 \text{ BTUs}}{1 \cancel{kWh}} =$$

In this problem, the numbers are already in their simplest form.

5. **Solve the math.**

$$\frac{48 \text{ million}}{\text{day}} \Bigg| \frac{10,000 \text{ BTUs}}{1} = \frac{480,000 \text{ million BTUs}}{\text{day}}$$

6. **Rewrite the answer including the units.**

$$\frac{480,000 \text{ million BTUs}}{\text{day}} \text{ or simplified: } \frac{480 \text{ billion BTUs}}{\text{day}}$$

Helpful Hints

❏ In the 13 years of the AP Environmental Science exam, no one has ever lost points for failing to include the units. However, it is *highly recommended* that units are included at every step to ensure that you're solving the problem correctly.

❏ When solving the problem, be sure to fully document all of your work, including the dimensional analysis in the book that will be scored. If the problem is solved in the test pages for making notes and the only answer is in the scored booklet, you won't receive any points, even if the answer is correct. In addition, often in the data-based question, partial points are given for showing the setup of the equation.

❏ Scientific notation can be used.

Now answer the second question in the example:

1. **Read the question to determine the final units.**

   The final units are coal cars per day.
2. **Set the final units at the end of a dimensional analysis equation.**
3. **Check that the problem is set up so that starting units are converted into ending units.**
4. **Simplify the math, cancel out zeros, and simplify the numbers.**

$$\frac{480,00\cancel{0}\ \cancel{\text{million}}\ \cancel{\text{BTU}}}{\text{day}} \Bigg| \frac{1\ \cancel{\text{lb}}\ \text{coal}}{5,00\cancel{0}\ \cancel{\text{BTU}}} \Bigg| \frac{1\ \cancel{\text{ton}}}{2,00\cancel{0}\ \cancel{\text{lb}}\ \cancel{\text{coal}}} \Bigg| \frac{1\ \text{coal car}}{12\cancel{0}\ \cancel{\text{tons}}}$$

5. **Solve the math.**

$$\frac{48,000}{\text{day}} \Bigg| \frac{1}{5} \Bigg| \frac{1}{2} \Bigg| \frac{1 \text{ coal car}}{12} = \frac{48,000 \text{ coal cars}}{120 \text{ day}} = \frac{400 \text{ coal cars}}{\text{day}}$$

6. **Rewrite the answer including the units.**

$$\frac{400 \text{ coal cars}}{\text{day}}$$

Now try the final question in the example.

1. **Read the question to determine the final units.**
   The final units are trains per day.
2. **Set the final units at the end of a dimensional analysis equation.**
3. **Check that the problem is set up so that starting units are converted into ending units.**
4. **Simplify the math, cancel out zeros, and simplify the numbers.**
5. **Solve the math.**
6. **Rewrite your answer including the units.**

$$\frac{400 \text{ coal cars}}{\text{day}} \quad \Big| \quad \frac{\text{trains}}{100 \text{ coal cars}} \quad = \quad \frac{4 \text{ trains}}{\text{day}}$$

Laws of Thermodynamics

There are four laws of thermodynamics, two of which are especially applicable in natural systems. The **first law of thermodynamics** states that energy can be changed from one form to another, but it cannot be created or destroyed. Energy input is equal to energy output. The **second law of thermodynamics** (see the following figure) deals with order and has many implications including the fact that systems naturally flow from states of high energy (low entropy), to states of low energy (high entropy). Systems do not naturally move toward higher states of order, and when energy flows through the components of a system, some energy is made unavailable at each transfer. Think of a food chain: the sun's energy is photosynthesized in plant material, which may then be eaten by (for example) a deer. However, the deer uses much of this energy for heat and movement, rather than growth, so when the deer is eaten by a mountain lion, the lion receives only a fraction of the initial energy provided by the sun.

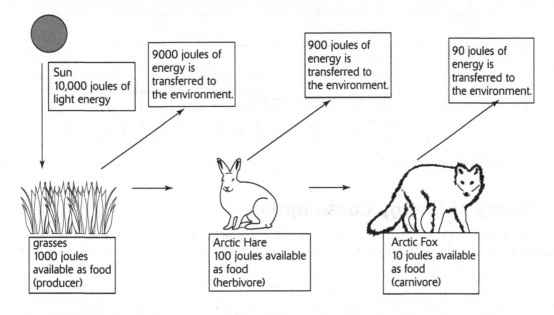

Progressive loss energy in the food chain due to the Second Law of Thermodynamics

Energy Consumption

Biomass, usually in the form of wood, was humanity's fuel for thousands of years, until the Industrial Revolution. Although wood is considered a renewable resource, the need for wood grew along with the human population, and as the Industrial Revolution put more demands on wood consumption, forests could no longer regrow as fast as they were being cut, leading to overall depletion. This depletion meant that humans had to go farther and farther to reach forests to satisfy their energy needs, but the energy cost of transporting wood from faraway forests was great compared to the amount of energy derived from the wood. These two factors prompted a switch from wood to coal as the energy source of choice.

At the beginning of the Industrial Revolution, coal was abundant and cheap. It has a higher energy yield per pound than wood. Around 1885, as the Industrial Revolution became widespread not only in the United Kingdom and the United States but also in much of Europe and Japan, the worldwide energy produced by burning coal exceeded the energy produced by burning wood. In turn, coal was replaced by petroleum in the middle of the 20th century. Petroleum remains the dominant source of energy worldwide (see U.S. Energy Consumption Graph below). However, during the latter half of the 20th century and the first decade of the 21st century, coal and natural gas have seen rapid expansions in use, due in part to the increase in the cost of petroleum and the decline in petroleum reserves.

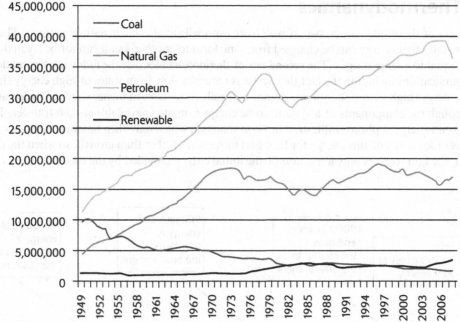

U.S. Energy Consumption by Source

Source: Kenneth R. Szulczyk, Ph.D.

The History of Energy Consumption

Until the late 1950s, the United States was able to meet its energy needs with domestic production. At the end of that decade, however, energy consumption exceeded domestic production, and the United States began to import energy, generally in the form of petroleum. Why was there a change in energy consumption? Because prior to World War II, the United States was just coming out of the Great Depression and energy consumption was comparably low. During the early stages of war, the United States increased the manufacturing of ships, planes, and vehicles built to fight and transport American troops and ammunition for war. After the war, only limited manufacturing remained during the Cold War, and other manufacturing was converted to peace time activities. The shift from agricultural to industrial professions also continued during this time. In the 1930s, approximately 21 percent of the work force worked on farms. By the 1950s, that number had decreased to just over 12 percent; it had decreased to 3.4 percent of the work force by the 1980s.

The average home size also began to get larger, from 938 square feet of floor space in 1950 to 2,266 square feet in 2000, a 141.6 percent increase over 50 years. Larger homes require more energy for heating and cooling. Additionally, the population began to shift toward warmer climates, requiring increased use of air conditioning to cool homes, business, and public buildings. Even in temperate climates, people started using air conditioners more often. Other energy-using appliances were developed, modified to become more automated requiring more energy, or increased in size and, thus, energy consumption. For example, refrigerators were developed, became ubiquitous, and then became larger. TVs first appeared in the late 1940s, and by the late 1950s became common household products, and then became larger. Washing machines, dryers, and dishwashers replaced hand washing and wringing, automating the cleaning of clothes and dishes. All these changes required more energy.

Square Footage Increase in Average Home Size (1950s to 2000s)						
	1950s	1960s	1970s	1980s	1990s	2000s
Square Feet	938	1,225	1,500	1,740	2,080	2,266
Change in Square Feet		287	275	240	340	186
Percent Increase		30.6	22.4	16	19.5	8.9

Energy consumption is typically divided into four end users: industry, transportation, residential, and commercial. Since 1950, industry has been the largest end-user of energy. Industry is defined as the production of economic goods and services. This includes mining and refining; farming; construction; manufacturing; services such as law and medicine; the distribution of manufactured goods; and, most recently, research, design, and the development of technology.

The transportation of people and goods is the second largest consumer of energy. Types of transportation include air, rail, road, water, and pipeline. Transportation can be divided into three broad categories: infrastructure, vehicles, and operations. Infrastructure needed for transportation: roads, railways, airways, waterways, pipelines, airports, rail, bus, warehouses, trucking terminals, and refueling depots. Vehicles include automobiles, bicycles, motorcycles, buses, trucks, trains, and aircraft. Operations include the financing, legalities, and policies related to operating vehicles.

Residential energy use takes place in single-family homes, multifamily residences, and mobile homes. Multifamily homes include apartments, condominiums, and town houses. Residential areas may include schools, hospitals, and parks that are used by the residents.

Commercial end users of energy include the places where goods and services are exchanged for money.

The following graph shows the energy delivered to each sector starting in 2003 and projected delivery past 2010.

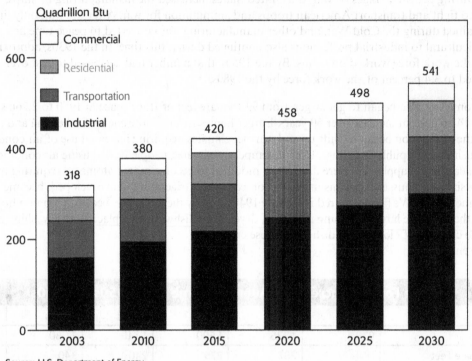

World Delivered Energy Consumption by End-Use Sector, 2003-2030

Source: U.S. Department of Energy

Present Global Energy Use

Worldwide, most energy comes from nonrenewable sources, primarily the consumption of fossil fuels (petroleum, coal, and natural gas) and the use of nuclear power. Fossil fuels are described as *nonrenewable* because their supply is finite. Their current high rate of use means that eventually we will run out of these energy sources. Renewable energy sources are replenished in a short period of time and include biomass (peat, trees, and other plant material), geothermal, hydroelectric, solar, and wind.

Future Energy Use

The energy needs of the United States and the world are increasing, primarily due to population growth, industrialization, and technology. The world population is increasing, and as the population increases, the need for additional energy increases. Approximately 38 nations are developed, and the remaining countries are in various stages of development. As they develop, their energy needs increase to meet the increase in production of goods and services. Technology usually leads to an increase in energy needs as well. The current technological revolution, with more powered items including computers and cellphones, has brought about great changes in society with a resulting increase in energy consumption, even with the development of low-energy technology.

The four fuel sources of clean coal, methane hydrates, oil shale, and tar sands may help meet future global energy needs.

Fossil Fuel Resources and Use

Fossil fuels including coal, oil, and natural gas are nonrenewable. The journal *International Energy Outlook* (2004) predicts that by the year 2025 about 87 percent of human energy needs will be provided by fossil fuels. Formed from plants and animals, fossil fuels are buried beneath the Earth's surface.

Societies around the world are dependent upon fossil fuels. Therefore, it is extremely useful to know how long these resources are likely to last. Scientists are trying to answer just that question. Just as important is the question of how much longer recovering fossil fuels will be technologically and economically viable. Many of the Earth's most accessible fossil fuel deposits are already being depleted, forcing energy companies to go farther, dig deeper, and work harder to recover remaining reserves, which adds to the remaining costs.

Coal, Oil, and Natural Gas

Coal, oil, and natural gas are the most commonly used fossil fuels. Although supplies are diminishing, consumption is still increasing due to a growing worldwide population and increasing industrialization in developing countries.

Clean Coal

Coal is the dirtiest and most abundant of the fossil fuels. Clean coal refers to the process of removing the pollutants that have a harmful effect on the environment. Technologies include washing coal to remove minerals and impurities and removing the sulfur dioxide and carbon dioxide from the flue gases. Cleaner-combustion technologies are being developed to make the burning of coal more efficient and help reduce contaminants during the combustion process. For example, coal can be converted into synthetic gas (syngas) in a process called **gasification.** Or the impurities in coal can be removed and used in other products. Treating coal-produced flue gases with steam can remove SO_2 and CO_2. Finally, researchers are developing carbon capture and storage (CCS) technologies to capture and store CO_2 emissions from coal.

The world's first "clean coal" power plant began generating energy in September 2008 in Germany. Due to the high cost of the technology, the German government owns the plant. The power plant captures CO_2 and acid-rain-producing sulfides. The CO_2 is compressed into liquid and stored. Future plans may inject liquid CO_2 into depleted natural gas fields.

Formation of Coal

Coal is formed in an **anaerobic environment,** one in which there is no oxygen. A swampy, heavily vegetative environment is ideal for forming coal. As plant matter falls into the swamp, it is quickly covered in mud. Over time it becomes deeply buried, and the plant matter becomes compressed as more and more mud is deposited on top of it. The pressure from the weight squeezes the liquid out of the dead plant material, leaving behind the carbon matter to form the complex chains found in coal. Some 300 million to 360 million years ago, such environments were widespread throughout the world, and much of the coal we use today was formed then.

To form coal, plant matter must first become peat. Peat is a low-energy fuel that is still used today in some parts of the world, generally when coal is unavailable. Peat varies from compressed matter to semihard substances that still look vegetative. It is cut from open pits, usually still wet, and must be dried to be used. The less compressed the peat, the higher the water content.

After millions of years under high pressure and temperatures, the peat turns into **lignite,** often called brown coal. This coal is drier and has a higher energy content than peat. Brown coal can still contain up to 70 percent moisture. Of the three types of coal, it has the lowest heat content. Lignite is used in power generators in locations where it is found in large quantities.

A denser, drier fuel with a higher energy content than lignite is formed with further compression and time. This black coal, called **bituminous** coal, is valuable as a fuel source for generating electricity and to manufacture coke for use in the steel industry. Rarer than lignite, bituminous coal is soft with a higher sulfur content and represents approximately 50 percent of the U.S. coal reserves.

After more compression, time, and exposure to extreme heat, black coal can be transformed into **anthracite.** Anthracite is a glossy, almost metallic-looking substance. With the highest energy content of the three types of coal, it has a low sulfur content and makes up approximately 2 percent of the U.S. reserves. Anthracite is the rarest of the three types of coal.

Graphite is the final stage of the carbon compression and heating process but is not considered a fossil fuel since it is difficult to ignite. Graphite is commonly used as the "lead" in pencils and as a dry lubricant.

Extraction and Purification of Coal

Two primary methods of mining coal are underground mining and surface mining. Most coal seams are too deep for surface mining, so underground mines must be dug. Approximately 60 percent of the world's coal production is from underground mining. Seams of coal, are found in long strands. When the seams of coal are near the Earth's surface, it may be more economical to extract the coal through open cuts in the surface of the Earth's crust. This method recovers a greater proportion of the coal deposit compared to underground mining. Globally, about 40 percent of coal production involves surface mining, but in the United States and Australia the technique is more prevalent, with 67 percent in the United States and around 80 percent in Australia. Mined coal may go through a variety of processes to remove sulfur and contaminants.

Oil

Oil Shale

Oil shale is a sedimentary rock that is rich in kerogen, an organic compound from which liquid hydrocarbons are extracted when heated. For use as an energy source, kerogen requires more processing than crude oil. It is, thus, more costly than oil, and the processing increases the negative environmental impacts, including damage to the surrounding environment due to surface mining and the disposal of waste material. The net-energy yield is considered moderate because energy is needed to mine the deposits, to heat the mined material, and to restore the mined area. There are major deposits of oil shale around the world, with several in the United States. These large deposits are found in Colorado, Utah, and Wyoming, but the world's largest reserves are in Australia, Estonia, Germany, Israel, and Jordan. China and Estonia have well-established oil-shale industries, while Brazil, Germany, Israel, and Russia have smaller oil-shale industries.

Tar Sands

Tar sands (also known as oil sands, extra-heavy oil, and bituminous sands) are a type of unconventional petroleum deposit. Note that the word *petroleum* means "rock oil" or "oil from the Earth." Tar sands contain naturally occurring mixtures of sand, clay, water, and an extremely dense and viscous form of petroleum. Technically, tar sands are referred to as bitumen and are found in large quantities in many countries, including Canada and Venezuela. Bitumen is an extremely viscous form of petroleum that can be extracted by heating tar sands. The resulting hydrocarbon requires more processing for use than crude oil, increasing both cost and environmental impact. Additional environmental impacts include damage to the surrounding environment due to surface mining and the disposal of waste material.

Like oil shale, tar sands yield moderate energy. Liquefying the crude oil from the sands requires injecting steam into the sand, which takes energy. The oil is then refined much like crude oil is refined. The process of generating useable oil from tar sand creates two to four times the amount of greenhouse gases as the production of conventional oil. The sulfur content is also higher, so larger amounts of sulfur dioxide are produced when the oil from tar sands is burned, resulting in an increase in acid rain.

Only since 2003 has oil shale been considered part of the world's oil reserves. The higher price of crude oil and the new technologies developed to obtain the oil from the oil sands has made it profitable to extract this unconventional oil. There are major deposits of oil shale in many places around the world, including deposits in the United States (Colorado, Utah, and Wyoming). The world's largest reserves are in Canada and Venezuela, each of which has oil sand reserves approximately equal to the world's total reserves of conventional crude oil supplies. Oil sands may represent as much as two-thirds of the world's total petroleum reserves.

Extraction and Purification of Crude Oil

Crude oil is a naturally occurring, complex mixture of hydrocarbons (with a variety of molecular weights) and other organic compounds found in geological formations at varying depths beneath the Earth's surface. Crude oil is obtained by drilling through the Earth's surface into deposits. Often, natural gas is found with these deposits but is usually not recovered.

Crude oil is refined into a large number of products, including gasoline and motor-vehicle fuels, kerosene, asphalt, and a variety of chemical reagents that can be used to make plastics, pharmaceuticals, and other chemical by-products. This is accomplished mostly by heating the crude oil and separating the different components by their boiling points.

Natural Gas

Formation of Natural Gas

Natural gas formation is similar to that of crude oil, from the remains of tiny aquatic plants and animals. When huge amounts of these organisms die over many years, they sink to the ocean floor and then are covered with silt and mud, decaying anaerobically (without oxygen). Over time, mud accumulates, and the pressure and heat on the organic materials increases. Eventually, the pressure squeezes out most of the liquid, leaving behind the dry carbons to form the long carbon chains in crude oil. The shorter chains, such as those in methane, ethane, propane, and butane, also form and become natural gas. Usually, natural gas and crude oil are found together. In some areas, natural gas is more abundant, and in other areas crude oil is found in larger amounts. Thus, in any given field, a company usually drills for either natural gas or crude oil, but not both.

Methane Hydrates

Methane hydrates are a recently discovered source of natural gas locked in ice formed at low temperatures and high pressures (often called "burning ice") and found in unique settings on Earth. On land, methane hydrates are found in the tundra, where cold temperatures persist in the shallow regions of the permafrost. The tundra's methane comes from decomposing plants and animals trapped in the permafrost. Methane hydrates also are found deep in the ocean, where the pressures are high and the temperatures are low, forming at depths greater than 500 meters and, in some parts of the deep oceans, may be very thick. The following figure shows the locations of known methane hydrate deposits. If used at their current rate, there may be a 350- to 3,500-year supply. Although not recognized as a fossil fuel at this time, another source of methane gas is that which escapes from pockets of fossil fuels in the deep oceans.

Two major issues are associated with the use of methane hydrates as a source of energy:

- The cost of locating and "mining" the methane hydrates
- The concern that methane, a greenhouse gas, will be released while obtaining and processing the methane, thus speeding up global warming

Locations of Large Amounts of Methane Hydrates

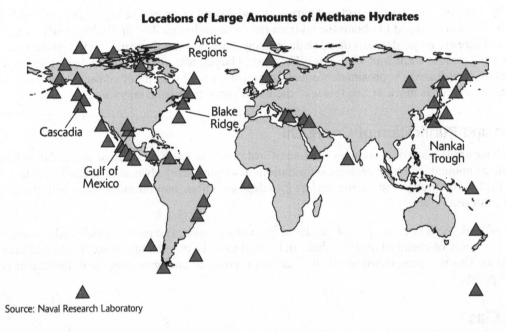

Source: Naval Research Laboratory

Methane hydrates made the news during the attempts to contain the *Deepwater Horizon* oil spill in the Gulf of Mexico in 2010. As the crude oil poured out of the broken well, methane also leaked out, and at the low-temperature depth of the broken oil well, methane hydrates formed. The methane hydrates made it difficult to install a containment system to help control the flow of crude oil and blocked the openings to the containment system.

Extraction and Purification of Natural Gas

Once a hole is punctured into a natural gas reservoir, the gas usually flows from wells under its own pressure. Natural gas is collected by small gas lines that are then connected to larger gas lines. These transmission pipelines move the natural gas great distances to areas where natural gas is present in low quantities or does not exist at all, or where the population and demand exceed the natural supply. Natural gas requires processing that includes the removal of water or water vapor, acid gas, and mercury. Natural gas also can be processed to obtain methane, ethane, propane, butane, and pentane. A small amount of odorant is added to give the gas a smell reminiscent of rotten eggs. Since natural gas is odorless, an odorant is added to help detect leaks that could otherwise create fires and explosions or be harmful if inhaled.

Synfuels

Synthetic fuels, or **Synfuels,** are liquefied fuels obtained from nonpetroleum sources such as coal, natural gas or biomass feedstocks through chemical conversion. For example, diesel and jet fuel that is made from coal are synfuels. Some synfuels are derived from waste, such as plastic or rubber. Daily production of synfuels is over 240,000 barrels with additional projects in development.

Advantages and Disadvantages of Synfuels	
Advantages	**Disadvantages**
Once converted, synfuels can be transported	Synfuels are not efficient, with minimal net energy yield.
Synfuels cause less air pollution than conventional coal when combusted.	Expensive production facilities.
Synfuels are uneconomical.	Synfuels would diminish coal reserves.
	There is an increased environmental impact due to mining of coal, processing into synfuels, and the burning of synfuels.

World Reserves and Global Demand

Fossil fuels (coal, crude oil, and natural gas) are nonrenewable resources, and eventually their reserves will run out. There has been much discussion and debate about how much of each fossil fuel remains. Adding to the difficulty in predicting a date at which fossil fuel reserves will run out is the difficulty in predicting demand as the world's need for energy increases with population growth and the industrialization of more countries. The world reserves and global demand for three fossil fuels are:

- **Coal:** By far the largest reserves of natural fuels are the various types of coal. The known reserves of coal are estimated to last about 200 years at the current rate of consumption. However, if consumption increases at the conservative rate of 5 percent per year, that figure drops to 86 years. Unknown reserves are estimated to last another 1,000 years. The largest reserves of coal are in Australia, China, Russia, and the United States.

- **Crude oil:** Of the three fossil fuels, the known reserves of crude oil are estimated to last about 45 years at current consumption and will dramatically decrease if consumption increases. The largest reserves are in the Middle East, which increases the potential for disruption in the world oil supply due to unstable governments, friction between the countries in the Middle East, and the recent wars in Iraq.

- **Natural gas:** At current consumption rates, the known reserves of natural gas are estimated to last 60 years. Europe has approximately 42 percent of the known reserves, while the Middle East has about 34 percent and the United States has about 3 percent.

Environmental Advantages and Disadvantages of Fossil Fuels

Following are the advantages and disadvantages of using coal, oil, and natural gas as sources of energy.

Advantages and Disadvantages of Coal	
Advantages	**Disadvantages**
Coal produces a relatively high amount of energy per pound.	Surface mining scars the Earth and destroys habitat.
Prices are relatively inexpensive and stable.	Subsurface mining can cause respiratory problems for workers.
Technologies to generate electricity are readily available.	Sixty percent of mining operations are done deep beneath the Earth's surface, increasing risks for mine collapses.
There is a large supply of undiscovered coal.	The estimated CO_2 (greenhouse gas) produced by an uncontrolled natural fire burning in coal beds around the world is greater than all of the CO_2 produced from automobiles in the United States.
Emissions can be reduced with the use of current technological advancements.	Coal is a non-renewable energy source.
	Delivery methods and pollution technologies can be costly.
	Runoff pollutes the rivers, lakes and oceans.
	Coal releases sulfur which can contribute to acid deposition and industrial smog.

Advantages and Disadvantages of Crude Oil	
Advantages	**Disadvantages**
There is established infrastructure for transport and use as a fuel.	Combustion of crude oil releases CO, CO_2, and other emissions.
Crude oil can produce fairly high net-energy compared to other products.	Crude oil is diminishing. Estimations are from 40 to 90 years.
Crude oil has a proven processing system.	Drilling, storing, processing, and transporting crude oil can cause a disruption to ecosystems.
Products have many uses.	Used oil is difficult to recycle.
	Spills can be devastating to ecosystems and the economy.

Advantages and Disadvantages of Natural Gas	
Advantages	**Disadvantages**
Natural gas is in a relative abundance.	Natural gas is a non-renewable energy source.
Delivery transport systems already exist.	Combustion of natural gas releases CO_2.
Natural gas has high net-energy per volume.	When pressurized, liquefied natural gas is extremely dangerous and can result in extreme explosions (BLEVE).
Natural gas emissions are cleaner burning than coal and oil.	Environmental damage can occur from extraction and pipelines, including releasing contaminated wastewater.
Natural gas has a variety of uses including home heating, cooking, and transportation.	Leaks can cause fires and explosions.
Natural gas cannot spill and contaminate soil, groundwater, or surface waters.	Liquefying the gas into liquefied natural gas can be costly.

Nuclear Energy

Nuclear Power

Currently, 31 countries produce electricity using nuclear power. Another ten countries have announced plans to build nuclear-generating power plants. The United States is the single largest producer of electricity from nuclear power, at 101,111 MW of capacity, which in 2008 accounted for approximately 19.7 percent of the United States production of electricity. France is the second largest producer of electricity generated by nuclear power plants, accounting for 76.2 percent of its total electrical power. Following are the top five countries in capacity and the top five countries in percentage of electrical production. Only France makes both lists. The dates for the data are 2007 and 2008.

Top Five Countries in Capacity and Percentage of Electrical Production				
Country	**Megawatt Capacity**	**Country**	**Percentage of Electricity from Nuclear Power**	
United States	101,119	France	76.2%	
France	63,473	Slovakia	56.4%	
Japan	46,239	Belgium	53.8%	
Russia	21,743	Ukraine	47.4%	
Germany	20,339	Armenia	43.5%	
World	**371,348**	**World**	**14.0%**	

The use of nuclear-generated electrical power grew rapidly in the United States from the early 1960s until the late 1980s. However, since the late 1980s, the use of nuclear power in the United States has declined. Reasons for the decline include huge cost overruns, higher-than-expected operating costs, safety concerns, issues with the disposal of nuclear waste, shorter-than-expected life of nuclear power plants, and a perception that nuclear power is a risky financial investment. Two historical nuclear incidents that played a role in the decrease in nuclear power in the United States were the accident at Three Mile Island in Pennsylvania on March 28, 1979, and the accident at Chernobyl, in what was then the Soviet Union and is now the Ukraine on April 26, 1986. The 2011 nuclear accident at the Fukushima Daiichi plant in Japan, resulting from an earthquake and subsequent tsunami, may change the face of nuclear energy. This event will most likely alter the public's perception of nuclear energy, as well as the safety controls and procedures of nuclear power plants near coastlines and major fault lines.

There was a renewed interest in building additional or replacement nuclear power plants in the United States until the incident at the Fukushima Daiichi power plant in Japan. This interest was due to the increased need for electrical power, which outstrips the current capacity of traditional power plants, an increase in fossil-fuel prices, and a concern about the release of carbon dioxide by fossil-fuel plants and the subsequent link to global warming.

Advocates of nuclear power claim that it is sustainable, reduces carbon dioxide emissions, and increases national energy security by decreasing the reliance on foreign crude oil. Supporters also argue that the risk of storing nuclear radioactive waste is small and can be further reduced by advances in nuclear power plant technology. In addition, the overall safety record for nuclear power plants is better than that for traditional fossil-fuel power plants.

Critics of new nuclear power plants believe that nuclear power is dangerous and not worth the cost or the risk. These critics are generally skeptical that new technology can decrease the hazards of nuclear radioactive waste. Critics also point out the problems of storing the nuclear waste, the lack of a national policy on nuclear storage, the potential radioactive contamination by accidents or terrorism, and the long-term storage of the nuclear waste before it is safe to be disposed of.

Nuclear Fission Process

Nuclear-power-generated electricity is usually produced by a process called nuclear fission. During the nuclear fission reaction, shown below, an atom is split into two smaller elements along with by-products (neutrons, photons, gamma rays, and beta and alpha particles). The fission reaction is exothermic, giving off great quantities of heat. The heat is used to convert water into steam that turns a generator, which produces electricity. This reaction must be carefully controlled to ensure that it does not critically overheat.

Converting Nuclear Fission into Electrical Energy

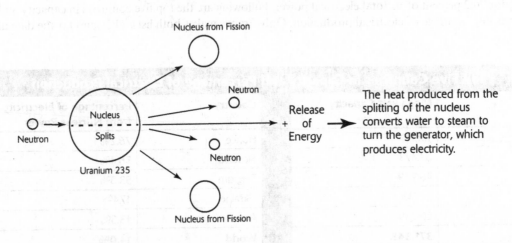

The potential energy per pound of nuclear fuel is exponentially greater than that of most established fuels (coal, petroleum, and natural gas). However, it is impossible to create a nuclear fission reaction without producing radioactive waste, which remains highly radioactive for thousands or even millions of years. Currently, most nuclear waste is stored on-site because there is no national program in the United States to dispose of nuclear waste. By traditional standards, nuclear waste must be stored for the length of time it takes for the material to go through ten half-lives. U-235, one of the most common nuclear fuels, has a half-life of 704 million years, and U-238 has a half-life of about 4.47 billion years. In other words, nuclear waste must be stored forever in a secure location.

Nuclear Fuel

There are two primary forms of fuel used in nuclear power plants: uranium and plutonium.

Uranium

Uranium has an atomic number of 92 and its chemical symbol is U. It has between 141 and 146 neutrons, meaning there are six isotopes, the most common being U-238 (146 neutrons), which makes up 99.284 percent of the uranium found in nature. U-235 (143 neutrons) and U-234 (142 neutrons) also occur naturally, at 0.711 percent and 0.0058 percent of natural reserves, respectively. All six forms of uranium are at least weakly radioactive, meaning that they shed particles. Uranium is commercially extracted from uranium-containing minerals such as uraninite. Uranium decays slowly by emitting an alpha particle.

U-235 is the only naturally occurring isotope capable of nuclear fission. Only 3 percent of U-235 is used in power plants to generate electricity, while 85 percent is used for weapons. Power plants convert U-238, which is not fissile, into plutonium-239 (Pu-239), which is fissile.

Plutonium

Plutonium, whose chemical symbol is Pu, is the heaviest naturally occurring element and has an atomic number of 94. As fission occurs in a nuclear reactor, Uranium (U-238) is said to be *fertile* and is able to capture one of the free neutrons flying around in the core of the reactor. This indirectly becomes plutonium (Pu-239). It is estimated that one-third of nuclear energy produced comes from his process, known as burning Pu-239.

International inspectors regularly inspect nuclear power plants to limit the production of Pu-239 and other radio-active isotopes that could be used to build nuclear weapons. One of the greatest fears is that if Iran and North Korea develop nuclear power plants (see an example in the following figure), they will not participate in these inspections and, thus, could build a supply of Pu-239 to be used in nuclear weapons.

Nuclear Power Plant

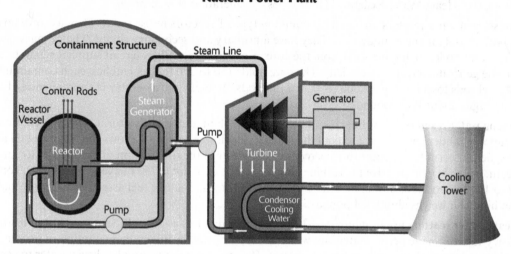

Nuclear Reactors

Reactors have several common components:

- **Fuel:** Uranium is the basic fuel used in all reactors. The uranium is enriched and processed into uranium oxide (UO_2). The UO_2 is formed into ceramic pellets and loaded into long tubes, usually zirconium alloy. When grouped together in a bundle, the tubes form a fuel assembly that is located in the core of the reactor.
- **Moderator:** It is usually water, occasionally heavy water, and rarely graphite. The moderator will slow down the release of neutrons in the core.
- **Control rods:** The rods are made of cadmium, hafnium, or boron. They are inserted and withdrawn from the core to control the rate of fission by absorbing neutrons.
- **Coolant:** The coolant is a liquid or gas that is circulated through the core to transmit heat away.
- **Containment:** Modern reactors have a containment structure that encapsulates the core. It is designed to prevent external intrusion and to protect everything surrounding it from the effects of radiation caused from a malfunction inside. It is usually constructed of steel and at least three feet of steel reinforced concrete.
- **Core:** The core may contain up to 75,000 fuel rods. The core is where fuel assemblies are located and where nuclear fission takes place.

Nuclear reactor types

Nuclear reactors have several common features in construction and operation, and are grouped into four generations. Each generation is grouped by age, and within each generation there are several reactor types.

- **Generation I** reactors were designed and built during the 1950s and 1960s. Very few of these early designs are still running. Generation I reactors are only expected to last about 40 years. The safety devices are primitive by today's standards and some do not have containment domes. For example, a Graphite-Moderated Reactor is a generation I type of reactor that uses water for cooling and steam and uses graphite as the moderator. Used in the former Soviet Union (USSR), these reactors were very unstable and are no longer being used. (see Chernobyl case study).

- **Generation II** reactors are in use today and are known as Pressurized Water Reactors, Boiling Water Reactors, and Heavy Water Reactors. Three types of generation II reactors are:

  - **Pressurized water reactors** are the most common type of reactors in use today. They use ordinary water as both a coolant and a moderator. They have a primary and secondary circuit. The primary circuit supplies water under high pressure to cool the core. A separate secondary circuit supplies steam to drive a turbine generator, creating electricity. The core holds 150 to 250 fuel assemblies, each containing 200 to 300 fuel rods for a total of 30,000 to 75,000 fuel rods. A single fuel assembly is approximately 13 feet high and weighs about 1,450 pounds.

  - **Boiling water reactors** use ordinary water as both a coolant and a moderator. Using a single circuit, water is supplied under low pressure to cool the reactor. The lower pressures allows the water to boil and is designed to permit 12 percent to 15 percent of the water in the top portion of the reactor to convert to steam, which is used to drive the turbine generator. The core holds 750 fuel assemblies, each containing 90 to 100 fuel rods, for a total of 67,500 to 75,000 fuel rods. A single fuel assembly is approximately 14.5 feet high and weighs about 704 pounds.

  - **Heavy water reactors** use uranium (U-235) as fuel and requires a more efficient moderator, heavy water. Heavy water is made up of deuterium, which is an isotope of hydrogen that contains an extra neutron, making it heavier than water. It has two circuits. The primary circuit supplies heavy water to cool the reactor. A separate secondary circuit transports steam to turn the turbine generator. The core holds 12 fuel assemblies, each containing 37 (2-foot) fuel rods for a total of 444 fuel rods.

- **Generation III reactors** incorporate the most current technologies but very few have gone online. These reactors are similar to generation II reactor designs but incorporate improved fuel technology, thermal efficiency, passive supply systems, and a standardized design. The standard design is meant to reduce construction and maintenance costs. The designers expect an operational life of 60 years.

- **Generation IV** reactors are mostly theoretical in nature at this time and are not expected to be feasible before the year 2030. Among the many types of experimental nuclear reactors are fast-breeder reactors. Fast-breeder reactors allow fission to propagate, meaning that as one radioactive atom decays, it is allowed to create other radioactive atoms. Left unchecked, these newly created atoms would themselves decay, creating heat and more radioactive atoms (and eventually a large explosion). The trick of fast-breeder reactors is to allow the production of additional radioactive atoms, but to disallow their decay. Thus, fast-breeder reactors create more fissionable material than they consume. Again, this is but one of many types of experimental nuclear reactors.

Advantages and Disadvantages of Nuclear Power	
Advantages	**Disadvantages**
Low emissions.	The waste from nuclear energy is radioactive and decomposes very slowly (over thousands and millions of years).
Usable technology is readily available.	Potential catastrophic consequences could befall nature and humans if a failure or serious accident should occur, including death.
It is possible to generate large amounts of energy from one plant.	There is an increased target risk for terrorism.
	Plants are licensed for 40 years and then can renew their licenses or shut down (decommission). It takes 20 years to build a nuclear power plant. Decommissioning of older plants is very expensive.
	Uranium is a scare resource and its supply is projected to last between 100 to 200 years.
	Special facilities are required for radioactive waste disposal.

Safety Issues

Safety is a major issue with nuclear power. Safety is evaluated in terms of both equipment and operator. For equipment there are three major areas of concern:

- Control of the radioactivity using control rods
- Maintenance of the core cooling system
- Maintenance of the barriers that prevent the release of radiation

The control rods can be adjusted to control the availability of released neutrons that drive the energy reaction used to create heat and, thus, electricity. The cooling system removes heat from the power plant, ensuring that it does not build to the point at which it can cause an explosion. Radiation barriers are constructed to hold radioactive material if it is released in an accident.

There are several precautions taken to prevent exposure to radioactive materials at a nuclear power plant:

- The equipment inside the core of the reactor is handled remotely. Employees are kept behind a physical shield.
- The time that an employee is in areas where exposure might be an issue is limited.
- The individual dose exposure is monitored, and limits are very strict.

Radiation and Human Health

The potential exists for a large-scale disaster at nuclear power plants, like that at Chernobyl. High, short-term exposure to radiation from a nuclear power plant accident leads to a very painful death. This was the case in Chernobyl, where several employees and many technicians brought in to control the accident were exposed to high levels of radiation and most of them died as a result. Most recently, the nuclear accident in Japan has not yielded major health problems from immediate radiation exposure, but there may be long-term effects that are not yet seen.

Scientists, policy makers, and the public also debate the safety of working in conditions of low-level radiation in nuclear power plants over a long period of time. Employees at nuclear power plants (like employees who may be exposed to radioactive material on the job, such as X-ray technicians, dentists, or scientists) wear dose exposure badges that monitor and display radiation doses received by the employees. These dose exposures are logged and there are limits on the dose that a person is allowed to receive in a year and in a lifetime. Reaching dose limits is more likely to occur working near radioactive material outside a nuclear power plant than it is working inside the plant itself.

Understanding Half-Life

If an isotope of an element is unstable, it experiences radioactive decay, or the process of losing energy from an unstable nucleus. The isotope's half-life is the amount of time that it takes for half of the isotope to decay. To be considered safe, a radioactive isotope must complete ten half-lives. Using an isotope's half-life, questions can be answered about quantities that remain after a given period of time, and also questions of how much time it takes to decay certain amounts of an isotope.

Calculating Using Half-Life Information

On the AP Environmental Science exam, there may be questions about half-life in both the multiple choice and free response sections.

EXAMPLES:

> 1. How long must an isotope be stored to be considered safe for disposal?

This type of question requires simple calculation. If given the isotope's half-life (in years), multiply it by 10 to find the number of years (or other unit) when the material will be considered safe. Below is a table of common isotopes, their half-lives, and the number of years it will take to be considered safe.

Isotope	Half-Life	Years to Be Considered Safe	Comment
C-14	5,730 years	57,300 years	Used in carbon dating to determine the age of organic material
P-32	14.29 days	142.9 days	Used in genetic and cellular research
Pu-239	24,100 years	241,000 years	Used in nuclear power plants and weapons
U-238	4.47 billion years	44.7 billion years	Used in nuclear power plants
U-235	700 million years	7 billion years	Used in nuclear power plants

> **2.** How much carbon-14 would be left after a set number of half-lives?

This type of question asks how much quantity would be left after a set number of half-lives.

Half-Life of Carbon-14		
Half-Life Spent	**Quantity (g)**	**Years**
0	10,240	0
1	5,120	5,730
2	2,560	11,460
3	1,280	17,190
4	640	22,920
5	320	28,650
6	160	34,380
7	80	40,110
8	40	45,840
9	20	51,570
10	10	57,300

Hydroelectric Power

Dams are built to create reservoirs that capture water, which is then released at a controlled flow, producing electricity as it flows over turbines. Hydroelectric power supplies approximately 12 percent of the power in the United States.

One major advantage of dams is the controlling of downstream flooding by containing the water produced by spring thaws and heavy storms. This is important because a population lives along rivers and streams that flood. Controlling flooding prevents deaths, property destruction, and damage to crops used for human food or animal feed. One disadvantage is the buildup of silt behind the dam. As silt builds up behind the dam, the dam holds less water, making the dam less reliable as a reservoir for water. This could increase water shortages and decrease the potential to produce hydroelectric power.

Hydroelectric power plants are similar to coal-fired power plants in that both turn a turbine, which then turns the shaft of an electric generator, producing electricity. Coal-fired plants use steam to turn the blades of the turbine, while hydroelectric plants use water to turn the turbine. The result is the production of electricity.

For hydroelectric power generation, a dam is built across a river that has a large change in elevation (which creates more water energy). The dam stores water behind it in the form of a lake or reservoir. The water intake is near the bottom of the dam (see the figure below). Gravity pulls the water through the penstock. Lower in the penstock is a turbine propeller, which is turned by the moving water. The shaft of the turbine is connected to the generator. The shaft turns the generator, and the generator produces the electrical power. Power lines carry the electricity to the power grid. The water continues past the propeller and into the river on the downstream side of the dam.

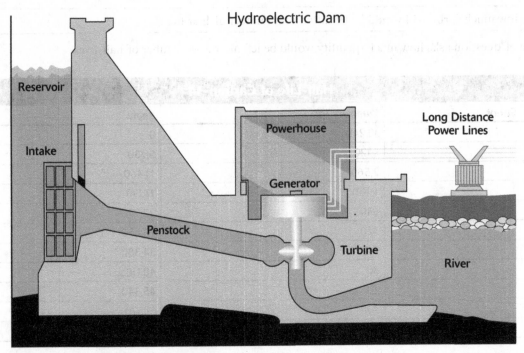

Source: Tennessee Valley Authority

Advantages and Disadvantages of Hydroelectric Power (Dams)	
Advantages	**Disadvantages**
No fossil fuel is needed.	There is flooding of land behind dams, sometimes including towns.
Dam reservoirs can store rainwater for use in the case of drought.	Dams disrupt natural seasonal changes in rivers, and ecosystems can be destroyed.
Hydroelectric plants are relatively inexpensive to maintain.	Impacts downstream water flow, often diminishing available water.
Hydroelectric is a renewable energy source because the Earth's water cycle replenishes upstream flow.	Silt accumulates and prevents mineral-enriched sediment to reach farmlands.
Dams can be shut down immediately if needed.	Water evaporation increases due to an increase in water surface area of the reservoir behind the dam.
Dams create lakes for recreation (fishing and boating).	The mating cycle of fish, such as salmon and steelhead trout, can be altered.
Dams control downstream flooding and provide a uniform source of water year round.	Sediment is altered downstream, impacting water flow and silt deposition.
There are no CO_2 emissions during operations.	
Provides electricity for a large number of people.	

Case Study: The Colorado River

The Colorado River starts in the Rocky Mountains and passes through seven states and two Mexican states, covering approximately 1,450 miles before emptying into the Gulf of California. There are six dams along the river and much of the water is taken out for agricultural and domestic uses along the way. Some of the water is moved hundreds of miles from the original river to distant cities. At the end of the river, the once large volume is often a trickle, and the water return is frequently contaminated with pesticides, fertilizers, drugs, and other contaminants.

Case Study: Salmon

Salmon are migrating fish, returning from the ocean to spawn in the stream where they were hatched. When they hatch, salmon slowly make their way downstream toward the ocean. Later, they return to the river, swim upstream to find the place they hatched, spawn, and die. Salmon usually return three years after they hatch to spawn and die. Steelhead trout usually return in two or three years and may head back out to the oceans and make several trips over their lifetime. Damming a river makes this migration difficult or impossible.

Almost every river system in the West has been blocked by a dam, often with more than one dam along the length of a single river. These dams have destroyed important habitat for fish spawning, along with areas important for salmon's growth. For example, the Columbia River has less than 110 km (70 miles) of remaining free-flowing water, which is not enough to sustain wild salmon. Of the estimated 130 West Coast salmon runs, 81 percent are extinct, and the remaining 19 percent are endangered. California has severely limited fishing on several of its salmon runs and has even eliminated fishing altogether in some years.

To help mitigate this loss, fish passage facilities and fish ladders have been built to bypass dams. While juvenile fish are moving downstream toward the ocean, dams may allow water to pass over the spillway to encourage the fish to swim over the tops of dams instead of through the turbines. Juvenile fish also may be collected and transported downstream.

Some salmon is farm raised. Fish farms often consist of holding pens in the ocean where the fish are kept and fed for upwards of three years. There is concern that these farm-raised fish may escape and mate with the wild salmon and contaminate the gene pool. Another issue with farm-raised salmon is the amount of waste produced by the fish, which is concentrated below the pens in the ocean. There is concern that this waste may be harming the environment in the area.

In 2010, scientists announced that eggs of Atlantic salmon had been genetically modified by the insertion of the gene from an ocean pout and a growth gene from the Pacific Chinook salmon, allowing the fish to grow year-round. Commonly, native salmon do not grow in the winter months. With gene insertion, the fish can grow to market size in approximately two years instead of three. There are claims that the modified eggs are reproductively sterile because they are **triploidic** (having three sets of haploid genetic information), eliminating the interbreeding amongst themselves and with native, wild stocks. The company plans to sell only female eggs and raise fish in inland systems away from the oceans. FDA studies claim that up to 5 percent of the eggs may be fertile and the resulting fish may, in fact, be able to breed with wild-type salmon. The FDA must approve the fish for sale in the marketplace because the genes have been altered. There is some concern that these larger genetically modified salmon could eventually displace the natural salmon.

Energy Conservation

Strategies to conserve energy are an important aspect of the AP Environmental Science exam. In the free-response questions asking for suggestions on different ways to save energy at home, in an office building, or in transportation. There are many energy conservation methods, which may vary in effectiveness across states and regions of the United States, due in part to climate and cultural differences. Here is a common list of energy-saving ideas with brief explanations:

- Add **insulation** to help hold in warm air in the winter and cool air in the summer, while blocking the unwanted heating and cooling effects of outside air.
- Add **weather stripping** to reduce drafts around door frames.

- Lower the **thermostat** in the winter and raise it in the summer to use less energy. Instead, compensate by wearing warmer clothing in the winter and cooler clothing in the summer. Also, install thermostats on each floor to more efficiently regulate temperature.

- Replace single-pane windows with **double- or triple-pane windows** filled with noble gases, which cut down heat exchange through windows.

- Replace older equipment with more **energy-efficient appliances.** This may include water heaters, washers and dryers, dishwashers, heaters, air conditioners, stoves, and refrigerators.

- Cut down on energy loss through items that are plugged in but not turned on. **Unplug electrical equipment** when not in use.

- Add **ceiling fans.** A reversible ceiling fan can change the direction of the circulating air, and any ceiling fan can redistribute the hot air during the winter or the cool air during the summer.

- Use **electronic switches** to turn on and off the heater and air conditioner.

- Buy a more **fuel-efficient vehicle.**

- **Maintain vehicles** with proper tire inflation and tune-ups.

Energy Efficiency

The U.S. Department of Energy recently established the **Office of Energy Efficiency and Renewable Energy (EERE),** with the goal of reducing U.S. dependence on foreign crude oil and developing technologies that promote energy efficiency for buildings, homes, transportation, power generation, and industry.

The EERE's role is to promote the research, development, and implementation of energy-efficient technologies through investing in speculative research and development that may provide for the future energy needs of the United States. Private investment in this sector is limited because of the high cost of research and the high risk of the investments. The EERE works with state and local governments, national laboratories, universities, and the private sector.

Energy Star

The U.S. Environmental Protection Agency created the Energy Star program in 1992 in an attempt to reduce energy consumption and, thus, greenhouse gases emitted by power plants. Starting as a voluntary labeling program to identify and promote energy-efficient products, Energy Star first labeled computer products and expanded in 1995 to include residential heating and cooling systems. More than 40,000 Energy Star products are available today, including major appliances (refrigerators, washers, dryers), heating and cooling systems, office equipment, electronics, lighting, and more. In addition, the label can be found on new homes as well as on commercial and industrial buildings. In 2006, 12 percent of new homes were labeled Energy Star compliant. The Energy Star program is credited with the spread of LED traffic lights, compact fluorescent lighting, and power management systems for office equipment.

Energy Star has become an international standard for energy-efficient consumer products originating in the United States. Other countries, including Australia, Canada, Japan, New Zealand, and the European Union, have developed similar programs. Products carrying the U.S. Energy Star logo generally use 20 percent to 30 percent less energy than required by federal standards.

Many programs are available to help homeowners take advantage of converting to Energy Star appliances and other energy-saving devices. These include state and federal tax rebates for installing new refrigerators, washers and dryers, heating and cooling systems, and multi-paned windows; also, there are programs to help mitigate the cost of installing solar panels on homes.

However, even with rebates and assistance programs, solar panels can be expensive, and the payback in reduced energy costs may take many years. To create similar energy conservation, homeowners may well be advised to start by determining ways to reduce energy usage. Can insulation be added to reduce energy for heating and cooling? Are windows single-paned? How old is their heating and cooling system? How old are the appliances? It might be more cost-effective and energy wise to make these changes before installing solar panels.

Corporate Average Fuel Economy

The Corporate Average Fuel Economy (CAFE) regulations were first enacted by the U.S. Congress in 1975, partly in response to the 1973 Arab oil embargo, and with the goal of improving the fuel economy of cars and light trucks. The "light trucks" group includes trucks, vans, and sport utility vehicles (SUVs) sold in the United States. Fuel economy is expressed in miles per gallon (mpg) and the CAFE is based on the manufacturer's fleet of current-year-model passenger cars or light trucks under 8,500 pounds (3.856 kg) manufactured for sale in the United States.

The United States and Canada have the least strict CAFE standards among developed nations. The U.S. standard is 25 mpg, while the European Union standard is 45 mpg, and the Japanese standard is even higher. However, the United States and Canada have the strictest emissions standards in terms of parts per million (ppm) of pollutants. Some high-mileage vehicles in Europe would not meet the U.S. emissions standards; California has even tighter emissions standards. There may be a tradeoff between improved gas mileage and pollution control.

The National Highway Traffic Safety Administration (NHTSA) regulates the CAFE standards, while the Environmental Protection Agency (EPA) measures the vehicle fuel efficiency for the fleets. Congress has specified that the CAFE regulations must be set at a "maximum feasible level" and consider the following criteria:

- Technological feasibility
- Economic practicality
- Effect of other standards on fuel economy
- Need of the nation to conserve energy

The EPA and NHTSA are often at odds with each other over the intent of the CAFE regulations. The EPA encourages consumers to purchase more fuel-efficient vehicles, while the NHTSA is concerned that smaller, more fuel-efficient vehicles may lead to more traffic deaths.

For CAFE purposes, cars and light trucks are considered separate and have different standards. As of 2004, cars must exceed 27.5 mpg, and light trucks must average 20.7 mpg. The standard for trucks under 8,500 pounds was 22.5 mpg in 2008, 23.1 mpg in 2009, and 23.5 mpg in 2010. Starting in 2011, new standards will take effect, and the targets will be based on the truck size footprint.

How to Calculate Percent Change

A vehicle's change in weight can be used as an example demonstrating how to calculate percent change.

Percent Change $= \frac{V_2 - V_1}{V_1} \cdot 100$, where V_1 is the initial value, and V_2 is the second value.

If vehicles' average weight went from 3,220 pounds to 4,066 pounds, you would calculate the percent change as follows:

$$\text{Percent Change} = \frac{4,066 - 3,220}{3,220} \cdot 100$$

$$= \frac{846}{3,220} \cdot 100$$

$$= 0.263 \cdot 100$$

$$= 26.3\%$$

CAFE Standards in Miles per Gallon for Passenger Cars until 2011			
Model Year	Passenger Car (mpg)	Model Year	Passenger Car (mpg)
1978	18	1995	27.5
1979	19	1996	27.5
1980	20	1997	27.5
1981	22	1998	27.5
1982	24	1999	27.5
1983	26	2000	27.5
1984	27	2001	27.5
1985	27.5	2002	27.5
1986	26	2003	27.5
1987	26	2004	27.5
1988	26	2005	27.5
1989	26.5	2006	27.5
1990	27.5	2007	27.5
1991	27.5	2008	27.5
1992	27.5	2009	27.5
1993	27.5	2010	27.5
1994	27.5	2011	30.2

Hybrid Electric Vehicles

Hybrid cars were invented by Porsche in 1900 and were subsequently dropped in favor of gasoline-only vehicles. Today's hybrid cars were first developed by the Japanese companies Honda and Toyota. Hybrid vehicles contain smaller gasoline engines, which are supplemented as needed by electric motors. When you apply the brake in a hybrid car, the energy from braking is captured and the car's kinetic energy is converted into electrical energy that charges the battery. If the battery is low, the electric motor will also convert energy from the gasoline engine to charge the batteries.

Honda's technology uses an electric motor to provide assistance to a constantly running gasoline engine as needed, commonly when the car is accelerating or climbing hills. Toyota's technology allows the car to run completely on the battery at low speeds and to assist the gasoline engine during accelerations and hill climbing. The Honda Civic gets better gas mileage on the highway than surface streets, while the Toyota Prius gets better gas mileage driving city streets than the highway. Both technologies produce about 65 percent less CO_2.

In 2010, Toyota had a limited number of plug-in Prius vehicles that were being used as test cars, and the company planned to release consumer versions soon thereafter. The plug-in hybrid has a larger battery and allows the owner to plug the car into a 110-volt outlet at home, work, or another location to completely charge the battery. The plug-in hybrid will allow the owner to drive up to 13 miles on a charge at a maximum speed of 62 mph.

Several companies and individuals have modified Prius cars to get 100 mpg. These changes have usually involved converting the car to be a plug-in vehicle and adding lithium-ion batteries. Conversion kits are available, and specialists can be found to install the high-voltage lithium-ion batteries. However, the cost for such a conversion is approximately $10,000, which is likely more than the savings in gasoline costs across the life of the vehicle.

These savings in gas costs are also counterbalanced by maintenance costs, which are generally higher for hybrid engines than for gasoline-only engines. The hybrid battery is under warranty for 100,000 miles in some states and 150,000 miles in others, with some owners reporting battery life over 200,000 miles. However, new batteries cost approximately $5,000 to replace, including installation. Many people believe that these batteries are hazardous. Toyota has a program to completely recycle its batteries.

Electric Cars

Electric cars in one form or another have been a part of car culture since the vehicle's inception. In fact, the first cars were electric, developed before the internal combustion engine was constructed. The development and subsequent improvements of the combustion engine ultimately pushed electric cars from the market. Then, as now, electric cars faced the problems of limited mileage on a single battery charge and the lengthy time needed to charge the battery.

Other attempts at reviving the electric car include the EV1, released on a lease-only basis by General Motors in 1996. The last of these vehicles were leased in 1998, with lease terms and extensions expiring in 2003. Subsequently all returned EV1s were crushed, though a few remain in museums. To learn more about the EV1 program and its death, watch the movie *Who Killed the Electric Car?* (2006).

With the recent increase in gasoline prices, interest in electric cars is once again on the rise. Despite technological advancements, these cars still face the same problems: battery technology that limits the total miles a car can drive on a single charge and the long time it takes to recharge. Several companies are developing electric car technology. For example, Chevrolet has recently released its all-electric car, the Volt. The Volt gets about 40 miles per charge and is emissions free (not taking into account the method used to generate the electricity the car uses to charge its battery). Currently, electric cars work well for owners who plan to use them only for short commutes.

Tesla is a car company devoted only to electric cars. Tesla was started in 2003 and released its first car in 2008, the Roadster. The Roadster gets about 275 miles per charge with zero tailpipe emissions. A second model, the Model S, will be released in 2012 and get about 300 miles per charge. Charging the Tesla roadster with a 110-volt plug takes about 32 hours. However, plugging the car into a 220-volt outlet allows the car to charge its batteries in only 3.4 hours.

Detractors point out that electric car technology trades one form of CO_2 and other gas emissions for another, as the electricity to charge these cars still must be generated. Traditional gasoline cars are **mobile-source** forms of pollution, meaning that emissions can be moved from one location to another as the vehicle drives. However, the emissions of electric cars are considered **point-source** emissions, localized at the electric power plant where the car's electricity originates, which may burn coal, natural gas, or petroleum (or may depend on renewable technologies including wind, solar, or geothermal).

Other Vehicle Options

Traditional gasoline is no longer the only option for powering cars. The new energy-efficient diesel cars that account for approximately 45 percent of new car sales in Europe are 30 percent more fuel efficient and emit 20 percent less CO_2 than conventional gasoline-powered cars. Besides making diesel from crude oil, diesel can be made from coal (synfuels). Diesel cars also can be converted to run on biodiesel. Biodiesel can be made from either plant material or from vegetable oil. Brazil runs 45 percent of its cars on ethanol. Other countries are experimenting with E85, which is 85 percent gasoline mixed with 15 percent ethanol. Ethanol can be made from corn, soy, or plant waste material.

Advantages and Disadvantages of Biodiesel	
Advantages	**Disadvantages**
Reduced CO and CO_2 emissions.	Increased NO_x emissions and increased photochemical smog.
Reduced hydrocarbon emissions.	Higher cost than regular diesel.
Better gas mileage.	Low net-energy yield for soybean crops.
Has the potential to be renewable if the source for the biodiesel is renewable.	Loss and degradation of biodiversity due to land being used for increased crop production.
Sources such as algae and oil palms offer high net-energy yield.	May compete with growing food for land use and raise food prices.
Sources from other crops offer moderate net-energy yield.	

Advantages and Disadvantages of Ethanol	
Advantages	**Disadvantages**
Reduced CO emissions.	Low net-energy yield with some crops.
Some reduction in CO_2 emissions if sugarcane is used.	Increased NO_x emissions and increased photochemical smog.
Can be mixed with gasoline and sold as E85 or as pure ethanol.	May compete with growing food for land use and raise food prices.
Potentially renewable.	Higher cost than regular diesel.
High net-energy yield for bagasse and switchgrass.	Higher CO_2 emissions using corn.

Another new fuel used to power vehicles is the hydrogen fuel cell, which coverts hydrogen into energy. There are various ways to access the hydrogen and convert it into useable form. One such way is electrolysis, where electricity is passed through water, separating the hydrogen and oxygen. The by-product of hydrogen fuels cells is water.

Mass Transit

The goal of public transportation is to move large numbers of people in one vehicle. When asked about mass transit, most people think of buses, subways, and light rail. Other forms include air, trains, and ships. People in Japan, Europe, and a few places in the United States, including the San Francisco Bay area and New York City, frequently take into account the accessibility of mass transit when evaluating where to live and work. Ridership in Japan is close to 50 percent, with the percentage of riders even higher in Tokyo. In a 2006 survey, 5 percent of the U.S. population used mass transit, while 20 percent had easy access to mass transit. Public transportation is more likely to be used by people living in cities with a population greater than 100,000. For example, ridership in New York City is over 50 percent; Washington, D.C., at 39 percent; Chicago at 25 percent; and Los Angeles at 11 percent. In the five years of 2006 to 2010, the use of mass transit increased in the United States partly in response to increases in gasoline prices, incentives of employers to increase the use of mass transit, expansion of some mass transit systems, and the idea of being more "green."

Buses are the most commonly used form of mass transit, partly because they can easily adjust their routes and time schedules to meet the needs of the population they serve. As transit systems have replaced their aging buses, they often choose buses that run on compressed natural gas (CNG). CNG burns cleaner than diesel, reducing CO_2 and particulates emissions. Bus systems offer low fares to attract riders, often operating at a loss and, thus, must rely on governments to subsidize their expenses.

Some cities have subway systems, most of which are underground electric light-rail systems. Chicago and a few other cities have elevated systems. One distinction between buses and subways is that subway systems are removed from the flow of traffic and, thus, can provide a faster form of transportation when city streets are clogged. Subways use less energy and generate less pollution than cars, require less land for tracks and parking, cause fewer accidents and deaths than cars, and reduce congestion in the cities. Disadvantages include a fixed track system that cannot be adjusted to meet changes in society, the cost of building and maintenance, and the noise and vibrations can impact nearby residents and businesses.

Light-rail systems are usually powered by electricity but can also use diesel. Like subways, their tracks are fixed, making it difficult to adjust routes. Light-rail systems can be mixed with traffic in systems where cars and buses share the road with the light-rail system. They also can have designated lanes and stops to allow passengers to get on and off the system easily. Light-rail systems are more expensive to build than bus systems, but cheaper than subway systems. Their schedules are easier to adjust than those of a subway system but not as flexible as a bus system.

Renewable Energy

Renewable energy can be replenished without depleting supplies. There are several forms of renewable energy, each with pros and cons. As shown below, approximately 6 percent of the total energy usage in the United States is generated by renewable energy, which includes biomass, geothermal, hydroelectric, solar, and wind. Other forms of renewable energy are being investigated.

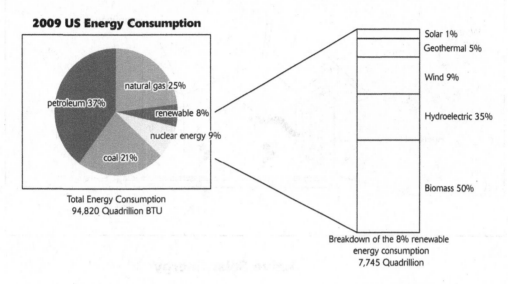

2009 US Energy Consumption

petroleum 37%
natural gas 25%
renewable 8%
nuclear energy 9%
coal 21%

Total Energy Consumption
94,820 Quadrillion BTU

Solar 1%
Geothermal 5%
Wind 9%
Hydroelectric 35%
Biomass 50%

Breakdown of the 8% renewable
energy consumption
7,745 Quadrillion

Solar

The sun's radiant energy is used both to create heat directly and for conversion into electrical energy. There are two types of systems:

- **Passive solar energy systems** require no moving parts and, thus, no input of electrical activity. These include both gravity-fed heating systems and photovoltaic cells, which capture the sun's energy to generate electricity. In a solar electricity system, sunlight hits the transparent solar cells causing them to emit electrons, and many cells wired together produce electricity. The electricity can be used immediately, cells can be connected to batteries to store the energy for later use, or cells can be connected to the power grid to share electricity with other users. Detractors point to the inefficiency of solar cells, but newer photovoltaic cells have increased this efficiency.

  Additional passive heating systems include the use of materials that allow the heat from the sun to be captured in the winter and reflected in the summer. Generally, these buildings are constructed to face the primary direction of the sun, maximizing the potential to trap heat in the winter.

- **Active solar energy systems** use pumps and fans to move water heated by the sun throughout buildings, requiring some input of electrical energy. This hot water can be used to heat the house and can be used as hot water for cleaning and bathing.

See the following figures for illustrations of passive and active solar energy.

Five Elements of Passive Solar Design

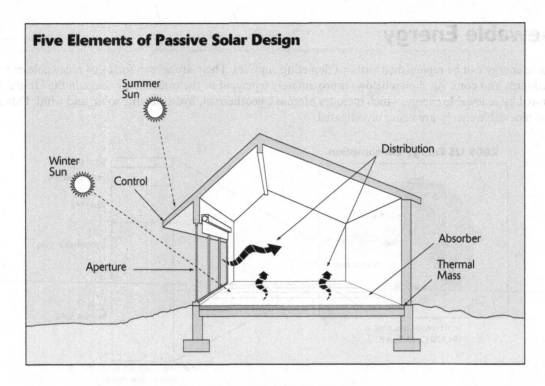

Active Solar Energy

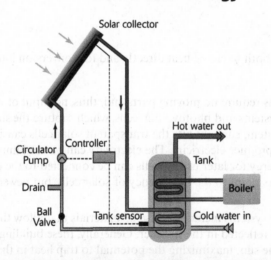

Solar	
Advantages	**Disadvantages**
There is an infinite, free supply of solar energy.	Solar energy is most efficient where sunlight is most consistent.
Solar energy is clean, renewable, and sustainable.	Initial costs for installation and building are high.
The energy collected can be stored in batteries.	Solar panels require a large area for efficiency.
There is limited or no maintenance.	Sunlight can be blocked by trees and buildings.
	Some people consider the solar panels to be unsightly.

Hydrogen Fuel Cells

The basic concept of a hydrogen fuel cell is to use hydrogen and oxygen in a chemical reaction to produce energy and water. Like a typical battery, a hydrogen fuel cell uses an anode and a cathode that are separated by an electrolyte. Hydrogen reacts with a catalyst on the anode electrode, splitting into negatively charged electrons and positively charged hydrogen ions. The electrons flow out of the cell and are used as electrical energy. The positively charged hydrogen ions move through the membrane to the cathode, where they combine with oxygen to produce water. Unlike in a typical battery, as long as the fuel cell is fed with hydrogen and oxygen, it will never run down or run out. Hydrogen fuel cell technology is being developed for cars and other forms of transportation. These fuel cells are being used to generate small amounts of electricity to supplement larger power systems. They are also being used in isolated areas where running transmission lines may be difficult or expensive.

Basic Fuel Cell Reaction

$$2\,H_2 + O_2 \rightarrow 2\,H_2O + energy$$

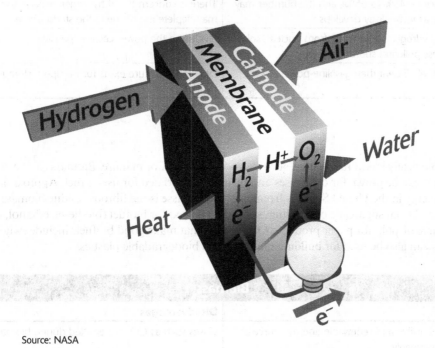

Source: NASA

Hydrogen Fuel Cells	
Advantages	**Disadvantages**
Hydrogen has three times the energy (pre-mass) of natural gas.	Hydrogen production is very energy-intensive in order to separate it from a water molecule.
Hydrogen can be obtained from splitting water. Hydrogen is the most abundant element in the universe.	Hydrogen gas is highly flammable and burns extremely hot.
The use of hydrogen as a fuel has minimal environmental impact. The only emissions from hydrogen combustion are water and heat.	An efficient method to store hydrogen has not yet been developed.
Hydrogen can be produced domestically, reducing dependence on foreign energy supplies.	Production may indirectly produce harmful emissions, depending on what energy source provides the electricity to split the water molecule.
They are highly efficient (45% to 65%), and the number may be likely to increase as technology develops.	There is concern that if hydrogen leaks in the atmosphere, it may deplete the ozone in the stratosphere.
Energy to produce hydrogen could come from nuclear, solar, wind, or another less polluting source of energy.	Producing the power cell is expensive.
Hydrogen is more fuel efficient than gasoline-powered cars.	Little infrastructure exists for transport, storage, and retrieval of hydrogen.

Biomass

Biomass is any biologically based fuel source, such as wood, charcoal, or manure. Biomass can be grown specifically for use as a fuel or it can be grown for other uses and then reappropriated for use as fuel. Approximately 50 percent of the renewable energy in the United States is from biomass. Bagasse is the fibrous residue biomass that remains after juice is extracted from sugarcane or sorghum stalks and is used for biofuel (biodiesel, ethanol, or methanol) or as a renewable source of pulp for paper products. Other crops that make good biofuels include switchgrass, hemp, and corn. Biomass can also be used for building materials and biodegradable plastics.

Biomass	
Advantages	**Disadvantages**
Biomass is an inexhaustible and renewable energy source as long as it is used sustainably.	Gases such as CO_2 are emitted during biomass burning.
There is a large potential supply worldwide.	Recycling of wastes requires greater amounts of water.
It is cost effective.	The process for biomass extraction, harvesting, and storage is costly.
Biomass briquettes are much cleaner than fossil fuels.	Only less than 30% efficient.
Plantations can be developed to provide a sustainable supply.	There is a moderate to high impact on the environment because they are monoculture crops.
	It can lead to soil erosion, water pollution, loss of habitat, and loss of biodiversity.
	Growth of biomass requires large amounts of land and other inputs, such as water, fertilizers, and pesticides.
	Growth of the crops may utilize land and other resources needed for food production.

Wind

Historically, windmills were used to pump water for farms and ranches. For example, the many windmills in Holland were built to help remove water from low-lying areas reclaimed by the dikes. Today's windmills are giant wind-powered turbines that generate electricity as they turn. More specifically, wind turns blades that are attached to a generator, which converts the mechanical energy (wind) into electricity. Cables carry the electricity to the transmission line. Wind turbines clustered together are called wind farms.

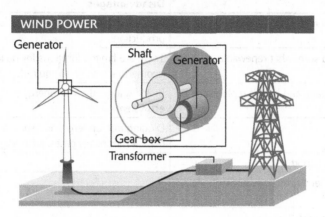

WIND POWER

- Wind causes blades to rotate.
- A shaft turns a generator to produce electrical energy.
- A transformer converts electrical energy to high voltage.
- Electricity is transmitted via the power grid.

Wind	
Advantages	**Disadvantages**
No harmful pollutants.	Turbines can be damaged in storms.
Easily constructed.	Wind does not always flow at the same speed. Backup systems need to be in place to compensate for periods of decreased production.
Wind farms can be located placed off of coastlines, where there are large amounts of steady winds.	Rotating blades of turbines have killed birds and bats.
Land beneath turbines can be used for other uses.	The appearance of wind turbines has been criticized.
Highly efficient.	Plastic components are produced from crude oil sources.
Wind farms can produce energy for several homes simultaneously.	Large amounts of space are necessary for wind farms.
No waste disposal.	Farms located in the ocean may have negative unintended impacts on the ecosystem.

Geothermal

Geo means "of the Earth," and *thermal* means "heat"; therefore, geothermal energy is using the Earth's heat to generate electricity. Geothermal heat in the form of hot underground rock formations, molten rock, and hot subterranean water is used to turn a water source into steam, which drives electrical turbines. The top three countries in geothermal energy production are the United States, the Philippines, and Mexico. The system can be used to heat a house in the winter and to cool the house in the summer. Currently less than 1 percent of human energy use is generated by geothermal. Scientists estimate that using 1 percent of the energy stored in the top 5 kilometers of the Earth's crust would provide 250 times more energy than all the Earth's crude oil and natural gas reserves combined.

Geothermal	
Advantages	**Disadvantages**
Lower CO_2 emissions than fossil fuels.	Water and heat can be depleted, diminishing energy production.
Geothermal energy is clean and somewhat renewable.	There are limited locations for building plants since access to geothermal activity is required.
Water supply is replenished by rain, and heat is replenished by the Earth's interior.	Building a geothermal energy plant can diminish a fragile local ecosystem.
It is relatively inexpensive.	Digging into underground sources of geothermal energy can release hazardous gases, including hydrogen sulfide.
There is no waste disposal or transport.	
There is low land disturbance. Geothermal power plants do not have to be large.	
Energy source (fuel) does not require transport.	

Ocean and Tidal Waves

Although the concept is not new, the collection of energy from ocean and tidal waves is not widely used at this time. As shown in the figure below, this type of energy generation starts when the wave hits a platform, which in turn pushes on air in a chamber, pushing on the turbine. This turns a generator to convert the energy into electromagnetic energy. There are also other methods that capture ocean and tidal waves to generate electricity.

Ocean and Tidal Wave

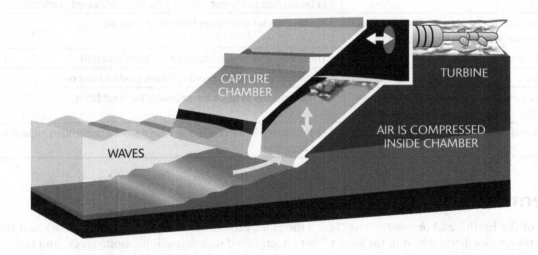

WAVES

CAPTURE CHAMBER

TURBINE

AIR IS COMPRESSED INSIDE CHAMBER

Only a few places are currently using waves to generate electricity: off the northern coast of France, in the Bay of Fundy, on the northeast end of the Bay of Maine between the United States and Canada, and in Strangford Lough off the coast of Northern Ireland. A wave farm is being installed off the coast of Reedsport, Oregon. Other ocean-wave or tidal-wave projects are being planned throughout the world.

Ocean and Tidal Waves	
Advantages	**Disadvantages**
Wave technology is clean and renewable.	Dependent upon proximity to oceans.
Wave technology is reliable.	Subject to corrosion from saltwater.
No harmful environmental pollutants.	The environmental effect on species and habitats is unknown.
No waste disposal.	Visual or noise effects may occur.
Low land disturbance.	There may be conflicts between the needs of commercial shipping and recreational boaters.

Practice

Questions 1–3 refer to the following answer choices.

    A.   Potential energy
    B.   Kinetic energy
    C.   Electrical energy
    D.   Electromagnetic energy
    E.   Nuclear energy

1. The gasoline stored in tanks at the gas station contains which type of energy?

2. Which type of energy involves both fusion and fission?

3. Which type of energy comes to our homes through wires?

4. The loss of energy in subsequent levels of a food web is due to which of the following?

    A.   First Law of Thermodynamics
    B.   Second Law of Thermodynamics
    C.   Law of Conservation
    D.   Law of Conservation of Mass
    E.   Law of Conservation of Momentum

5. Energy consumption is divided into four categories: industry, transportation, residential, and commercial. Which of the following is NOT part of the transportation sector?

    A.   Air, rail, roads, and waterways
    B.   Services such as law and medical
    C.   Personal vehicles such as automobiles, bicycles, and motorcycles
    D.   Operations including the financing, legalities, and policies for vehicles
    E.   The infrastructure of roads and railways

6. Which fuel source is NOT being considered for future energy use?

    A.   Clean coal
    B.   Methane hydrates
    C.   Oil shale
    D.   Petroleum
    E.   Tar sands

7. Which of the following is NOT considered a fossil fuel?

    A.   Graphite
    B.   Coal
    C.   Petroleum
    D.   Natural gas
    E.   Methane hydrates

8. Which of the following is NOT an advantage of coal production?

    A.   High net-energy yield
    B.   Subsidies to keep the prices low
    C.   Non-explosiveness
    D.   Estimated large supply of undiscovered reserves
    E.   Decreased biodiversity

9. Which of the following is NOT an advantage of nuclear power?

    A.   No air pollutants are produced.
    B.   Decommissioning is expensive.
    C.   Water pollution is low.
    D.   Little carbon dioxide is released during processing.
    E.   Disruption of the land is moderate.

10. Dams have both advantages and disadvantages. Which of the following is an advantage of building a dam across a river?

    A. Large flooded area behind the dam
    B. Controlled downstream flooding
    C. Sediments building up behind the dam
    D. Increased water evaporation
    E. Building expenses

11. If you live in the Southwest and you want to make your house more energy-efficient, which of the following would NOT be a way to do so?

    A. Replacing your 25-year-old air conditioner
    B. Replacing your single-paned windows with double-paned windows
    C. Removing ceiling fans because you replaced your air conditioner
    D. Adding weather stripping
    E. Adding insulation

12. What is the percentage change in average passenger car fuel mileage from 1978 at 18 mpg to 2010 at 27.5 mpg? (You may NOT use a calculator.)

    A. 18
    B. 26.2
    C. 27.0
    D. 37.5
    E. 52.8

13. Which of the following is NOT a disadvantage of solar energy?

    A. It is inefficient where sunlight is seasonal.
    B. Battery technology is limited.
    C. It is great for remote locations.
    D. Efficiency is low.
    E. Systems get old and need to be replaced.

14. Which of the following is NOT produced by the combustion of fossil fuels?

    A. Carbon dioxide
    B. Water
    C. Pollutants
    D. Energy
    E. Glucose

15. Historic energy consumption changed dramatically in the 1800s. Which is NOT a reason for this change?

    A. Industrial Revolution
    B. Population growth
    C. Development of the combustion engine
    D. Switching from wood to coal as a primary energy source
    E. Building of cross-country railroads

Answers

1. **A** Potential energy is stored energy; gasoline in the tank is stored, so it is potential energy.

2. **E** Only nuclear energy can include both fusion and fission.

3. **C** Electrical energy is the alternating current that is transmitted to homes, businesses, and other locations by power lines.

4. **B** As energy flows up a food chain, approximately 10 percent of the energy moves to the next level, while the other 90 percent is heat transferred to the environment. See the following illustration.

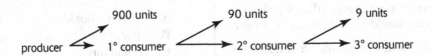

5. **B** Services such as law and medicine are part of the industry sector.

6. **D** Petroleum is currently being used as a fuel source. The other four choices are in development or expansion to fulfill a bigger part of our energy needs.

7. **A** Although graphite's basic source is the same compacted carbon that creates coal, it is the final stage *beyond* the three types of coal. Because it does not combust, it is not considered a fossil fuel.

8. **E** This question asks which is *not* an advantage or, put differently, "Which is a *disadvantage?*" Mining coal can destroy habitats and, thus, decrease biodiversity. It also produces air pollutants, especially sulfur dioxide, which combines with water to form sulfuric acid, a major component of acid rain, which can lower the pH of soil and lakes (among other consequences).

9. **B** This question also asks for a *disadvantage*. Decommissioning is a very expensive process, which makes it a disadvantage. The others are all advantages of nuclear power.

10. **B** Controlling downstream flooding prevents property damage and may save lives; thus, it is an *advantage* of building a dam across a river. (However, some areas historically have depended on seasonal flooding to distribute the rich topsoil used for growing crops.)

11. **C** Although ceiling fans use energy to operate, they help keep the house cool in the summer by improving air circulation, and they help lower energy costs.

12. **E** $V_1 = 18$ mpg and $V_2 = 27.5$ mpg and use the following formula:

$$\text{percent change} = \frac{V_2 - V_1}{V_1} \cdot 100$$
$$= \frac{27.5 - 18}{18} \cdot 100$$
$$= \frac{9.5}{18} \cdot 100$$
$$= 0.528 \cdot 100$$
$$= 52.8\%$$

13. **C** Solar panels work well in remote locations where it may be difficult or too expensive to run power lines to transport electricity. Santa Cruz Island in the Channel Islands off the coast of California runs one of its facilities using solar panels, storing electricity collected during the day in batteries to be used at night when solar energy cannot be collected.

14. **E** The following equation is the combustion reaction for fossil fuels (coal, natural gas, crude oil). Only glucose is not produced in this reaction; the other four choices are produced in the reaction.

$$\text{Fossil Fuel} + O_2 \xrightarrow{\text{burns}} CO_2 + H_2O + \text{Pollutants} + \text{Energy}$$

15. **D** The shift from wood to coal as the world's primary energy source is the change that occurred, not a *cause* of the change.

Chapter 6

Pollution

The wide variety of human activities on the planet is accompanied by the unintended consequences of environmental pollution. Air, water, and soil all can become polluted. With an ever-increasing number of people being added to the planet, noise, light, and genetic pollution are becoming more common as well. Pollution can harm wildlife, ecosystems, and humans, and its presence requires efforts to reduce and eliminate it.

Pollution Types

Pollution comes in various forms and can adversely affect the biosphere's land, atmosphere, and water. Though the sources of pollution and the areas it affects are many, pollution is categorized two ways: **point-source pollution** or **non-point-source pollution.** Point-source pollution is emitted from a specific place, such as wastewater from a plant, acid drainage from a mine, noise from a jet plane, or oil from a tank. Identifying the main source of non-point-source pollution can be difficult, because it may come from a multitude of smaller sources. Examples of non-point-source pollution include emissions from vehicles, runoff from a group of farms, and emissions from widely dispersed factories.

Air, water, and soil are forms of pollution but are accompanied by noise, light, and genetic pollution as well.

Measuring units

To express pollutant amounts present in air, in water, on land, and in tissue, the term **parts per million (ppm)** is commonly used. Ppm is the concentration of a very dilute toxin or substance in relative proportion to another substance (in this case, meaning one part per million). For example, 2 ppm chlorine corresponds to 2 parts chlorine to 1,000,000 parts water. Parts per billion (ppb) and parts per trillion (ppt) also are used as measurements of concentration.

Air Pollution

Human-caused air pollution has been a problem since the Industrial Revolution, when combustion of fossil fuels became the world's primary source of energy. Air pollution is composed of unwanted gases and particulate matter and can be created through natural means or through human actions. Natural polluting events include wildfires, wind-blown debris and dust storms, and volcanic activity.

Airborne chemicals can travel far, so even though a pollutant is emitted from one source, it can affect an ecosystem hundreds or thousands of miles away, potentially in countries other than its source.

Major Air Pollutants

Six common air pollutants monitored by the Environmental Protection Agency (EPA) are considered to be **criteria pollutants** and are measured to gauge air quality. These criteria pollutants are carbon monoxide, nitrogen dioxide, sulfur dioxide, ozone, lead, and particulate matter.

Carbon monoxide (CO) is a colorless, odorless gas that results from the incomplete combustion of organic matter, especially fossil fuels. The use of fossil fuels in the internal combustion engines of vehicles accounts for the majority of CO emissions. Boats, lawn mowers, and construction equipment also contribute large amounts. Other sources include industrial equipment, the burning of wood, cigarette smoke, forest fires, and volcanoes. Indoor sources of CO include gas stoves, wood-burning fireplaces, older furnaces and boilers, and gas and kerosene space heaters.

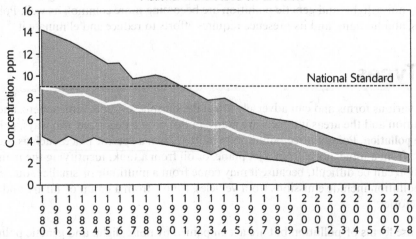

CO Air Quality, 1980 - 2008
(Based on Annual 2nd Maximum 8-hour Average)
National Trend based on 124 Sites

1980 to 2008 : 79% decrease in National Average

Source: Environmental Protection Agency

Nitrogen dioxide (NO₂) is a reddish-brown gas with a strong odor. It is created from combustion at high temperatures, most commonly in vehicles and electric utilities. Once in the atmosphere, NO_2 reacts to form nitrous acid and nitric acid, which are components of acid rain. NO_2 also reacts with the catalyst of the sun's heat in the form of UV radiation to form **photochemical smog.** This is especially common in the summers of warm, sunny regions with large volumes of automobile traffic, such as Los Angeles, California.

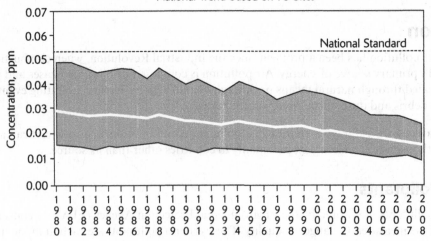

NO₂ Air Quality, 1980 - 2008
(Based on Annual Arithmetic Average)
National Trend based on 75 Sites

1980 to 2008 : 46% decrease in National Average

Source: Environmental Protection Agency

Sulfur dioxide (SO$_2$) is formed when sulfur is released from burning coal and oil, and then reacts with oxygen in the atmosphere to form sulfur dioxide. The majority of atmospheric SO$_2$ is due to emissions from coal-fired power plants. SO$_2$ can react with water vapor to form sulfuric acid (H$_2$SO$_4$) and sulfate salts, which can cause acid rain. Acid rain can harm vegetation and speed the deterioration of structures such as buildings and statues. Also, SO$_2$ absorbs ultraviolet radiation in the atmosphere to form **industrial smog.** It also can produce **aerosols,** which are solid particles and droplets suspended in the atmosphere. Naturally, SO$_2$ can be released from volcanic activity.

Control of SO$_2$ emissions is a major goal of the National Ambient Air Quality Standards established by the EPA under the authority of the Clean Air Act. These standards regulate emissions and develop plans to reduce and monitor pollutants. One successful mandate of the National Ambient Air Quality Standards required the extraction of sulfur from coal prior to combustion. Through extensive efforts, sulfur dioxide in the atmosphere has decreased, but it is by no means eradicated.

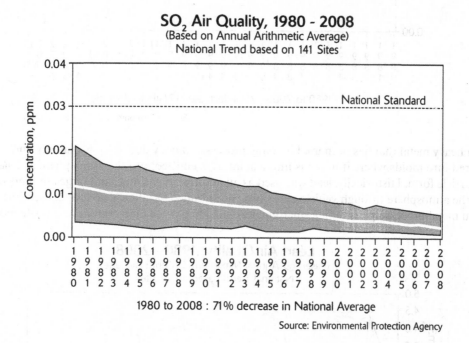

SO$_2$ Air Quality, 1980 - 2008
(Based on Annual Arithmetic Average)
National Trend based on 141 Sites

1980 to 2008 : 71% decrease in National Average

Source: Environmental Protection Agency

Ozone (O$_3$) is a colorless gas found in both the stratosphere and the troposphere. "Good" ozone is located naturally in the stratosphere and protects the Earth from excess levels of harmful ultraviolet radiation from the sun. "Bad" ozone is located close to the ground in the troposphere. The main component of smog, ozone is created at ground level when human-created nitrogen oxides (NO$_x$) react with **volatile organic compounds (VOCs),** sunlight, and heat. VOCs are highly reactive organic compounds and can be found in thousands of products including dry-cleaning products, paint, cleaning supplies, varnishes, vehicle emissions, solvents, and pesticides.

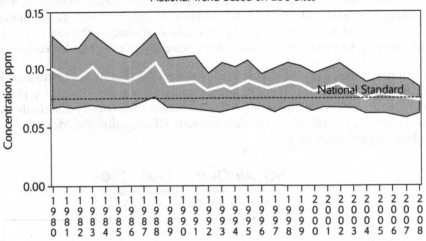

Ozone Air Quality, 1980 - 2008
(Based on Annual 4th Maximum 8-Hour Average)
National Trend based on 258 Sites

1980 to 2008 : 25% decrease in National Average

Source: Environmental Protection Agency

Lead (Pb) is a heavy metal that has been used in many processes, mostly due to its availability and the fact that it can be poured into molds where it hardens into a solid. It is emitted into the atmosphere as a **particulate,** meaning in particle form. Historically, lead was used as an additive in gasoline, and large amounts of lead were released into the atmosphere through vehicle emissions. Since leaded gasoline is no longer used, the main source of lead is from metal processing, including smelting, lead-acid battery manufacturers, and waste incinerators.

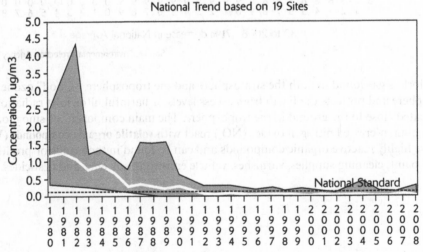

Lead Air Quality, 1980 - 2008
(Based on Annual Maximum 3-Month Average)
National Trend based on 19 Sites

1980 to 2008 : 92% decrease in National Average

Source: Environmental Protection Agency

Particulate matter (PM) includes solid or liquid particles in the atmosphere and can be either a primary pollutant from direct emissions, or a secondary pollutant formed from the chemical reactions of substances such as SO_2 and NO_x. Dust, soot, smoke, dirt, metals, and liquid particles are all examples of particulate matter. Particle size tends to vary depending on the source. As a primary pollutant, PM can come from wood burning, trucks, factories, buses, stone crushing, construction sites, unpaved roads, and bare fields. Secondary or indirect forms of PM can come from vehicle, factory, or power plant emissions.

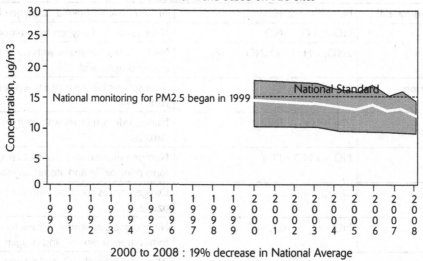

PM2.5 Air Quality, 2000 - 2008
(Based on Seasonally-Weighted Annual Average)
National Trend based on 728 Sites

National monitoring for PM2.5 began in 1999

National Standard

2000 to 2008 : 19% decrease in National Average

Source: Environmental Protection Agency

Smog

The two common types of smog—photochemical smog and industrial smog—are formed from the interactions of pollutants with the atmosphere, catalyzed by solar radiation. For example, to form photochemical smog, nitrogen dioxide, NO_2, reacts with the heat of UV radiation from the sun. To form industrial smog, sulfur dioxide, SO_2, absorbs ultraviolet radiation in the atmosphere. Sulfur dioxide can also produce aerosols, which are solid particles and droplets suspended in the atmosphere.

Acid Deposition

Acid deposition, also known as acid precipitation or (most commonly) acid rain, occurs when chemical reactions occur in the atmosphere between pollutant emissions and atmospheric components. Ultimately, acidic (below 7 on the pH scale) particulate matter falls to Earth's surface as either as precipitation, particulate, or gas. The main contributors to acid deposition are sulfur dioxide and nitrogen dioxide. In the atmosphere, NO_2 reacts to form nitrous and nitric acids, which can fall as acid rain. In addition, sulfur dioxide can react with water vapor to form sulfuric acid (H_2SO_4) and sulfate salts, resulting in acid precipitation.

The following table shows basic chemical reactions of pollutants in the atmosphere and their production of smog and acid precipitation.

Atmospheric Chemical Reactions		Explanation
Acid rain (sulfur-based)	$S + O_2 \rightarrow SO_2$	Sulfur and oxygen form sulfur dioxide.
	$2SO_2 + O_2 \rightarrow 2SO_3$	Sulfur dioxide reacts with oxygen to form sulfur trioxide.
	$SO_3 + H_2O \rightarrow H_2SO_4$	Sulfur trioxide and water react to form sulfuric acid, which can produce acid precipitation.

(continued)

(continued)

Atmospheric Chemical Reactions		Explanation
Acid rain (nitrogen-based)	$N_2 + 2O \rightarrow 2NO$	Atmospheric nitrogen and oxygen form nitric oxide.
	$NO + \frac{1}{2} O_2 \rightarrow NO_2$	Nitric oxide and oxygen form nitrogen dioxide.
	$2NO_2 + H_2O \rightarrow HNO_2 + HNO_3$	Nitrogen dioxide reacts with water to create nitrous acid and nitric acid.
Photochemical smog	$N_2 + O_2 \rightarrow 2NO$	Atmospheric nitrogen reacts with oxygen to produce nitric oxide.
	$2NO + O_2 \rightarrow 2NO_2$	Nitric oxide combines with oxygen to form nitrogen dioxide.
	$NO_2 \rightarrow NO + O$	Nitrogen dioxide absorbs light energy and splits to form nitric oxide and atomic oxygen.
	$O + O_2 \rightarrow O_3$	Oxygen atoms combine with the O_2 in air to produce ozone.
	$NO + O_3 \rightarrow NO_2 + O_2$	Nitric oxide can remove ozone by reacting with it to form nitrogen dioxide and oxygen.
		When the ratio of NO_2 to NO increases, formation of ozone is the main reaction. If the ratio is on the lower side, then the nitric oxide reaction destroys ozone at almost the same rate as it is formed, keeping ozone concentration below harmful levels.
*Note: The mixture of nitric oxide (NO) and nitrogen dioxide (NO_2) is sometimes referred to as NO_x.		
Industrial smog	$C + O_2 \rightarrow CO_2$	Coal (mostly carbon) is burned, and carbon dioxide, carbon monoxide, and soot are produced (soot is uncombusted carbon).
	$2C + O_2 \rightarrow 2CO$	
	$S + O_2 \rightarrow SO_2$	Coal containing sulfur produces sulfur dioxide.
	$2SO_2 + O_2 \rightarrow 2SO_3$	Sulfur dioxide is further oxidized to sulfur trioxide.
	$SO_3 + H_2O \rightarrow H_2SO_4$	Sulfur trioxide can then react with water, forming sulfuric acid.

It should also be noted that **peroxyacetyl nitrate** ($CH_3CO_3NO_2$), known as **PAN,** can be produced by the reaction of some volatile organic hydrocarbons with oxygen and nitrogen dioxide. PAN, ozone, and organic compounds called aldehydes are responsible for many of the harmful effects of smog.

Heat Islands

A problematic phenomenon, but one much less discussed than many other pollutants, is the phenomenon of **heat islands,** which are urban areas with long-term increased temperatures due to human activity. They result from the heat released from activities such as vehicle use, air conditioning, lights, and appliances. Pavement and building materials also may absorb more heat than would a natural ecosystem, therefore the heat island effect can be especially strong in summertime. Unfortunately, higher summertime temperatures encourage additional use of air conditioning, which, in turn, increases the effect of the heat island. Not only does this increased air-conditioning usage contribute to heat islands by producing heat as a by-product of the operation of the units, but it also increases electrical usage, and therefore increases air pollutants.

Indoor Air Pollution

Not only are air pollutants found in the atmosphere, but they also can be a threat indoors. Indoor air pollutants are found in most buildings and can become a problem in large concentrations or when there is poor ventilation.

Indoor air pollutants can include, but are not limited to, tobacco smoke, radon, asbestos, lead and other heavy metals, mold, carbon monoxide, and emissions from burning wood. Indoors, people may also be exposed to harmful chemicals including those in cleaning products, volatile organic compounds (VOCs), and polybrominated biphenyl ether (PBDEs).

Here is a brief description of each of the main indoor air pollutants:

- **Tobacco smoke** produced from cigarettes, pipes, and cigars is a known carcinogen. The inhalation of tobacco smoke can lead to respiratory issues and potentially harmful or fatal cancers.
- **Radon** is an extremely toxic, naturally occurring radioactive gas. It is produced from the decay of radium, which is, in turn, produced from the decay of uranium and can seep into basements from the bedrock. Like installing a smoke alarm, a radon detector can help people recognize the danger before becoming affected.
- **Asbestos** is a naturally occurring mineral. At one time it was used as insulation for pipes, soundproofing, roof tiles, and as a fire retardant. Asbestos fibers can float in the air and if inhaled can cause respiratory problems. Though no longer widely used, it is still found in older buildings.
- **Lead and mercury** can sometimes be found indoors in the form of dust particles or fumes. Lead is mainly found indoors in lead pipes and lead paint. While lead is no longer widely used, it can still be found in older buildings and furniture. Mercury also can become airborne indoors, and mercury fumes can occur from the use of latex paints.
- **Biological threats,** such as mold, dust mites, and pet dander, are often found indoors. They are not universally toxic, but some people are sensitive to these allergens.
- **Carbon monoxide (CO)** is a colorless, odorless gas that is emitted from broken or incorrectly used heating appliances such as clothes driers and water heaters. It is also emitted in vehicle exhaust and the combustion of wood.
- **Wood-burning** emits particulate matter and carbon monoxide.
- **Volatile organic compounds (VOCs)** can be released as gases from a wide variety of products including carpeting, paints, aerosol sprays, cleaning products, building supplies, pesticides, printers, glues, wood preservatives, mothballs, and air fresheners. Some VOCs are also used in dry cleaning processes.
- **Polybrominated biphenyl ether (PBDEs)** are chemicals that are used as flame-retardants in household items such as televisions, furniture, fabrics, wire insulation, drapes, small appliances, and other electronics. During manufacture, PBDEs are mixed with materials in order to raise the temperature at which they burn, but unfortunately they are released into the air in small quantities throughout the life of the product. Some forms of PCDEs have been banned in places such as the United States and the United Kingdom, but others are still in use.

Noise Pollution

Noise pollution encompasses all human activities that produce enough sound to be considered a nuisance. Common sources of noise pollution consist of vehicle traffic, railways, aircraft, car alarms, machinery, barking dogs, yard equipment, loud motorcycles, and music. Poor urban planning can result in an increased amount of aggravating noise for the people who reside or work in these locations.

This issue is serious enough that federal laws have been enacted in response to noise pollution. Such laws include the Noise Pollution and Abatement Act of 1970 and the Noise Control Act of 1972.

Light Pollution

Light pollution results from the excessive use of artificial light and can cause glare, over-illumination, sky glow, and decreased night visibility, and can consume excessive amounts of energy. In addition to being a distraction and an annoyance, light pollution can block terrestrial views of the night sky, interfering with organisms that depend on this view. Reducing light pollution requires conscious conservation efforts by all.

Genetic Pollution

Genetic pollution is a new concern that refers to the unintended spread of altered genetic information from genetically engineered organisms to natural organisms. **Genetically engineered organisms** are organisms that have had their DNA intentionally altered by combining their genetic material with that of another, most commonly in hopes of creating traits that are commercially desirable, including size, growth, or disease resistance. The use of these genetically engineered organisms is quickly increasing, especially in industrialized agriculture, in which genetically modified seeds are used to grow crops. This process has proponents and opponents and is seen to have both positive and negative impacts. Benefits of genetically engineered foods can include increased yield and crop efficiency. Dangers of these organisms include their potential to leak into the wild due to pollination or wind, where they may out-compete native species. Another concern is that only a few companies may have access to certain types of genetically modified products, allowing these few companies to control markets, restricting the freedom of competition.

Economic impacts of genetic engineering (both positive and negative) are dramatic and far-reaching, affecting farmers, fishermen, ranchers, markets, and nations.

Water Pollution

Water pollution can be very harmful to the environment as well as to people and wildlife. This section addresses freshwater and marine water.

Cultural Eutrophication

Eutrophication is the addition of excess nutrients to water. If these excess nutrients are due to human activity, it is called **cultural eutrophication.** Nutrients are added to an ecosystem through runoff, including excess nitrogen and phosphorus from fertilizers, untreated sewage, detergents, animal waste, or fossil fuel combustion. Nitrogen has a greater impact on marine ecosystems, and phosphorus has a larger impact on freshwater ecosystems.

Groundwater Pollution

Groundwater and surface water can be polluted by anthropogenic sources such as leaking oil tanks, agricultural runoff, chemical spills, untreated sewage, storm runoff, development, and mining operations.

Pollutants that affect freshwater sources are:

- **Toxic chemicals:** These can run off or leak into waterways. Toxic chemicals include pesticides; volatile organic compounds; petroleum products; heavy metals such as arsenic, chromium, mercury, and lead; and other dangerous substances.

- **Nutrient pollution:** This results from nutrient runoff from agricultural practices, sewage, lawns, golf courses, and fields. Excess nutrients can cause eutrophication in both freshwater and marine environments, resulting in an alteration of the balance of the ecosystem.

- **Temperature pollution:** This results from the release of water that is either warmer or colder than normal for the specific environment. This temperature change can affect individual species as well as the balance of an entire ecosystem. Thermal (heat) pollution occurs when water is used in factories and manufacturing processes. The water becomes heated as it cycles through the manufacturing processes and is then discharged into the local water source. Heating of water also can occur when vegetation is removed from the banks of a river, allowing more sunlight to hit the water's surface. Cold water pollution can occur when a dam releases cold water from the bottom of a reservoir into a river, as in the case of most hydroelectric power stations. Both extremes affect ecosystem balance.

- **Sediment** can become excessive in freshwater systems. Although it is a natural part of aquatic ecosystems, sediment in disproportionate amounts can change the aquatic balance. Excess sediment suspended in the water causes cloudiness that is called **turbidity.** Turbidity affects some fish that cannot adjust to changes in sediment levels and leads to a lack of sunlight and, thus, available energy in deeper waters. Once sediment settles it also can impact the benthic environment and alter the flow of water. Contaminants, such as heavy metals, can accumulate in sediment as well, ultimately settling on the bottom where they can be ingested by benthic organisms.

- **Pathogens and waterborne diseases** exist in surface waters and can enter the drinking water supply if water is untreated. Protists, bacteria, and pathogenic viruses can cause serious health effects in humans, entering the water supply through runoff from sewage and animal manure.

Marine Ecosystems

Marine environments also suffer from the impacts of pollution. For many decades, the oceans were thought to be endless, so waste was dumped into them without thought of repercussion. Now the issues of polluting marine environments are being addressed and understood. Forms of pollution include oil pollution, excess nutrients, sewage, and trash such as plastics, debris, and fishing equipment.

Most oil pollution reaches the oceans through runoff from hard surfaces on the land, especially roads. Other sources include maintenance of ships, natural seepage from the ocean floor, and spills such as the *Exxon Valdez* supertanker rupture and the *Deepwater Horizon* (BP) drilling rig explosion. Oil spills can drastically impact the economy, most directly through the loss of fisheries and decreased tourism. Losses to these industries ripple through a local economy. Additionally, spilled oil carried in currents can reach sites far from the original disaster.

Trash reaches the ocean from the occupants of boats, damaged or sunken boats, barges dumping the refuse of coastal cities, offshore winds, and water runoff. To exacerbate the problem, trash is then carried by ocean currents, waves, and gyres, sometimes traveling hundreds of miles from the original source of the trash. One especially visible effect of trash on the marine ecosystem is to sea turtles, which frequently eat and are killed by floating plastic bags, which look much like their natural prey, jellyfish.

Maintaining Water Quality

The United States government has put in place water quality standards to maintain water quality in both freshwater and marine ecosystems. Drinking, ground, and surface water quality is tested for potential threatening levels of nutrient concentrations, fecal coliform bacteria (from sewage), hardness, pH, turbidity (suspended particles), and dissolved oxygen content. Additionally, during the past few decades, The Environmental Protection Agency (EPA) and other organizations have made efforts to reduce sources of water pollution. These sources include leaking underground storage tanks, illegal dumping of toxic chemicals, and proper management of landfills, runoff, and other waste. The EPA also has set standards for concentrations of over 80 contaminants likely to be found in drinking water. The Clean Water Act also has reduced water contamination, helping to maintain safer water quality for both humans and ecosystems.

Clean Water Act

The Clean Water Act was created in 1972 and amended in 1977 to protect the America's freshwater sources. Specifically, it was established to regulate the discharge of pollutants into waterways while also establishing quality standards for surface waters, including wastewater standards for industries.

Wastewater Purification and Sewage Treatment

Wastewater is generated by humans. After water is used and before it is released back into the environment, it is put through a cleaning process, commonly using a septic system or a municipal sewer system.

Septic systems are constructed directly on the property where they are used. Wastewater travels from the house to a septic tank buried underground, where solids, oils, and water naturally separate by density. The wastewater then travels to an empty field, or lawn area, where the waste products continue to be decomposed by microbes. The remnants left in the tank undergo decomposition as well. If the tank gets full, it is pumped and the contents taken to a landfill for disposal. Septic systems are usually found in rural areas, although as more remote locations have been developed, septic systems can now be found in areas considered to be urban or suburban.

In a **municipal sewer system,** wastewater is taken by pipes from local homes and businesses and sent to a central treatment plant where it undergoes clarification processes. During **primary treatment** suspended solids are physically removed in settling tanks. The wastewater then goes through **secondary treatment** where oxygen enters the water from continual mixing and movement, encouraging aerobic decomposition. By the end of this process, the majority of suspended solids have been removed. Some treatment facilities also use a third step, or a **tertiary treatment,** where there is additional filtration of the water. The final step is the treatment of the clarified water with UV light treatment or chlorine to kill bacteria. The water is then discharged into a river or an ocean. The solids (sludge) that were extracted are placed in large tanks where decomposition occurs. When the solids dry, the remainder is incinerated, sent to a landfill, or used as fertilizer for crops. Unfortunately, in many developing countries, the bulk of domestic and industrial wastewater is discharged without any treatment, or with only limited primary treatment. Without adequate sanitation systems, ecosystems can be destroyed and human populations threatened.

Solid Waste

Soil can be polluted through industrial waste, agricultural runoff, acid precipitation, underground storage tanks, and radioactive fallout. The most prominent contaminants are heavy metals, petroleum hydrocarbons, solvents, and pesticides. For management purposes, solid waste is considered one of four types:

- **Hazardous waste** is flammable, corrosive, toxic, or reactive.
- **Industrial waste** is created during industrial processes such as agriculture, mining, consumer goods production, and the extraction and refining of petroleum products.
- **Municipal solid waste** comes from homes, business, schools, hospitals, and other types of institutions.
- Also classified as waste is **wastewater**, which is post-consumer water that is flushed or goes down the drain, or water that runs into sewers from streets.

Disposal

Waste material from industry, municipalities, mining, agriculture, and medical operations requires disposal in a way that does not contaminate the soil. These solid wastes include, but are certainly not limited to, tailings and overburden from mining processes, agricultural remnants, medical wastes (biohazards), and radioactive and toxic substances, each of which requires its own protocol for disposal. Landfills, open dumps, or incineration facilities are often the final destination for these materials.

Landfills are areas where solid waste is disposed of by being buried in the ground or piled in a mound. Once a landfill is full, it is capped, or covered. In the United States, landfill regulations help to protect human health, wildlife, and ecosystems. For example, landfills must be located away from wetlands and cannot be built on an earthquake fault. Also, the bottoms of landfills are lined with plastic and clay to prevent leakage into the environment. Waste in a landfill experiences aerobic and anaerobic decomposition, allowing some of the waste to break down.

In some locations, solid waste is incinerated, or burned, at high temperatures in facilities built for this purpose. Prior to incineration, metals are removed for recycling. The ash that remains after incineration is then sent to a landfill.

This process reduces the mass and volume of waste being placed in a landfill. Unfortunately, incineration is likely to produce some quantity of hazardous waste, which requires specialized handling. Most likely, this special handling includes disposal in a hazardous waste landfill. In the United States, incineration plants have air emission guidelines aimed at the reduction of the amount of acid-causing chemicals, heavy metals, and other toxic and harmful substances released during incineration.

Most incineration plants operating in the United States are considered to be **waste-to-energy** facilities, where the heat that is generated during combustion is captured and used to heat water, which creates steam at high temperatures. Just as in a coal-fired power plant, this steam is then used to turn turbines, generating electricity.

Reduction

Certainly the most energy efficient and environmentally friendly way to address waste is by producing less of it. While recycling is becoming more common and economical, not all products are recycled. Even products that are recycled must be disposed. Composting of organic substances is also becoming more widely accepted and used, but it still requires time, effort, and space to conduct it properly. By reducing what we purchase and use, reusing existing products, recycling used products, and composting people can reduce the amount of waste entering landfills or being incinerated.

Many efforts have been made at the international, federal, state, and local levels to control pollution, both at the source and in the areas where it concentrates. Subsidies, green taxes, and permit trading have been used to help lessen pollution. For more information on these efforts refer to Chapter 4. Innovative technological advancements also have helped to reduce pollution from a range of sources. To protect human health and the environment, the **Clean Air Act** set standards governing the release of criteria pollutants. The act was created in 1970 and most recently amended in 1990, with the goal of protecting public health and welfare. The **Clean Air Act** regulates emissions from mobile and stationary sources, as well as hazardous emissions. It focuses on reducing air emissions, reducing concentrations of air pollutants, and ultimately reducing the production of destructive chemicals. National Ambient Air Quality Standards (NAAQS) were set by this act.

U.S. Laws and Treaties

- ❏ National Environmental Policy Act (NEPA)
- ❏ Clean Air Act (CAA)
- ❏ Clean Water Act (CWA)
- ❏ Comprehensive Environmental Response, Compensation, and Liability Act (CERCLA)
- ❏ Toxic Substances Control Act (TSCA)
- ❏ Resource Conservation and Recovery Act (RCRA)
- ❏ Emergency Planning and Community Right-to-Know Act (EPCRA)
- ❏ Oil Pollution Prevention Act (OPP)
- ❏ Pollution Prevention Act (PPA)

International Laws and Treaties

- ❏ The 2001 Stockholm Convention on Persistent Organic Pollutants (POPs)
- ❏ United Nations Framework Convention on Climate Change
- ❏ Kyoto Protocol
- ❏ Convention on Long-Range Transboundary Air Pollution
- ❏ United Nations Convention on the Law of the Sea
- ❏ Convention on the Prior Informed Consent (PIC) Procedure for Certain Hazardous Chemicals and Pesticides in International Trade
- ❏ International Convention on Oil Pollution Preparedness, Response, and Cooperation
- ❏ International Atomic Energy Agency Convention on Nuclear Safety
- ❏ Protection of the Arctic Marine Environment (PAME)

Impacts on the Environment and Human Health

Pollution can break down quickly in the environment and cause relatively little harm, or it can persist for years, decades, centuries, or millennia depending on the pollution type and quantity. Detrimental affects of pollution can impact human, wildlife, and ecosystem health.

Hazards to Human Health

Exposure

Exposure to health hazards can be long-term or short-term, in high or low doses. **Acute exposure** occurs when someone is exposed to a high dose for a brief period of time, whereas **chronic exposure** occurs repeatedly over a long period of time but in small doses. Historic examples of chronic exposure include the many people who had frequent contact with lead, asbestos, or mercury, all of which were considered harmless at the time. In fact, low-dose, one-time exposure to these substances is unlikely to be harmful. However, chronic exposure to lead, mercury, or asbestos can lead to life-threatening conditions. There are many examples of acute exposure, including a one-time experience of high radiation or inhalation of toxic gas. Generally, it is easier to identify the source of acute exposure, since it is usually related to an event, as opposed to exposure over an extended period of time.

Environmental Risk Analysis

A **risk analysis** assesses the environmental risks potentially associated with an event or action. Any environmental risk is balanced against the associated monetary value, and recommendations are included for mitigating risk. A risk analysis also helps concerned parties better understand the toxins and pollutants involved in the event and their effects on humans and ecosystems, the potential for human exposure to the threat, and people's perceptions of the risk. A **dose-response analysis** can be used to determine the toxicity and threat to human and wildlife health, and a **cost-benefit analysis** provides the final overview of the proposed action.

Despite research and testing, the effects of substances are not fully known until they are used; therefore, some countries and companies use the **precautionary principle** when evaluating a substance's toxicity. This means assuming the product is harmful until proven otherwise. In contrast to this is the **innocent-until-proven-guilty** approach, in which a product is assumed to be harmless until proven otherwise. Obviously, the latter approach is somewhat riskier (and usually less expensive) and can potentially lead to health problems or death. The United States often uses the innocent-until-proven-guilty approach, while Europe commonly uses the precautionary principle.

In the United States, some substances do not require Food and Drug Administration (FDA) approval prior to being released to the market, although many of these substances are then tracked and regulated through the FDA, EPA, and other agencies. Many substances that are not regulated through laws are monitored by the EPA. A key law that addresses the monitoring of toxic chemicals is the Toxic Substances Control Act (TSCA). Workplace hazards and safety, including exposure to toxins, are monitored through the Occupational Safety and Health Administration (OSHA).

Dose-Response

A **dose-response relationship** is used to represent the effect of a toxin on an organism or population. A **dose** is the amount or concentration of a substance, while the **response** is an organism's reaction to a substance. Thus, dose-response describes the effects of certain levels of a toxin, illustrating the tipping point at which a safe level and exposure time becomes hazardous. In order to show this relationship, a **dose-response curve** can be used, as illustrated in the following figures. The term LD_{50} describes the lethal dose of a substance for 50 percent of the test population. When 50 percent of the population is affected (but not killed) by a certain dose of a substance, it is labeled ED_{50} or effective dose-50 percent. The **threshold** dose is the amount of a substance that has any effect on an organism or population.

Dose-Response Curve Showing Threshold

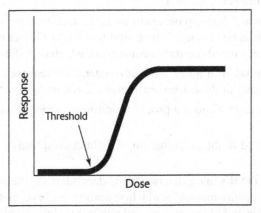

Dose-Response Curve Showing LD_{50}

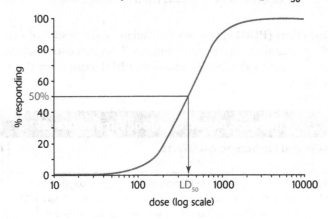

Acute and Chronic Effects

The health and environmental effects of pollution vary depending on levels, the individual, the location, vegetation types, climate, and many other factors.

Indoor Air Pollutants

Indoor air pollution can have a wide range of health effects. Here are the major hazards:

- **Radon** is an extremely toxic radioactive gas that occurs naturally. Exposure generally occurs after it seeps into basements from the bedrock. Radon can be detected with the proper equipment, but without a detection kit it can build up in an enclosed space and eventually lead to lung cancer. Radon exposure is considered the second leading cause of lung cancer, next to tobacco smoke.

- **Asbestos** threats occur when a product containing asbestos is damaged, which releases the tiny asbestos particles into the air. When inhaled, these particles can lodge in the lungs, which produce acid to fight the invaders, ultimately scarring the lung tissue. Long-term exposure can lead to asbestosis, which is a decrease in lung function due to scarred lungs. Asbestos is also classified as a carcinogen. Mesothelioma is the result of asbestos damaging major organs of the human body. It is often a fatal condition. Before its impact on human health was discovered and acknowledged, asbestos was widely used to insulate pipes, for sound-proofing, as vehicle brake shoes, as a fire retardant, among many other uses.

- **Tobacco smoke** is produced from cigarettes, pipes, and cigars and is the leading cause of lung cancer. There are many toxic chemicals found in tobacco smoke including butane, hydrogen cyanide, arsenic, lead, carbon monoxide, and ammonia. Both the smoking of tobacco and exposure to secondhand smoke are dangerous, and secondhand smoke actually contains higher concentrations of chemicals because it does not pass through cigarette filters before being inhaled.

- **Lead and mercury** can be toxic if buildup occurs in body tissue. Exposure to small amounts of lead can cause minor symptoms such as headaches, fatigue, and nausea, but larger exposure to lead can affect brain development of fetuses. Heavy metals contain neurotoxins, which can affect the nervous system.

- **Biological threats,** such as mold, dust mites, and pet dander, can create respiratory issues, congestion, headaches, and infections, especially in those who are allergic. Some molds are toxic and can be very harmful.

- **Carbon monoxide** is undetectable without a proper monitoring device and can lead to asphyxiation, as it disrupts blood oxygenation.

- **Wood-burning indoors** can lead to the exacerbation of asthma symptoms, respiratory problems, and respiratory illness.

- **Volatile organic compounds (VOCs)** have diverse effects depending on the product and amount of exposure. Less severe symptoms of exposure include headaches; nausea; and eye, nose, and throat irritation. More severe exposure can lead to liver, kidney, and central nervous system damage. Some VOCs are known carcinogens and can lead to potentially fatal cancers. VOCs such as those used in dry-cleaning processes can have negative impacts on the environment if leaked from a storage source into the soil, air, groundwater, or other water source.

- **Polybrominated biphenyl ethers (PBDEs)** can bioaccumulate in the tissues of organisms and biomagnify throughout a food web as organisms eat other organisms. They can cause neurological problems and are cancer-causing, especially affecting the thyroid and liver. PBDEs can enter the water, soil and air, and then make their way into wildlife.

Effects of Major Outdoor Air Pollutants		
Environmental Air Pollutant	**Health and Environmental Effects**	**Major Sources of Environmental Pollution**
Carbon monoxide (CO)	Carbon monoxide inhibits the blood's ability to carry oxygen to body tissues including vital organs such as the brain and heart. CO can cause headaches and dizziness with continuous exposure. Higher concentrations can cause nausea, impaired vision, confusion, fatigue, seizures, respiratory failure, and death.	Motor vehicle exhaust
Nitrogen dioxide (NO_2)	NO_2 can irritate eyes, nose, and lungs and lower resistance to respiratory infection. Sensitivity increases for people with asthma and bronchitis. Environmental effects include eutrophication in aquatic systems, acid rain, and photochemical smog.	Motor vehicle exhaust, heat and power generation, explosives, fertilizer

Environmental Air Pollutant	Health and Environmental Effects	Major Sources of Environmental Pollution
Sulfur dioxide (SO_2)	SO_2 can cause respiratory and cardiovascular health problems. It is a precursor of fine particulate soot. Sulfur dioxide is a major component of acid rain, which accelerates corrosion of buildings and can disturb water and soil pH levels and can produce industrial smog.	Industry (heat and power) that uses oil or coal containing sulfur
Ozone (O_3)	Ozone can lead to respiratory problems, especially in people with existing respiratory ailments. Environmental effects include destroying vegetation (crops and forests) and, thus, ecosystems. It is a foundation of smog.	Formed from a reaction of NO_2 and VOCs (nitrogen oxides, hydrocarbons, and sunlight)
Lead (Pb)	Lead damages the nervous system by accumulating in the bloodstream over time. It is not easily removed and can bioaccumulate in organisms and is a neurotoxin. Lead can kill fish and animals and, thus, affect ecosystems.	Motor vehicles (burning leaded gasoline) and battery plants
Particulate matter (PM)	Particles can enter the bloodstream through the lungs. Health effects include lung and heart problems, chronic bronchitis, asthma, and other respiratory system issues. It can contribute to acid precipitation and smog. When it settles in land or in water, it depletes the soil of nutrients, causes groundwater sources to become acidic, changes the nutrient content of groundwater, and damages vegetation and crops. Particulates also decrease visibility.	Soot from motor vehicles industry

Water Pollutants

The contamination of freshwater can have harmful effects on human and ecosystem health. As discussed earlier, pollution can occur from excessive nutrients, excessive heat, pathogens and waterborne disease, toxic chemicals, and sediment. Since all life depends on water, when sources become polluted, there are far-reaching effects. Effects of water pollution on ecosystems include poisoning of organisms, loss of biodiversity, and potentially ecosystem death. Groundwater and surface water are used for drinking, crop irrigation, cleaning, recreation, and other human activities.

Coral reefs are especially fragile and sensitive to pollutants. Eutrophication, excess sediment, and oil spills can smother coral. Temperature changes can be lethal, because coral needs a consistent water temperature. Acid precipitation and other forms of pollution can kill coral as well.

Soil Contaminants in Water

When soils are contaminated, the contaminant can percolate down through the soil, transported by water, and ending up in a groundwater source. Contaminated groundwater and aquifers can be a serious issue in areas of dense human population. With population density comes the threat of accidents, leaks, and human carelessness. Contaminated soil and water may result in the inability to support life and the degradation of an ecosystem. Humans can be at risk from direct contact with the soil, inhalation of fumes, or consumption of contaminated water. Health effects vary from mild to extreme, depending on the substance and concentration.

Oil Spills

The effects of an oil spill can be destructive, far-reaching, and long-term. Once oil is released in water, it can float on the surface, partially submerge and stay suspended in midlevel waters, or sink to the bottom, depending on the density of the oil. In an ecosystem, oil spills can:

- Poison or suffocate life
- Affect breeding cycles and locations

- Damage nesting sites
- Weaken egg shells and harm or kill larvae
- Damage coastlines
- Contaminate algae and phytoplankton, which serve as the basis of food webs
- Coat organisms with oil, potentially leading to loss of body heat, smothering, drowning, and starvation
- Get trapped between rocks, gravel, and sand particles and persist for many years

The amount of oil released by the *Deepwater Horizon* spill is one of the largest oil spills in history. The devastation of wildlife and ecosystems, combined with the economic losses to people such as fishermen and the tourism industry, is dramatically higher than that of most spills due to the proximity to the coastline and barrier islands, and to the biologically productive nature of the Gulf of Mexico.

Waterborne Diseases and Pathogens

Health effects from pathogens and waterborne diseases are more immediately devastating than those from any other form of water pollution. These waterborne diseases include cholera, typhoid, hepatitis A, *E. coli,* dysentery, SARS, giardiasis, and many others. An increasing number of people worldwide have access to safe and clean drinking water, but an unreasonably high number of people still do not, mainly in developing countries.

Nutrients

Nutrient overload from fertilizers and sewage runoff can create eutrophication, hypoxia, and dead zones in both marine and freshwater ecosystems, affecting wildlife, ecosystems, and humans. **Eutrophication** occurs when excess nitrogen or phosphorous enters an aquatic system, leading to an excessive growth of phytoplankton, algae, and other plants. As organisms die off and decompose, the bacteria consuming them use large amounts of oxygen, which ultimately can deprive an ecosystem of oxygen. A **hypoxic** environment, lacking oxygen, can form, and much of the ecosystem life cannot survive or will leave the area. An extreme hypoxic environment can become devoid of any life and become a **dead zone.**

Trash

Trash that ends up in oceans can end up in organisms, as some fish and marine organisms consume small pieces in the assumption that it is food. Some items, such as plastics, do not break down in the organisms' digestive tracts and if it cannot be passed, will remain inside the organism for its lifespan. This can shorten an organism's life span through a slow release of synthetic chemicals or through the lodging of the trash inside their bodies. Organisms also can become tangled in fishing gear and other debris, trapping them and ultimately leading to starvation and death.

Noise

Noise pollution can cause immediate irreversible hearing loss in the event of an extremely loud instantaneous burst, or it can gradually impact hearing through long-term repeated exposure. Other effects include increased stress levels, hypertension, aggression, sleep deprivation, short-term hearing loss, and tinnitus. Organisms in ecosystems are also impacted by noise pollution and may lead to a decline in biodiversity in some areas.

Light

Anthropogenic light can affect organisms by causing distractions or by altering their natural cycles. Light can alter feeding cycles, prompt unnatural periods of attraction that lead to disruptions in reproductive cycles, disorient migratory birds, and interfere with intraspecies communication. Thus, bright lights are a form of habitat destruction, altering behaviors, with effects that can be passed throughout an ecosystem.

Also, using more light requires more electricity, which uses more energy and leads to increased emissions.

Genetic

Since genetic pollution is still relatively new, we are still discovering its long-term effects, both good and bad. Known adverse effects of genetically modifying crops and organisms include the following:

- Decrease in crop diversity
- Increase in pest and disease resilience
- Abnormalities and mutations occurring that would not occur naturally
- Possible species extinctions due to natural species being out-competed by modified ones

Hazardous Chemicals in the Environment

When substances are considered to be **toxins,** or poisonous substance, they are classified based on their potential health impacts.

Types of Hazardous Waste	
Neurotoxins	Neurotoxins target the nervous system, affecting motor control and brain function. Heavy metals such as lead, cadmium, and mercury are classified as neurotoxins.
Carcinogens	Carcinogens are cancer-causing toxins, such as asbestos, formaldehyde, radioactive substances, and some organic compounds like benzene.
Teratogens	Teratogens can affect embryo development, harming or killing the fetus. Known teratogens include alcohol and thalidomide.
Mutagens	Mutagens create mutations in the DNA of organisms and include radiation, nitrous oxide, and UV light. Many mutagens including benzene are also carcinogens.
Endocrine disruptors	Endocrine disruptors alter the hormone (endocrine) system, usually by binding to hormone receptors in place of the existing, desired hormone or by otherwise blocking hormone effects. DDT, the pesticide once used in the United States, is an endocrine disruptor.
Allergens	Allergens overactivate the immune system, stimulating a disproportionate response in those who are allergic. Examples range from pollen and dust mites to peanuts.

Biomagnification and Bioaccumulation

Over time, toxins may build up, or **bioaccumulate,** in organisms' muscles, organs, and other tissues. Especially if a substance is fat- or oil-soluble, it can dissolve into fatty tissues and accumulate in the organism. This accumulation can magnify through the food chain as predators consume organisms, each with accumulated toxins, which then pass to the predator. Thus, toxin levels tend to increase dramatically with each step higher in the food chain. The buildup of toxins within an organism through the consumption of other organisms is called **biomagnification.**

Treatment and Disposal of Hazardous Waste

Disposal of hazardous chemicals poses a serious threat to human and environmental health. Some hazardous substances degrade over time until they are no longer dangerous, but some substances **persist,** or remain in the environment for an extended period of time. Heavy metals, many organic compounds, and radioactive waste all persist in the environment. Hazardous waste substances can be classified as:

- **Toxic:** Harmful to human health
- **Corrosive:** Can wear away and break down metals
- **Reactive:** Easily react with other substances and can cause a serious reaction such as explosions or toxic gases
- **Ignitable:** Easily combustible

Some hazardous waste is treated prior to disposal in order to neutralize it. Usually, treatment involves the incineration of the waste, which breaks down the toxic organic components and reduces the volume of the waste. As specified in the Clean Air Act, the emissions from these incineration facilities are monitored through the National Emissions Standards for Hazardous Air Pollutants (NESHAP), with levels established by the EPA.

Proper disposal of hazardous waste requires special facilities designed to hold these substances, often designed to permanently contain the waste. Most hazardous substances are placed into landfills, injection wells, land treatment units, or surface impoundments. Liquids are usually placed into injection wells deep within the earth. Hazardous waste disposal is monitored by the Resource Conservation and Recovery Act (RCRA) and the Safe Drinking Water Act (SDWA).

Remediation and Cleanup of Contaminated Sites

Polluted waters and soils can be **remediated,** or cleaned up, through extensive effort and at high costs. Remediation is the removal of contaminants from water or soil. Prior to the start of remediation, an environmental site assessment is created to determine what activities occurred on the site and in the area, what pollutants are present, and what can be done to remove and clean up the pollutants. Generally, the parties who contaminated the site are responsible for the remediation and removal of contaminated soils and water within the contaminated area. If the contamination is found on an abandoned site and cannot be traced to any person or company, funds are provided by the federal government through the EPA's Superfund program. Taxes imposed on polluting industries are placed into the Superfund to be used for the remediation of contaminated areas.

Remediation can involve either treating the contaminated area without removing any soil **(in situ),** or removing contaminated soil **(ex situ),** or a combination of both. Possible remediation techniques include excavation, extraction, pump and treat, bioremediation, aeration, phytoremediation, and thermal remediation, with the optimal treatment depending on the type of pollution, what is contaminated, and how much is affected.

Economic Impacts

Pollution affects many economic sectors, so it can be difficult to put an exact dollar amount on the effects of pollution. Because pollution can travel from the point of origin, it impacts both human health and ecosystem health, sometimes in locales widely removed from the original source of contamination. Effects may not be seen for years or decades, and not all effects are reported or known. Thus, the economic impact of pollution is estimated, including combinations of many factors including the following:

- Medical costs, loss of income, and loss of productivity due to pollution-related human illness
- Lost profits due to impacts on agriculture
- Loss of income due to impacts on resources, including fisheries and timber
- Potential decrease in tourism
- Costs related to cleanup and control of pollution
- Loss of revenues due to businesses moving from or refusing to move to polluted areas
- Lost income of all services that depend on monies generated in communities affected by pollution

However, it is beneficial for some businesses to move specifically to areas that allow higher levels of pollution, in which their emission and pollution standards may not be as tight and permitting for pollution may be simpler. Thus, allowing pollution can have beneficial effects on local economies.

Cost-Benefit Analysis

Many industries use **cost-benefit analysis (CBA)** to determine beneficial courses of action. For example, an office might ask if the ease and decreased cost over time is worth the purchase price of a new printer. Similar analysis applies when industries pollute or evaluate the remediation of a polluted area. Simply, do the benefits outweigh the costs?

For example, benefits of remediation may include improved air or water quality, species preservation, increased recreational opportunities, reduced wildlife mortality, increased job opportunities, and reduced pollution. Costs may include higher prices of goods passed on to the consumer; increased taxes, fees, or costs associated with the action; and lost opportunities to create marketable products. Aside from assessing the immediate economic gains and losses of an action, a cost-benefit analysis takes into account long-term effects and the impact on human well-being.

Market effects are the effects that can be expressed in dollars, whereas **nonmarket effects** do not necessarily have a fixed dollar amount but may have tangible and intangible benefits to ecosystem or human well-being. Sometimes, for the purpose of comparison in a cost-benefit analysis, these intangibles are represented as dollar amounts; however, some people argue that assigning dollar values to nature, ecosystems, and human lives is unethical.

Assessing the relative desirability of actions is a difficult and often subjective process, and one in which finite monetary resources must be allocated to the places in which they do the most good. Is preserving a unique forest ecosystem just as valuable as providing increased healthcare options to individuals? Also, how is the value of an ecosystem or a resource assessed? Therefore, CBA is used not only to define whether a single action should take place, but also to compare the benefits of many possible actions, allowing more informed decisions on where limited resources can be the most useful.

Marginal Costs

It isn't very difficult to clean up "grade F" air to "grade D" air, but it is much harder to make B+ air into A+ air. This is the idea of **marginal cost:** As more units are produced, as air gets cleaner, or as grades get higher, it is increasingly difficult to add the same amount as you did before. So, although the effort of cleaning very dirty air may be worthwhile, the effort of cleaning air that is already relatively clean may not be worthwhile. Add to this the idea of **marginal benefit**—the fact that making those first air-quality improvements can drastically increase quality of life, but making further improvements tends to have decreasing benefits. One piece of pizza is great, but 15 pieces are not so great—each subsequent piece has a decreasing marginal benefit. So, how much air should you clean or how much pizza should you eat? To create economic efficiency, you should clean or eat exactly until the marginal benefit becomes less than the marginal cost—you want to continue until the cost outweighs the gain. At this point of equilibrium, between marginal cost and marginal benefit, is economic efficiency.

The cost benefit analysis in the diagram below shows the optimal point of equilibrium (Q), between marginal cost and marginal benefit. To the right of equilibrium, items' production cost outweighs their gain; to the left of equilibrium, the relatively high combination of high marginal benefit and low marginal cost means that you should be producing more than you are to take advantage of these conditions (again, producing in exactly the quantity at which you reach equilibrium between these factors).

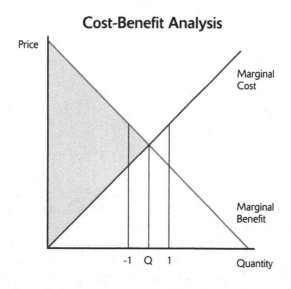

Cost-Benefit Analysis

Cost of Pollution Control

There are costs associated with most efforts to limit and control pollution. Thus, rather than depending on businesses to police their own pollution control, pollution-control mechanisms often come in the form of laws and regulations. This approach is considered a **command-and-control strategy,** where the government sets and enforces legal limits. Although this method is very common and has led to success in some sectors, it is not always the most efficient and/or economical method. For example, emissions standards vary depending on the country, the state, the industry, the age of the factories, and a variety of other factors; the costs of new technologies and other adjustments needed to create compliance may simply be passed on to consumers. There are also costs to the government (and, thus, to taxpayers) for the enforcement of laws.

In addition to regulating pollution standards, there exist market-based strategies to pollution control. For example, making companies responsible for the cleanup of any pollution of their land creates incentives for companies to pollute the land less in the first place. Another way to create incentives for pollution reduction (used mainly in Europe) is to mandate that companies pay **pollution fees,** which are taxes levied on polluters relative to the amount of pollution discharged, frequently with a cap on the total amount of pollution allowed. This cap-and-trade system allows relatively clean companies to sell pollution permits to companies that exceed the cap (which buy the permits to avoid penalties). With **permit trading,** including **marketable emissions permits**, companies can buy, sell, and trade credits for the amount of pollution they are allotted to emit. Some companies will pollute more, while others will pollute less, but cap-and-trade ensures that all companies have an economic incentive to pollute less. This approach was used to successfully reduce sulfur-dioxide emissions in the United States.

In yet another approach, instead of creating laws and regulations to control pollution, federally funded programs provide grants to support local remediation programs. An example of this in the United States is the Superfund, which contributes federal dollars to clean up hazardous waste sites in situations in which a responsible party is not identified or is unable to pay.

Sustainability

In the long tem, economics is dependent on environmental sustainability. A situation of maximum pollution is one without the resources that businesses need. Thus, economics and the environment are interwoven, dependent on each other, and the concept of sustainability applies to both. Short-term economic success may come more easily by polluting and over-utilizing the environment, but businesses that operate in this way will eventually create excessive harm to humans and the environment. Therefore, economic goals must be aligned with environmental sustainability in order for both to continue indefinitely.

Practice

Questions 1–4 refer to the following air pollutants.

    A.   Carbon monoxide
    B.   Sulfur dioxide
    C.   Nitrogen dioxide
    D.   Ozone
    E.   Particulate matter

1. Which criteria pollutant contributes to the creation of industrial smog?

2. Which criteria pollutant is a component of photochemical smog and acid precipitation?

3. Which criteria pollutant can lead to eutrophication in an aquatic system?

4. Which criteria pollutant helps to create smog when in the troposphere but protects life from UV radiation when in the stratosphere?

5. Which of the following best describes the way carbon monoxide interacts in the body to cause asphyxiation?

    A.   Carbon monoxide binds with hemoglobin in the bloodstream, displacing oxygen and preventing it from binding with the hemoglobin.
    B.   Carbox monoxide is inhaled into the lungs, where it replaces oxygen.
    C.   The carbon and oxygen atoms in carbon monoxide separate, and the carbon bonds with hemoglobin.
    D.   Excess carbon monoxide cannot cause asphyxiation.
    E.   Carbon monoxide combines with oxygen and forms a toxic substance in the body.

6. Endocrine disruption occurs when

    A.   Heavy metals bioaccumulate in the body.
    B.   An ecosystem is disrupted by the removal of vegetation.
    C.   Carbon monoxide replaces a hormone in a molecule within the body, impeding the necessary reaction process.
    D.   A toxin replaces a hormone in a molecule within the body, impeding the necessary reaction process.
    E.   Allergens over-activate the immune system.

7. Which of the following chemical reactions best represents the process of the creation of acid precipitation?

   A. $N_2 + O_2 \rightarrow 2NO$
       $2NO + O_2 \rightarrow 2NO_2$
       $NO_2 \rightarrow NO + O$
       $O + O_2 \rightarrow O_3$
       $NO + O_3 \rightarrow NO_2 + O_2$
   B. $H_2SO_4 + Ca(OH)_2 \rightarrow CaSO_4 + 2H_2O$
   C. $S + O_2 \rightarrow SO_2$
       $2SO_2 + O_2 \rightarrow 2SO_3$
       $SO_3 + H_2O \rightarrow H_2SO_4$
   D. $C + O_2 \rightarrow CO_2$
       $2C + O_2 \rightarrow 2CO$
       $S + O_2 \rightarrow SO_2$
       $2SO_2 + O_2 \rightarrow 2SO_3$
       $SO_3 + H_2O \rightarrow H_2SO_4$
   E. $4FeS_2 + 11O_2 \rightarrow Fe_2O_3 + 8SO_2$

8. The most harmful form of water pollution affecting human health is

   A. An oil spill
   B. Heavy metals
   C. Waterborne diseases and pathogens
   D. Eutrophication
   E. Thermal pollution

9. Genetic pollution occurs when

   A. Speciation occurs.
   B. Mutations occur as cells replicate within an organism.
   C. Toxins are spread by wind.
   D. Artificial selection is used to select desired traits.
   E. There is an unintended spread of altered genetic information from genetically engineered organisms to natural organisms.

10. Which of the following toxins can produce birth defects and affect embryo development?

    A. Mutagens
    B. Teratogens
    C. Allergens
    D. Neurotoxins
    E. Carcinogens

11. Why can asbestos be lethal?

    A. Small inhaled fibers can get lodged in the lining of the lungs, which can cause the lungs to develop scar tissue and can ultimately lead to death.
    B. The gaseous form causes lungs to create acid to combat the invader, which causes the development of scar tissue and can ultimately lead to death.
    C. It is a mutagen.
    D. Asbestos fibers are inhaled and get lodged in the throat, causing asphyxiation.
    E. Asbestos is not lethal but can act as an allergen.

12. Which of the following is a common source of lead pollution today?

    A. The use of leaded gasoline
    B. Vehicle emissions
    C. Metal processing
    D. Acid precipitation
    E. Smog

13. When a factory uses water to help cool its operational processes and then releases this water into a local river, pollution can occur as which of the following?

    A. Carcinogens
    B. Pathogens
    C. Thermal pollution
    D. Heavy metal pollution
    E. Cold discharged water

Questions 14–15 refer to the following cost-benefit analysis curve.

Cost-Benefit Analysis Curve

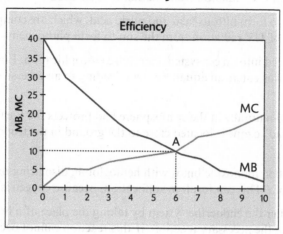

MB = marginal benefits   MC = marginal costs

14. Which is a valid reason why marginal costs exceeded marginal benefits?

    A. An increase occurred in the cost of production.
    B. There is potential for an increase in biodiversity.
    C. Profits are high.
    D. Prices are higher than marginal cost.
    E. It was pushed in this direction due to an increase in production.

15. At which point on the graph does maximal economic efficiency occur?

    A. On the line representing marginal costs
    B. On the line representing marginal benefits
    C. Where marginal costs exceed marginal benefits
    D. At point A
    E. Where marginal benefits exceed marginal costs

Answers

1. **B** Sulfur dioxide reacts with UV radiation from the sun to form industrial smog.

2. **C** Nitrogen dioxide reacts to form nitrous acid and nitric acid, which are components of acid precipitation. It also reacts with the heat of UV radiation from the sun to form photochemical smog.

3. **C** Excess nitrogen introduced into an ecosystem can cause eutrophication. Eutrophication occurs when excess nitrogen or phosphorus enters an aquatic system, leading to an excessive growth of phytoplankton, algae, and other plants.

4. **D** "Good" ozone is located naturally in the stratosphere and protects the Earth from harmful ultraviolet radiation from the sun. "Bad" ozone is located close to the ground in the troposphere and is the main component of smog.

5. **A** In the bloodstream, carbon monoxide binds with hemoglobin, displacing oxygen and inhibiting it from binding with the hemoglobin. This can result in suffocation, because oxygen is not circulating in the blood.

6. **D** Endocrine disruptors alter the endocrine system by taking the place of a hormone molecule, blocking the hormone, and impeding the necessary reaction. If this reaction cannot occur, the endocrine (hormone) system cannot function as necessary.

7. **C** Once sulfur is released into the atmosphere, it reacts with oxygen to form sulfur dioxide, which reacts with oxygen to form SO_3. Sulfur trioxide and water react to form sulfuric acid, which can fall as acid precipitation. The chemical reaction is as follows:

$$S + O_2 \rightarrow SO_2$$
$$2SO_2 + O_2 \rightarrow 2SO_3$$
$$SO_3 + H_2O \rightarrow H_2SO_4$$

8. **C** Waterborne diseases and pathogens bring health-related issues such as cholera, typhoid, hepatitis A, *E. coli*, dysentery, SARS, giardiasis, and many others. These diseases and pathogens are passed through water sources and are in higher abundance in unsanitary water. Often, fecal matter is the source of the contaminant. When consumed, or sometimes when a person comes in contact with the water, contamination occurs.

9. **E** When altered genetic material is unintentionally transported to neighboring areas via wind and pollination, the altered material can become part of the genetic makeup of local wildlife and other crops. This is genetic pollution.

10. **B** Teratogens are toxins that can affect embryo development, harm the fetus, or lead to death. When pregnant or breastfeeding, it is important for women to be aware of potential health threats from toxic substances.

11. **A** Small fibers of asbestos can get lodged in the lining of lungs. The lungs produce acid to try to get rid of the fibers, causing scarring of tissue and decreased lung function. This alteration of the lungs can lead to lung cancer.

12. **C** In the past, lead was used as an additive in gasoline, so it was emitted as a pollutant through car emissions. Due to its toxicity, leaded gasoline is no longer used, so the main source of lead is metal processing, including smelting, lead-acid battery manufacturers, and waste incinerators.

13. **C** When water is used as part of the cooling process in a factory, it gets heated due to the transfer of heat from the energy produced by the processes. This heat transfer increases the temperature of the water, so when the water is discharged into a local river, it creates thermal pollution, impacting the ecosystem and wildlife.

14. **A** The marginal costs curve continues to rise after equilibrium, meaning costs are increasing. Costs associated with the production process could be one reason why the overall costs increase. For example, the price of raw materials used in the production process could have increased or increased production could require specialized machinery.

15. **D** At point A, marginal costs and marginal benefits are at equilibrium, which is where economic efficiency is maximized.

Chapter 7

Global Change

With an increasing number of people inhabiting this planet, the atmosphere is experiencing rapid changes, which impacts all life. In this chapter, the focus is on global change, starting with the protective ozone layer and followed by global warming, climate change, and the greenhouse effect. Finally, the impacts on other species and biodiversity are presented, along with conservation efforts. Each of these components of the Earth has been altered by human activities. Although changes in the ozone, climate, and biodiversity all occur naturally, human involvement has increased the rate at which destruction and alteration is occurring.

Stratospheric Ozone

Formation of Stratospheric Ozone

Stratospheric ozone shields life on Earth from the sun's ultraviolet (UV) radiation. There are three forms of UV radiation: UVA (long wavelength), UVB (medium wavelength), and UVC (short wavelength). Ozone (O_3) is formed in the upper stratosphere by a photochemical reaction between an existing oxygen molecule (O_2) and an additional oxygen atom (O), with the catalyst of ultraviolet (UV) radiation. UVC, the strongest of the three types of UV radiation, has enough energy to **photolyze** (break apart with light) the oxygen molecule.

The UVC splits apart the oxygen molecule into atomic oxygen.	$O_2 + UVC \rightarrow O + O$
Atomic oxygen then reacts with the oxygen molecule to form ozone.	$O + O_2 \rightarrow O_3$

This is a reversible reaction. When UVC strikes the ozone molecule, atomic oxygen and molecular oxygen are formed. Atomic oxygen can react with an ozone molecule to form two oxygen molecules.

The UVC splits apart the ozone molecule into atomic oxygen and the oxygen molecule.	$O_3 + UVC \rightarrow O + O_2$
Atomic oxygen now reacts with an ozone molecule to form two oxygen molecules.	$O + O_3 \rightarrow 2\,O_2$

For millions of years, the formation and destruction of ozone remained balanced so that the amount of ozone in the atmosphere stays fairly constant. It filters out much of the UV radiation reaching to the Earth from the sun. Keeping the UV radiation relatively constant for millions of years, has allowed life to evolve on Earth that is equipped to handle this (and only this) level of UV radiation.

The layer of the Earth's atmosphere known as the **stratosphere** extends from about 6 miles to about 31 miles above the Earth's surface. The highest part of the stratosphere houses 97 percent to 99 percent of the atmosphere's ozone molecules; thus, it is often referred to as the **ozone layer.** The remaining small percentage of ozone in the ground-level atmospheric layer known as the **troposphere** is considered a pollutant. The majority of ozone is formed above the tropics near the equator where the sun is almost directly overhead most of the year. Ozone is produced above the temperate and polar regions, too, but in less volume and concentration. As you would expect, there are strong seasonal variations in the production of ozone (more in the summer months and less in the winter months).

Ozone does not necessarily remain in the area where it is produced. Air currents distribute the ozone away from the tropics toward the North Pole and South Pole. Generally, winds carry ozone toward the North Pole during the Northern Hemisphere's winter and toward the South Pole during the Southern Hemisphere's winter. Ozone above the poles builds slowly over time because, while little is generated in the polar regions, a correspondingly small amount is destroyed, so the ozone that moves in from more tropical regions accumulates. Ozone reaches its highest concentration and thickness during the spring. As the spring moves into summer, the ozone layer starts to thin, becoming its thinnest in the fall.

Ultraviolet (UV) Radiation

While all light is electromagnetic radiation, radiation comes in different wavelengths, frequencies, and energies. The higher the frequency and shorter the wavelength, the higher the energy. **Ultraviolet radiation (UV)** is light on the electromagnetic spectrum with wavelengths shorter than the minimum that the human eye is designed to see. However, some insects can see UV light. In fact, the sun emits many kinds of electromagnetic radiation we cannot see, including radio, microwave, infrared, ultraviolet, X-ray, and gamma radiations. The three most common bands of energy are **visible light, infrared,** and **ultraviolet.**

The three types of ultraviolet radiation (UV) are labeled by their wavelengths: **UVA** (long wavelength), **UVB** (medium), and **UVC** (short). UVA is not absorbed by ozone, and UVB is absorbed only partially by ozone, with some reaching the Earth's surface. UVC (short wavelength) is completely absorbed by ozone and normal oxygen. In the case of UVA and UVB, the more ozone, the more absorption. If there is less ozone, more of these types of radiation reach the Earth. Additional factors that affect how much radiation reaches the Earth include the amount of cloud cover and the angle at which the Earth faces the sun (which varies seasonally). The following table illustrates the amount of radiation that reaches the Earth's surface.

Types of UV Radiation			
	Wavelength	**How Much Reaches the Earth's Surface**	**Description**
UV-A	Long Wavelength (320 to 400 nm)	Most	UVA is closest to blue/violet in the visible light spectrum. UVA absorption through human skin plays an essential role in the formation of natural vitamin D and is also responsible for tanning. That said, overexposure can be harmful and cause sunburn and premature aging. Many species of birds, insects, and reptiles can see UVA.
UV-B	Medium Wavelength (290 to 320 nm)	About 5 percent	The power of UVB radiation can alter human DNA. Over-exposures also can cause "snow blindness" (photokeratitis), cataracts, immune deficiencies, and skin tumors. The strongest risk to human health of overexposure to UVB radiation is non-melanoma skin cancer. Many animals as well as humans are harmed if exposed to high doses of UVB radiation.
UV-C	Short Wavelength (100 to 290 nm)	None	UVC is found only in the stratosphere and is completely absorbed by the ozone. UVC radiation drives the reactions that both form and destroy ozone.

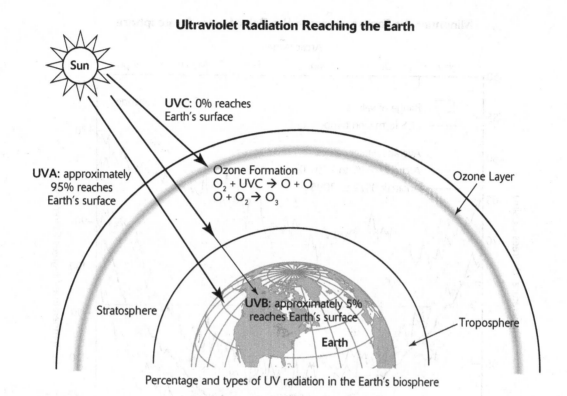

Ultraviolet Radiation Reaching the Earth

UVC: 0% reaches Earth's surface

UVA: approximately 95% reaches Earth's surface

Ozone Formation
$$O_2 + UVC \rightarrow O + O$$
$$O + O_2 \rightarrow O_3$$

Ozone Layer

Stratosphere

UVB: approximately 5% reaches Earth's surface

Troposphere

Earth

Percentage and types of UV radiation in the Earth's biosphere

Ozone Depletion

The ozone layer shields the Earth from the harmful effects of UV radiation. Ozone becomes depleted when the natural balance of production and destruction of ozone in the stratosphere is skewed toward destruction. Periodically occuring natural phenomena can create a temporary decrease of ozone. Of immediate importance are man-made chemical compounds released in the atmosphere that can cause ozone depletion. These compounds contain halogens (chlorine, bromine, iodine, and fluorine) and are known as **ozone-depleting substances,** such as chlorofluorcarbons (CFCs).

The global awareness and concern of ozone depletion started in 1985 with the discovery of a thinning of the ozone layer above the Antarctic by British scientists Joesph Farman, Brian Gardiner, and Jonathan Shanklin. Further research revealed that this thinning is twofold: First, overall levels of ozone in Antarctica have dropped 30 percent since the 1970s. This depletion continues at a rate of about 3 percent per year. The second depletion has been commonly described as the **ozone hole.** The ozone hole is not technically a "hole" devoid of ozone; it is an area of seasonal depletion over Antarctica that, once formed, tends to travel northward toward the equator and may linger over landmasses such as Australia, New Zealand, South America, and South Africa. When present, this ozone hole increases the UVB levels in affected areas by 3 percent to 10 percent, and in some years, by as much as 20 percent. The severe depletion of ozone above the Antarctic occurs because of special weather conditions. Very low temperature in the Antarctic winter months of below −78°C create ice clouds called **polar stratospheric clouds (PSCs).** Consolidation of greenhouse gases in these clouds helps drive ozone-depletion reactions. The more extremely cold days, the more PSCs and the larger that year's ozone hole will likely be.

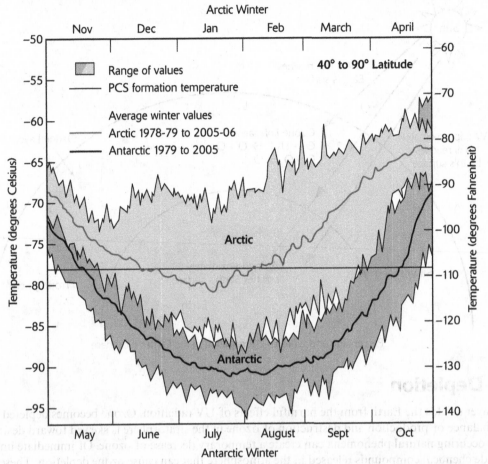

Minimum Air Temperatures in the Polar Lower Stratosphere

Source: National Oceanic and Atmospheric Administration

In 1988, a similar but less severe hole was found in the ozone layer above the Arctic, occurring between February and June. The Arctic hole caused an 11 percent to 38 percent ozone loss (as compared to the 50 percent seasonal loss in Antarctica). As the ozone hole breaks up, it may move and linger over North America, Europe, and Asia. However, because the hole is not yet as thin as that in Antarctica, the increase in UVB radiation will not be nearly as extreme, so the effect on humans and local ecosystems will be less dramatic.

Chlorofluorocarbons (CFCs) are the primary man-made compounds involved in the depletion of ozone. They have commonly been used as refrigerants in air conditioners, refrigerators, and aerosol propellants. CFCs also are used as cleaning solvents for electrical parts and in the manufacturing of insulation. Prior to the 1980s, at least one million tons of CFCs were manufactured for consumer use every year, and the production and distribution of CFCs was a billion-dollar industry. The largest sources of environmental CFCs were leaks from car air conditioners and aerosols used in spray paints, deodorants, hairspray products, and other aerosol cans. Today, the use of CFCs as propellants is forbidden in the United States and most developed countries due to the strong link between CFCs and ozone depletion.

How Do CFCs Destroy Ozone?

When CFCs are released into the atmosphere, they rise through the troposphere and into the stratosphere. UV radiation breaks down the CFC molecule, releasing atomic chlorine (Cl). The released chlorine then detaches an oxygen molecule from ozone (O_3) to create **chlorine monoxide** (ClO) and molecular oxygen (O_2). Then the chlorine monoxide further reacts with another ozone molecule to produce two molecular oxygen molecules, freeing the chlorine to react with another ozone molecule and continue the cycle of ozone destruction. One freed atomic chlorine molecule from CFCs can destroy over 100,000 ozone molecules. The CFC may take many years to reach the stratosphere, where it can stay for 20 to 120 years, depending upon the exact compound. CFCs were first manufactured in 1931 as safer substitutes for ammonia and sulfur dioxide, the toxic refrigerants used at the time. The CFCs currently in the stratosphere may have been released any time since the development of CFCs.

Bromine levels in the stratosphere are about 150 times less than chlorine levels, but bromine is 10 to 100 times more influential in destroying ozone. This is because there is no stable, binding form of bromine in the stratosphere, and it is very easily photolyzed so that almost all the atmospheric bromine remains in a form that reacts with ozone. Approximately 20 percent of observed ozone depletion is caused by bromine. Bromine compounds are found in halons that are often used in dry-cleaning and fire-suppression equipment. Bromomethane (commonly known as methyl bromide [CH_3Br]) is produced industrially and naturally. It was used extensively as a pesticide until it was phased out in most countries in the early 2000s due to its being recognized as an ozone-depleting chemical. Methyl bromide is also produced by phytoplankton in the world's oceans and is found in the smoke plumes of burning biomass.

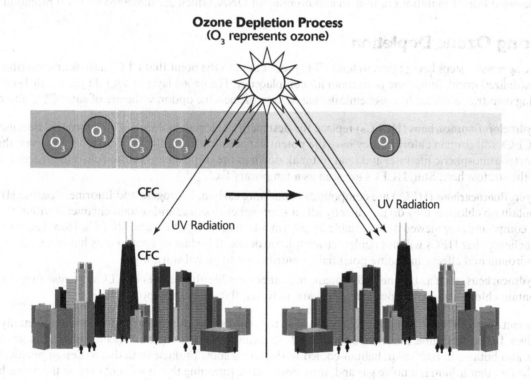

Ozone Depletion Process
(O_3 represents ozone)

Environmental Effects of Ozone Depletion

Ozone depletion and the resulting increase in ultraviolet radiation harm the Earth, humans, plants, and animals. Some of these adverse effects include the following:

- Changes in weather patterns
- Increased cooling of the stratosphere and warming of the troposphere due to less ozone to absorb the UV radiation, allowing more to reach the Earth's surface
- Increased formation of ground-level smog
- Increased damage to the skin (for example, sunburns)
- Increased UV radiation (UVB), which plays a major role in malignant melanoma skin cancer
- Increase of eye diseases (for example, cataracts)
- Increased damage to plants (including hardwood forests)
- Increased damage to agricultural crops, reducing food availability
- Increased harmful effects on animals, which may threaten the extinction of some species
- Disruption of productivity of ecosystem food chains, such as reduced growth of phytoplankton (tiny floating algae in the ocean, which are the base of the marine food chain)
- Weakening the efficiency of humans immune system
- Increased rate of mutations in human and nonhuman DNA, which are damaged by UVB radiation

Reducing Ozone Depletion

There are aggressive steps being taken to limit CFC production, to the point that CFCs have nearly vanished from the industrialized world. Still, there is no room for complacency. The ozone layer is not safe yet, partly because some developing countries continue to use chemicals that destroy ozone. One option is the use of safer CFC alternatives:

- **Hydroclorofluorocarbons (HCFCs)** replace the destructive chlorine molecule with hydrogen. Because HCFCs still contain chlorine, they have the potential to react with stratospheric ozone. However, they have shorter atmospheric lifetimes and tend to break down in the troposphere before delivering reactive chlorine to the stratosphere. Still, HCFCs are seen as a temporary fix.
- **Hydrofluorocarbons (HFCs)** are compounds containing carbon, hydrogen, and fluorine. Because HFCs contain no chlorine, they do not directly affect stratospheric ozone, and certain chemicals within this class of compounds are viewed as acceptable long-term alternatives to CFCs and HCFCs. However, though it is believed that HFCs will not deplete stratospheric ozone, this class of compounds has other adverse environmental effects, including potentially contributing to global warming.
- **Hydrocarbons,** such as butane and propane are other possible alternatives to CFCs because they do not contain chlorine and are ozone safe. They are, however, flammable and poisonous.

Replacements for CFCs, HCFCs, and HFCs continue to be investigated in the search for environmentally safe alternatives. In the meantime, alternative compounds that can be used as coolants include helium, ammonia, propane, and butane. In particular, helium-cooled refrigerators show promise both due to design practicality and to the fact that helium is a noble gas and, thus, nonreactive (meaning that it will not deplete the ozone layer).

Amendments to the **Clean Air Act** include requirements for the disposal of old refrigerators and air-conditioner units and may require that older units be modified to use newer, environmentally safer coolants. Home air conditioners are designed to have a lifetime of 20 years or more, so many older units still use the ozone-depleting Freon (R12). New products continue to be developed that are less harmful to the stratospheric ozone layer and less harmful to the environment.

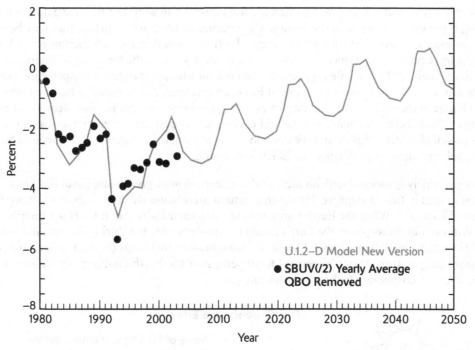

Percent of Ozone Change (50°N–50°S) Since 1980 and Projected to 2050

U.1.2–D Model New Version

● SBUV(/2) Yearly Average QBO Removed

Source: Environmental Protection Agency

Relevant Laws and Treaties

There are many laws and treaties pertaining to the cleanliness and safety of the air and to the protection of Earth's atmosphere and ozone layer. Those relating to ozone depletion are the Clean Air Act and Montreal Protocol.

- **United States Clean Air Act (amended in 1990):** The United States signed the Montreal Protocol in 1987, and the 1990 amendments to the Clean Air Act contained provisions for implementing the protocol. The Clean Air Act mandated that governments reduce smog and air pollution. It was supposed to curb three major threats to the nation's environment and to the health of millions of Americans: acid rain, urban air pollution, and toxic air emissions.

- **Montreal Protocol (1987):** The Montreal Protocol was a ground-breaking, international treaty signed by several countries in 1987 that aimed to protect stratospheric ozone by reducing and phasing out the production of ozone-destroying compounds used in refrigeration, aerosols, and foam, most notably CFCs. The protocol projected that the recovery of the ozone would return to pre-1980 levels as early as 2050; however, contributing factors such as greenhouse gases make this estimate less certain. The treaty has been modified seven times since its origination and continues to emphasize the importance of a total phase-out of CFCs. Since the protocol came into effect, the atmospheric concentrations of CFCs and related hydrocarbons have either leveled or decreased. The Montreal Protocol has been called the most successful international environmental agreement in history.

Global Warming and Climate Change

The terms *global warming* and *climate change* often are used interchangeably, but they have different meanings. **Global warming** is the steady increase in the average temperature of the Earth's surface that may be caused by man-made greenhouse emissions, which lead to increased infrared and thermal radiation near the Earth's surface. Global warming has been observed since the 1980s and continues to be at the forefront of international environmental research and debate. This debate is generally centered on whether the steady temperature increase of the Earth's surface is a natural occurrence or whether it has been accelerated as a result of human activity. **Climate change** is any change in the state of the climate (for example, temperature) that persists steadily for many years—decades or longer. Global climate change is a natural process and is best illustrated by the five known ice ages. Questions about global climate change and the contributions of human activities will continue to be discussed and evaluated, but regardless of its origins, the Earth is warming.

Global warming is widely associated with an increased concentration of **greenhouse gases** that soak up infrared radiation and trap heat in the atmosphere. However, a **natural greenhouse effect** is necessary to keep the Earth's climate warm and habitable. When the Earth's atmosphere traps solar radiation, it heats up, distributing this heat to the Earth. Without our atmosphere, the Earth would be uninhabitably hot during the day and uninhabitably cold at night. Thus, the atmosphere is much like an insulting blanket that traps the heat to keep the planet at a relatively constant temperature. About 80 percent to 90 percent of the Earth's natural greenhouse effect is due to water vapor in the atmosphere, which is a greenhouse gas.

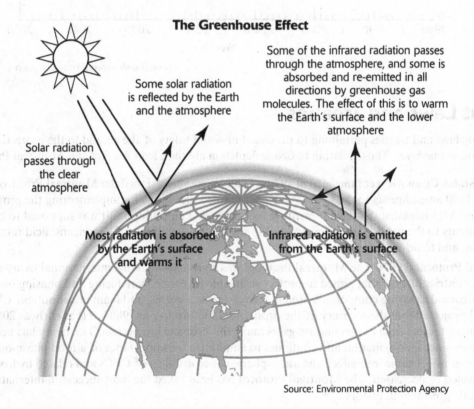

Source: Environmental Protection Agency

Other gases found naturally in the atmosphere also are considered greenhouse gases, insulating and acting as positive factors in the atmosphere in moderate concentrations and having a negative impact at increasing concentrations. Here are some of the most prominent of the greenhouse gases:

- **Carbon dioxide (CO_2)** is the most prominent greenhouse gas in the Earth's atmosphere. The primary sources of CO_2 are the burning of fossil fuels, decomposition, deforestation, and cellular respiration. This means that burning fires, motor vehicles, and smokestacks of factories that burns coal all emit carbon dioxide. Without carbon dioxide in the air, the Earth would be very cold. Carbon dioxide can spend an average of 50 to 100 years (or more) in the troposphere.

- **Carbon tetrachloride (CCl_4)** was primarily used in the production of cleaning fluids, especially in the manufacture of military airplanes and spacecrafts. It has an average time in the troposphere of about 50 years.

- **Chlorofluorocarbons (CFCs)** spend a relatively short 15 years in the troposphere but a much longer time in the stratosphere, where they damage ozone (as previously discussed). Historically, the primary sources of CFCs included coolants used in air conditioners and refrigerators, foam and insulation production, and aerosol spray cans. For the most part, these sources have been eliminated or are in the process of being eliminated.

- **Halons** are used in fire suppression and dry-cleaning supplies. Halons also are found naturally in the smoke plumes of burning biomass and in phytoplankton in the world's oceans. The relative warming effects of halons is 6,000 times that of carbon dioxide.

- **Hydrochlorofluorocarbons (HCFCs)** are modified CFCs, having fewer chlorine atoms and are considered less dangerous than CFCs. HCFCs tend to stay in the troposphere longer than CFCs. HCFCs are used as replacement coolants in air conditioners and refrigerators and in foam and insulation production.

- **Hydrofluorocarbons (HFCs)** are modified CFCs, having no chlorine atoms. HFCs like HCFCs tend to stay in the troposphere longer than CFCs—in the case of HFCs, 15 to 400 years. HFCs are used as coolants in air conditioners and refrigerators and in production of foam and insulation. HFCs tend to be less effective than CFCs as coolants.

- **Methane** is a naturally occurring gas with a lifespan of approximately 15 years in the troposphere and a warming factor of 25 times that of carbon dioxide. There are many sources of methane, including the production of rice, cattle, and coal, as well as natural gas leaks, especially during the transporting of natural gas in pipelines. Interestingly, organisms currently frozen in permafrost produce methane if thawed, and as the tundra melts due to global warming, these organisms will begin to contribute their methane, increasing the rate of warming.

- **Nitrous oxide (N_2O)** can stay in the troposphere for about 115 years. Its relative warming potential is 300 times greater than carbon dioxide. The sources of nitrous oxide include the burning of fossil fuels, livestock waste, fertilizers, and the manufacturing of plastics.

- **Sulfur hexafluoride (SF_6)** is used largely in heavy industry to insulate high-voltage equipment and to assist in the manufacture of cable cooling systems. It is used as a replacement for the highly carcinogenic pollutant PCBs. Of the ten greenhouse gases described here, it has the longest potential time in the troposphere at 3,200 years and the highest relative warming potential (24,000 times that of carbon dioxide).

- **Water vapor** concentrations fluctuate by geographic regions, but human activity does not significantly affect water vapor concentrations except in local areas of large agricultural irrigation. Although as temperatures increase on the planet, more water evaporates and can cause additional water vapor to rise into the atmosphere. Water vapor is naturally occurring.

The **man-made greenhouse effect** is the process by which manmade, "greenhouse" gases are released into atmosphere, where they act like an insulating blanket, trapping heat in the troposphere that would otherwise reflect into space. The majority of the scientific community believes that human activities contribute to global warming, but the topic is widely debated, partly due to the fact that many businesses produce greenhouse gases and reducing the emission of these gases costs money. Most of the greenhouse effect takes place in the troposphere, where levels of several greenhouse gases have increased since large-scale industrialization began 150 years ago. Carbon dioxide is increasing due to the burning of fossil fuels and deforestation. Nitric oxide is increasing due to the burning of fossil fuels. Part of the methane increase is due to the decomposition of organic material in the permafrost, increased cattle production, and the melting of methyl hydrates as ocean temperatures rise (scientists are searching for additional causes of increased methane). CFCs were not manufactured until the 1930s so all atmospheric CFCs are human-made.

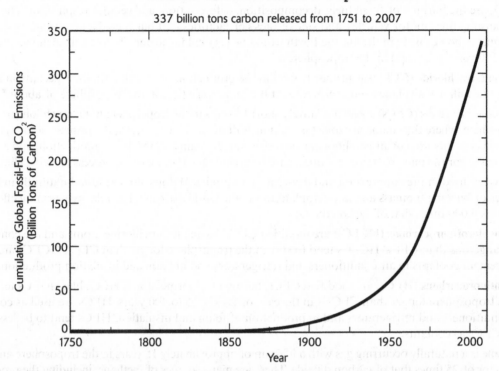

Cumulative Global Fossil-Fuel CO₂ Emissions

337 billion tons carbon released from 1751 to 2007

Source: Boden, T.A., G. Marland, and R.J. Andres. 2010. Global, Regional, and National Fossil-Fuel CO₂ Emissions. Carbon Dioxide Information Analysis Center, Oak Ridge National Laboratory, U.S. Department of Energy, Oak Ridge, Tenn., U.S.A. doi 10.3334/CDIAC/00001_V2010

The natural concentration of carbon dioxide in the Earth's atmosphere is constantly changing due to seasonal variations. Plants take in carbon dioxide for photosynthesis and then release it during cellular respiration and decomposition. The world's oceans absorb slightly more than they release. This natural waxing and waning of carbon dioxide concentrations is known as the **carbon cycle.** However, humans have altered the carbon cycle by contributing excess carbon dioxide from the burning of fossil fuels in power plants and for transportation, excessive deforestation and through other carbon-dioxide-producing activities. Plants and the world's oceans can absorb some of this excess, but the imbalance between emissions and absorption leads to a net increase in atmospheric CO_2 over time. The amount of carbon dioxide in the atmosphere has increased almost 39 percent since 1750, shortly before the beginning of the Industrial Revolution (see the following table).

Increase in Greenhouse Gases				
Greenhouse Gas	**Preindustrial Levels (ppm)**	**Current Level (ppm)**	**Increase Since 1750 (ppm)**	**Percent Increase**
Carbon dioxide	280	388	108	38.6
Methane	700	1,745	1,045	149.3
Nitric oxide	270	314	44	16.3
CFCs	0*	533	533	

* CFCs were first manufactured in 1931.

One factor accelerating the amount of carbon dioxide that humans add to the atmosphere is the increased contributions of developing nations, especially China and India. As these countries undergo industrialization, they burn more fossil fuels, especially in coal-burning power plants (though many newer coal power plants are somewhat cleaner than the older designs). The overall increase of CO_2 emissions between 2003 and 2008 was over 30 percent for the world and over 61 percent for China. The following table shows the change in coal production from 2003 to 2008 for the larger coal producers. To date, humans have developed no way to successfully capture carbon dioxide once it is emitted into the atmosphere.

Production of Coal (in million tonnes, 1 tonne = 1,000 kg)					
	2003	2008	Change	% Change	Reserves (years)
World	5,187.6	6781.2	1,593.6	30.7	142
China	1,722	2782	1,060	61.6	41
United States	972.2	1062.8	90.5	9.3	224
European Union	638	587.7	−50.3	−7.9	51
India	375.4	521.7	146.3	39	114

Impacts and Consequences of Global Warming

Atmospheric levels of carbon dioxide (CO_2) have increased steadily since the Industrial Revolution and continue to rise at a pace consistent with the steady increase of the global economy. Historically, natural climate changes have caused large-scale geographical shifts in weather patterns and in the habitats of all living organisms. However, the current pace of global climate change is unprecedented. If greenhouse gases continue on pace to double in the next 65 years, the global temperature could rise at least 1°C to 5°C. If this rise continues into the next century, the global average temperature may reach higher values than have occurred in the last million years. This rapid environmental change can cause glaciers to melt, surface temperature changes, alteration of weather patterns, rising sea levels, changes in biodiversity, and the extinction of species.

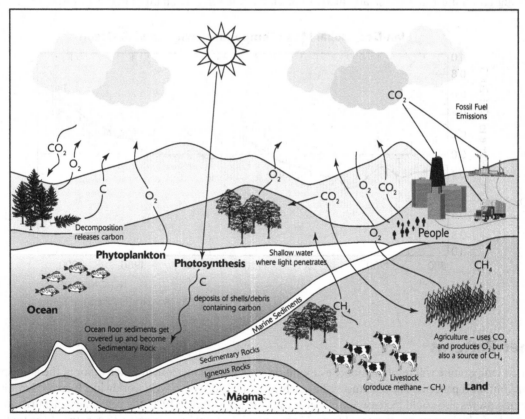

Source: NASA

Global Carbon Cycle

Oceans

Carbon dioxide reacts with water in a reversible reaction to form carbonic acid (H_2CO_3). As the carbon dioxide increases in the atmosphere, the ocean absorbs more carbon dioxide, and more carbonic acid is formed, lowering the pH of seawater. This affects all the living organisms in the world's oceans, both plant and animal.

Temperature

Determining changes in the Earth's temperature is difficult because accurate temperature data only dates back to about 1850. One way to measure historic air temperatures is to study ice cores. Ice core samples are often collected on ice sheets in Antarctica, in Greenland, or on glaciers found in higher elevations. As ice forms, it traps gases found in the atmosphere, allowing analysis of historic levels of atmospheric gases. Collected ice core samples range from just a few years old, to as old as 800,000 years. Analysis of these samples shows that historic increases in air temperature have averaged less than 2°C per 1,000 years. However, since the Industrial Revolution, we've seen a dramatic increase in the concentration of greenhouse gases in the Earth's atmosphere. And since the Industrial Revolution, the average air temperature on Earth has increase between 3°C and 5°C. The temperature increase in the past 260 years is double the amount we have historically seen in any 1,000-year period.

There are many possible consequences of higher air temperatures, including changes in weather patterns, a decrease in glaciers and polar ice caps, and rising sea levels. Additionally, as the polar regions warm, there will be an increase in greenhouse gases released from organisms currently frozen in permafrost and from the decomposition of organic matter currently preserved in permafrost. In ocean water, recent studies show that CO_2 dissolved in the water is released into the atmosphere as the oceans warm. This action is similar to the release of carbon dioxide when opening a bottle of warm soda.

The following graph illustrates the steady increase of global temperature changes in the atmosphere.

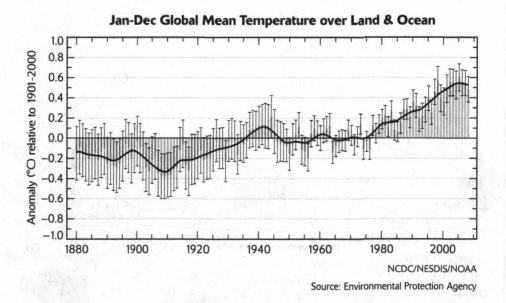

Jan-Dec Global Mean Temperature over Land & Ocean

NCDC/NESDIS/NOAA

Source: Environmental Protection Agency

Weather Patterns

An increased temperature will result in higher evaporation rates and an increase in water vapor in the atmosphere, altering precipitation patterns. These changes ultimately alter the hydrologic cycle worldwide. Increased evaporation and sea temperatures also could increase the frequency of hurricanes. Since 1970, the percentage of hurricanes that are category 4 or 5 hurricanes has increased from 20 percent of the total hurricanes to 35 percent of the total hurricanes. Increased rainfall in areas degraded by deforestation and plowing will lead to an increase in soil erosion, which may lead to decreased land productivity and, as sediment washes into water sources, decreased productivity in both freshwater and saltwater ecosystems. Other areas may see an increase in desertification and a loss of biodiversity.

Rise in Sea Level

The most obvious contribution to rising sea levels due to global warming is from the melting of ice, most notably in the polar regions. Additionally, warmer water expands, and with higher temperatures, the existing ocean waters would take up more space. Increased hurricanes also could cause seasonal swelling of the oceans. Oceans cover approximately 70 percent of the Earth's surface, and the sea level is currently rising at a rate of $1/10$ inch per year. Due to the CO_2 already in the atmosphere, the sea level is projected to continue rising for many centuries.

The impacts of a rising sea level include loss of coastal ecosystems, flooding of cities (such as New Orleans and Venice), disappearing islands, disappearing wetlands, displacement of coastal inhabitants, and increased vulnerability to storm surges because coral reefs and barrier islands, which protect the coastland, may be submerged. Some of these effects could be magnified if the frequency of severe storms increases. Bangladesh, for example, is an impoverished nation that is projected to lose 17.5 percent of its land if the sea level rises 40 inches. Louisiana would lose its freshwater wetlands. Economic challenges of a rising sea include decreased tourism and reduced local agriculture.

El Niño and La Niña

El Niño and La Niña patterns also have been altered by global climate change. El Niño events produce increased warming of the Pacific Ocean every two to seven years, while La Niña events produce cooling of surface waters near the equatorial region of the Pacific Ocean every two to seven years. During the last several decades, the frequency of El Niño events has increased while the frequency of La Niña has decreased. Studies of historic data show that the recent increase in the El Niño variation is most likely linked to global warming. However, these cycles are still not fully understood, so future changes in these cycles are difficult to predict. For example, stronger El Niño events may occur in the early stages of global warming but may become weaker as the lower layers of the ocean get warmer. Some scientists believe these patterns will stabilize on their own.

Melting Glaciers

Over time, in areas where more snow falls than melts, the accumulation of snow compresses the lower layers into glacial ice. This ice slowly slides toward lower elevations like an ice river, and at a certain elevation, the ice starts to melt. Many people worldwide depend upon melting glaciers for survival. However the warming Earth means that over the past century, Earth's glaciers have increased their melt rate, decreasing in total land coverage by 50 percent. Glacial melting in areas unaccustomed to water causes landslides, flash flooding, and increased variation of water flows into rivers. Much of Asia relies on the waters from seasonal melting of the glaciers in the Himalayan Mountains, where global warming has increased the overall flow of water, which has, in turn, increased flooding and disease. Once the source glaciers are depleted, it is expected that the flow of water to much of Asia will decrease, leading to droughts and decreased potential to produce hydroelectric power.

Current estimates put the number of people living within 1 vertical meter of the coastline at about 150 million, and current estimates predict a rise in sea level of between 0.5 and 1.5 meters by the end of the century. The resulting worldwide flooding of islands and coastal areas will force these 150 million people to relocate.

Since the end of the last ice age 18,000 years ago, the sea level has risen 122 meters, most of that in the first 15,000 years. It is estimated that the rate of ocean rise for the 3,000 years prior to the Industrial Revolution had slowed to about 0.2 mm per year. Since the Industrial Revolution, the pace of ocean rise has increased to about 3 mm per year.

If all the glaciers, the ice sheets, and the polar ice cap melted in the Northern Hemisphere, combined with the thermal expansion of water, the sea level would rise 6.5 to 7.5 meters. If the ice cap and ice sheets in Antarctica melted, the sea level would rise another 61 meters. (However, extreme melting in Antarctica is unlikely as the mean air temperature of –37°C is still much below the melting point of water at 0°C.)

Biodiversity

Humans are not the only organisms affected by global warming. A decrease in polar ice in the Northern Hemisphere has decreased both the food supply and the hunting areas of polar bears. Plants and animals have moved their ranges towards the poles. Grasses have become established in Antarctica for the first time. Bird migration patterns have changed, with migrations starting an average of two days earlier per decade. As the thermal temperature of the water increases, phytoplankton, krill, and fish populations have been affected, changing population size and location. It is interesting to note that many migratory patterns have evolved with codependence on other species. For example, a migratory bird population may depend on the timing of seasonal food sources along its route. With global climate change, many of these coevolved behaviors are altered. Birds may arrive to find plant or animal food sources nonexistent, which, in turn, can impact reproduction and offspring. Current research is exploring the ways in which interdependent populations are likely to be affected by continuing climate change.

Global warming and the resultant rise in sea levels will affect not only land ecosystems, but also sea life. Corals are dependent on a narrow temperature range for survival and are sensitive to temperate variations. Therefore, small increases in temperature can kill corals. In recent years, we have seen this happen, as corals die in warmed seas. Also, increasing acidification of the oceans due to changing CO_2 concentrations can harm and kill coral. Other marine life may be forced to migrate northward or southward to find the same water temperature. These displaced animals may find that, while their migration allows them to keep a constant water temperature, many of the habitats and food sources on which they depend are scarce.

Sea water circulation patterns also are disturbed by global warming. Cold water moves along the sea floor toward the equator, and warm water around the equator moves toward the poles across the surface of the ocean. This is known as *thermohaline circulation*. One result of this circulation process is the delivery of oxygenated water to the sea floor and nutrient-rich waters to the surface. Without this circulation, oxygen levels in the deeper parts of the ocean and on the sea floor would be depleted and nutrient upwellings on the surface would decrease.

Fish, such as salmon, are also sensitive to water temperature. During the summer, when the water is warm, salmon have a higher metabolic rate. During the winter months, their metabolism slows down, an adaptation that allows them to survive longer on less food (like a bear's hibernation when food is scarce). With global warming and increased water temperatures, salmon would be forced to maintain a higher metabolic rate, even in the winter months of food shortage. Many salmon would starve.

Reducing Climate Change

In the 1990s, CO_2 emissions increased 1.3 percent per year, but with the current rate of global growth and industrialization, scientists predict that the annual growth rate of CO_2 emissions is likely to climb to approximately 1.9 percent to 2.5 percent annually. According to the EPA, total emissions from the developing world are expected to exceed those from the developed world by the year 2015. Asia is leading the way in the growth rate of CO_2 emissions, with an increase in a consumer-oriented economic middle class and new coal power plants. The rise in carbon dioxide is also due to the inability of natural **carbon sinks** such as plants and oceans to absorb carbon dioxide at the rate at which it is being produced.

This means that before we can achieve a true reduction in carbon dioxide levels, we have to first stabilize the rate of the current emissions *increase*. The three gases specifically targeted for stabilization and then reduction are carbon dioxide, methane, and nitrous oxide.

Since cars currently produce almost 30 percent of carbon dioxide emissions in the United States, increasing efficiency measured in miles per gallon will help decrease emissions. Another way to reduce carbon dioxide emissions is switching electricity production from fossil-fuel-based power plants to renewable sources such as wind, solar, and hydroelectric. Methane emissions can be reduced by repairing leaks in pipelines and by reducing the world dependency on rice and livestock production. Other ideas to reduce global warming include supporting laws, treaties, and protocols that reduce the emissions of greenhouse gases, and slowing down the rate of deforestation while encouraging the replanting of forests.

Laws and Treaties

Enacted by the United Nations Framework Convention on Climate Change, the goal of the **Kyoto Protocol (1997)** is to achieve stabilization of greenhouse-gas concentrations in the atmosphere at a level that would prevent climate change. The protocol was adopted in 1997 and signed by 187 nations. Under the protocol, 39 industrialized countries and the European Union are committed to the reduction of four greenhouse gases (carbon dioxide, methane, nitrous oxide, and sulfur hexafluoride), along with two groups of gases (hydrofluorocarbons and perfluorocarbons). They agreed to a reduction of their greenhouse gas emissions by 5.2 percent from 1990 levels. The United States is one of the few countries in the world that has not signed the Kyoto Protocol.

Loss of Biodiversity

Massive Extinctions from Human Activity

Biodiversity is the variety of organisms found within a specific geographic area. Increased biodiversity allows an ecosystem to remain stabile when pressured. A variety of species, for example, provides ecosystems and humans with many benefits and services.

In addition to diversity of species, biodiversity includes genetic diversity within any single species. For example, wild cheetahs have very low gene diversity, so they may be at risk for population decimation by one kind of pathogen. As each species in an ecosystem finds its role in a community, its **niche,** then a complex ecosystem structure is formed. This promotes ecosystem stability and provides a variety of food sources and habitat for flora and fauna. An example of biodiversity is found in Yosemite National Park, which is home to one-third of all the bird species represented in North America.

As humans have interfered with ecosystems, we have caused biodiversity to decline. The factors that make an area's biodiversity likely to decline are represented by the acronym HIPPCO, used by many conservation biologists. HIPPCO stands for **H**abitat destruction, degradation, and fragmentation; **I**nvasive species (nonnative, exotic); **P**opulation and resource use increases; **P**ollution; **C**limate change; and **O**verexploitation.

Issues Related to Loss of Biodiversity

Issues related to loss of biodiversity as described by the World Resource Institute (2005) are linked to human activity:
- Overuse and overexploitation
- Pollution and sedimentation
- Introduced species
- Endangered and extinct species
- Habitat loss

Losses Due to Overuse and Overexploitation

Overexploitation of species creates loss of biodiversity. Among the most common overused and overexploited groups of species are marine fish and invertebrates. Overexploitation, including overfishing and over-harvesting, has resulted in 75 percent of the world's marine species being depleted. Several species—including cod off Newfoundland in Canada, anchovy off the coast of Peru, sole in the Irish Sea, and deep-sea fish such as orange roughy and sablefish—have been depleted to such an extent that they are no longer a viable food or economic resource. Nearly 100 million tons of fish and shellfish are removed from the world's oceans every year. As the world's population grows and as diets increasingly shift from beef and pork to more fish and shellfish, even more fish and shellfish will be removed. Overfishing also impacts species, such as dolphins and seals, which are caught unintentionally as part of netting or long-lining techniques. So-called **bycatch** is thrown away when fish are harvested. For every pound of shrimp catch, over 5 pounds of bycatch is discarded. The loss of marine life impacts the world's coastal populations (nearly 2 billion people), many of whom depend upon marine life for food and other products.

Aquatic species are not alone in their growing use. Worldwide beef consumption doubled from 1950 to 2000, from approximately 44 pounds per capita to nearly 88 pounds per capita. The acreage needed to grow beef is immense. Land is needed to grow food (usually corn) to feed the cattle, and land is needed to house the cattle until they are taken to market. Many corporations that use beef in their fast-food restaurants have cut down large areas of trees in the tropical rain forest to meet the needs of beef production.

Losses Due to Pollution

Pollution comes in five primary forms: air, soil, water, noise, and light. Humans release pollutants into the Earth's atmosphere, soil, or natural water systems, causing degradation in both local areas and sources to which pollution can be transported. Light and noise pollution can interfere with the natural cycles of species and adversely affect behavior. A sixth form of pollution, genetic pollution, is still under investigation.

Pollutants can have many negative affects on **animal species:** interfering with metabolic and endocrine functions, impairing development, shortening life spans, and compromising immune systems. Pollutants also can alter species' reproductive function, causing changes in mating behaviors, genetically affecting offspring, or causing an organism to become sterile. Pollution is often a contributing factor in the decline or ultimate extinction of a species. The loss of one species then has a ripple effect throughout an ecosystem.

There are many mechanisms by which pollutants enter species: through the air they breathe, the water they drink, the food they digest, or through their skin percutaneously. Marine fish and other aquatic species are especially defenseless when exposed to pollutants in the water. Air pollutants include carbon monoxide, sulfur dioxide, and oxides of nitrogen. Water and soil pollutants include heavy metals, pesticide and herbicide compounds, and the thermal pollution of man-made heat sources.

Plant species also can be adversely affected by pollutants. **Lichen** is especially fragile and, thus, susceptible to destruction by **air pollutants.** Therefore, the presence of lichen is often a good indicator of clean air. Air pollutants also can cause damage to the water and soil, frequently in the form of adjusting the pH level. When an air pollutant, such as sulfuric acid, combines with the water droplets that make up clouds, the water droplets become acidic. **Acid rain** causes harm to living organisms. When those droplets fall to the ground as rain or snow, the acidity of the water can have damaging effects on plants and the environment. Acid rain can destroy leaves on plants (reducing photosynthesis) and trees, and can harm animals, fish, and other wildlife. When acid rain penetrates into the soil, it can change soil chemistry, making it unfit for many living things that rely on soil as a habitat or for nutrition. Acidified soil can leach out nutrients that plants need for their development, growth, or maintenance. Plants exposed to pollutants can deteriorate from disease and insect infiltration.

Light pollution (luminous pollution) is excessive artificial lighting of the type often seen in any major industrialized city. This artificial lighting interferes with animal species that depend on natural lighting phenomena (such as the stars and moon) to find their way in the night. Lights may interfere with mating and nesting of species, migration patterns, and hunting for food. In some satellite photos of sections of the Earth at night, it is difficult to identify specific cities due to the overall glow of light pollution—especially in Europe, the east and west coasts of the United States, Japan, China, and India.

Noise pollution is another pollutant that is especially prevalent in urban areas. Noise pollution adversely affects the health and lives of millions of people and is related to sleep disruption, hearing loss, high blood pressure, and stress-related illnesses. The constant drone of vehicles on the roads, the flight of airplanes in and out of airports, manufacturers, power plants, and others man-made sources produce noises that can impair animal species. In animals, noise can cause stress, alter the delicate balance of detection and avoidance of predators and prey, and interfere with animals' use of sounds in communication and reproduction.

Genetic pollution is a term popularized by environmentalist Jeremy Rifkin in his 1998 book *The Biotech Century.* Biologists have used the term to describe the flow of genes from two genetically distinct organisms resulting in a genetically modified organism (GMO). For example, the flow of genes from domestic, feral, nonnative, and invasive species into wild, native species. Today, the term *genetic pollution* is associated with the genetic exchange of undesirable genes from GMOs to wild native species. In addition, genetic pollution often refers to crops and aquaculture. Several GMO animal products have been developed, but none has yet been approved for market by the U.S. Food and Drug Administration (FDA).

Losses Due to Introduced Species

Introduced species originate in one location and end up in another, either by chance or by human intervention. There are several words used to describe introduced species including *nonnative, invasive, alien,* and *exotic.* There are more than 4,500 *nonnative* species in North America. *Invasive* species infest an area and can do harm to it. They may kill other species, drive them out of the area, or cause economic damage for humans. Examples of invasive species include kudzu, zebra mussels, the Mediterranean fruit fly, and sudden oak death. The spread of invasive species has caused widespread damage to native habitats, including the elimination of native species. Invasive species have interfered with crop production, causing losses of crops and money.

There are many ways an invasive species can be transported to new areas. Some are left over from farming and animal raising (such as feral pigs), others arrive by accident (for example, the zebra mussel in the ballast water of ships), and some are introduced intentionally to provide a service but then grow out of control (such as kudzu in the southeastern United States and cane toads in Australia). Their adverse effects are many. The zebra mussel can clog the openings to water intakes for water filtration plants. Kudzu, sometimes referred to as "the vine that ate the South," was planted along freeways to prevent erosion. Unfortunately, kudzu can grow up to 3 feet in a single day, and since there are no known organisms that keep kudzu in check in its invasive habitat, it has grown rampant. Invasive species' case studies are further discussed in Appendix B.

Losses Due to Endangered and Extinct Species

An **endangered species** is a population of organisms that is at risk of becoming extinct. Many species become endangered due to habitat loss, changes in environment, hunting/poaching, introduction of a nonnative species, disease, pollution, or a combination of factors. Many countries have established their own criteria for labeling a species "endangered." In the United States, these criteria are put forth in the Endangered Species Act, which describes two categories of danger:

- **Endangered:** Plants and animals that are so rare that they are in danger of becoming extinct.
- **Threatened:** Plants and animals that are projected to become endangered within the foreseeable future.

The International Union for Conservation of Nature (IUCN) was established to promote natural resource conservation. The IUCN has developed its Red List, which has three broad categories and smaller breakdowns within those categories. The categories are:

- **Extinct**
  - Extinct: The last remaining member of the species has died or is presumed to have died.
  - Extinct in the wild: Only captive individuals of the population remain; no individuals of the species are known to live in the wild.
- **Threatened**
  - Critically endangered: The species faces an extreme risk of becoming extinct.
  - Endangered: The species faces a high risk of extinction in the near future.
  - Vulnerable: The species faces a high risk of extinction in the medium term.
- **At Low Risk**
  - Near threatened: The species may be considered threatened in the near future.
  - Least concern: There is no immediate threat to the survival of the species.

Three hundred known plant and animal species have gone extinct in North America since European colonization. Approximately 750 North American plants and 1,200 animals are listed as endangered, with another 3,000 species proposed for listing. Only a few species have been removed from the list. As of May 2007, the populations of endangered species have increased from historic lows and several species that were once endangered have been removed from the list, while others have been moved from endangered to threatened. Five species had recovered and been removed from the list entirely, including bald eagles, peregrine falcons, American alligators, gray whales, and grizzly bears. However, as of 2007, seven species had also been removed from the list after becoming extinct, including Florida's dusky seaside sparrow, the Santa Barbara song sparrow, the Tecopa pupfish, the Sampson's pearly mussel, the blue pike, the longjaw cisco, and the Amistad gambusia.

Losses Due to Habitat Destruction

According to researchers, the greatest threat to species is the loss, degradation, and fragmentation of habitats. Perhaps the greatest loss is the deforestation of the tropical areas. Large areas of forest have been cut down for their timber, or to plant grasses and corn for cattle production. Additionally, the destruction and degradation of coral reefs resulting especially from harvesting for home aquariums and coral bleaching has created devastating habitat loss. The draining and filling of the world's coastal wetlands including mangrove swamps and saltwater marshes has resulted in an over 50 percent loss of these habitats. Many countries' inland wetlands have experienced a loss of more than 80 percent.

Large areas of grasslands have been plowed to grow food for animal and human consumption, to house large farms to raise cattle and other farm animals, and, most recently, for the development of large cities. These grasslands include the prairie in the United States, the pampas in Argentina, the steppes of Eurasia, and the veldt in Africa. Less than 1 percent of the original prairie is left in the United States.

Pollution of land and water also can result in habitat destruction. And this destruction is not limited to the areas in which pollution first occurs. For example, cities have storm drains that collect pollutants from a variety of sources, including oils and other fluids from cars; feces from pets; fertilizers from our yards, playing fields, and golf courses; and trash such as plastic bottles and bags. These pollutants flow downstream to the oceans, destroying habitats and harming species along the way.

Historically, the lack of development in the majority of the Earth's tropical biomes has kept them relatively safe from habitat destruction (in comparison with the greater habitat destruction born of development in temperate biomes in the United States, Canada, most of Europe, Japan, and elsewhere). However, the recent increase in development in tropical biomes has resulted in the accelerated habitat destruction in these regions.

Island species are especially vulnerable, because they have no place to go when their habitat is destroyed, degraded, or fragmented, and many face extinction as the island is developed. Many of those species are endemic to their island (meaning, they are found nowhere else on Earth).

Maintenance through Conservation

As described in *Sustaining the Earth: An Integrated Approach,* by G. Tyler Miller and Scott Spoolman, there are two major approaches to maintaining and protecting wildlife:

- **Species approach:** Protecting individual endangered species, usually by laws and international treaties, or by establishing breeding programs to help sustain these species and reintroducing them back into the wild. The California condor is a good example of this approach.
- **Ecosystem approach:** Increasingly, scientists and conservationists are finding that the best way to preserve species is to preserve the ecosystem they inhabit. The ecosystem approach employs a four-point plan:
  - Locate and map the ecosystem. Develop an inventory of its species and the role they play in the ecosystem.
  - Protect the most endangered ecosystems and their species.
  - Repair degraded ecosystems.
  - Design biodiversity-friendly developments that help protect endangered ecosystems.

One place this ecosystem approach has been especially effective is on California's Santa Cruz Island, within Channel Islands National Park. On Santa Cruz Island, two native species were close to extinction. But instead of working directly to increase these species through breeding or species-specific protection, conservation efforts focused on returning the environment to conditions in which these endangered species formerly thrived. On Santa Cruz Island, the introduced golden eagle had decimated the rodent population on which the endemic Channel

Island fox depended for survival. Conservationists reintroduced the bald eagle, which had become nearly extinct on the island due to the historic use of DDT as a pesticide. The bald eagle greatly displaced the invasive golden eagles, allowing rodent and, thus, fox populations to rebound. Additionally, conservationists worked to eradicate the island's introduced and invasive wild pig population, which had been decimating both plant and terrestrial animal populations. It took 26 months to eradicate the introduced wild pigs on the island, but after focusing on habitat and restoring native species while eradicating invasive ones, the ecosystem of Santa Cruz Island was overwhelmingly restored.

Another strong example of an ecosystem approach to habitat and species restoration was in Yellowstone National Park, where a rampant elk population was over-grazing aspen trees, leading to overall ecosystem degradation. With the reintroduction of gray wolves to the park, the elk was soon culled to a population size the ecosystem could sustainably support.

Other ideas to slow habitat destruction include expanding current wildlife refuges and sanctuaries and adding new ones, expanding federal public lands to preserve and protect habitats of endangered species, managing existing habitats and monitoring their use for changes, expanding breeding programs for additional plant and animal species, and passing new laws and international treaties to protect threatened and endangered species and protect their habitats.

However, many of these initiatives cost money either directly or through the decreased ability to make money. The economic challenges, combined with a general lack of knowledge about the benefits of habitats and biodiversity and the ways they can be protected or saved, makes conservation challenging. Much of the money needed to save species such as the California Condor, Santa Cruz Kit Fox, and the Giant Panda comes from governments, private donations, grants, and zoos. For example, it has cost an average of $5 million per year to help the condors recover from 22 birds in 1987, when all the condors were in captivity, to over 350 birds today, with approximately 150 in the wild.

Practice

1. What type of radiation is involved in the formation of ozone?

   A. Visible radiation
   B. UVA
   C. UVB
   D. UVC
   E. Infrared radiation

2. Which of the following human conditions can be caused by UVB radiation?

   I.   Blistering of the skin with severe sunburns
   II.   Skin cancer
   III. Cataracts

   A. I only
   B. II only
   C. III only
   D. I and III
   E. I, II, and III

3. Which of the following gases is involved in the destruction of the ozone layer?

   A. NO
   B. CFCs
   C. CO_2
   D. CH_4
   E. H_2O

4. Which of the following is NOT an effect of ozone depletion?

   A. An increase in sunburns and other damage to the skin that may result in more cases of skin cancer
   B. Higher UV radiation causing damage to the leaves of plants and reducing the crop production
   C. Cooling of the troposphere as less UV radiation reaches the Earth's surface
   D. Harmful effect to the skin of animals (even animals with fur) and to their eyes
   E. Increase in the rate of mutations as UVB damages DNA in living organisms

5. Which of the following is NOT a source of CFCs?

   A. Aerosol cans
   B. Air conditioners
   C. Foam production
   D. Cleaning solutions
   E. Refrigerators

6. Which greenhouse gas is the cause of 80 percent to 90 percent of the natural greenhouse effect?

   A. Water vapor
   B. Carbon dioxide
   C. Methane
   D. Nitrous oxide
   E. Halons

7. Which of the following is the greatest overall threat to species survival?

   A. Climate change
   B. Pollution
   C. Overuse
   D. Invasive species
   E. Habitat loss

8. Which of the following are examples of habitat fragmentation?

   I.   A large area is cut into smaller patches by the development of ranches.
   II.   Farms are removed to reconnect land areas.
   III. Major highways divide the land, making it difficult for species to cross.

   A. I only
   B. II only
   C. III only
   D. I and III
   E. I, II, and III

9. Which of the following is NOT a reason for the huge loss of species in the world's oceans?

    A. Over 60 percent of the world's population living near a coastal area

    B. Two billion people relying on the world's oceans for the majority of their protein

    C. Bycatch, the unintended capture of fish that are not the target species

    D. The high number of fish caught for sport fishing

    E. People changing their diets to include more fish and less beef and pork

10. Which of the following is NOT a form of pollution that may result in the loss of biodiversity?

    A. Air

    B. Food

    C. Land

    D. Noise

    E. Water

11. Which of the following is NOT a reason why invasive species cause the loss of biodiversity?

    A. Invasive species may kill native species.

    B. Invasive species outcompete native species for food.

    C. Invasive species may drive out native species.

    D. Invasive species may be food for native species.

    E. Invasive species may damage the habitat and make it uninhabitable for native species.

12. Which of the following is an example of the ecosystem approach to maintaining biodiversity?

    A. Protect individual species by passing laws to help sustain the species.

    B. Develop breeding programs to increase the population of the species.

    C. Map an ecosystem and develop an inventory of the species and the role they play in the ecosystem.

    D. Manage the species for sustainable yield through national laws and international treaties.

    E. Develop quotas for the capture of fisheries and game species.

13. Which U.S. act was created to protect species that are threatened or endangered?

    A. Endangered Species Act

    B. Fish and Wildlife Act

    C. Fur Seal Act

    D. Marine Mammal Protection Act

    E. Migratory Bird Treaty Act

14. Which of the following is NOT true about UVA?

    A. UVA has a frequency of 320 nm to 400 nm.

    B. UVA causes tanning in humans.

    C. Most UVA reaches the Earth's surface.

    D. UVA is involved in the formation of ozone.

    E. Many species of birds, bees, and reptiles can see UVA.

15. Which of the following treaties controls international trade in endangered species?

    A. Endangered Species Act

    B. CITES

    C. Montreal Protocol

    D. Kyoto Protocol

    E. Basel Convention

Answers

1. **D** UVC is the form of UV radiation that is involved in the formation of ozone.

2. **E** All three are the result of UVB radiation.

3. **B** All five are greenhouse gases, but only CFCs destroy ozone and cause the thinning of the ozone layer.

4. **C** The troposphere will see an increase of UV radiation and, thus, should heat up, not cool down.

5. **D** Cleaning solutions do not contain CFCs, unless they were used with aerosols; most cleaning supplies are either poured out of a container or sprayed from pump-type bottles.

6. **A** Water vapor is the cause of 80 percent to 90 percent of the natural greenhouse effect. Halons are not part of the natural greenhouse gases.

7. **E** Based on multiple studies, scientists suggest that habitat loss is the greatest threat to species survival.

8. **D** Removing farms allows segmented land to come together, thus reversing habitat fragmentation.

9. **D** Most fish that are sold at a market are caught by commercial fishing boats, not by sport fishing. All the other answers are reasons why fisheries have declined.

10. **B** Food is not considered a form of pollution. Air, land, noise, and water are forms of pollution that may result in the loss of biodiversity.

11. **D** If an invasive species happened to be food for a native species, the population of the native species would be likely to increase rather than decrease.

12. **C** Choices A and B demonstrate the species approach to saving biodiversity. Choices D and E are part of the wildlife management approach. Choice C, mapping an ecosystem, is part of the ecosystem approach to maintaining biodiversity.

13. **A** Although the other four acts may be used to protect specific species, the Endangered Species Act encompasses all endangered and threatened species.

14. **D** UVC is not involved in the formation of ozone, while UVA is not included.

15. **B** The Convention on International Trade in Endangered Species of Wild Fauna and Flora, often called CITES, is the international treaty that was designed to regulate international trade in endangered species.

PRACTICE EXAMS

Chapter 8

Practice Exam 1

Answer Sheet

Remove this sheet and use it to mark your answers for the multiple-choice section of Practice Exam 1.

Section I

1 Ⓐ Ⓑ Ⓒ Ⓓ Ⓔ	26 Ⓐ Ⓑ Ⓒ Ⓓ Ⓔ	51 Ⓐ Ⓑ Ⓒ Ⓓ Ⓔ	76 Ⓐ Ⓑ Ⓒ Ⓓ Ⓔ
2 Ⓐ Ⓑ Ⓒ Ⓓ Ⓔ	27 Ⓐ Ⓑ Ⓒ Ⓓ Ⓔ	52 Ⓐ Ⓑ Ⓒ Ⓓ Ⓔ	77 Ⓐ Ⓑ Ⓒ Ⓓ Ⓔ
3 Ⓐ Ⓑ Ⓒ Ⓓ Ⓔ	28 Ⓐ Ⓑ Ⓒ Ⓓ Ⓔ	53 Ⓐ Ⓑ Ⓒ Ⓓ Ⓔ	78 Ⓐ Ⓑ Ⓒ Ⓓ Ⓔ
4 Ⓐ Ⓑ Ⓒ Ⓓ Ⓔ	29 Ⓐ Ⓑ Ⓒ Ⓓ Ⓔ	54 Ⓐ Ⓑ Ⓒ Ⓓ Ⓔ	79 Ⓐ Ⓑ Ⓒ Ⓓ Ⓔ
5 Ⓐ Ⓑ Ⓒ Ⓓ Ⓔ	30 Ⓐ Ⓑ Ⓒ Ⓓ Ⓔ	55 Ⓐ Ⓑ Ⓒ Ⓓ Ⓔ	80 Ⓐ Ⓑ Ⓒ Ⓓ Ⓔ
6 Ⓐ Ⓑ Ⓒ Ⓓ Ⓔ	31 Ⓐ Ⓑ Ⓒ Ⓓ Ⓔ	56 Ⓐ Ⓑ Ⓒ Ⓓ Ⓔ	81 Ⓐ Ⓑ Ⓒ Ⓓ Ⓔ
7 Ⓐ Ⓑ Ⓒ Ⓓ Ⓔ	32 Ⓐ Ⓑ Ⓒ Ⓓ Ⓔ	57 Ⓐ Ⓑ Ⓒ Ⓓ Ⓔ	82 Ⓐ Ⓑ Ⓒ Ⓓ Ⓔ
8 Ⓐ Ⓑ Ⓒ Ⓓ Ⓔ	33 Ⓐ Ⓑ Ⓒ Ⓓ Ⓔ	58 Ⓐ Ⓑ Ⓒ Ⓓ Ⓔ	83 Ⓐ Ⓑ Ⓒ Ⓓ Ⓔ
9 Ⓐ Ⓑ Ⓒ Ⓓ Ⓔ	34 Ⓐ Ⓑ Ⓒ Ⓓ Ⓔ	59 Ⓐ Ⓑ Ⓒ Ⓓ Ⓔ	84 Ⓐ Ⓑ Ⓒ Ⓓ Ⓔ
10 Ⓐ Ⓑ Ⓒ Ⓓ Ⓔ	35 Ⓐ Ⓑ Ⓒ Ⓓ Ⓔ	60 Ⓐ Ⓑ Ⓒ Ⓓ Ⓔ	85 Ⓐ Ⓑ Ⓒ Ⓓ Ⓔ
11 Ⓐ Ⓑ Ⓒ Ⓓ Ⓔ	36 Ⓐ Ⓑ Ⓒ Ⓓ Ⓔ	61 Ⓐ Ⓑ Ⓒ Ⓓ Ⓔ	86 Ⓐ Ⓑ Ⓒ Ⓓ Ⓔ
12 Ⓐ Ⓑ Ⓒ Ⓓ Ⓔ	37 Ⓐ Ⓑ Ⓒ Ⓓ Ⓔ	62 Ⓐ Ⓑ Ⓒ Ⓓ Ⓔ	87 Ⓐ Ⓑ Ⓒ Ⓓ Ⓔ
13 Ⓐ Ⓑ Ⓒ Ⓓ Ⓔ	38 Ⓐ Ⓑ Ⓒ Ⓓ Ⓔ	63 Ⓐ Ⓑ Ⓒ Ⓓ Ⓔ	88 Ⓐ Ⓑ Ⓒ Ⓓ Ⓔ
14 Ⓐ Ⓑ Ⓒ Ⓓ Ⓔ	39 Ⓐ Ⓑ Ⓒ Ⓓ Ⓔ	64 Ⓐ Ⓑ Ⓒ Ⓓ Ⓔ	89 Ⓐ Ⓑ Ⓒ Ⓓ Ⓔ
15 Ⓐ Ⓑ Ⓒ Ⓓ Ⓔ	40 Ⓐ Ⓑ Ⓒ Ⓓ Ⓔ	65 Ⓐ Ⓑ Ⓒ Ⓓ Ⓔ	90 Ⓐ Ⓑ Ⓒ Ⓓ Ⓔ
16 Ⓐ Ⓑ Ⓒ Ⓓ Ⓔ	41 Ⓐ Ⓑ Ⓒ Ⓓ Ⓔ	66 Ⓐ Ⓑ Ⓒ Ⓓ Ⓔ	91 Ⓐ Ⓑ Ⓒ Ⓓ Ⓔ
17 Ⓐ Ⓑ Ⓒ Ⓓ Ⓔ	42 Ⓐ Ⓑ Ⓒ Ⓓ Ⓔ	67 Ⓐ Ⓑ Ⓒ Ⓓ Ⓔ	92 Ⓐ Ⓑ Ⓒ Ⓓ Ⓔ
18 Ⓐ Ⓑ Ⓒ Ⓓ Ⓔ	43 Ⓐ Ⓑ Ⓒ Ⓓ Ⓔ	68 Ⓐ Ⓑ Ⓒ Ⓓ Ⓔ	93 Ⓐ Ⓑ Ⓒ Ⓓ Ⓔ
19 Ⓐ Ⓑ Ⓒ Ⓓ Ⓔ	44 Ⓐ Ⓑ Ⓒ Ⓓ Ⓔ	69 Ⓐ Ⓑ Ⓒ Ⓓ Ⓔ	94 Ⓐ Ⓑ Ⓒ Ⓓ Ⓔ
20 Ⓐ Ⓑ Ⓒ Ⓓ Ⓔ	45 Ⓐ Ⓑ Ⓒ Ⓓ Ⓔ	70 Ⓐ Ⓑ Ⓒ Ⓓ Ⓔ	95 Ⓐ Ⓑ Ⓒ Ⓓ Ⓔ
21 Ⓐ Ⓑ Ⓒ Ⓓ Ⓔ	46 Ⓐ Ⓑ Ⓒ Ⓓ Ⓔ	71 Ⓐ Ⓑ Ⓒ Ⓓ Ⓔ	96 Ⓐ Ⓑ Ⓒ Ⓓ Ⓔ
22 Ⓐ Ⓑ Ⓒ Ⓓ Ⓔ	47 Ⓐ Ⓑ Ⓒ Ⓓ Ⓔ	72 Ⓐ Ⓑ Ⓒ Ⓓ Ⓔ	97 Ⓐ Ⓑ Ⓒ Ⓓ Ⓔ
23 Ⓐ Ⓑ Ⓒ Ⓓ Ⓔ	48 Ⓐ Ⓑ Ⓒ Ⓓ Ⓔ	73 Ⓐ Ⓑ Ⓒ Ⓓ Ⓔ	98 Ⓐ Ⓑ Ⓒ Ⓓ Ⓔ
24 Ⓐ Ⓑ Ⓒ Ⓓ Ⓔ	49 Ⓐ Ⓑ Ⓒ Ⓓ Ⓔ	74 Ⓐ Ⓑ Ⓒ Ⓓ Ⓔ	99 Ⓐ Ⓑ Ⓒ Ⓓ Ⓔ
25 Ⓐ Ⓑ Ⓒ Ⓓ Ⓔ	50 Ⓐ Ⓑ Ⓒ Ⓓ Ⓔ	75 Ⓐ Ⓑ Ⓒ Ⓓ Ⓔ	100 Ⓐ Ⓑ Ⓒ Ⓓ Ⓔ

Section II

Section I: Multiple-Choice Questions

Time: 90 minutes
100 questions

Directions: Each of the questions or incomplete statements in this section is followed by five answer choices. Select the best answer choice and fill in the corresponding circle on the answer sheet.

Questions 1–3 refer to the following answer choices.

    A.   Sulfur
    B.   Nitrogen
    C.   Carbon
    D.   Phosphorus
    E.   All four cycles

1. This nutrient is stored mainly in sediment.

2. The release of this element into the atmosphere is due, in large part, to fossil fuel combustion and deforestation.

3. This cycle has been altered dramatically by humans.

4. One issue with the use of freshwater aquifers in otherwise arid regions is:

    A.   Constant flow of water from the aquifer into a surface water source
    B.   Slow recharge of the aquifer
    C.   Intrusion of saltwater from oceans
    D.   Waterlogging of the soil
    E.   Eutrophication

5. Which of the following has shifted the storage of carbon from sediment to the atmosphere?

    A.   Mining of coal
    B.   Combustion of fossil fuels
    C.   Increased occurrence of acid precipitation
    D.   Extraction of crude oil
    E.   Industrial smog

6. The protective ozone layer is located in the:

    A.   Troposphere
    B.   Exosphere
    C.   Lithosphere
    D.   Stratosphere
    E.   Mesosphere

7. If soil has the ability to hold high amounts of water and gases in its pore spaces, it is said to have:

    A.   High soil porosity
    B.   Low soil porosity
    C.   High soil permeability
    D.   Low soil permeability
    E.   Waterlogging

8. Which of the following are naturally occurring indoor air pollutants?

    A.   Radon and asbestos
    B.   Asbestos and tobacco smoke
    C.   Radon and CFCs
    D.   Chloroform and radon
    E.   Formaldehyde and chloroform

9. Atmospheric convective currents are due to the:

    A.   Intensity of hurricanes
    B.   Rising of warm, less dense air, which then cools and becomes more dense at it rises, causing the air to sink back toward the Earth
    C.   Rising of cool, less dense air, which then warms and becomes more dense at it rises, causing the air to sink back toward the Earth
    D.   Rising of cool air
    E.   Increasing velocity of tornadoes

10. If the population is growing at a rate of 1.4 percent annually, the population will double in how many years?

    A.   20
    B.   50
    C.   65
    D.   100
    E.   140

11. K-selected species often are regulated by density-dependent factors. A population of K-selected elephants is experiencing a recent rapid decline in numbers. Which of the following is the most likely cause?

    A. Declining predator populations
    B. Lack of food and water
    C. Climate change
    D. Increase in vegetation
    E. Inbreeding

12. Positive feedback loops

    A. Keep the environment in dynamic equilibrium
    B. Are closed systems
    C. Are becoming more common in nature because of human impact on the environment
    D. Are open systems
    E. Never occur in nature

13. Tropical rain forests are considered to have high net primary productivity because of the:

    A. Rapid rate at which solar energy is converted to biomass
    B. Ability of the soils to hold water
    C. Alkaline soils
    D. Rapid rate at which biomass decomposes
    E. Rapid pace at which organisms reproduce

14. Which of the following greenhouse gases are most abundant?

    A. Carbon dioxide, water vapor, and methane
    B. Carbon monoxide and methane
    C. Methane, water vapor, and sulfur dioxide
    D. Sulfur dioxide and nitrous oxide
    E. Carbon dioxide and sulfur dioxide

15. Which of the following best describes the process of photosynthesis?

    A. Oxygen, water, and solar energy are used to produce carbon dioxide and sugar.
    B. Oxygen, sugar, and solar energy are used to produce carbon dioxide and water.
    C. Carbon dioxide, water, and solar energy are used to produce oxygen and sugar.
    D. Carbon dioxide and oxygen combine to form water and sugar.
    E. Carbon dioxide and water are used to produce oxygen, sugar, and more carbon dioxide.

16. The Monteverde golden toad was in danger of extinction with minimal environmental change because it was _____ to the Monteverde cloud forest.

    A. indigenous
    B. endemic
    C. native
    D. introduced
    E. extirpated

17. Which of the following can be considered a keystone species?

    A. Garter snake
    B. Mosquito
    C. Poison oak
    D. Barn owl
    E. Beaver

Questions 18–20 refer to the following answer choices.

    A. Tundra
    B. Chaparral
    C. Boreal forest
    D. Desert
    E. Temperate grassland

18. Organisms have evolved to survive the environment in this biome through adaptations such as spines for protection and the ability of photosynthesis to take place in stems as opposed to leaves.

19. This biome is dominated by coniferous trees.

20. In this biome, permafrost keeps the soil frozen most of the year.

21. A company has developed a new type of pesticide. Prior to use, the company tests the health effects on humans, wildlife, and ecosystems. Upon completion of the tests, it is determined that the pesticide is safe and harmless. This process is an example of:

    A. A cause-and-effect relationship
    B. A dose-response analysis
    C. The innocent-until-proven-guilty approach
    D. The precautionary principle
    E. Tragedy of the commons

22. A forest community remained stable and unaffected for many decades. In a dramatic turn of events, a volcano erupted, covering the forest with lava and killing all organisms in the area. The first species to appear on the barren lava rock was lichen, which was followed by the growth of small plants and an influx of insects. Eventually, the community contained mature trees and remained stable for a long period of time.

    Which of the following best describes the order in which these events took place?

    A. Disturbance, pioneer species, secondary succession, climax community
    B. Climax community, disturbance, pioneer species, secondary succession
    C. Disturbance, primary succession, pioneer species, climax community
    D. Secondary succession, disturbance, primary succession, climax community
    E. Climax community, disturbance, pioneer species, primary succession

23. One way in which scientists study climate change is through ice core samples. What information does this tell us about the climate?

    A. The impact of changing sea levels on the climate.
    B. The frequency of thermal inversions in the atmosphere.
    C. Greenhouse gas concentrations, atmospheric composition, and trends in atmospheric temperature.
    D. The rate of the solidification of greenhouse gases in the atmosphere.
    E. Nothing. This is not a way to study climate change.

24. Which of the following helps to create the greenhouse effect?

    I. Solar radiation reflecting off the Earth's surface
    II. Greenhouse gases reflecting some solar radiation back to Earth
    III. Greenhouse gases emitting heat as a byproduct of chemical reactions

    A. I only
    B. II only
    C. III only
    D. I and II only
    E. I, II, and III

25. Due to the large amount of vegetation in tropical rain forests, the soil is:

    A. High in nutrient content
    B. Prone to erosion
    C. Low in nutrients
    D. Waterlogged
    E. Dry

26. A pollutant has entered a body of water at the concentration of 0.5 ppm. If it dissipates by 20 percent every five days, how much is left after 15 days?

    A. 0.44 ppm
    B. 0.30 ppm
    C. 0.26 ppm
    D. 0.15 ppm
    E. 0 ppm

27. What is the main source of energy for Earth's organisms?

    A. Wind
    B. The sun
    C. Fossil fuels
    D. Geothermal activity
    E. Biomass

28. Which of the following countries has the largest ecological footprint?

    A. Afghanistan
    B. Mexico
    C. India
    D. Japan
    E. The United States

29. In a country with an inverted population pyramid, there is a

    A. Growing population
    B. High rate of disease affecting the working-age population
    C. Smaller labor market as well as more stress on social systems to support the elderly
    D. Strong military and labor market
    E. High rate of death among older ages in the population

30. A population of mule deer was growing very quickly until starvation reduced the number of individuals. The mule deer passed the condition or point of

    A. Overcrowding
    B. Exponential growth
    C. Carrying capacity
    D. Limited growth
    E. Extirpation

31. China's one-child policy has been successful in reducing population growth but has had negative consequences as well. All of the following are potential problems with the declining population due to this policy EXCEPT

    A. Increased pressure on social systems such as Social Security and healthcare
    B. A decrease in the number of individuals in the labor market
    C. Increased abortion rates of female fetuses
    D. An uneven sex ratio
    E. More people entering the military

Questions 32–33 refer the following information.

A country has a crude birth rate of $\frac{32}{1,000}$, a crude death rate of $\frac{9}{1,000}$, an immigration rate of $\frac{2}{1,000}$, and an emigration rate of $\frac{4}{1,000}$.

32. What is the growth rate of this country?

    A. 1.8 percent
    B. 2.9 percent
    C. 2.6 percent
    D. 2.1 percent
    E. 3.4 percent

33. What do these numbers tell you about the country's population?

    A. It is declining slowly.
    B. It is stabilizing.
    C. There are a large number of individuals in the older age groups.
    D. There are high death rates at young ages.
    E. The population is still growing.

34. How is wind harnessed for use as energy?

    A. The kinetic energy produced by the wind is converted into electrical energy.
    B. Solar energy is converted into kinetic energy.
    C. Kinetic energy is converted into electrical energy through photovoltaic (PV) cells.
    D. Wind energy is captured and used to heat water, which then produces steam to turn turbines.
    E. Wind's potential energy turns turbines, which then produce electrical energy.

35. Global fossil fuel use has shifted in recent decades. Which statement accurately reflects this shift?

    A. Coal has overtaken natural gas as the most widely used fossil fuel.
    B. Oil has overtaken natural gas as the most widely used fossil fuel.
    C. Coal has overtaken oil as the most widely used fossil fuel.
    D. Oil has overtaken coal as the most widely used fossil fuel.
    E. Natural gas has overtaken coal as the most widely used fossil fuel.

36. Acute exposure to a substance means that an organism has been exposed to

    A. High levels over a long period of time
    B. High levels over a brief period of time
    C. Low levels over a brief period of time
    D. Low levels over a long period of time
    E. Moderate levels over a lifetime

Questions 37–38 refer to the following logistic growth curve.

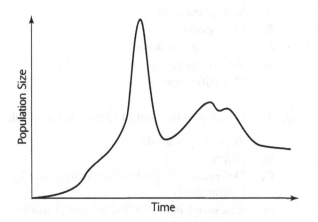

37. This curve represents a population that

    A. Rises quickly and then stabilizes at carrying capacity

    B. Depicts the theoretical model of logistic growth

    C. Experiences a destabilization of the population

    D. Grows exponentially

    E. Fluctuates and lessens in extremes over time but does not reach carrying capacity

38. What could have led to this extreme destabilization?

    A. A natural disaster

    B. Carrying capacity

    C. Disease

    D. Introduced predation

    E. All of the above

39. Which of the following would be included in the risk assessment of a substance accidentally released from a local factory?

    A. Conducting a dose-response analysis

    B. Determining who is at fault in the factory

    C. Determining who will pay for the remediation of the substance

    D. Assessing the cost of the lost chemical as well as the cost of the remediation

    E. Conducting an analysis of local flora and fauna

40. Succession in an aquatic environment can occur

    A. As a result of eutrophication

    B. Only in areas of excessive erosion

    C. In the absence of life

    D. In the open ocean

    E. Only during summer months

Questions 41–43 refer to the following graph.

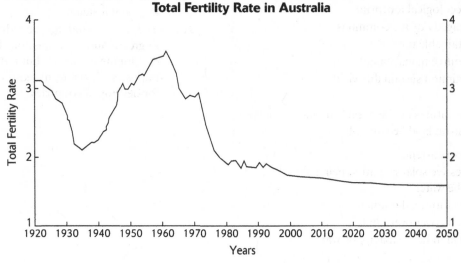

Source: Australian Government, The Treasury

41. What lead to the decline in total fertility rate in Australia in the 1920s and 1930s?

    A. War
    B. Economic depression
    C. Widespread disease
    D. An increase in the use of contraception
    E. An aging population

42. What contributed to the increase in total fertility rate in Australia in the 1940s and 1950s?

    A. Immigration
    B. Economic growth
    C. High infant mortality rates
    D. Lack of contraception
    E. Lack of female empowerment

43. If the total fertility rate continues to decrease and stabilize in the future as projected, what could be a social and/or economic repercussion?

    A. An increase in productivity and an economic boom
    B. An uneven sex ratio
    C. A decrease in the labor market and slower economic growth
    D. Decreased female empowerment
    E. None of the above

44. The overfishing of the world's ocean fisheries is considered an example of

    A. An ecological footprint
    B. A tragedy of the commons
    C. Sustainable use
    D. Resource management
    E. Maximum sustainable yield

45. The temperatures of the oceans are more stable than those on land because of

    A. Ocean currents
    B. Excessive solar radiation being absorbed by the water
    C. The latitudinal gradient
    D. Cloud cover over land
    E. The high heat capacity of water

46. Overworking and overuse of land can lead to all of the following issues EXCEPT

    A. Soil salinization
    B. Dust storms
    C. An increase in disease
    D. Waterlogging
    E. Desertification

47. The dead zone in the Gulf of Mexico is a result of:

    A. Toxic-waste runoff
    B. Hurricane Katrina
    C. Destruction of the benthic environment by fishing trawls
    D. Excess nutrients, leading to eutrophication and eventually hypoxia
    E. The *Deepwater Horizon* oil spill

48. Why did the United States not ratify the Kyoto Protocol?

    A. U.S. emissions are lower than that of other countries.
    B. The treaty mandates the reduction in greenhouse-gas emissions for developed countries, but it does not impose such stringent requirements for developing countries.
    C. Each state in the United States has set emission standards, so there was no need to sign an international treaty.
    D. The United States signed the Montreal Protocol instead.
    E. The treaty mandates the reduction in greenhouse-gas emissions for developing countries, but it does not impose such stringent requirements for developed countries.

49. A proposed dock that would be built over a wetland into a portion of a bay is controversial. An environmental impact statement (EIS) is required, and the local community has numerous concerns about this project. Which law or laws most likely pertain to the building of this proposed dock?

    I.   Endangered Species Act
    II. Comprehensive Response Compensation and Liability Act (CERCLA)
    III. National Environmental Policy Act

    A. I only
    B. II only
    C. III only
    D. I and III only
    E. II and III only

50. Which of the following best describes the current state of the world's largest aquifer, the Ogallala Aquifer, in the Midwestern United States?

    A. It continues to decrease in volume as water is pumped for human use.
    B. It is recharging quickly as a result of increased rainfall.
    C. It is recharging slowly but still faster than water is being taken out.
    D. It is experiencing saltwater intrusion.
    E. It is completely dried as a result of overpumping.

Questions 51–53 refer to the following answer choices.

    A. Soil salinization
    B. Desertification
    C. Waterlogging
    D. Saltwater intrusion
    E. Eutrophication

51. This results from the over pumping of an aquifer in coastal areas.

52. This occurs when the water table rises and denies plant roots of essential gases.

53. This is a result of salt buildup in the top layer of soil.

54. The incorporation of the preservation of biodiversity with sustainable development is created through the use of:

    A. Wildlife reserves
    B. Biosphere reserves
    C. Land trusts
    D. National parks
    E. Wildlife refuges

55. The building of a dam can have many ecological implications. Which of the following is an issue with a river being dammed?

    I.   Excess sedimentation
    II. Disruption of mating patterns of fish
    III. Decreased water flow as the river reaches its termination point

    A. I only
    B. II only
    C. I and III only
    D. I, II, and III
    E. None of the above

56. Habitat islands can occur as a result of

    A. A decrease in permafrost
    B. The development of roadways
    C. A decreasing sea level
    D. The creation of national parks
    E. Industrial smog

Questions 57–58 refer to the following map.

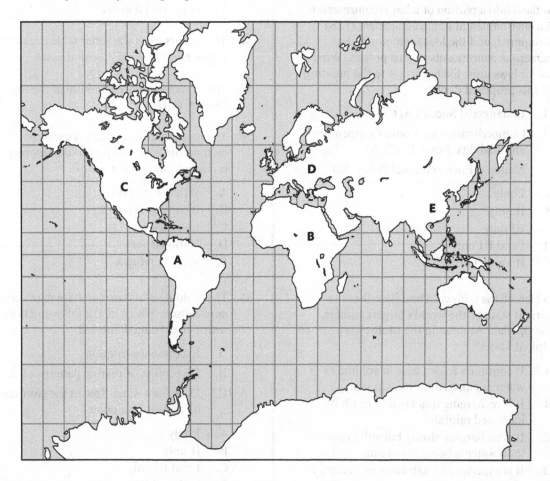

57. Which regions represent the highest rate
    of deforestation?

    A. A and B
    B. B and C
    C. C and D
    D. D and E
    E. None of the noted regions

58. Which regions are seeing an increase in forested
    area due to conservation efforts?

    A. A and B
    B. B and C
    C. C and D
    D. D and E
    E. None of the noted regions

59. Photovoltaic cells produce energy by

    A. Converting solar energy into electrical
        energy, which creates an electrical current
        as a result of the movement of electrons
    B. Converting light energy into electrical
        energy, which creates an electrical current
        as a result of the movement of protons
    C. Using mechanical energy from wind to
        create an electric current
    D. Absorbing sunlight and heating water,
        which then produces steam to turn
        a turbine
    E. Splitting water molecules and converting
        the hydrogen into electrical energy

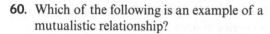

60. Which of the following is an example of a mutualistic relationship?

  A. A tapeworm living in an organism's stomach
  B. A duck eating algae
  C. A dolphin searching for a mate
  D. Algae living in coral
  E. A frog consuming an insect

61. There are many arguments in support of the development of wind farms as a source of energy, but there are also many arguments against it. Which of the following is a common argument against the development of wind farms?

  A. Wind energy does not produce a high output of energy.
  B. Wind can be inconsistent, varying daily, seasonally, and in different locations.
  C. It is necessary to have multiple turbines in order to generate any energy from wind.
  D. Wind farms cannot be placed in the high salinity of the oceans.
  E. The technology is not yet fully developed.

62. Which of the following nations have the largest oil reserves?

  A. Saudi Arabia, Iran, and the United States
  B. Saudi Arabia, Iran, and Iraq
  C. Russia, Iran, and Qatar
  D. The United States, Russia, and China
  E. Iran, Iraq, and Russia

63. Biomass is a renewable fuel and burns cleaner than fossil fuels, but one of the downsides of using biomass is the

  A. Addition of ethanol
  B. Large amounts of carbon emission from biodiesels
  C. Unequal distribution globally
  D. Expense of producing it
  E. Creation of a monoculture on crop land that could be used for food production.

Questions 64–66 refer to the following answer choices.

  A. Lignite
  B. Sub-bituminous
  C. Bituminous
  D. Peat
  E. Anthracite

64. What is a wet, moderately compressed organic matter?

65. What has the highest energy content per unit volume?

66. What is formed under minimal heat and pressure and is moderately wet?

67. In which ways can natural gas be produced?

  I. Anaerobic decomposition
  II. Aerobic decomposition
  III. Extreme heat and pressure

  A. I only
  B. II only
  C. III only
  D. I and III
  E. I, II, and III

68. In developing countries (as compared to developed countries), the largest use of energy is for?

  A. Transportation
  B. Manufacturing
  C. Preparing food
  D. Technology
  E. Recreational activities

69. How does carbon monoxide lethally act upon an organism?

  A. Carbon monoxide binds to hemoglobin and blocks carbon dioxide from binding, preventing carbon dioxide from circulating in the blood.
  B. Carbon monoxide binds to hemoglobin and blocks oxygen from binding, preventing oxygen from circulating in the blood.
  C. Carbon monoxide acts as a neurotoxin.
  D. Carbon monoxide mutates cells and causes cancer.
  E. Carbon monoxide binds with the endocrine receptor sites on cells and blocks hormones and oxygen from entering cells.

70. How is crude oil separated into its various components?

    A. Through a filtration system
    B. In separation tanks as it is pumped from the ground and collected
    C. Through boiling and distillation
    D. Through a series of steps, including heating, cooling, and filtration
    E. None of the above

71. Nuclear energy is produced through the process of

    A. Fusion
    B. Fission
    C. Splitting of hydrocarbons
    D. Combustion
    E. Steam generation

72. When organisms within an ecosystem consume others that contain mercury in their tissues, the toxin can build up over time within the organism. This is considered

    A. Endocrine disruption
    B. Dose-response
    C. Bioaccumulation
    D. LD_{50}
    E. Biomagnification

73. Thermal inversions occur when

    A. Cool air is trapped beneath a layer of warm air, trapping pollutants as well.
    B. Warm air is trapped beneath a layer of cool air, trapping pollutants as well.
    C. Ocean surface waters are heated.
    D. Tornadoes form.
    E. Cool air is trapped beneath a layer of warm air, but pollutants are allowed to escape.

74. Which criteria pollutants contribute to acid precipitation?

    I. Nitrogen dioxide
    II. Ozone
    III. Sulfur dioxide

    A. I only
    B. II only
    C. III only
    D. I and III only
    E. I, II, and III

75. Endocrine disruptors interfere with the endocrine system by

    A. Causing cells to mutate
    B. Mimicking hormones and binding to the hormone receptor sites on cells
    C. Becoming a carcinogen
    D. Mimicking glucose molecules and binding to receptor sites on cells
    E. Impeding the absorption of nutrients by an organism

76. The main contributor to ozone depletion prior to the signing of the Montreal Protocol was

    A. Sulfur dioxides
    B. Nitric oxides
    C. CFCs
    D. Particulate matter
    E. Carbon-dioxide emissions

77. Salvage logging can harm an ecosystem through all of the following EXCEPT

    A. Taking nutrients out of an ecosystem
    B. Accelerating soil erosion
    C. Loss of habitat
    D. Increasing the risk of large-scale fires
    E. Decreasing biodiversity

78. Noise pollution can become a serious nuisance in areas where the following situations occur EXCEPT where there is

    A. High vehicle traffic
    B. Poor urban planning
    C. Frequent construction
    D. Congestion of sailboats
    E. A loud nightclub

79. Cultural eutrophication is a result of

    A. A mixing of multiple cultures in one area
    B. Excess nutrients entering aquatic environments from sources such as sewage and fertilizers
    C. Excess nutrients entering aquatic environments from weathering rocks
    D. Genetic pollution
    E. Increasing vehicle traffic

80. The following chemical reactions describe the process of the formation of _____.

$$C + O_2 \rightarrow O_2$$
$$2C + O_2 \rightarrow 2CO$$
$$S + O_2 \rightarrow SO_2$$
$$2SO_2 + O_2 \rightarrow 2SO_3$$
$$SO_3 + H_2O \rightarrow H_2SO_4$$

A.   Photochemical smog
B.   Industrial smog
C.   Acid precipitation
D.   Ozone
E.   Peroxyacetyl nitrate

81. When water is used in factory processes, it cycles through and absorbs heat as it cycles. The water is then discharged into a local water source. This can lead to

A.   Acidic water
B.   Basic water
C.   Toxic pollution
D.   Thermal pollution
E.   Nutrient pollution

82. During which step in the sewage treatment process is oxygen added to start aerobic decomposition?

A.   Pretreatment
B.   Primary treatment
C.   Secondary treatment
D.   Tertiary treatment
E.   Final treatment

Questions 83–84 refer to the following dose-response curve.

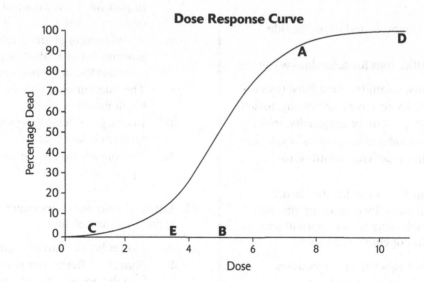

83. Which point represents the LD$_{50}$?

A.   A
B.   B
C.   C
D.   D
E.   E

84. Which point represents the threshold?

A.   A
B.   B
C.   C
D.   D
E.   E

85. Which of the following affects how solar radiation hits the Earth's surface?

    A. El Niño and La Niña
    B. Perihelion
    C. Aphelion
    D. The vernal equinox
    E. Milankovitch cycles

86. A species of insect develops resistance to a pesticide. This occurs

    A. Within one generation, through the process of natural selection
    B. Through acute exposure
    C. Through chronic exposure
    D. Gradually over time, through the process of natural selection
    E. Never in nature

87. In developing countries, the indoor burning of fuel wood as a source of energy is very common and is a cause of many health problems and deaths in these countries. The issues arise from the combustion of wood, which produces

    A. Carbon monoxide and particulate matter
    B. Nitrogen dioxide
    C. Carbon dioxide and carbon monoxide
    D. Sulfur dioxide
    E. Carbon monoxide and sulfur dioxide

88. The four classifications for hazardous waste are

    A. Ignitability, volatility, corrosivity, toxicity
    B. Radioactivity, reactivity, corrosivity, toxicity
    C. Ignitability, reactivity, corrosivity, toxicity
    D. Ignitability, radioactivity, corrosivity, toxicity
    E. Ignitability, reactivity, volatility, toxicity

89. There are many ways in which the Earth's systems are impacted by a changing climate. Which of the following is an important and prominent effect of climate change?

    A. Increased frequency of earthquakes
    B. Extreme freeze of permafrost
    C. More gases released during volcanic activity
    D. Increasing occurrence of the bleaching of coral reefs
    E. Rapid development of mountaintop glaciers

90. A farmer has experienced large crop loss due to insects this growing season. If this is not dealt with, he will lose most of his crop and most of his income for the year. What is the best solution to this issue?

    A. Apply large amounts of pesticides.
    B. Bring in a predator to consume the insects.
    C. Use the integrated pest management (IPM) approach.
    D. Change crops.
    E. Create mixed crops throughout his land.

91. A potential threat of climate change on human health could be

    A. Increased heart disease
    B. Faster transmission of AIDS in Africa
    C. Higher threat of frostbite throughout the globe
    D. Reduced sun exposure due to an increase in the number of overcast days
    E. An increase in the range of tropical diseases such as malaria due to a larger range of warmer temperatures

92. The IPCC is

    A. An organization in the Unites States responsible for the control of emissions nationally
    B. An international group of scientists and government officials that assesses, summarizes, and reports on climate change
    C. The International Pollution Control Commission
    D. In charge of developing solutions to resolve climate change
    E. Responsible for regulating greenhouse gases internationally

93. Equatorial ocean waters usually have lower salinity because of the

    A. Slower breakdown of sediment
    B. Numerous freshwater rivers that empty into the ocean in these regions
    C. High amount of dissolved gases
    D. High level of precipitation in the region
    E. None of the above

Questions 94–96 refer to the following table.

Per Capita Energy Consumption (Kilograms of Oil Equivalent [kgoe] per Person)					
Developed	**2005**	**1990**	**Developing**	**2005**	**1990**
Australia	5,898	5,106	Bangladesh	171	123
Austria	4,135	3,263	Brazil	1124	897
Bulgaria	2,592	3,306	Cambodia	354	0
Canada	8,473	7,564	China	1,316	760
Finland	6,555	5,758	Cuba	905	1,597
France	4,397	3,913	Egypt	828	573
Germany	4,187	4,481	Ethiopia	304	296
Hungary	2,757	2,755	Haiti	293	231
Iceland	12,209	8,476	India	491	377
Ireland	3,656	2,943	Iran	2,381	1,264
Israel	2,816	2,599	Iraq	1,067	1,029
Italy	3,169	2,611	Kuwait	11,102	3,985
Japan	4,135	3,595	Mexico	1,701	1,514
Lithuania	2,515	4,377	Mongolia	916	1,525
Russia	4,519	5,923	North Korea	943	1,670
Spain	3,340	2,338	Philippines	538	428
Switzerland	3,599	3,650	Qatar	19,466	13,554
United Kingdom	3,895	3,709	Senegal	261	281
United States	7,886	7,700	South Korea	4,415	2,178

Source: Data from http://earthtrends.wri.org

94. Which of the following could be a valid explanation for the increase in per capita energy consumption in many developing countries between 1990 and 2005?

    A. The increased number of females in the labor market
    B. An increase in imports
    C. National economic growth
    D. Advancements in medical care
    E. An increase in population

95. In some developing and developed countries, per capita energy consumption is declining. Which of the following could explain this?

    A. Fewer people
    B. Incorrect data
    C. Inefficiencies of energy-generating facilities
    D. Increasing energy efficiency
    E. Access to cheaper oil

96. Explain the overall difference in per capita energy consumption between developed and developing countries.

    A. Developed nations consume more energy due to affluence and access to energy.
    B. Developed nations consume less energy due to poverty.
    C. Developing nations consume less energy due to increasing wealth.
    D. Developing nations consume more energy due to increasing affluence and access to energy.
    E. Developing and developed nations consume about the same amount of energy.

97. Nitrogen fixation is a necessary part of the nitrogen cycle because

    A. Atmospheric nitrogen cannot be used directly by organisms.

    B. There is not enough nitrogen in the atmosphere.

    C. Nitrogen needs to be combined with phosphorus.

    D. Bacteria needs to be created to help with plant growth.

    E. Nitrogen in the soil needs to be fixed to go back to the atmosphere.

98. When referring to energy, Earth is considered to be

    A. A closed system

    B. An open system

    C. A positive feedback loop

    D. In homeostasis

    E. Unbalanced

99. A newly developed wind farm is working at full capacity. One wind turbine generates 2000 kW of power per day. If there are 50,000 turbines, how many megawatts of energy could be produced in one day?

    A. 1×10^4

    B. 1×10^6

    C. 1×10^8

    D. 2.5×10^6

    E. 2.5×10^8

100. Geothermal energy is considered to be renewable, but why is it not truly a sustainable supply of energy?

    A. Geothermal energy relies on the sun's energy.

    B. Geothermal energy can be harnessed only from geysers.

    C. Geothermal energy provides less power than solar, wind, and biomass energy.

    D. Geothermal activity shifts naturally, so the location of the heat produced may not always be the same.

    E. Geothermal energy produces more emissions than fossil fuels.

IF YOU FINISH BEFORE TIME IS CALLED, CHECK YOUR WORK ON THIS SECTION ONLY. DO NOT WORK ON ANY OTHER SECTION IN THE TEST.

Section II: Free-Response Questions

Time: 90 minutes

4 questions

Directions: Each question is equally weighted. Plan to budget your time and allow yourself approximately 20 minutes per question. Write clearly to show any calculations when computations are necessary. Calculators are not allowed. Where an explanation or discussion is required, support your answers with relevant information, facts, and/or specific examples.

Question 1 refers to the following article by Martha Baskin of Green Acre Radio (Seattle, Washington).

An Urban Superfund Site, an Urban River, and the South Park Community

Ten years ago, the Duwamish was declared a Superfund site. The Superfund law was enacted to clean up hazardous substances that endanger public health and the environment. So far, "help" for the Duwamish has involved lengthy study and negotiations with the principal parties responsible for cleanup: the city, King County, the port, and Boeing. Cleanup of two hot spots is underway. They contain the river's most persistent toxins: PCBs, PAHs or polynuclear aromatic hydrocarbons, arsenic, and dioxin. But the EPA won't decide about action for the rest of the waterway until 2013. The EPA's Tristan Gardner uses LEGOs to demonstrate options on the table: dredging, removal, containment, and natural recovery. "We're using the blue LEGOs to represent the Duwamish, the gray to represent mud and the sediments, and the red to represent the pollution." Containment involves putting 10 to 20 feet of sand, clay, and other materials on top of the pollution. "Now this doesn't remove the contamination, but it prevents it from being taken up by fish or disturbed by human activity. So, when the clean water from upstream is coming down, it's not going to pick up the contamination and deposit it somewhere else."

1. Answer the following questions:

   A. Explain what it means when a site is listed as a Superfund site.
   B. Name and explain the law that is also called the "Superfund."
   C. Describe three likely consequences to the Duwamish River ecosystem as a result of the contamination.
   D. Select one of the listed contaminants and cite a possible source and its potential health effects on humans.
   E. Cite and explain at least two possible issues associated with the proposed method of pollution containment.

2. A house is located in Southern California in an inland chaparral valley. The house is 2,000 square feet and is cooled by a 5-ton central air-conditioning system. (A 1-ton air-conditioning unit subtracts 12,000 BTUs, the amount needed to melt 1 ton of ice in one day.) One kWh of electricity costs $0.10, and the air conditioner uses an average of 25 kWh per day from June 1 through September 30.

   A. Calculate the following, showing all the steps of your calculations.
      a. The number of kWh of electricity used to cool the house for the summer.
      b. The cost of cooling the house for the summer.
   B. Identify and describe two actions the owner of the house could take to conserve electrical energy, aside from replacing the air-conditioning unit with a more energy-efficient model.
   C. The owner has been considering replacing the air-conditioning unit because it is more than 25 years old. Discuss one environmental cost and one environmental benefit of replacing the air-conditioning unit, and one economic cost and one economic benefit of replacing the unit.

3. A type of bacterium called fire blight is destroying partial and full trees in a large portion of a pear orchard. Fire blight is spread via insects, pruning tools, and water splash. As always, the orchard owner uses a fungicide spray that has been effective at controlling the blight in previous seasons. Recent applications, though, have not been as successful, with each application killing a lower and lower percentage of the bacterium. It is apparent that the blight has become resistant to the used fungicide.

    A. Explain how bacteria could develop resistance to a fungicide.

    B. Give two examples of how bacterial resistance to fungicide can economically impact orchard owners.

    C. Explain one alternative to fungicide that may help the orchardist manage the spread of fire blight.

    D. Describe an example of how the development of bacterial resistance can affect human health.

4. A forest ecosystem is destroyed by a volcanic eruption. There are many steps involved in the process of regrowth.

    A. Discuss which type of succession would follow this disturbance.

    B. Explain the role of a pioneer species in succession. What is an example of a pioneer species? Why are some organisms successful as pioneer species?

    C. Discuss a climax community.

    D. Explain the concept of resilience.

    E. Discuss how humans have impacted the cycle of succession.

IF YOU FINISH BEFORE TIME IS CALLED, CHECK YOUR WORK ON THIS SECTION ONLY. DO NOT WORK ON ANY OTHER SECTION IN THE TEST.

Answer Key

Section I: Multiple-Choice Questions

1. D	26. C	51. D	76. C
2. C	27. B	52. C	77. D
3. E	28. E	53. A	78. D
4. B	29. C	54. B	79. B
5. B	30. C	55. D	80. B
6. D	31. E	56. B	81. D
7. A	32. D	57. A	82. C
8. A	33. E	58. C	83. B
9. B	34. A	59. A	84. C
10. B	35. D	60. D	85. E
11. B	36. B	61. B	86. D
12. C	37. C	62. B	87. A
13. A	38. E	63. E	88. C
14. A	39. A	64. D	89. D
15. C	40. A	65. E	90. C
16. B	41. B	66. A	91. E
17. E	42. B	67. D	92. B
18. D	43. C	68. C	93. D
19. C	44. B	69. B	94. C
20. A	45. E	70. C	95. D
21. D	46. D	71. B	96. A
22. C	47. D	72. C	97. A
23. C	48. B	73. A	98. B
24. D	49. D	74. D	99. B
25. C	50. A	75. B	100. D

Answer Explanations

Section I: Multiple-Choice Questions

1. **D** Phosphorus is found mainly in sediment, with large amounts also found in oceans. Very small amounts are found in the atmosphere in dust particles and sea spray.

2. **C** Vast quantities of carbon are stored in vegetation. The cutting down of forests and removal of vegetation releases this stored carbon into the atmosphere. Fossil fuels contain a large amount of carbon as well, because they are made from the remains of organic matter. With the combustion of fossil fuels, the trapped carbon is released.

3. **E** The carbon, sulfur, phosphorus, and nitrogen cycles all have been altered by humans. Carbon has been altered through the burning of fossil fuels and removal of large amounts of the Earth's vegetation; phosphorous, through its use in fertilizers and detergents and its presence in untreated sewage; sulfur, in coal combustion and industrial processes; and nitrogen, through extensive use of fertilizers, the combustion of fossil fuels, and massive production of animal waste.

4. **B** Aquifers recharge slowly if there is inconsistent rainfall. Water percolates from the soil surface down through soil and sediment, ultimately reaching the aquifer. With limited rainfall, this process is slow and limits the amount of water that reaches the aquifer.

5. **B** Because fossil fuels are stored in the sediment of the Earth, when they are removed and then combusted for energy, the carbon is emitted into the atmosphere. Deforestation and the removal of vegetation also release carbon into the atmosphere in the form of carbon dioxide. Deforestation releases carbon dioxide into the atmosphere because trees act as carbon sinks, storing carbon. Once they are cut down, the stored carbon is re-released. Conversion of carbon dioxide back into vegetation and eventually sediment is not happening at the same rate at which carbon is being removed, leading to a shift in the balance of carbon from sediment to atmosphere, and resulting in the current climate change.

6. **D** The ozone layer is located in the stratosphere, where it creates a shield against much of the harmful ultraviolet radiation from the sun. Ozone emitted into or formed in the troposphere contributes to climate change.

7. **A** Soil porosity is the amount of space between soil particles and is expressed as the ratio of void space to total volume. Water, air, and other gases fill these pore spaces. More pore space means a high water-holding capacity.

8. **A** Radon and asbestos are both naturally occurring substances but can become indoor air pollutants. Radon is a radioactive gas that can seep into basements from the surrounding bedrock. Because it is radioactive, chronic exposure can lead to negative health effects, including lung cancer. Asbestos is a mineral with a fibrous crystal that is mined from the lithosphere. When inhaled, these fibers can lodge in the alveoli of the lungs. The body then produces acids to fight the invasive particles, sometimes leading to diseases including mesothelioma and asbestosis.

9. **B** The Earth absorbs and slowly releases solar energy, warming air near its surface. This warm air is less dense that cool air above, so the warm air rises. As it rises, it cools, thereby becoming denser and sinking back toward the Earth's surface. This continual rising and falling creates convection currents.

10. **B** To calculate the doubling time of a population, use the equation 70 ÷ annual growth rate (in which "percent" is removed from the growth rate). Therefore, if a population is growing at a rate of 1.4 percent annually, the answer is found as follows: 70 ÷ 1.4 = 50. This means that the population will double in 50 years.

11. **B** Populations of K-selected species usually stay near carrying capacity, competing for limited resources. Fewer resources lead to a diminished carrying capacity. Although climate change may contribute to lack of food and water, it is this lack and not climate change itself that diminishes carrying capacity.

12. **C** Negative feedback loops are the most common in nature, as the inputs and outputs into a system stabilize each other and create equilibrium. (For example, more of something "turns off" its production.) Within positive feedback loops, a system moves in one direction, toward an extreme, and one reaction causes another, which causes another, creating instability (like a snowball picking up more snow). Positive feedback loops in nature are usually due to human involvement. Examples include the changing climate, melting of polar ice, erosion, and human population growth.

13. **A** Net primary productivity is the rate at which solar energy is converted into biomass, so high net primary productivity means energy is converted to biomass quickly. Coral reefs, wetlands, and algal beds also have high net primary productivity.

14. **A** Water vapor, carbon dioxide, and methane are the most abundant greenhouse gases in the atmosphere. All three gases occur naturally, but their levels have increased in the last century due to human activity. They all have the ability to trap heat, so the greater the concentration of gases the more heat that can be trapped within the atmosphere.

15. **C** In photosynthesis a plant takes in carbon dioxide and water, which react with light energy from the sun to produce glucose and oxygen. The chemical equation for photosynthesis is: $6CO_2 + 6H_2O \xrightarrow{\text{light}} C_6H_{12}O_6 + 6O_2$.

16. **B** The golden toad was endemic to the Monteverde cloud forest in Costa Rica. An endemic species is found in only one location on the planet. Therefore, if it vanishes from this region it becomes extinct. This is what happened to the golden toad when the climate began to shift in its habitat, drying the forest. (It was indigenous and native as well, but neither of those conditions contributed to its extinction.)

17. **E** A beaver is a keystone species in North America because many other species depend on it for survival. Beaver dams help to maintain river flow, provide habitat for other organisms, and reduce the effects of flooding. Also, their dams create wetlands and ponds vital to the maintenance of biodiversity.

18. **D** Survival in an extremely dry desert environment requires adaptations, including spines to help protect exposed organisms from being eaten, deep roots to access water, and waxy outer coatings on plants to prevent water loss.

19. **C** Boreal forests are dominated by coniferous trees, which are needle-containing trees such as evergreens. Coniferous trees are well-suited for the cold, dry climate of this region since their leaves require less water and sunlight for photosynthesis.

20. **A** Tundra is found in high latitudes and is very cold through most of the year. Water that remains frozen in the soil through most of the year is known as permafrost. Unfortunately, in recent years, more permafrost has been melting and remaining melted for longer periods of time due to climate change.

21. **D** When using the precautionary principle to assess a newly developed substance, it is assumed that the substance is harmful until proven otherwise. This process takes a cautious approach so harmful substances are not introduced to people, wildlife, or the environment.

22. **C** This example describes a disturbance (volcanic eruption) that completely destroyed all life. This means that primary succession takes place, with all life in the area essentially starting over. Lichens are a pioneer species starting the process, followed by the growth of small plants and then the presence of insects. Eventually larger vegetation develops and, finally, there are mature trees. Over time, this community remains stable, unaffected by disturbance, and is considered a climax community.

23. **C** Ice has been accumulating in glaciers and ice caps for millions of years, trapping air bubbles as it freezes. The composition of these bubbles in an ice core sample tells scientists what was in the atmosphere at the time the ice froze. Concentrations of greenhouse gases, variations in temperature, volcanic activity, and the composition of the atmosphere can all be determined from ice core samples.

24. **D** Much solar radiation penetrates the Earth's atmosphere and reflects off of the planet. Some of this heat escapes back into space and some is reflected back to Earth by greenhouse gases. This double reflection, first from the Earth and then from atmospheric gases, is known as the greenhouse effect.

25. **C** Tropical rainforests store the majority of their nutrients in vegetation. Therefore, the soil contains minimal nutrients. The runoff from extensive rain in these regions also contributes to the removal of nutrients from the soil.

26. **C** The pollutant starts with a concentration of 0.5 ppm. The pollutant dissipates over a five-day period by 20 percent. Twenty percent of 0.5 ppm is $0.5 \times 0.20 = 0.1$ ppm. And so, after five days, the concentration is 0.4 ppm. But 20 percent of *this* is 0.08. So, after ten days, there is 0.32 ppm remaining. Twenty percent of this is 0.064. So, after 15 days, there is 0.256, rounded to 0.26 ppm remaining.

27. **B** The sun supplies the energy that fuels the beginning of the food webs on Earth. Plants, algae, and some bacteria use solar energy to make their own food in the process of photosynthesis. This process also produces the chemical energy that serves as fuel for herbivores. Herbivores are then consumed by carnivores, and so on. Without solar radiation, there would be no energy to start this process.

28. **E** The United States has the largest ecological footprint, consuming more resources, using more land, using more water, and producing more waste than any other nation.

29. **C** An inverted population pyramid describes a population with more people in the older age brackets as opposed to younger age brackets. This age structure has an impact on social and economic systems. Socially, this affects the labor market, military recruitment, and reproduction. An inverted population pyramid also weighs heavily on social systems that support the elderly, such as Social Security and healthcare.

30. **C** Carrying capacity is the population that an ecosystem can support. In this case, the number of mule deer exceeded that which the food supply could support. The starvation deaths of individuals brought the population in line with the ecosystem's carrying capacity.

31. **E** The effects of China's one-child policy are in some ways different than they would be in other populations. Males are still valued more than females in Chinese culture, so it is desirable to have a son. Sometimes people abort female fetuses because there are limits on having more than one child. This leads to an uneven sex ratio. The policy also leads to an inverted population pyramid, with an inordinate percentage of elderly citizens, which increases pressures on healthcare and Social Security. Because there are fewer young people in the country, there are fewer people entering the military.

32. **D** To find the growth rate of a population the following equation is used:

    (Crude Birth Rate + Immigration) – (Crude Death Rate + Emigration) = Growth Rate per 1,000 Individuals

    The answer is then multiplied by 100 to convert it to a percent. The terms *crude birth rate* and *crude death rate* mean per 1,000 individuals.

    For the question, calculate as follows:

    $$\left(\frac{32}{1,000} + \frac{2}{1,000}\right) - \left(\frac{9}{1,000} + \frac{4}{1,000}\right) = \frac{21}{1,000} = 0.021$$

    Then convert it to a percent by multiplying by 100.

    The answer is 2.1 percent.

33. **E** With a growth rate of 1.8 percent, the population is growing. In fact, the population will double in about 39 years. If there is even a small positive growth rate, the population will continue to grow exponentially.

34. **A** Wind has kinetic energy (energy of motion). This kinetic energy is converted into electrical energy through the use of turbines. Wind turns the turbine blades, which rotate an internal shaft. This connects to a generator that produces electrical energy.

35. **D** In the 1960s, oil overtook coal as the most commonly used fossil fuel. Oil is used for many purposes, including home heating, transportation, and power plants. Currently the use of natural gas is increasing at the fastest rate.

36. **B** Exposure to a substance in large doses within a brief period of time is termed acute exposure, while exposure to small doses over a long period of time is considered chronic exposure. Acute exposure is usually related to a specific incident or event. Chronic exposure affects an organism gradually over time, and because of this the source is usually harder to identify.

37. **C** The dramatic dip in population size represents population destabilization, likely due to limiting factors in the environment.

38. **E** Any number of factors could have contributed to this destabilization and drop in population numbers. Such factors include disease; temperature extremes; or competition for space, food, and water.

39. **A** A risk assessment includes a dose-response analysis, which assesses the toxic effects of a substance on an organism.

40. **A** In an aquatic environment, succession can occur due to eutrophication. As excess nutrients enter a lake or pond, plants and organisms grow rapidly. Eventually plants fill the area. With extensive growth comes a large amount of death and decomposition. Water accumulates dead organic matter over time, and a moving water source also deposits sediment. Ultimately, this area is likely to become terrestrial because it has essentially been filled in by dead organic matter and sediment.

41. **B** Australia suffered an economic depression in the 1920s and 1930s, as did the United States. When there is a severe economic depression, the total fertility rates typically decline because most people cannot afford to have children.

42. **B** As in the United States, Australia experienced an economic boom in the 1940s and 1950s following World War II. This led to increased total fertility rates and a baby boom.

43. **C** As with any declining human population, a decrease in population growth could lead to a decrease in the labor market because there are fewer young people entering the workforce. With fewer people in the population working and making money, there could be an economic decline.

44. **B** A tragedy of the commons occurs when an unregulated resource is overexploited unsustainably. Fisheries cannot always be managed and controlled globally. Therefore, the resource can be over-harvested and depleted without proper regulation and monitoring. Because it is in each individual actor's best interest to act unsustainably, all suffer in the long run.

45. **E** Heat capacity is the amount of heat necessary to change the temperature of a substance. Thus, it describes the ability of a substance to retain heat. Water has a high heat capacity, meaning it heats and cools slowly, and only with the addition or subtraction of large amounts of heat energy. Therefore, oceans remain at a more constant temperature than land because oceans heat and cool slowly, while land temperatures change more quickly.

46. **D** Overworking and overuse of the land can lead to soil salinization in arid regions where high evaporation rates pull salt-laden waters from deeper in the soil to the surface, where salts remain after the water content evaporates. Also, dust storms occur when dry, overworked soil becomes airborne. Waterlogging occurs when soils are overwatered and become saturated. Desertification occurs when land in arid regions is overworked and the soil becomes unusable and depleted of nutrients. Only the increase in disease is not related to the overworking and overuse of soils.

47. **D** The dead zone in the Gulf of Mexico is a result of excess nutrients entering the water from sources along the Mississippi River. Agriculture, sewage, urban areas, and industry all add excess nutrients into the river through runoff, which then carries the nutrients and pollution into the Gulf of Mexico. Excess nutrients in a water source spur the increase in growth of algae and plankton. More organisms means more death, and this increased decomposition consumes large amounts of oxygen. When this happens on a large scale, a hypoxic environment (one that is lacking in oxygen) is created. This lack of oxygen creates a dead zone.

48. **B** Countries that sign the Kyoto Protocol are mandated to reduce greenhouse gas emissions of six gases by 2012, when they must be at or lower than 1990 levels. The United States did not sign this treaty because the requirement was placed on developed, industrialized countries and not on developing nations. Some developing nations are emitting large amounts of greenhouse gases.

49. **D** The Endangered Species Act protects threatened and endangered species and their habitats, and the National Environmental Policy Act requires that proper consideration be given to the environment when federal actions are being taken. The National Environmental Policy Act mandates the use of an environmental impact statement. In building the dock, endangered species may be affected by its construction and location, so it's important to assess these issues prior to development. If endangered species are in the area and if their habitat would be affected by the dock, then the species is protected by the Endangered Species Act.

50. **A** The Ogallala Aquifer is located under eight states in the Midwestern United States. It is the world's largest aquifer, but for many decades much of its water has been pumped out and used for farmland crop irrigation. As a result, the aquifer's volume has been reduced. The recharge of the aquifer is slow because it is located in an arid region with minimal annual rainfall.

51. **D** Saltwater intrusion can occur when an aquifer is over-pumped and, therefore, decreases in volume. If this happens near a saltwater source, the saltwater will eventually move in to fill the empty space in the aquifer.

52. **C** Waterlogging is a result of the overwatering of soils, leading to a rise in the water table and eventually suffocation of plant roots. Because of the excess water in the soil, plant roots do not get the important gases necessary for survival.

53. **A** Soil salinization results from salts building up in the top layer of soil. Because of low precipitation in arid regions, when evaporation occurs, it pulls salts up through the soil. Once the water evaporates, it leaves the salts on the soil.

54. **B** Biosphere reserves have been created in an effort to incorporate sustainable development with preservation of biodiversity. Managed by the United Nations, they are international efforts. In a biosphere reserve, the center is used for preservation; the middle area is used for research, tourism, and recreation (along with limited development); and the outer area is used for sustainable living and agriculture.

55. **D** While dams provide for electricity generation and drinking water, and can control flooding, they also can have harmful ecological effects. The alteration of the flow of water can impact sedimentation, mating patterns of fish, and flooding of terrestrial ecosystems. Dams also potentially slow the river's flow to the point that it has difficultly pushing sediment from its end point in an ocean, lake, or larger river.

56. **B** Habitat islands are sections of one type of habitat or ecosystem that are disconnected from larger areas of the same ecosystem, essentially creating "islands" of an ecosystem. A habitat island can be surrounded by various man-made structures such as roadways, canals, shopping centers, and other developments. Other activities such as deforestation, agricultural development, and rerouting of a water source also can create habitat islands.

57. **A** Deforestation is occurring at a rapid rate in both South America and Africa. The tropical rain forests in these regions provide many economic resources, so the sale of trees and other resources are a way to bring revenue to the countries. In addition, the rapid rate of population growth in these areas increases the need for land. This results in forests being cut down to make space for people.

58. **C** Deforestation was once occurring at a very rapid rate in both Europe and North America, but the destruction has slowed and some forest land is actually being regained through successful conservation and preservation efforts.

59. **A** In photovoltaic cells, solar energy is converted into electrical energy. Electrons are released as a result of sunlight illuminating metal within the cell. The electrons then travel toward another piece of metal, creating an electric current.

60. **D** In mutualism, organisms interact in a way that gives each a fitness benefit—in this case, coral providing shelter for algae, which in turn provides food for the coral through photosynthesis.

61. **B** Wind varies dramatically from place to place, day to day, and season to season, leaving humans with no control over when and how much wind is available at a given time.

62. **B** Large amounts of oil reserves are located in Iran, Iraq, and Saudi Arabia, with close to two-thirds of the world's oil supply being located in the Middle East.

63. **E** The use of biomass as a fuel source offers many benefits, but there are downsides as well. One of the drawbacks is the production of biomass crops used for energy on land that could potentially be used as crop land for food production. Also, the biomass crops are usually monoculture, with little biodiversity.

64. **D** The types of coal are defined by their water content, as well as how the coal was formed. The more heat and pressure under which coal is formed, the more energy per unit volume and the less water it contains. Peat is wet, moderately compressed organic matter that forms near the surface.

65. **E** The types of coal are defined by their water content, as well as how the coal was formed. The more heat and pressure under which coal is formed, the more energy per unit volume and the less water it contains. Anthracite is the deepest and most compressed form of coal, so it has the highest energy content per volume.

66. **A** The types of coal are defined by their water content, as well as how the coal was formed. The more heat and pressure under which coal is formed, the more energy per unit volume and the less water it contains. Lignite is formed relatively close to the surface under minimal heat and pressure, so it retains more water than anthracite but not as much as peat.

67. **D** Resulting from the decomposition of organic matter, natural gas is produced in an anaerobic environment within the Earth. It can form either near the surface of the lithosphere or deep within the Earth. Within the Earth, natural gas is formed under extreme heat and pressure. (If organic matter decomposes aerobically, it simply rots.)

68. **C** Developed nations use a disproportionate percentage of energy for transportation, industrial processes, and agriculture. In developing countries, energy is still invested mainly in daily activities such as cooking, indoor heating, industry, and agriculture. As many of the world's nations develop, more energy is used for transportation and industry.

69. **B** Carbon monoxide binds to hemoglobin in red blood cells, blocking oxygen from binding with the hemoglobin and, ultimately, depriving the cells and the body of oxygen.

70. **C** Crude oil is separated through boiling and distillation. In fact, the term *distillation* refers to the separation of the components of a substance through boiling. In oil distillation, components that boil at high temperatures collect toward the bottom of a distillation column, while parts that boil at lower temperatures rise and collect near the top.

71. **B** Fission is the reaction used in the process of generating nuclear energy. In a nuclear power plant, heavy, unstable atoms are bombarded with neutrons, causing the nuclei to split. This split releases heat as well as radiation in the form of additional neutrons, which cause other atoms to split, continuing the reaction.

72. **C** Bioaccumulation occurs within an organism when it consumes other organisms containing a toxicant, eventually concentrating the toxin in its body. In the situation described in this question, mercury is the toxicant.

73. **A** A thermal inversion occurs when a layer of cool air is trapped beneath a layer of warm air. Usually, air is warmed near the Earth's surface and, being less dense than cool air, travels upward, bringing with it surface pollutants. In a thermal inversion, there is no convection current, thus no vertical mixing, so pollutants remain trapped in the cool air near the Earth's surface.

74. **D** Both sulfur dioxide and nitrogen dioxide contribute to acid precipitation. Nitrogen dioxide (NO_2) is created from combustion processes at high temperatures, such as vehicle emissions. Once in the atmosphere, NO_2 reacts to form nitrous and nitric acid, which are components of acid precipitation. Sulfur dioxide (SO_2) emissions are mainly due to the emissions from electric utilities that burn coal for energy. SO_2 can react with water vapor to form sulfuric acid (H_2SO_4) and sulfate salts, which can cause acid precipitation.

75. **B** Endocrine disruptors disturb the endocrine system (hormone system) by imitating hormones. The endocrine disruptors bind to receptor sites on cells, both blocking hormones from binding to these sites and

making the cell function as if a hormone is attached. This hormone displacement can lead to health and reproductive issues.

76. **C** Chlorofluorocarbons (CFCs), which later were found to deplete the ozone layer, were emitted in extremely high amounts in the 1970s. In the atmosphere, a CFC molecule breaks apart, releasing a chlorine atom. This atom of chlorine breaks apart an ozone molecule (O_3) by ripping away one oxygen atom to form chlorine monoxide (ClO) and leaving an oxygen molecule (O_2). In 1987, the Montreal Protocol was signed by over 150 nations, successfully cutting CFC production in half and allowing regeneration of the ozone layer.

77. **D** Salvage logging is the removal of dead trees and brush after a wildfire. This dead vegetation could serve as fuel for an additional fire. However, the environmental impacts of salvage logging include the removal of nutrients from an ecosystem, the loss of habitat for other organisms, the acceleration of soil erosion, and the resulting decrease in biodiversity.

78. **D** In a growing modern society, noise pollution has become an increasing issue. Some sources of noise pollution are vehicle traffic, construction, and nightclubs. It is also a result of poor urban planning, where housing may be too close to noise-pollution sources. Sailboats emit a very minimal amount of sound, so they are not considered a source of noise pollution.

79. **B** Eutrophication occurs when excess nutrients enter the water from runoff. When, as is frequently the case, these nutrients are due to human sources including agriculture, sewage, urban areas, and industry, it is considered cultural eutrophication.

80. **B** Industrial smog is created when coal is burned and carbon dioxide, carbon monoxide, and soot are produced. Sulfur dioxide is produced from the combustion of sulfur-containing coal. Sulfur dioxide is oxidized to sulfur trioxide, which can react with water, forming sulfuric acid. Sulfuric acid is a component of industrial smog.

81. **D** Thermal pollution results from the heating of a water source beyond its natural temperature range, commonly resulting from the release of water from a factory. Often, water is used to cool industrial processes, thereby absorbing heat. When the water is discharged, it may still be hot or warm, thus heating the water into which it is released. Thermal pollution can harm ecosystems by killing organisms and, thus, affecting biodiversity, food webs, and ecosystem structure.

82. **C** During secondary treatment in the sewage treatment process, oxygen is added to start aerobic decomposition. This results in the removal of most suspended solids, breaking down the organic matter.

83. **B** Point B represents the LD_{50}, which is the lethal dose for 50 percent of the population. It corresponds to the death of 50 percent of the population on the y-axis.

84. **C** The threshold value is the amount of a toxicant that begins to affect the population being tested. Therefore, on the graph the threshold value is the point at which a response starts registering on the y-axis, point C.

85. **E** Milankovitch cycles have an impact on the amount of solar radiation affecting various latitudes on the Earth's surface. There are three different changes to the Earth's rotation; each change occurs in a cycle between every 23,000 and 100,000 years, resulting in changes in climate.

86. **D** Resistance to a pesticide or other substance occurs over many generations through natural selection. When a pesticide is applied to a crop, many insects die, but the ones that survive have a natural resistance to the pesticide. More insects of the next generation survive because they have a natural resistance inherited from their parents. Through selection acting across generations, the population gradually becomes more and more resistant until almost the entire population is resistant to the pesticide.

87. **A** The combustion of wood produces carbon monoxide and particulate matter in the form of ash. These both can be health hazards; carbon monoxide can lead to cardiovascular disease or asphyxiation and particulate pollutants can lead to irritation, asthma, respiratory issues, and cancer.

88. **C** Hazardous waste can be classified as ignitable if the substance can catch fire easily, reactive if the chemical is unstable and can react with other compounds easily, corrosive if a substance can deteriorate metal easily, or toxic if a chemical can harm human health.

89. **D** Coral reef ecosystems are especially sensitive to climate change. As water temperatures increase as a result of global warming, the algae (zooxanthalae) that live in a mutualistic relationship with the coral leave. This leaves the coral without food and nutrients, ultimately killing them.

90. **C** The integrated pest management (IPM) approach uses many techniques together to combat the threat of pests. Techniques include crop rotation, habitat alteration, some chemical use, transgenic crops, and biological controls. Because every method has negatives, combining the benefits of each leads to a more successful and safer approach to pest management.

91. **E** With the changing climate, tropical diseases are having an impact on a broader scale. Because the ranges of warm climate are increasing, tropical diseases are able to move into areas that previously would have been too cold for their vectors to survive. Rodents, mosquitoes, and other warm-climate insects carry these diseases and spread them to humans. Tropical diseases like malaria, dengue fever, yellow fever, and cholera now have farther reach.

92. **B** The International Panel on Climate Change (IPCC) is a group of scientists and government officials that assesses, summarizes, and reports information regarding climate change. This organization was established by the United Nations Environmental Program (UNEP) and the World Meteorological Organization (WMO) in 1988.

93. **D** In regions close to the equator, precipitation is higher. This larger amount of fresh water entering the ecosystems decreases the salinity of equatorial ocean waters.

94. **C** As a country experiences economic growth, energy consumption may increase because more people may purchase items such as vehicles, increasing the use of oil. The trick in this question is the inclusion of the term *per capita*. Yes, overall energy consumption increases due to population growth and medical care that keeps energy consumers alive longer, but in this list, only economic growth increases per-capita consumption.

95. **D** Because of improved technologies, the production and use of energy is becoming more efficient. This means more usable energy is obtained from the same amount of a substance. For example, vehicles now can get more miles per gallon than in the past. Also, power plants are more efficient in producing energy today than they were previously. These efficiencies can reduce a country's per-capita energy consumption.

96. **A** People in affluent nations have the financial means to consume more energy. These people also tend to have increased access to energy infrastructure.

97. **A** Atmospheric nitrogen (N_2) cannot be used directly by organisms and must be fixed prior to being absorbed. Nitrogen fixation can occur through lightning or through nitrogen-fixing bacteria located in nodules on the roots of legumes. When nitrogen is fixed, it is combined with hydrogen to form ammonia (NH_3). Ammonia's water-soluble ion (NH_4^+) can be used by plants.

98. **B** Earth is considered an open system in terms of energy because its main source of energy is the sun, which contributes from outside the Earth's system.

99. **B** If each wind turbine generates 2,000 kW of energy per day, and there are 50,000 turbines, 1×10^8 kW of energy is produced each day (assuming all turbines are operating at 100 percent). This then needs to be converted to MW.

$$1 \times 10^8 \, kW = 1 \times 10^6 \, MW \text{ or } 100,000 \, MW$$

100. **D** The source of geothermal energy is the extreme heat generated deep within the Earth as a result of radioactive decay of elements. This heat increases the temperature of water it comes in contact with, creating steam and heated water under pressure. To create usable electricity, this water and steam are then captured and used as a direct heat source, or the steam can be used to turn turbines to generate electricity. Because geothermal energy occurs only in areas where heat is being generated by radioactive decay, not all areas can use this form of energy. Also, over time the activity can shift and an area that once had access to geothermal energy may no longer have access to it.

Section II: Free- Response Explanations

1. This question is worth a maximum of 10 points, as follows:

A. Explain what it means when a site is listed as a Superfund site (2 points maximum):
- 1 point: Superfund sites are areas contaminated with hazardous waste, including both groundwater and soil pollution.
- 1 point: Superfund sites are administered by the Environmental Protection Agency (EPA).

B. Name and explain the law that is also called the "Superfund" (2 points maximum):
- 1 point: Comprehensive Response Compensation and Liability Act (CERCLA).
- 1 point: The "Superfund" provides for federal money to be used for the cleanup of hazardous-waste sites, including accidents and spills. If a party responsible for the spill can be identified, the EPA has the power to ensure that the party is held accountable for the cleanup. If the responsible party cannot be identified or if they refuse to pay for cleanup, the "Superfund" monies will pay for the remediation of the hazardous waste site.

C. Describe three likely consequences to the Duwamish River ecosystem as a result of the contamination (3 points maximum):
- 1 point: Loss of vegetation, leading to the loss of other organisms dependent upon plant life for food, shelter, and breeding grounds.
- 1 point: Poisoning of organisms, which can reduce the populations of species and may result in some species being threatened or endangered.
- 1 point: Loss of biodiversity in the river ecosystem if some species are lost or populations are diminished.
- 1 point: Loss of nurseries for the laying and protection of eggs.
- 1 point: Bioaccumulation and biomagnifications of the contaminants in organisms, causing a range of health-related issues.
- 1 point: Potential for contaminants to act as endocrine disruptors, affecting reproduction and offspring.

D. Select one of the listed contaminants and cite a possible source and its potential health effects on humans (1 point maximum):
- 1 point: Polychlorinated biphenols (PCBs) are industrial chemicals commonly added to plastics, paints, and sealants. They can act as endocrine disruptors, carcinogens, and neurotoxins, and affect the reproductive and immune systems.
- 1 point: Polynuclear aromatic hydrocarbons (PAHs) are created from the incomplete combustion of fossil fuels, garbage, and other products. They are found in plastics, pesticides, some medicines, and dyes. PAHs can be found naturally or can be man-made. It is thought that PAHs can affect the reproductive and immune systems and may also act as carcinogens, teratogens, and mutagens, while also damaging the skin.
- 1 point: Arsenic occurs naturally in some soils and can infiltrate water sources when leached out of sediment and carried via runoff and percolation through the soil. Exposure can occur through consumption of contaminated foods or via inhalation of particles. It can lead to skin disorders, lung and skin cancer, internal and organ damage, gastrointestinal problems, and neurological issues.
- 1 point: Dioxins are unintentionally created as a result of many processes, including incomplete combustion in reactions during smoking of cigarettes, vehicle emissions, and wood and coal burning. They are created during paper bleaching and metal recycling. Air, soil, water, and foods all can carry dioxins. Health effects of dioxins include skin disease and negative impacts on the immune and endocrine systems; they also can act as teratogens.

E. Cite and explain at least two possible issues associated with the proposed method of pollution containment (2 points maximum):
- 1 point: Contaminants are not being removed from the water source.
- 1 point: The covered contaminants could be disturbed by natural events including flooding of the river, shifting of the river bed, or earthquake.

- 1 point: The contaminants could be disturbed by human activities such as dredging.
- 1 point: If the sediment is disturbed, the pollution will be disturbed, reintroducing the contaminants into the river ecosystem.

2. This question is worth a maximum of 10 points, as follows:

A. Calculate the following, showing all the steps of your calculations.

a. The number of kWh of electricity used to cool the house for the summer (2 points maximum—1 point for setup, 1 point for correct answer):

Number of Days = 30 (June) + 31 (July) + 31 (August) + 30 (September) = 122 days

kWh used = Number of Days × kWh per day = 122 days × 25 kWh per day = 3,050 kWh

b. The cost of cooling the house for the summer (2 points maximum—1 point for setup, 1 point for correct answer):

Cost = kWh × \$0.10 per kWh = \$305

Make sure to include proper units in each step.

B. Identify and describe two actions the owner of the house could take to conserve electrical energy, aside from replacing the air-conditioning unit with a more energy-efficient model (2 points maximum):

- 1 point: Replace single-paned windows with double- or triple-paned windows.
- 1 point: Add or increase insulation in the walls.
- 1 point: Add or increase insulation in the ceiling.
- 1 point: Turn the thermostat up to a higher temperature and wear less clothing to stay cool.
- 1 point: Replace light bulbs with compact florescent light (CFL) bulbs or install dimmer switches.
- 1 point: Turn off lights when not in use.
- 1 point: Unplug appliances when not in use. (Some appliances plugged into the outlets still use a little electricity.)
- 1 point: Turn down the water temperature on the water heater.
- 1 point: Buy a more energy-efficient appliance such as a refrigerator, electric stove, dishwasher, washing machine, or electric dryer.
- 1 point: Any other reasonable energy-saving strategy.

C. The owner has been considering replacing the air-conditioning unit because it is more than 25 years old. Discuss one environmental cost and one environmental benefit of replacing the air-conditioning unit and one economic cost and one economic benefit of replacing the unit (4 points maximum):

- Environmental cost (1 point):

  1 point: Replacing the unit requires production of a new unit, especially including mining for metals, so it increases CO_2 emissions from mining equipment and the transport of raw materials, and contributes to greenhouse-gas emissions and global climate change.

  1 point: Transportation of the final product to the store increases CO_2 from combustion of fossil fuels, contributing to greenhouse-gas emissions and global climate change.

  1 point: Increasing dust from mining operations decreases air quality.

  1 point: Increasing soil runoff from erosion into streams increases turbidity in the stream and decreases photosynthesis.

- Environmental benefit (1 point):

  1 point: A newer unit will reduce electricity usage, resulting in less CO_2 emissions if electricity is produced from the combustion of coal.

  1 point: A newer unit will reduce electricity usage, which will result in a reduction of waste generated from nuclear processes if energy is being created at a nuclear power plant.

  1 point: Decreased transport of coal lowers CO_2 emissions from diesel-powered trains.

1 point: Decreased demand for uranium for nuclear energy generation.

1 point: Less coal is needed, reducing the effects of mining such as habitat destruction from strip mining, air pollution from dust, runoff into streams that cause increased turbidity in the stream, and a lesser decrease of photosynthesis.

- Economic cost (1 point):

    1 point: The cost of purchasing the new air-conditioning unit.

    1 point: The cost of installing the new air-conditioning unit.

    1 point: The sales tax paid on the purchase.

- Economic benefit (1 point):

    1 point: Retains jobs (sales, manufacturing, transportation, mining).

    1 point: Taxes help cities, counties, and states.

    1 point: Eventually saves money by using less electricity.

    1 point: Any other reasonable cost or benefit.

3. This question is worth a maximum of 10 points, as follows:

A. Explain how bacteria could develop resistance to a fungicide. (5 points maximum):

- 1 point: When a fungicide is applied, most of the targeted bacteria die, but some survive.

- 1 point: The bacteria that survive have a natural resistance to the fungicide, and the genes containing this resistance are passed on during reproduction.

- 1 point: After several generations, only a population resistant to the fungicide remains, and the chemical becomes ineffective against the bacteria.

- 1 point: New and possibly more powerful fungicides need to be developed in order to target these resistant pests.

- 1 point: This creates a perpetual cycle of organisms evolving resistance to fungicides and humans developing different means to control the bacteria.

- 1 point: The process of the development of resistance is natural selection.

B. Give two examples of how bacterial resistance to fungicide can economically impact orchard owners. (2 points maximum):

- 1 point: Loss of fruit due to tree loss means loss of sales profits for the orchardist.

- 1 point: Each tree lost means a new tree needs to be planted. The costs associated with this replacement include purchasing the new tree and paying for labor to remove the old tree and plant a new one.

- 1 point: Cost of fungicides.

- 1 point: Labor costs associated with the application of fungicides and the maintenance of the trees to control and minimize damage from the blight.

C. Explain one alternative to fungicide that may help the orchardist manage the spread of fire blight (1 point maximum):

- 1 point: An orchardist can try to control the insects that contribute to the spread of the blight.

- 1 point: The orchardist can alternate between types of fungicide to reduce the likelihood of bacteria developing resistance to any one fungicide.

- 1 point: The affected limbs and trees can be removed.

- 1 point: The orchard can be divided into smaller sections, separated by vegetation that is not impacted by fire blight. This will reduce the possibility of the transfer of the bacteria and will help to contain a breakout when one does occur.

D. Describe an example of how the development of bacterial resistance can affect human health (2 points maximum):

- 2 points: With continued use of antibiotics or other medications to control or destroy pathogens that carry disease—including viruses, bacteria, and fungi—resistance to that product can develop over time. The result is the development of a superbug that is exceptionally hardy and unaffected by current medications.

4. This question is worth a maximum of 10 points, as follows:

A. Discuss which type of succession would follow this disturbance (2 points maximum):

- 1 point: Primary succession.
- 1 point: Following a major disturbance in which all life is removed from an area, a community begins again and life redevelops.

B. Explain the role of a pioneer species in succession. What is an example of a pioneer species? Why are some organisms successful as pioneer species? (3 points maximum)

- 1 point: A pioneer species is the first species to colonize an area after complete destruction of life in an ecosystem.
- 1 point: Examples include lichen, moss, grasses, and algae.
- 1 point: The seeds and spores of some organisms are carried easily through air and water. These species tend to be pioneer species because they can easily be transported into a desolate area and establish themselves, growing in an extreme environment, devoid of life.

C. Discuss a climax community (2 points maximum):

- 1 point: The climax community is the stable community resulting from succession.
- 1 point: This community remains relatively unaltered for an extended period of time, until another disturbance occurs.
- 1 point: An ecosystem may never reach a climax community if it is continually disturbed or altered dramatically by human interference.

D. Explain the concept of resilience (1 point maximum):

- 1 point: Resilience is an ecosystem that changes due to a disturbance but eventually returns to its original state.

E. Discuss how humans have impacted the cycle of succession (2 points maximum):

Humans have altered ecosystems dramatically, which in turn can alter succession. Examples include:

- 1 point: Complete deforestation.
- 1 point: Timber harvesting, including sustainable methods.
- 1 point: Conversion of land for agricultural purposes.
- 1 point: Extreme erosion, which can lead to a positive feedback loop.
- 1 point: Extreme sedimentation in an aquatic environment, leading to aquatic succession.
- 1 point: Vegetation removal.
- 1 point: Fragmentation of habitats.
- 1 point: Any other reasonable human impact on succession.

Practice Exam 2

Answer Sheet

Remove this sheet and use it to mark your answers for the multiple-choice section of Practice Exam 2.

Section I

1 ⒶⒷⒸⒹⒺ	26 ⒶⒷⒸⒹⒺ	51 ⒶⒷⒸⒹⒺ	76 ⒶⒷⒸⒹⒺ
2 ⒶⒷⒸⒹⒺ	27 ⒶⒷⒸⒹⒺ	52 ⒶⒷⒸⒹⒺ	77 ⒶⒷⒸⒹⒺ
3 ⒶⒷⒸⒹⒺ	28 ⒶⒷⒸⒹⒺ	53 ⒶⒷⒸⒹⒺ	78 ⒶⒷⒸⒹⒺ
4 ⒶⒷⒸⒹⒺ	29 ⒶⒷⒸⒹⒺ	54 ⒶⒷⒸⒹⒺ	79 ⒶⒷⒸⒹⒺ
5 ⒶⒷⒸⒹⒺ	30 ⒶⒷⒸⒹⒺ	55 ⒶⒷⒸⒹⒺ	80 ⒶⒷⒸⒹⒺ
6 ⒶⒷⒸⒹⒺ	31 ⒶⒷⒸⒹⒺ	56 ⒶⒷⒸⒹⒺ	81 ⒶⒷⒸⒹⒺ
7 ⒶⒷⒸⒹⒺ	32 ⒶⒷⒸⒹⒺ	57 ⒶⒷⒸⒹⒺ	82 ⒶⒷⒸⒹⒺ
8 ⒶⒷⒸⒹⒺ	33 ⒶⒷⒸⒹⒺ	58 ⒶⒷⒸⒹⒺ	83 ⒶⒷⒸⒹⒺ
9 ⒶⒷⒸⒹⒺ	34 ⒶⒷⒸⒹⒺ	59 ⒶⒷⒸⒹⒺ	84 ⒶⒷⒸⒹⒺ
10 ⒶⒷⒸⒹⒺ	35 ⒶⒷⒸⒹⒺ	60 ⒶⒷⒸⒹⒺ	85 ⒶⒷⒸⒹⒺ
11 ⒶⒷⒸⒹⒺ	36 ⒶⒷⒸⒹⒺ	61 ⒶⒷⒸⒹⒺ	86 ⒶⒷⒸⒹⒺ
12 ⒶⒷⒸⒹⒺ	37 ⒶⒷⒸⒹⒺ	62 ⒶⒷⒸⒹⒺ	87 ⒶⒷⒸⒹⒺ
13 ⒶⒷⒸⒹⒺ	38 ⒶⒷⒸⒹⒺ	63 ⒶⒷⒸⒹⒺ	88 ⒶⒷⒸⒹⒺ
14 ⒶⒷⒸⒹⒺ	39 ⒶⒷⒸⒹⒺ	64 ⒶⒷⒸⒹⒺ	89 ⒶⒷⒸⒹⒺ
15 ⒶⒷⒸⒹⒺ	40 ⒶⒷⒸⒹⒺ	65 ⒶⒷⒸⒹⒺ	90 ⒶⒷⒸⒹⒺ
16 ⒶⒷⒸⒹⒺ	41 ⒶⒷⒸⒹⒺ	66 ⒶⒷⒸⒹⒺ	91 ⒶⒷⒸⒹⒺ
17 ⒶⒷⒸⒹⒺ	42 ⒶⒷⒸⒹⒺ	67 ⒶⒷⒸⒹⒺ	92 ⒶⒷⒸⒹⒺ
18 ⒶⒷⒸⒹⒺ	43 ⒶⒷⒸⒹⒺ	68 ⒶⒷⒸⒹⒺ	93 ⒶⒷⒸⒹⒺ
19 ⒶⒷⒸⒹⒺ	44 ⒶⒷⒸⒹⒺ	69 ⒶⒷⒸⒹⒺ	94 ⒶⒷⒸⒹⒺ
20 ⒶⒷⒸⒹⒺ	45 ⒶⒷⒸⒹⒺ	70 ⒶⒷⒸⒹⒺ	95 ⒶⒷⒸⒹⒺ
21 ⒶⒷⒸⒹⒺ	46 ⒶⒷⒸⒹⒺ	71 ⒶⒷⒸⒹⒺ	96 ⒶⒷⒸⒹⒺ
22 ⒶⒷⒸⒹⒺ	47 ⒶⒷⒸⒹⒺ	72 ⒶⒷⒸⒹⒺ	97 ⒶⒷⒸⒹⒺ
23 ⒶⒷⒸⒹⒺ	48 ⒶⒷⒸⒹⒺ	73 ⒶⒷⒸⒹⒺ	98 ⒶⒷⒸⒹⒺ
24 ⒶⒷⒸⒹⒺ	49 ⒶⒷⒸⒹⒺ	74 ⒶⒷⒸⒹⒺ	99 ⒶⒷⒸⒹⒺ
25 ⒶⒷⒸⒹⒺ	50 ⒶⒷⒸⒹⒺ	75 ⒶⒷⒸⒹⒺ	100 ⒶⒷⒸⒹⒺ

Section II

CUT HERE

Section I: Multiple-Choice Questions

Time: 90 minutes

100 questions

Directions: Each of the questions or incomplete statements in this section is followed by five answer choices. Select the best answer choice and fill in the corresponding circle on the answer sheet.

1. Which of the following is responsible for reducing global CFC production by half?

   A. Copenhagen Protocol
   B. Montreal Protocol
   C. Pollution Prevention Act
   D. Kyoto Protocol
   E. Convention on Long-Range Transboundary Air Pollution

2. The main global contributing factors to greenhouse-gas emissions are

   A. Electricity production and transportation
   B. Industrial processes
   C. Agricultural processes
   D. Agriculture and transportation
   E. None of the above

3. Which of the following is a way to potentially avoid a tragedy of the commons?

   A. People sharing the resource work to manage the resource
   B. Private ownership
   C. Regulation by the government
   D. All of the above
   E. None of the above

4. In the transitional stage of demographic transition, why does the death rate fall?

   A. Movement of people into urban areas
   B. Less disease on a global scale
   C. More efficient and reliable food production and medical advancements
   D. Fewer births
   E. Fewer work-related accidents

5. What is the most abundant greenhouse gas in the atmosphere?

   A. Methane
   B. Nitrogen dioxide
   C. Water vapor
   D. Carbon dioxide
   E. Sulfur dioxide

6. How does a nuclear meltdown occur?

   A. Radiation is released when temperatures in the core of the reactor increase and the uranium fuel rods melt.
   B. Radiation escapes from the core of the reactor due to the shutdown of the generator.
   C. The nuclear core collapses.
   D. The fission process halts instantaneously.
   E. None of the above.

7. As a whole, industrialized nations use _____% more energy than developing nations.

   A. 10
   B. 25
   C. 50
   D. 75
   E. 100

8. $N_2 + O_2 \rightarrow 2NO$

   $2NO + O_2 \rightarrow 2NO_2$

   $NO_2 \rightarrow NO + O$

   $O + O_2 \rightarrow O_3$

   The above reactions describe the chemical process that forms:

   A. Photochemical smog
   B. Industrial smog
   C. Acid precipitation
   D. Ozone
   E. Peroxyacetyl nitrate

9. Which of the following is the main advantage of breeder nuclear fission over conventional nuclear fission?

    A. Breeder nuclear fission is less expensive.
    B. Breeder nuclear fission is a more efficient use of the fuel.
    C. Breeder nuclear fission is safer.
    D. Breeder nuclear fission creates less emission.
    E. Breeder nuclear fission uses less land to build the reactor.

10. In what products are PBDEs commonly used?

    A. Fire retardants
    B. Food preservatives
    C. Cosmetics
    D. Pesticides
    E. Paint thinners

11. Which of the following biomes is comprised mainly of trees that lose their leaves in the winter?

    A. Tundra
    B. Boreal forest
    C. Temperate rain forest
    D. Temperate deciduous forest
    E. Tropical rain forest

12. Invasive species are able to survive and thrive in new environments because of all of the following EXCEPT:

    A. The ability to travel long distances
    B. The increased risk of predation
    C. The decreased threat of disease
    D. The ability to outcompete native species
    E. The abundance of food sources

Questions 13–15 refer to the following answer choices.

    A. Biomass
    B. Hydrogen
    C. Tidal
    D. Solar
    E. Hydropower

13. Uses electrolysis to split a water molecule into oxygen and hydrogen atoms.

14. Uses heat-absorbing material for part of its process.

15. Uses reservoirs as a storage mechanism.

16. The green revolution brought which of the following to modern society?

    A. Increased movement into urban areas
    B. New farming techniques, new crop varieties, and increased food production
    C. A return to traditional agriculture
    D. New breeds of animals capable of the strenuous work on a farm
    E. Suburban areas

17. Soil degradation is an increasing global problem. Two main reasons for this are

    A. Agriculture and deforestation
    B. Deforestation and industrialization
    C. Industrialization and overgrazing
    D. Overgrazing and climate change
    E. Climate change and agriculture

18. Which of the following types of electricity generation produces the least amount of greenhouse-gas emissions from cradle to grave?

    A. Coal
    B. Nuclear
    C. Natural gas
    D. Biomass
    E. Oil

19. The biome that is adapted to and dependent upon frequent fires is:

    A. Chaparral
    B. Tundra
    C. Desert
    D. Boreal forest
    E. Savannah

20. In an ecosystem, what represents the amount of energy available as food to heterotrophs?

    A. Gross primary production
    B. Biomass
    C. Net primary production
    D. Photosynthesis
    E. Cellular respiration

21. Which of the following is an invasive species that has had devastating effects on freshwater ecosystems, while also clogging pipes and boat engines?

    A. Bullfrogs
    B. Blue mussels
    C. Cheatgrass
    D. Brown tree snakes
    E. Zebra mussels

22. Species that fulfill a narrow niche and depend on specific requirements for survival are considered:

    A. Generalists
    B. K-selected
    C. Specialists
    D. r-selected
    E. Survivors

23. Essential to the process of natural selection and evolution are:

    A. Survival and adaptations
    B. Adaptations and reproduction
    C. Adaptations and mutations
    D. Survival and reproduction
    E. Adaptations and reproduction

24. In a population of anteaters, in order to reach ants far underground, each generation has successively longer tongues than the preceding generation. Which of the following types of selection does this adaptation reflect?

    I. Directional selection
    II. Disruptive selection
    III. Stabilizing selection

    A. I only
    B. II only
    C. III only
    D. I and II
    E. II and III

Questions 25–27 refer to the following graph.

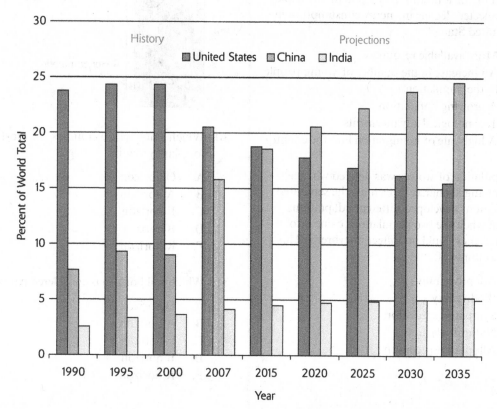

Source: U.S. Energy Information Administration

25. Which statement best explains the trend of energy consumption in India?

    A. Both past and projected consumption remain stable into the future.

    B. Both past and projected consumption are steadily increasing.

    C. Projected consumption appears to decline.

    D. Though past consumption increased dramatically, consumption is projected to nearly level out in the future.

    E. Both past and projected consumption increase at a rapid rate.

26. Which of the following most likely explains the projected increase in energy consumption in China?

    A. Fewer available resources

    B. An increase in the number of elderly in the population

    C. A growing population

    D. Decline in technological advancements

    E. A high rate of immigration into the country

27. Which of the following could potentially explain the projected decline in energy consumption in the United States?

    A. More available resources

    B. An increase in the number of young people in the population

    C. A growing population

    D. Technological advancements

    E. A high rate of immigration into the country

28. A population of wolves was divided when a river changed course. Over time, the separated populations developed different adaptations, so that when the two populations came into contact, they could no longer interbreed. This is an example of:

    A. Adaptive traits

    B. Biodiversity

    C. Sympatric speciation

    D. Natural selection

    E. Allopatric speciation

29. Which of the following nations consume the most oil?

    A. The United States, China, and Japan

    B. Saudi Arabia, Iran, and Iraq

    C. Russia, China, and India

    D. The United States, Russia, and China

    E. Iran, Iraq, and Russia

Questions 30–31 refer to the following diagram.

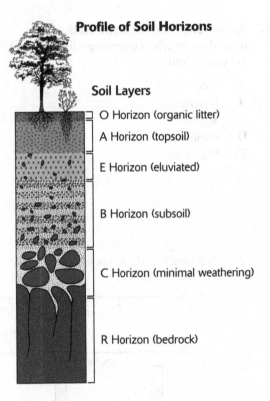

Profile of Soil Horizons

Soil Layers

O Horizon (organic litter)
A Horizon (topsoil)
E Horizon (eluviated)
B Horizon (subsoil)
C Horizon (minimal weathering)
R Horizon (bedrock)

30. Which soil horizon contains the most nutrients for plant growth?

    A. O horizon

    B. A horizon

    C. E horizon

    D. B horizon

    E. R horizon

31. Which soil horizon is considered parent material?

    A. O horizon

    B. A horizon

    C. E horizon

    D. B horizon

    E. R horizon

32. Where is acid precipitation most commonly found?

    A. Downwind of industrial emissions
    B. Upwind of industrial emissions
    C. Where industrial emissions are released
    D. Where excessive fertilizer and pesticides are sprayed
    E. Next to nuclear power plants

33. Which of the following is the most abundant gas in the Earth's atmosphere?

    A. Oxygen
    B. Nitrogen
    C. Argon
    D. Hydrogen
    E. Helium

34. What is meant by the phrase *fishing down the food chain?*

    A. Humans have harvested the majority of the smaller fish and are now fishing for larger fish.
    B. Techniques such as long-lining and drift-netting are catching fish of all sizes, so humans are depleting the entire fish population.
    C. Humans are depleting larger fish stocks, leading to the harvesting of smaller and smaller fish.
    D. Fishing efforts are now focusing on the benthic environment, depleting the organisms at this level.
    E. Only small fish are being harvested.

35. The Hawaiian Islands were formed from which of the following processes?

    A. Diverging plates
    B. Hot spots
    C. Earthquakes
    D. Plate subduction
    E. Sea-level change

36. Which part of the ocean contains most of the ocean's primary productivity?

    A. Benthic zone
    B. Abyssal zone
    C. Hadal zone
    D. Photic zone
    E. Intertidal zone

37. The main goal of the creation of golden rice is to provide

    A. A more nutritious rice that contains vitamin B
    B. A frost-resistant rice
    C. A form of rice that contains a preservative
    D. A more nutritious rice that contains vitamin A
    E. Pest-resistance

38. Permit trading is used as a way to

    A. Provide capitalistic incentives for companies to reduce emissions
    B. Create a top-down approach to emission standards
    C. Enable different countries to trade
    D. Enforce socialism
    E. Provide incentives for companies to work cooperatively

39. All the following are important and unique properties of water EXCEPT:

    A. Cohesiveness
    B. The ability to resist temperature change
    C. The low density of ice
    D. The ability to bond
    E. Neutral pH

40. In which of the following ecosystems do tree roots serve as important havens for biodiversity?

    A. Salt marshes
    B. Coral reefs
    C. Mangrove forests
    D. Estuaries
    E. Freshwater wetlands

41. An energy source that is difficult to extract but contains a large amount of energy is:

    A. Natural gas
    B. Methane hydrate
    C. Manganese nodules
    D. Anthracite
    E. Hydrogen

42. In the United States, the largest component of the municipal solid waste stream is:

    A. Yard clippings
    B. Plastics
    C. Food remnants
    D. Glass and wood
    E. Paper

43. Which of the following changes most likely acted as a key step toward the dramatic and steady decline in levels of lead in human blood between the 1960s and 1990s?

    A. Decreased use of lead in water pipes
    B. Removal of lead as a gasoline additive
    C. Reduction in emissions containing lead
    D. Decreased use of lead in paint
    E. Reduction in the usage of lead in building materials

44. Which organization is responsible for the safety of workers at their jobs?

    A. Occupational Safety and Health Administration
    B. Environmental Protection Agency
    C. Organization of Safety and Health
    D. Food and Drug Administration
    E. Department of Labor

Questions 45–47 refer to the following answer choices.

    A. Toxic Substances Control Act
    B. CERCLA
    C. National Environmental Policy Act
    D. Resource Conservation and Recovery Act
    E. Clean Water Act

45. Called the "Superfund" Act, this law mandated a federal hazardous-waste cleanup program.

46. This law manages and monitors the movement of hazardous waste.

47. This law mandates the preparation of environmental impact statements (EISs).

48. Which of the following organisms has high biotic potential?

    A. Whale
    B. Human
    C. Elephant
    D. Frog
    E. Gorilla

49. A resource manager attempts to harvest as many trees as possible without depleting the overall supply. This is applying the concept of

    A. Profit margin
    B. Maximum sustainable yield
    C. Adaptive management
    D. Selective management
    E. Ecosystem-based management

50. Persistent organic pollutants (POPs) are dangerous because they

    A. Remain in the environment, bio-accumulate in organisms, and bio-magnify throughout the food chain
    B. Are considered carcinogens
    C. Are corrosive and toxic
    D. Persist in the environment and contribute to an increase in greenhouse gases
    E. Are radioactive

51. Why has Haiti experienced repeated earthquakes throughout history?

    A. The area experiences recurring volcanic eruptions.
    B. The nation is on a fault line.
    C. It is an island, and islands are more prone to earthquakes.
    D. The sediment is unstable.
    E. The island is close to the North American plate

52. Which of the following reflects why there is concern over BPA found in foods?

    A. BPA is considered a carcinogen.
    B. BPA is considered a teratogen.
    C. BPA is considered an endocrine disruptor.
    D. BPA is considered a mutagen.
    E. BPA is considered an allergen.

53. What is one difficulty when conducting a cost-benefit analysis relating to an environmental action?

   A. Benefits usually outweigh costs.
   B. The environmental costs and benefits associated with an action cannot necessarily be quantified.
   C. The benefits are usually exceptionally high with respect to costs.
   D. This is not a tool that is used in the environmental field.
   E. The costs and benefits of an environmental action cannot be assessed.

54. Which of the following are repercussions experienced by the regions affected by the *Deepwater Horizon* oil spill in 2010?

   I. Economic loss to fishermen
   II. Destruction of nesting sites for bird species
   III. Endocrine disruption in organisms

   A. I only
   B. II only
   C. III only
   D. I and II only
   E. I, II, and III

Questions 55–57 refer to the following answer choices.

   A. Subsidy
   B. Marketable emissions permit
   C. Laws and regulations
   D. Lobbying
   E. Green tax

55. Uses market capitalism to reduce pollution.

56. Deters environmentally destructive activities.

57. Offers incentives to act in an environmentally friendly way.

58. The disposal of waste, including hazardous waste in a landfill, is mandated and controlled by the:

   A. Comprehensive Response Compensation and Liability Act
   B. Pollution Prevention Act
   C. Superfund Amendments and Reauthorization Act
   D. Toxic Substances Control Act
   E. Resource Conservation and Recovery Act

59. If a population is growing at a rate of 0.7 percent annually, the population will double in how many years?

   A. 20
   B. 50
   C. 65
   D. 100
   E. 140

60. Negative feedback loops

   A. Maintain the stability of systems
   B. Are closed systems
   C. Are becoming more common in nature because of human impact on the environment
   D. Are open systems
   E. Never occur in nature

61. Which of the following best describes the process of cellular respiration?

   A. Oxygen, water, and solar energy are used to produce carbon dioxide and sugar.
   B. Oxygen, sugar, and solar energy are used to produce carbon dioxide and water.
   C. Carbon dioxide, water, and solar energy are used to produce oxygen.
   D. Oxygen and sugar are used to produce carbon dioxide, water, and energy.
   E. Carbon dioxide and water are used to produce oxygen, sugar, and more carbon dioxide.

62. Often an endemic species is more prone to extinction than other species because it:

   A. Is endangered
   B. Is found only in one location on the planet
   C. Lives in a disaster-prone region
   D. Is an introduced species
   E. Has a limited food source

63. Which of the following is often considered a pioneer species?

   A. Brown tree snake
   B. Mosquito
   C. Lichen
   D. Red-tailed hawk
   E. Beaver

64. If soil is comprised of large particles and, therefore, has large pore spaces, it allows water to flow through more easily and is said to have:

    A. High soil porosity
    B. Low soil porosity
    C. High soil permeability
    D. Low soil permeability
    E. Waterlogging

65. Which of the following countries has the smallest ecological footprint?

    A. Canada
    B. Mexico
    C. Chile
    D. Pakistan
    E. China

66. In a country with a pyramid-shaped age structure diagram, there is a:

    A. Growing population
    B. High rate of disease affecting the working-age population
    C. Smaller labor market, as well as more stress on social systems to support the elderly
    D. Weak military and labor market
    E. High rate of death among younger age groups

67. In a country with 75 out of 1,000 people being added to the population through births and immigration and 50 out of 1,000 people leaving the population through death and emigration, what is the growth rate of this country?

    A. 1.8 percent
    B. 2.9 percent
    C. 2.5 percent
    D. 2.1 percent
    E. 3.4 percent

68. Chronic exposure to a substance means that an organism has been exposed to:

    A. High levels over a long period of time
    B. High levels over a short period of time
    C. Low levels over a short period of time
    D. Low levels over a long period of time
    E. Moderate levels over a lifetime

69. Minerals are transported through the soil via a process called:

    A. Active transport
    B. Waterlogging
    C. Leaching
    D. Porosity
    E. Permeability

70. Highway congestion is considered an example of:

    A. An ecological footprint
    B. Sustainable use
    C. Resource management
    D. A tragedy of the commons
    E. Maximum sustainable yield

Questions 71–73 refer to the following answer choices.

    A. Parasitism
    B. Commensalism
    C. Competition
    D. Amensalism
    E. Herbivory

71. A hookworm living inside a dog's intestine.

72. A blue jay living in a tree.

73. Sea lice living on a sunfish.

74. Which of the following is an example of a detritivore?

    A. Mushroom
    B. Bacteria
    C. Squirrel
    D. Millipede
    E. Ladybug

75. How can asbestos be harmful to humans?

    A. Asbestos binds to hemoglobin and blocks oxygen from binding, preventing oxygen from circulating in the blood.
    B. Asbestos acts as an endocrine disruptor.
    C. Asbestos lodges in the lining of the lungs, provoking the production of acid to destroy the invader, but over time it can potentially lead to cancer.
    D. In its gaseous form, asbestos can be inhaled and ultimately cause cancer.
    E. Asbestos can be absorbed into the blood, potentially poisoning the body.

76. In terms of matter, Earth is considered to be

   A. A closed system
   B. An open system
   C. A positive feedback loop
   D. In homeostasis.
   E. Unbalanced

77. Anthropogenic sources of methane include

   A. Methane hydrates
   B. Wetlands
   C. Landfills
   D. Termites
   E. Wildfires

78. Mercury enters the aquatic food web mainly through

   A. The processes of bio-accumulation and bio-magnification
   B. Deposition from atmospheric sources
   C. Decomposition of organisms
   D. Ocean dumping
   E. Fertilizer and pesticide runoff

79. During which step in the sewage treatment process are suspended solids removed?

   A. Pretreatment
   B. Primary treatment
   C. Secondary treatment
   D. Tertiary treatment
   E. Final treatment

80. Potential threats to biodiversity as a result of climate change include all the following EXCEPT:

   A. An increase in drought in some regions
   B. The possibility that vegetation types could shift throughout latitudes
   C. The possibility that specialized species may perish
   D. The possibility that glaciers will increase in size
   E. An increase in global average surface temperature

81. Which of the following is true of recombinant DNA technology?

   A. It is illegal under the Kyoto Protocol.
   B. DNA from different species is combined.
   C. There are few benefits seen from this technology.
   D. It is only used for crops at this point in time.
   E. It can cause mutated genes in humans.

82. In the oceans, upwellings generate areas of:

   A. High biotic potential
   B. Low primary productivity
   C. High primary productivity
   D. Nutrient-poor waters
   E. Strong currents

83. The process of mining can be very destructive to the environment. Which of the following best summarizes this destruction?

   A. Wildlife loss, toxic waste and runoff, air pollution
   B. Human death, wildlife loss, acid drainage
   C. Vegetation removal, acid drainage, toxic waste and runoff
   D. Toxic waste, displacement of wildlife, demolition of towns
   E. Earthquakes, acid drainage, vegetation removal

84. The IPAT model describes:

   A. The human impact on the environment through the effects of population numbers, affluence, and technological innovations
   B. The human influence on the environment through the effects of pollution, affluence, and technological innovations
   C. The human impact on the environment through the effects of population numbers on aquatic and terrestrial biomes
   D. The International Pollution and Atmospheric Team
   E. The human influence on the environment through the effects of pollution, atmosphere, and technological innovations

85. What is the important lesson modern society should learn from Easter Island?

   A. Unsustainable use of a resource will ultimately lead to the downfall of a civilization.
   B. It is not wise to inhabit an island.
   C. Lack of food can destroy a society.
   D. Sustainable resource use is not necessarily important to the survival of a civilization.
   E. Leaving behind relics is essential to having your civilization remembered throughout history.

86. The deterioration of soil by human actions can be considered a

   A. Negative feedback loop because, eventually, the system will stabilize and the soil will return to its previous state
   B. Positive feedback loop because once soil becomes degraded, further consequences occur as a result
   C. Negative feedback loop because once soil becomes degraded, further consequences occur as a result
   D. Positive feedback loop because eventually the system will stabilize and the soil will return to its previous state
   E. Both a positive feedback loop and a negative feedback loop because, at first, the system is unstable and moving toward an extreme, but eventually it balances out and becomes stable again

87. Family planning is a successful measure used to reduce population growth in many developing countries. All the following are frequent components of family planning EXCEPT

   A. Making contraceptives available
   B. Empowering females to make decisions
   C. Strengthening patriarchal households
   D. Improving reproductive healthcare options
   E. Education

88. Which of the following countries currently has the highest population?

   A. United States
   B. China
   C. India
   D. Brazil
   E. Bangladesh

89. How does soil compaction affect the use of the land?

   A. Compacted soils have negligible effects on land use.
   B. Compacted soils help reduce the threat of invasive species taking over.
   C. Although compacted soils reduce the flow of water through the soil, there is an increase in the availability of oxygen.
   D. Soil compaction helps to keep the topsoil from eroding.
   E. Compaction reduces space between soil particles, obstructing the flow of gases, nutrients, and water through the soil.

90. How do El Niño events cause economic loss to countries on the Pacific Coast of North America, Central America, and South America?

   A. Fewer upwellings bring fewer nutrients to the fisheries along the coasts, diminishing available catch for fishermen.
   B. There is an increase in tropical storms, which can be destructive when they hit land.
   C. Large amounts of money are spent in an effort to protect the coastlines.
   D. Ocean waters are warmed, thus killing large numbers of marine organisms that cannot survive in the increased temperatures.
   E. More upwellings bring large amounts of nutrients to the fisheries along the coasts, reducing available nutrients to the benthic environments.

91. Which element is consumed during decomposition in an aquatic environment, potentially leading to a hypoxic situation?

   A. Nitrogen
   B. Phosphorous
   C. Calcium
   D. Carbon
   E. Oxygen

Questions 92–94 refer to the following graph.

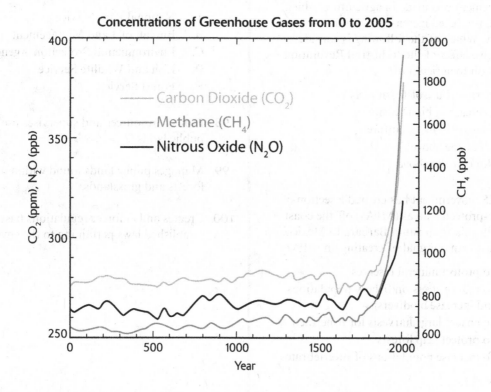

Concentrations of Greenhouse Gases from 0 to 2005

- Carbon Dioxide (CO_2)
- Methane (CH_4)
- Nitrous Oxide (N_2O)

92. Which of the following is the most likely cause of the recent trend noted for all three gases?

   A. Increased burning of wood and biomass for fuel
   B. Increasing number of livestock being raised
   C. Increased combustion of fossil fuels
   D. Global climate change
   E. More materials being disposed of in landfills

93. What are the repercussions of this trend on the environment?

   A. Decreased sedimentation in benthic zones
   B. Overall changes in climate patterns around the world, including more severe weather events
   C. Increased growth of vegetation on a global scale
   D. Growth of ice coverage over most of the Earth
   E. Global cooling

94. What is one way in which CO_2 emissions can be reduced?

   A. Sequester carbon in the lithosphere.
   B. Reduce the number of livestock globally.
   C. Keep ocean temperatures more constant.
   D. Reduce fertilizer use.
   E. Use alternative, renewable sources of energy.

95. If there are an estimated 84 billion barrels of oil left in a country's reserves, and the rate of production is 4 billion barrels per year, what is the reserves-to-production ratio of oil for this country?

   A. 49 years
   B. 33 years
   C. 21 years
   D. 336 years
   E. 500 years

96. During the Industrial Revolution, much advancement was made in agriculture, which, in turn, produced increased yields and food security. Which of the following is considered a negative effect of the Industrial Revolution in relation to agriculture?

    A. Increased use of fossil fuels
    B. Decrease in biodiversity
    C. Increase in monoculture
    D. All of the above
    E. None of the above

97. The U.S. government has created a section of marine-protected areas (MPAs) off the coast of California from Santa Barbara to Mexico. What is the major goal of creating an MPA?

    A. To protect mineral reserves
    B. To reduce stress on fishery populations and increase biodiversity
    C. To ensure large harvests for fishermen
    D. To protect kelp forests
    E. To increase populations of invertebrates

Questions 98–100 refer to the following answer choices.

    A. National Park Service
    B. Bureau of Land Management
    C. Environmental Protection Agency
    D. Fish and Wildlife Service
    E. Forest Service

98. Protects resources and supervises use of public lands.

99. Manages public lands found within national forests and grasslands.

100. Creates and enforces regulations based on established laws pertaining to the environment.

IF YOU FINISH BEFORE TIME IS CALLED, CHECK YOUR WORK ON THIS SECTION ONLY. DO NOT WORK ON ANY OTHER SECTION IN THE TEST.

Section II: Free-Response Questions

Time: 90 minutes

4 questions

Directions: Each question is equally weighted. Plan to budget your time and allow yourself approximately 20 minutes per question. Write clearly to show any calculations when computations are necessary. Calculators are not allowed. Where an explanation or discussion is required, support your answers with relevant information, facts, and/or specific examples.

Question 1 refers to the following article from Reuters (PARS International Corp.).

U.S. Coral Reefs under Threat, Report Finds

Reefs in the Caribbean, in particular, are under severe assault, and coral in the U.S. Virgin Islands and off Puerto Rico had not recovered from 2005, when unusually warm waters that led to massive bleaching and disease killed up to 90 percent of the marine organisms on some reefs.

"The evidence is warning us that many of our coral reef ecosystems are imperiled and we as a community must act now," said Kacky Andrews, program manager of the Coral Reef Conservation program at the National Oceanic and Atmospheric Administration.

The new NOAA report on the state of coral reefs in the United States and Pacific territories, including Palau and Guam, was presented at a meeting of coral reef scientists in Fort Lauderdale, Florida.

It was the third such report and the second to be based on actual monitoring of reefs. The reefs were classified as excellent, good, fair, or poor based on such things as water quality, fish population, and the threats they faced.

1. Answer the following questions:

   A. Explain two reasons why coral reefs are being threatened worldwide.
   B. Discuss the process of coral bleaching and its impact on coral reefs.
   C. What are two ways in which coral reefs can be protected from future destruction?
   D. Explain the importance of protecting coral reefs.

2. Populations continually experience growth or decline. The human population continues to increase exponentially, with environmental and societal consequences. Following is a table representing the growth rates of a few countries.

Country	Growth Rate
Turkey	1.0
Brazil	1.2
Philippines	2.0
Kuwait	3.6

   A. Calculate the doubling time for the population of Kuwait.
   B. Calculate the natural growth rate for a country with a birth rate of 350 out of 1,000 and a death rate of 380 out of 1,000.
   C. List and explain another statistic used by demographers to predict the population growth of a country.
   D. Explain why the extinct civilization of Easter Island is considered a warning for modern society.
   E. Describe two ways in which population growth can be slowed.

247

3. Persistent organic pollutants (POPs) are toxic chemicals that can cause health issues in humans and wildlife.

   A. What makes POPs so dangerous when released into the environment?
   B. Explain two ways in which POPs are harmful to humans and wildlife.
   C. How do POPs enter the environment? Explain POP reservoirs.
   D. Name and describe one of the international treaties related to POPs.
   E. Explain the purpose of DDT and issues with its use.

4. Coal mining is a major industry in Wyoming and provides energy for essential services throughout the country. As the third largest coal producer in the country, Wyoming's coal is either sub-bituminous or bituminous.

   A. Identify two environmental consequences of coal combustion.
   B. Discuss three positive economic effects of coal mining.
   C. Explain one way in which coal is mined.
   D. Discuss two uses for coal.
   E. Explain two terrestrial environmental impacts of coal mining.

IF YOU FINISH BEFORE TIME IS CALLED, CHECK YOUR WORK ON THIS SECTION ONLY. DO NOT WORK ON ANY OTHER SECTION IN THE TEST.

Answer Key

Section I: Multiple-Choice Questions

1. B	26. C	51. B	76. A
2. A	27. D	52. C	77. C
3. D	28. E	53. B	78. B
4. C	29. A	54. D	79. B
5. C	30. B	55. B	80. D
6. A	31. E	56. E	81. B
7. E	32. A	57. A	82. C
8. A	33. B	58. E	83. C
9. B	34. C	59. D	84. A
10. A	35. B	60. A	85. A
11. D	36. D	61. D	86. B
12. B	37. D	62. B	87. C
13. B	38. A	63. C	88. B
14. D	39. E	64. C	89. D
15. E	40. C	65. D	90. A
16. B	41. B	66. A	91. E
17. A	42. E	67. C	92. C
18. B	43. B	68. D	93. B
19. A	44. A	69. C	94. E
20. C	45. B	70. D	95. C
21. E	46. D	71. A	96. D
22. C	47. C	72. D	97. B
23. D	48. D	73. A	98. B
24. A	49. B	74. D	99. E
25. D	50. A	75. C	100. C

Answer Explanations

Section I: Multiple-Choice Questions

1. **B** The Montreal Protocol was a very successful international agreement to reduce CFCs, signed in 1987. It required participating nations to reduce CFC emissions by half. As a result, the ozone layer has been recuperating throughout the past two decades.

2. **A** The production of electricity and transportation are the two main contributors to global emissions of greenhouse gases. Fossil fuels power many electrical power plants and most forms of transportation, both of which are increasing along with the human population.

3. **D** A tragedy of the commons is the overexploitation of a resource due to unregulated use, and the best way to address this issue is through some form of regulation. This regulation can occur through private ownership, government regulation, or a cooperative effort of participants involved in the use of the resource.

4. **C** Death rates fall during the transitional stage of demographic transition due to more efficient and reliable food production and medical advancements, which reduce death due to starvation and health-related causes.

5. **C** Water vapor is the most abundant greenhouse gas, considered as such because of its ability to absorb reflected solar radiation that would otherwise escape into space.

6. **A** Radiation is released when temperatures in the core of the reactor increase and the uranium fuel rods melt. Water is usually used as a way to keep the reactor core cool in a nuclear power plant. If the coolant water is lost or leaks in some way, the core will quickly overheat, causing the melting of the metal in which the uranium fuel rods are located. This allows radiation from the uranium to escape from the core.

7. **E** Despite lower overall populations, industrialized nations use close to 100 percent more energy than developing nations do. This is because people in industrialized nations use relatively large amounts of energy for transportation; industry; and home heating, cooling, and lighting. Because industrialized nations have the economic ability to consume in excess, they do, and this consumption is currently not balanced by energy-saving technologies.

8. **A** Photochemical smog is produced when atmospheric nitrogen reacts with oxygen to produce nitric oxide, which then combines with oxygen to form nitrogen dioxide. Nitrogen dioxide absorbs light energy and splits to form nitric oxide and atomic oxygen. The oxygen atoms combine with the O_2 in air to produce ozone. Then nitric oxide can remove ozone by reacting with it to form nitrogen dioxide and oxygen.

9. **B** Breeder nuclear reactors make more efficient use of the fuel than conventional nuclear reactors do. This is because breeder reactors make use of the isotope U-238, which is discarded as a waste product in conventional reactors.

10. **A** Polybrominated diphenyl ethers (PBDEs) are used as fire retardants in consumer products ranging from computers and televisions to couches, curtains, and plastics. Unfortunately, PBDEs can be released when products are created and during disposal. PBDEs may cause cancer and neurological problems.

11. **D** A temperate deciduous forest is mainly comprised of deciduous trees, which are trees that lose their leaves in the winter months.

12. **B** Invasive species thrive in a new environment because of the lack of limiting factors, including lack of predators and disease, potentially abundant food sources, and the ability to outcompete native species for resources.

13. **B** Hydrogen power uses electrolysis to split water molecules into their component parts of hydrogen and oxygen. Although this process makes pure hydrogen without creating any harmful or polluting by-products, overall emissions depend on the source of the electricity used for electrolysis. The chemical equation for this reaction is: $2H_2O \rightarrow 2H_2 + O_2$.

14. **D** Both passive and active solar energy use some form of heat-trapping material to capture incoming solar radiation. With passive solar energy, the heat-trapping materials—including brick, concrete, and

tile—absorb solar radiation directly. In active solar collection, solar collectors are used to capture heat from the sun. The solar panels are made of a dark metal that absorbs the heat, which is then transferred to a liquid circulating throughout an area, heating a building or water.

15. **E** Hydropower uses a dam to control water flow, generating power as water is released from the dam to power turbines.

16. **B** The Green Revolution brought new farming techniques, crop varieties, and increased food production. During this time, agricultural techniques were industrialized and the processes made more efficient. Increased yield was attained from each plot of land. Selectively breeding crops for specific traits helped to make more pest- and disease-resistant strains.

17. **A** Agriculture and deforestation are the two main contributors to soil degradation worldwide. When forests are cleared, the soil is exposed to wind and water, which can lead to erosion. Agriculture removes the protective cover of vegetation on soil, making the soil prone to erosion as well. Topsoil erosion reduces soil nutrients and its ability to retain water.

18. **B** Nuclear energy produces the least amount of greenhouse gas emissions relative to fossil fuels and biomass since combustion is not part of the nuclear process. The downside of nuclear energy, though, is the production of radioactive toxic waste.

19. **A** Chaparral ecosystems are adapted to frequent wildfires. Some vegetation found there has a protective coating to help resist fire damage, while other types of plants and trees germinate from the extreme heat of fire.

20. **C** Net primary production is the amount of energy available to heterotrophs. This represents the amount of energy from a plant available to consumers after the plant has used some energy through cellular respiration to meet its own energy needs.

21. **E** Zebra mussels were introduced to the United States through ships entering the Great Lakes. Because they had few natural limiting factors in the new environment, this invasive species proliferated. The repercussions of this invasion have been far-reaching and expensive. The zebra mussels are small, so they can get inside pipes and clog them; cling to docks, buoys, and boat engines; and damage fishing equipment.

22. **C** Specialists fill a narrow niche and have specific requirements for survival. These organisms can be affected easily by environmental changes, so they are more prone to extirpation and extinction.

23. **D** Organisms pass on their genes through reproduction. To do so, organisms must survive to reproductive age. Adaptations that allow this survival are coded in an organism's genes, so well-adapted organisms survive to reproduce and pass on these successful genes to their offspring. This is the process of natural selection.

24. **A** The development of long tongues over generations reflects directional speciation, during which one extreme of a trait is selected. This is in contrast to disruptive selection, in which extreme traits are favored in either direction (extremely short *or* extremely long tongues), or stabilizing selection in which the middle ground between two versions of a trait is reflected (a mid-length tongue).

25. **D** With India's growing population and increasing wealth, it is consuming more resources. However, the graph shows that the country's growth is predicted to slow in the future.

26. **C** An increasing population could explain why energy consumption in China is predicted to increase. More people use more energy, and China's increasing wealth leads to more per-capita energy consumption.

27. **D** The projected decrease in consumption in the United States could be attributed to improvements in technological advancements, which includes increased use of alternative forms of energy.

28. **E** Allopatric speciation occurs when a population of organisms is separated due to a geographic barrier, such as a river changing course, mountain range forming, glaciers progressing, or sea level rising. When populations are separated, each adapts to specific environmental conditions and, over time, can become so different from each other that they lose the ability to interbreed. At this point, they are considered distinct species.

29. **A** The United States, China, and Japan consume the most oil worldwide. This is due to large population (China) and high economic ability (United States and Japan).

30. **B** Considered the topsoil, the A horizon contains the most nutrients for plant growth. When the organic matter from the O horizon decomposes, the nutrients are deposited on the A horizon right below it.

31. **E** The R horizon is the location of bedrock. It is also considered to be the parent material of soil and is often the deepest part of the soil horizon.

32. **A** Acid precipitation is formed from the chemicals released into the atmosphere during combustion in industrial processes and vehicle emissions. The chemicals react in the environment to form acid precipitation. Because emissions and particulate matter can be carried long distances in the atmosphere, acid precipitation can occur far from its source.

33. **B** Nitrogen is the most abundant gas in the Earth's atmosphere, making up 78 percent of its composition. Oxygen makes up 21 percent and other gases comprise the remaining 1 percent.

34. **C** Humans are depleting stocks of large fish, leading to the harvesting of smaller and smaller fish. This is considered fishing down the food chain because the largest fish make up the top of the food chain in an ecosystem, and the smaller fish are located at the bottom.

35. **B** Hot spots occur when magma breaks through the middle of a plate, emerging and hardening on the surface. As this occurs over time, the hardened magma continues to layer and ultimately may rise above sea level. This is how the Hawaiian Islands formed.

36. **D** The photic zone is the top layer of the ocean. It receives the most solar radiation and, in turn, provides energy for most of the ocean's primary productivity.

37. **D** Vitamin A deficiency is common in malnourished populations and can lead to blindness and reduced ability to battle infection. Golden rice is a genetically modified food created with the purpose of providing people in these regions with vitamin A.

38. **A** Permit trading allows companies to buy and sell emissions permits. A certain level of emissions is established within an industry for a particular pollutant. Companies are issued a certain number of permits for these emissions. They can buy, sell, and trade these permits as long as the overall standards are met. This is considered a way to meet environmental standards through the use of capitalism.

39. **E** Only pure water has a neutral pH. The minerals and other components of naturally occurring water alter its pH slightly to become either somewhat basic or somewhat acidic.

40. **C** Mangrove forests are populated by trees that thrive in a saline environment and are partially submerged by water through much of their lives. Some roots extend upward to access oxygen from the air, and other roots extend down to act as support for the tree. This unique shape also offers protection for fish eggs and young fish.

41. **B** Methane hydrate is a solid form of methane located deep on the ocean floor. In its molecular structure, the methane hydrate is surrounded by a crystal lattice of water molecules. Methane hydrates are difficult to extract because the structure can destabilize and release methane gas, a greenhouse gas. The release of gas can also cause instability in rock and sediment structures.

42. **E** Paper is the largest part of the waste stream in the United States. Despite the fact that paper can be recycled, it is still used in many products that are not put into the recycle bin.

43. **B** Lead was an additive in gasoline but was phased out as an additive in the 1970s due to its ability to bio-accumulate in organisms and act as a neurotoxin, particularly for younger humans. As lead use was reduced, so were emissions and, ultimately, blood level concentrations in people.

44. **A** Occupational Safety and Health Administration (OSHA) is a federally run agency responsible for worker safety on the job.

45. **B** CERCLA, the Comprehensive Response Compensation and Liability Act, also called "Superfund," provides a federal means to clean up, or remediate, soil and water contaminated with hazardous waste. If

possible, parties responsible for the contamination are made to pay for cleanup. If not, the cost of cleanup comes from federal taxpayer monies.

46. **D** In an effort to reduce illegal dumping, the Resource Conservation and Recovery Act (RCRA) manages the creation, movement, and disposal of hazardous waste as well as nonhazardous solid waste.

47. **C** The National Environmental Policy Act (NEPA) mandates that the environment be taken into account prior to any development, including requiring preparation of an environmental impact statement (EIS) prior to any federal action that will or could potentially disrupt the environment.

48. **D** A frog has high biotic potential because it reproduces many young at one time. High biotic potential means that an organism has the ability to produce many offspring. Since a frog is considered to be an r-selected species, it produces many eggs at once, with some surviving into adulthood but the majority perishing at some point prior to reproductive age.

49. **B** Maximum sustainable yield requires harvesting a renewable resource for use while also maintaining the resource at adequate levels for the future—in this case, harvesting trees only at the pace at which they grow back.

50. **A** Persistent organic pollutants (POPs) remain in the environment and can bio-accumulate in organisms and potentially bio-magnify through the food chain. Substances classified as POPs do not break down easily.

51. **B** Haiti is located on a fault line between the North American and Caribbean plates. The two plates slide past each other at a transform boundary.

52. **C** BPA stands for bisphenol-A, which is a chemical used to make polycarbonate plastics and epoxy resins. Polycarbonate plastic is used to make popular containers for many foods and drinks. Its advantage is that it is lightweight, has a high resistance to heat, is tough, and has excellent electrical resistance. However, BPA is an endocrine disruptor and humans can unknowingly have daily exposure to BPA that leaches out of plastic containers into foods and beverages.

53. **B** Environmental costs and benefits are not easily quantified, because many of the pros and cons are subjective or immeasurable.

54. **D** Fishermen have suffered massive economic losses due to the oil spill. Also, the oil has accumulated on some shores, affecting the nesting sites of shore birds, potentially impacting long-term populations. To date, endocrine disruption has not been noted as a result of the oil spill. Although the dispersant used was originally thought to be a potential endocrine disruptor, no such problems have been seen.

55. **B** Permit trading allows companies to buy and sell emissions permits. A certain level of emissions is established within an industry for a particular pollutant. Companies are issued a certain number of permits for these emissions. They can buy, sell, and trade these permits as long as the overall standards are still met. This is considered a way to meet environmental standards through the use of capitalism.

56. **E** A green tax is a tool used to discourage an environmentally harmful activity. It is a tax imposed on a company for harmful actions to the environment.

57. **A** A subsidy provides a financial incentive for a company to act in an environmentally responsible manner.

58. **E** The Resource Conservation and Recovery Act (RCRA) was established in an effort to reduce illegal dumping. It manages the creation, movement, and disposal of hazardous waste as well as nonhazardous solid waste.

59. **D** To calculate the doubling time of a population, use the equation $70 \div$ annual growth rate. Therefore, if a population is growing at a rate of 0.7 percent annually, the answer is found as follows: $70 \div 0.7 = 100$. This means the population will double in 100 years.

60. **A** Negative feedback loops maintain ecosystem balance. System outputs in excess of the norm turn off the mechanisms that create these outputs, realigning the system with its norms.

61. **D** In the process of cellular respiration, oxygen and sugar are used to produce carbon dioxide, water, and energy.

62. **B** An endemic species is native to only one location on the planet, which means that alterations to only one local ecosystem can make the species extinct.

63. **C** Lichens are considered a pioneer species. When a major disturbance occurs and destroys all living components of an ecosystem, one of the first species to arrive at the devastated area are lichens, which help to recolonize the area. They can do this because of their ability to be carried great distances in the air, as well as the unique mutualistic relationship between the fungi and algae that make up lichen. The fungi hold on to rocks and absorb moisture while the algae produce food via photosynthesis.

64. **C** Soil comprised of larger particles, which have larger pore spaces, allows water to flow through more easily. This means it has high soil permeability.

65. **D** Pakistan has a smaller ecological footprint than Canada, Chile, Mexico, or China because of its relatively low rates of consumption and waste.

66. **A** In a country with a pyramid-shaped age structure diagram there is a growing population. The pyramid shape represents a population with a large number of young and a progressively smaller number of people at older ages. Since the majority of the population are not yet at reproductive age, when they do reach this point, more people will have children and, therefore, the population will continue to increase.

67. **C** To find the growth rate of a population the following equation is used:

(Crude Birth Rate + Immigration) – (Crude Death Rate + Emigration) = Growth Rate per 1,000 Individuals

The answer is then multiplied by 100 to convert it to a percent.

In this case, the crude birth and immigration rates have already been added to equal $\frac{75}{1,000}$, and death and emigration have already been added to equal $\frac{50}{1,000}$, allowing the following calculation:

$$\frac{75}{1,000} - \frac{50}{1,000} = \frac{25}{1,000} = 0.025$$

Then convert it to a percent by multiplying by 100. The answer is 2.5 percent.

68. **D** Chronic exposure to a substance means exposure has occurred in small doses over a long period of time.

69. **C** Leaching is the process of minerals being transported down through the soil via water. As the water percolates through the soil, minerals are carried with it downward to other soil horizons. Unfortunately, pollution can be leached as well.

70. **D** Highway congestion is considered an example of a tragedy of the commons. Highways are used often and without regulation. A tragedy of the commons occurs when an unregulated resource is used unsustainably.

71. **A** A hookworm is an intestinal parasite, consuming nutrients from the host for survival. This will harm the host and may kill it.

72. **D** A blue jay living in a tree is an example of amensalism; the tree is providing habitat and shelter for the blue jay, and the tree is unaffected in this relationship.

73. **A** Sea lice living on a sunfish is a parasitic relationship. The sea lice feed off of the blood of the sunfish, harming it but not killing it, because it is beneficial for the parasite to keep its host alive.

74. **D** A millipede is considered a detritivore, physically breaking down dead organic matter through scavenging. Decomposers chemically break down dead organic matter.

75. **C** Asbestos is a fibrous mineral found in the lithosphere. People can potentially inhale small fibers of asbestos, which can lodge in the lining of the lungs, provoking the production of acid to destroy the invader. Over time, this chronic destruction can lead to cancer.

76. **A** A closed system is self-contained, without outside input. Despite minimal additions of space dust and occasional meteorites, the Earth is considered a closed system in relation to matter.

77. **C** Landfills produce methane through the anaerobic decomposition of organic matter. This methane is collected and reused for energy, burned, or released into the atmosphere.

78. **B** Mercury is added to the environment mostly as the particulate matter byproduct of combustion. As the heavy metal falls out of the air, it is deposited onto the ground and into aquatic sources. Runoff from land can transport this deposited mercury into aquatic environments.

79. **B** Primary treatment removes suspended solids in the sewage treatment process. Settling tanks are used, where solid particles sink to the bottom and are removed.

80. **D** During the planet's current climate alteration, glaciers are retreating rather than advancing due to warming temperatures. As the glaciers retreat, the species that depend on them for survival are threatened and face potential endangerment or extinction.

81. **B** Recombinant DNA technology combines DNA from different organisms, usually with the goal of producing desired traits in a new genetically modified organism (GMO).

82. **C** Upwellings in the oceans carry nutrients from the ocean bottom to the surface, creating areas of high primary productivity.

83. **C** As a result of the process of mining, the environment can be harmed in many ways, and the destruction varies depending on the type of mining employed. In general, though, mining can lead to the removal of vegetation, acid drainage, and the production of toxic waste and runoff.

84. **A** The IPAT model examines the human impact on the environment due to population, affluence, and technological innovations. Higher population means more resources consumed. Increased affluence results in the population's ability to consume more resources and, therefore, create more waste. Technological innovations can either help the environment with advancements or create new ways to pollute and deplete resources.

85. **A** The civilization on Easter Island overused its resources, using trees unsustainably. This led to the downfall of the island's civilization. If modern society is not careful, resources may be overused to the point where they cannot be replenished.

86. **B** Soil degradation is a positive feedback loop because depleted soil leads to an increasing pace of degradation.

87. **C** Family planning is an essential tool in reducing population growth and includes the availability of contraceptives, the empowerment of females in decision-making, and improved reproductive healthcare options for women. The key component in any family-planning initiative is education, providing information to women and families.

88. **B** China currently has approximately 1.3 billion people, while India has 1.1 billion, and the United States has about 300 million.

89. **D** Compaction reduces space between soil particles, obstructing the flow of gases, nutrients, and water through the soil. It also can increase the amount of water runoff and, thus, erosion. Soils can be compacted as a result of many factors, including the weight of grazing animals and the weight of heavy equipment.

90. **A** Usually upwellings from the Humboldt Current in the Pacific Ocean bring nutrient-rich cooler waters up from the ocean bottom. During El Niño periods, the surface waters are warmer and upwellings are reduced, limiting the amount of nutrients at the ocean's surface. This affects the productivity of the ocean's fisheries, which, in turn, reduces the catch for fishermen and, thus, negatively impacts their income.

91. **E** Decomposition usually requires oxygen. When extensive decomposition occurs in aquatic environments, a great deal of oxygen is consumed. This can deplete the area of oxygen, making it hypoxic.

92. **C** Carbon monoxide, methane, and nitrous oxide are all produced as a result of fossil fuel combustion. When fossil fuel use increased in the past few centuries, so did resulting emissions.

93. **B** An increase in the amount of greenhouse gases in the atmosphere increases the amount of heat in the atmosphere, potentially altering the world's weather and climate patterns. In some situations, more severe weather events can occur.

94. **E** Using alternative, renewable energy sources is one way the levels of atmospheric carbon dioxide could be reduced. The main contributor of carbon dioxide emissions is fossil fuel combustion, which shifts the lithospheric carbon into the atmosphere, increasing concentrations of the greenhouse gas, thus contributing to climate change.

95. **C** Dividing the amount of total remaining reserves (84 billion barrels) by the annual rate of production (4 billion barrels) yields a reserves-to-production ratio of 21 years.

96. **D** All the choices listed are considered negative consequences of the Industrial Revolution as it relates to agriculture. With improvements in technology and efficiencies of farming, large monocultures were created. This, in turn, reduced biodiversity in the areas. Also, the technological advancements included the use of machinery run on fossil fuels, which produce greenhouse gas emissions.

97. **B** Marine protected areas (MPAs) are created with the goal of protecting fisheries and the biodiversity of the area. Some MPAs allow harvesting of marine organisms, while others do not allow any commercial or recreational fishing. Worldwide, there are over 400 MPAs. The network of MPAs created off the coast of California from Mexico to Santa Barbara was approved in December 2010.

98. **B** The Bureau of Land Management (BLM) is responsible for protecting resources and supervising the use of public lands.

99. **E** The Forest Service manages public lands located within national forests and grasslands, with the goal of protecting the land and its resources.

100. **C** The main focus of the Environmental Protection Agency (EPA) is the protection of both human health and the environment. This is done through the creation and enforcement of regulations based on established laws pertaining to the environment.

Section II: Free-Response Explanations

1. This question is worth a maximum of 10 points, as follows:

A. Explain two reasons why coral reefs are being threatened worldwide (2 points maximum):
- 1 point: Overfishing affects the biodiversity of coral reef communities, altering the food chain and causing far-reaching impacts even beyond the reef.
- 1 point: Coral bleaching is caused by an increase in water temperatures and by pollution.
- 1 point: Tourism such as boating, diving, snorkeling, and fishing can harm reefs if people touch or collect the coral, disturb sediment, or otherwise impact the reef (for example, by dropping anchors). Some tourist resorts and infrastructure have been built directly on reefs, and some empty sewage or other waste directly into water around coral reefs.
- 1 point: Pollution from manufacturing waste, sewage, agricultural chemicals, and oil extraction and refining are toxic to reefs.
- 1 point: Excess nutrients such as nitrogen and phosphorus can cause eutrophication around a coral reef, depleting the oxygen in the aquatic environment and depriving the coral of the oxygen it needs to survive.
- 1 point: Erosion caused by construction, mining, logging, and farming leads to increased sediment in rivers. This sediment ends up in the ocean, where it can inhibit sunlight from reaching corals.
- 1 point: Harmful fishing practices such as cyanide fishing, dynamite fishing, and bottom trawling.
- 1 point: The extraction of live coral from reefs, which is used as bricks, road fill, or cement. Corals are also sold as souvenirs to tourists and for export.
- 1 point: Corals are extremely sensitive to water temperature, which is warming due to global climate change.

B. Discuss the process of coral bleaching and its impact on coral reefs (4 points maximum):
- 2 points: Coral lives in a symbiotic relationship with zooxanthalae, an alga. The coral provides shelter and habitat for the zooxanthalae and the alga provides food for the coral through photosynthesis. Coral bleaching occurs when the zooxanthalae leave the coral, frequently as a result of excess pollution or warming water temperatures.

- ▪ 2 points: This can leave the coral devoid of nutrients and may lead to the death of the coral. The reason this is considered bleaching is because the resulting dead coral loses its color and is white.

C. What are two ways in which coral reefs can be protected from future destruction? (2 points maximum)

- ▪ 1 point: The proper disposal of trash and waste products.
- ▪ 1 point: Reduction in overall water and air pollution starting at the source of pollution.
- ▪ 1 point: Consumers ceasing to purchase coral products, such as for souvenirs or to stock aquariums, which will eventually reduce harvesting.
- ▪ 1 point: Anchor boats away from reefs.
- ▪ 1 point: Encouraging tourists to enjoy the beauty and uniqueness of the reefs without touching or taking.
- ▪ 1 point: Fishing in areas not located near a reef.
- ▪ 1 point: Reduce fertilizer use and, thus, chemical runoff that can negatively impact coral reefs.

D. Explain the importance of protecting coral reefs (2 points maximum):

- ▪ 1 point: Coral reefs provide habitat for a wide range of organisms, offering a variety of niches, food, and shelter.
- ▪ 1 point: Coral reefs are considered areas of high primary productivity, contributing to the biodiversity of the oceans.
- ▪ 1 point: Reefs protect the shorelines by reducing the impact of waves and storms.
- ▪ 1 point: The reefs provide breeding grounds for organisms.
- ▪ 1 point: Coral helps to control carbon dioxide in the oceans.

2. This question is worth a maximum of 10 points, as follows:

A. Calculate the doubling time for the population of Kuwait (1 point maximum):

- ▪ 1 point: To calculate the doubling time of a population, use the equation 70 ÷ annual growth rate. If Kuwait is growing at a rate of 3.6 percent annually, the answer is found as follows: 70 ÷ 3.6 = 19.4. This means the population will double in a little over 19 years.

B. Calculate the natural growth rate for a country with a birth rate of 350 out of 1,000 and a death rate of 380 out of 1,000 (2 points maximum):

- ▪ 1 point: Use the following equation to find the population's natural growth rate:

Natural Growth Rate per 1,000 Individuals = Crude Birth Rate – Crude Death Rate

The answer is then multiplied by 100 to convert it to a percent.

For the question, calculate as follows:

$$\frac{350}{1,000} - \frac{380}{1,000} = \frac{-30}{1,000} = -0.03$$

Then convert it to a percent by multiplying by 100.

- ▪ 1 point: The answer is a –3 percent natural growth rate.

C. List and explain another statistic used by demographers to predict the population growth of a country (1 point maximum):

- ▪ 1 point: Rate of natural increase reflects changes in crude birth and death rates.
- ▪ 1 point: Infant mortality rate, which is the number of deaths of children under the age of 1 year old, per 1,000 individuals born.
- ▪ 1 point: Replacement fertility level (the total fertility rate that is necessary to maintain a stable population).

D. Explain why the extinct civilization of Easter Island is considered a warning for modern society (4 points maximum):

- 1 point: The inhabitants of Easter Island met their demise because of their unsustainable use of the island's resources, specifically the trees.

- 1 point: Modern society has the very real potential for similar overuse, as resources can be consumed at a faster pace than they regenerate.

- 1 point: The Earth contains both finite and renewable resources. Supplies of resources such as minerals and fossil fuels will eventually run out, necessitating the development of alternatives. Resources that are considered renewable must be used sustainably in order to ensure enough for future generations.

- 1 point: If modern society does not learn from the demise of Easter Island, the planet's entire population could end up in the same situation as the island's inhabitants.

E. Describe two ways in which population growth can be slowed (2 points maximum):

- 1 point: Family planning programs.

- 1 point: Increased education about and use of contraception.

- 1 point: Shift in cultural norms (reduction in socially expected family size).

- 1 point: Female empowerment.

- 1 point: Female employment opportunities.

- 1 point: Enforced government regulations on births per family, such as China's one-child policy.

3. This question is worth a maximum of 10 points, as follows:

A. What makes POPs so dangerous when released into the environment? (2 points maximum):

- 1 point: POPs are persistent in the environment.

- 1 point: POPs bio-accumulate in tissue and bio-magnify in the food chain.

- 1 point: POPs travel long distances via the atmosphere and water.

B. Explain two ways in which POPs are harmful to humans and wildlife (2 points maximum):

- 1 point: POPs can cause diseases such as cancer.

- 1 point: POPs can create reproductive abnormalities.

- 1 point: POPs can cause neurological issues.

- 1 point: POPs can act as endocrine disruptors.

- 1 point: The immune system can be altered by POP exposure.

- 1 point: POP exposure can lead to developmental and behavioral issues.

C. How do POPs enter the environment? Explain POP reservoirs. (2 points maximum):

- 1 point: Some POPs are released during combustion, including the burning of biomass and fossil fuels.

- 1 point: Insecticides and fungicides often are released through spraying.

- 1 point: Effluent release (for example, from factories or sewage treatment plants) introduces POPs into water supplies.

- 1 point: Once in the atmosphere, POPs can be deposited onto the land and into the water.

- 1 point: POPs can enter water through runoff from the land.

- 1 point: POP reservoirs are the long-term storage of POPs in the sediment of marine or freshwater ecosystems. POPs are not very soluble, so they bond to particulate matter and are then are deposited on the bottom of aquatic environments, where they can remain for long periods of time.

D. Name and describe one of the international treaties related to POPs (2 points maximum):

- 1 point: The Basel Convention.

- 1 point: The Basel Convention controls the transport of hazardous waste between nations, and particularly the transfer of waste from developed to less developed countries. It also focuses on management practices and the reduction of waste toxicity through monitoring of storage, transfer, reuse, recycling, and disposal of hazardous waste.

- 1 point: The Rotterdam Convention.

- 1 point: The Rotterdam Convention aims to protect human and ecosystem health through proper use of potentially harmful pesticides and industrial chemicals. It also promotes sharing of information and responsibility.
- 1 point: The Stockholm Convention.
- 1 point: The Stockholm Convention banned or set a schedule for phasing out 12 of the worst persistent organic pollutants (POPs), including DDT, eight other pesticides, PCBs, dioxins, and furans. These were called the "dirty dozen."

E. Explain the purpose of DDT and issues with its use (2 points maximum):
- 1 point: DDT is used as a pesticide, particularly for the eradication of mosquitoes.
- 1 point: DDT bio-accumulates in organisms and bio-magnifies throughout the food chain.
- 1 point: DDT was responsible for the decline of many predatory bird populations due to its thinning of eggs and resultant death of offspring.
- 1 point: DDT is persistent in the environment, remaining for long periods of time.
- 1 point: DDT can break down into DDE, which is also persistent and toxic.

4. This question is worth a maximum of 10 points, as follows:

A. Identify two environmental consequences of coal combustion (2 points maximum):
- 1 point: The particulate matter of mercury emissions deposits onto land and into aquatic environments. Runoff can carry mercury from the land into the aquatic environments where it enters the food chain and biomagnifies through the food web.
- 1 point: The combustion of coal releases sulfur into the atmosphere, where it reacts with oxygen to form sulfur dioxide, which in turn reacts to form acid precipitation and industrial smog.
- 1 point: Soot is made up of carbon and is released as particulate matter from the incomplete combustion of coal. This is a component of industrial smog.

B. Discuss three positive economic effects of coal mining (3 points maximum):
- 1 point: Job creation. For example, in Wyoming almost 7,000 people are employed in coal mining, and the average income for an employee is almost double that of the state's average annual income.
- 1 point: Taxes paid to the state and federal governments. This money is then used for programs such as education and infrastructure.
- 1 point: Money from exports. Because the United States is the second-largest coal producer in the world, the export of this resource is important for other countries. Some countries, such as Japan and South Korea, do not have their own supply or have a very minimal supply, but they still use coal as an energy source.
- 1 point: Commerce brought to local communities through living activities, such as home sales and rentals, food consumption, and entertainment.
- 1 point: Decreased reliance on heavily taxed, imported fuel sources.

C. Explain one way in which coal is mined (1 point maximum):
- 1 point: Surface mining removes the soil and rock surface over a large amount of land. This is used when deposits are located relatively close to the surface. Once the mineral deposit is completely extracted, the hole is refilled with the original soil and rock.
- 1 point: Mountaintop removal is just as it sounds: The tops of mountains are blasted off in order to access the resource. This technique is common in the coal mines of the Appalachian Mountains.
- 1 point: Placer mining uses water to separate the heavier minerals from lighter mud and debris. Because many deposits are formed in riverbeds, this process uses naturally running water to make the initial separation.
- 1 point: Open pit mining involves digging up the land in order to reach the desired resource. The pits can be so large that the sides are terraced in order to allow trucks to get in and out. Open pits are usually called quarries.
- 1 point: Subsurface mining creates shafts deep underground in order to extract resources from pockets or seams. Dynamite blasts and manual labor are used to remove rock and access the resource.

D. Discuss two uses for coal (2 points maximum):

- 1 point: Burning coal provides the heat source for the majority of electricity generation in the United States.
- 1 point: Coal is used in industrial and manufacturing plants for the production of products such as ceramics, paper, and chemicals.
- 1 point: Coal is used as coke in the steel industry.
- 1 point: Coal by-products are used for medicines, perfumes, wood preservatives, fungicides, linoleum, solvents, and insecticides.
- 1 point: Some indoor heating in commercial and residential buildings uses coal.

E. Explain two terrestrial environmental impacts of coal mining (2 points maximum):

- 1 point: Introducing oxygen and water to rock rich with sulfur allows the formation of sulfuric acid, which can run off into water sources and seep into the ground, potentially affecting wildlife.
- 1 point: Removal of vegetation and habitat on land above coal deposits can impact local wildlife.
- 1 point: Mining can cause soil erosion.
- 1 point: The runoff from mining can lead to a buildup of debris and sediment in lakes and rivers.
- 1 point: Surface mining or mountaintop removal may require deforestation.

Chapter 10

Practice Exam 3

Remove this sheet and use it to mark your answers for the multiple-choice section of Practice Exam 3.

Section I

CUT HERE

1 Ⓐ Ⓑ Ⓒ Ⓓ Ⓔ	26 Ⓐ Ⓑ Ⓒ Ⓓ Ⓔ	51 Ⓐ Ⓑ Ⓒ Ⓓ Ⓔ	76 Ⓐ Ⓑ Ⓒ Ⓓ Ⓔ
2 Ⓐ Ⓑ Ⓒ Ⓓ Ⓔ	27 Ⓐ Ⓑ Ⓒ Ⓓ Ⓔ	52 Ⓐ Ⓑ Ⓒ Ⓓ Ⓔ	77 Ⓐ Ⓑ Ⓒ Ⓓ Ⓔ
3 Ⓐ Ⓑ Ⓒ Ⓓ Ⓔ	28 Ⓐ Ⓑ Ⓒ Ⓓ Ⓔ	53 Ⓐ Ⓑ Ⓒ Ⓓ Ⓔ	78 Ⓐ Ⓑ Ⓒ Ⓓ Ⓔ
4 Ⓐ Ⓑ Ⓒ Ⓓ Ⓔ	29 Ⓐ Ⓑ Ⓒ Ⓓ Ⓔ	54 Ⓐ Ⓑ Ⓒ Ⓓ Ⓔ	79 Ⓐ Ⓑ Ⓒ Ⓓ Ⓔ
5 Ⓐ Ⓑ Ⓒ Ⓓ Ⓔ	30 Ⓐ Ⓑ Ⓒ Ⓓ Ⓔ	55 Ⓐ Ⓑ Ⓒ Ⓓ Ⓔ	80 Ⓐ Ⓑ Ⓒ Ⓓ Ⓔ
6 Ⓐ Ⓑ Ⓒ Ⓓ Ⓔ	31 Ⓐ Ⓑ Ⓒ Ⓓ Ⓔ	56 Ⓐ Ⓑ Ⓒ Ⓓ Ⓔ	81 Ⓐ Ⓑ Ⓒ Ⓓ Ⓔ
7 Ⓐ Ⓑ Ⓒ Ⓓ Ⓔ	32 Ⓐ Ⓑ Ⓒ Ⓓ Ⓔ	57 Ⓐ Ⓑ Ⓒ Ⓓ Ⓔ	82 Ⓐ Ⓑ Ⓒ Ⓓ Ⓔ
8 Ⓐ Ⓑ Ⓒ Ⓓ Ⓔ	33 Ⓐ Ⓑ Ⓒ Ⓓ Ⓔ	58 Ⓐ Ⓑ Ⓒ Ⓓ Ⓔ	83 Ⓐ Ⓑ Ⓒ Ⓓ Ⓔ
9 Ⓐ Ⓑ Ⓒ Ⓓ Ⓔ	34 Ⓐ Ⓑ Ⓒ Ⓓ Ⓔ	59 Ⓐ Ⓑ Ⓒ Ⓓ Ⓔ	84 Ⓐ Ⓑ Ⓒ Ⓓ Ⓔ
10 Ⓐ Ⓑ Ⓒ Ⓓ Ⓔ	35 Ⓐ Ⓑ Ⓒ Ⓓ Ⓔ	60 Ⓐ Ⓑ Ⓒ Ⓓ Ⓔ	85 Ⓐ Ⓑ Ⓒ Ⓓ Ⓔ
11 Ⓐ Ⓑ Ⓒ Ⓓ Ⓔ	36 Ⓐ Ⓑ Ⓒ Ⓓ Ⓔ	61 Ⓐ Ⓑ Ⓒ Ⓓ Ⓔ	86 Ⓐ Ⓑ Ⓒ Ⓓ Ⓔ
12 Ⓐ Ⓑ Ⓒ Ⓓ Ⓔ	37 Ⓐ Ⓑ Ⓒ Ⓓ Ⓔ	62 Ⓐ Ⓑ Ⓒ Ⓓ Ⓔ	87 Ⓐ Ⓑ Ⓒ Ⓓ Ⓔ
13 Ⓐ Ⓑ Ⓒ Ⓓ Ⓔ	38 Ⓐ Ⓑ Ⓒ Ⓓ Ⓔ	63 Ⓐ Ⓑ Ⓒ Ⓓ Ⓔ	88 Ⓐ Ⓑ Ⓒ Ⓓ Ⓔ
14 Ⓐ Ⓑ Ⓒ Ⓓ Ⓔ	39 Ⓐ Ⓑ Ⓒ Ⓓ Ⓔ	64 Ⓐ Ⓑ Ⓒ Ⓓ Ⓔ	89 Ⓐ Ⓑ Ⓒ Ⓓ Ⓔ
15 Ⓐ Ⓑ Ⓒ Ⓓ Ⓔ	40 Ⓐ Ⓑ Ⓒ Ⓓ Ⓔ	65 Ⓐ Ⓑ Ⓒ Ⓓ Ⓔ	90 Ⓐ Ⓑ Ⓒ Ⓓ Ⓔ
16 Ⓐ Ⓑ Ⓒ Ⓓ Ⓔ	41 Ⓐ Ⓑ Ⓒ Ⓓ Ⓔ	66 Ⓐ Ⓑ Ⓒ Ⓓ Ⓔ	91 Ⓐ Ⓑ Ⓒ Ⓓ Ⓔ
17 Ⓐ Ⓑ Ⓒ Ⓓ Ⓔ	42 Ⓐ Ⓑ Ⓒ Ⓓ Ⓔ	67 Ⓐ Ⓑ Ⓒ Ⓓ Ⓔ	92 Ⓐ Ⓑ Ⓒ Ⓓ Ⓔ
18 Ⓐ Ⓑ Ⓒ Ⓓ Ⓔ	43 Ⓐ Ⓑ Ⓒ Ⓓ Ⓔ	68 Ⓐ Ⓑ Ⓒ Ⓓ Ⓔ	93 Ⓐ Ⓑ Ⓒ Ⓓ Ⓔ
19 Ⓐ Ⓑ Ⓒ Ⓓ Ⓔ	44 Ⓐ Ⓑ Ⓒ Ⓓ Ⓔ	69 Ⓐ Ⓑ Ⓒ Ⓓ Ⓔ	94 Ⓐ Ⓑ Ⓒ Ⓓ Ⓔ
20 Ⓐ Ⓑ Ⓒ Ⓓ Ⓔ	45 Ⓐ Ⓑ Ⓒ Ⓓ Ⓔ	70 Ⓐ Ⓑ Ⓒ Ⓓ Ⓔ	95 Ⓐ Ⓑ Ⓒ Ⓓ Ⓔ
21 Ⓐ Ⓑ Ⓒ Ⓓ Ⓔ	46 Ⓐ Ⓑ Ⓒ Ⓓ Ⓔ	71 Ⓐ Ⓑ Ⓒ Ⓓ Ⓔ	96 Ⓐ Ⓑ Ⓒ Ⓓ Ⓔ
22 Ⓐ Ⓑ Ⓒ Ⓓ Ⓔ	47 Ⓐ Ⓑ Ⓒ Ⓓ Ⓔ	72 Ⓐ Ⓑ Ⓒ Ⓓ Ⓔ	97 Ⓐ Ⓑ Ⓒ Ⓓ Ⓔ
23 Ⓐ Ⓑ Ⓒ Ⓓ Ⓔ	48 Ⓐ Ⓑ Ⓒ Ⓓ Ⓔ	73 Ⓐ Ⓑ Ⓒ Ⓓ Ⓔ	98 Ⓐ Ⓑ Ⓒ Ⓓ Ⓔ
24 Ⓐ Ⓑ Ⓒ Ⓓ Ⓔ	49 Ⓐ Ⓑ Ⓒ Ⓓ Ⓔ	74 Ⓐ Ⓑ Ⓒ Ⓓ Ⓔ	99 Ⓐ Ⓑ Ⓒ Ⓓ Ⓔ
25 Ⓐ Ⓑ Ⓒ Ⓓ Ⓔ	50 Ⓐ Ⓑ Ⓒ Ⓓ Ⓔ	75 Ⓐ Ⓑ Ⓒ Ⓓ Ⓔ	100 Ⓐ Ⓑ Ⓒ Ⓓ Ⓔ

Section II

CUT HERE

Section I: Multiple-Choice Questions

Time: 90 minutes
100 questions

Directions: Each of the questions or incomplete statements in this section is followed by five answer choices. Select the best answer choice and fill in the corresponding circle on the answer sheet.

Questions 1–3 refer to the following answer choices.

    A. Active volcano
    B. Cinder cone volcano
    C. Dormant volcano
    D. Extinct volcano
    E. Shield volcano

1. A volcano that is considered inactive.

2. A slowly erupting volcano with a broad base.

3. A volcano with a large amount of seismic and thermal activity.

4. Using manual labor, animal labor, and simple tools to grow crops is known as:

    A. Agriculture
    B. Conventional agriculture
    C. Industrialized agriculture
    D. Subsistence agriculture
    E. Traditional agriculture

5. The Green Revolution of the 20th century is best characterized by which of the following:

    I. Development of high-yield crops
    II. Wide use of pesticides
    III. Augmentation of an irrigation infrastructure

    A. I only
    B. II only
    C. III only
    D. I and II only
    E. I, II, and III

6. Ozone can be beneficial or it can be a pollutant. What is the function of beneficial ozone?

    A. To act as a barrier for heat in the troposphere
    B. To block ultraviolet radiation in the mesopause
    C. To help hold in heat in the thermosphere
    D. To filter ultraviolet radiation in the stratosphere
    E. To filter ultraviolet radiation in the troposphere

Questions 7–9 refer to the following information.

    A CFL bulb using 25 watts of energy is expected to last 10,000 hours. The 100-watt incandescent bulb is expected to last 1,000 hours. Assume electricity costs 10¢/kWh.

7. How much will it cost to operate the CFL over its expected lifetime?

    A. $25
    B. $250
    C. $2,500
    D. $25,000
    E. $250,000

8. How much will it cost to operate the incandescent bulb over its expected lifetime?

    A. $1
    B. $10
    C. $100
    D. $1,000
    E. $10,000

9. What is the expected savings in operating costs between the CFL and the incandescent bulb over the expected life of the CFL bulb?

   A. The incandescent bulb will save $15 over the CFL bulb.
   B. The CFL bulb will save $15 over the incandescent bulb.
   C. The incandescent bulb will save $75 over the CFL bulb.
   D. The CFL bulb will save $75 over the incandescent bulb.
   E. The cost will be the same.

10. The type of treatment for sewage coming from a house is dependent upon the location of the house and its access to a municipal treatment system. If a house in the United States is located far from a treatment system, what form of sewage treatment would it most likely have?

    A. Primary treatment
    B. Secondary treatment
    C. Tertiary treatment
    D. Septic system
    E. No treatment

11. All the following are considered forms of noise pollution EXCEPT:

    A. Airports
    B. Freeways/highways
    C. Rock concerts
    D. Telephones
    E. Lawnmowers

12. Which type of plate boundary is the mid-Atlantic ridge?

    A. Subduction zone
    B. Convergent plate boundary
    C. Divergent plate boundary
    D. Transform plate boundary
    E. Thrust fault

Questions 13–14 refer to the following diagram.

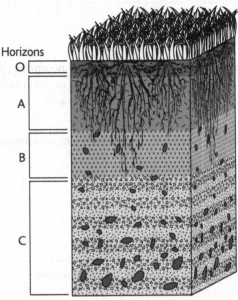

Source: Natural Resources Conservation Service, U.S. Department of Agriculture

13. Which of the following ecosystems best characterizes a thick O horizon?

    A. Chaparral
    B. Desert
    C. Grassland
    D. Semi-desert
    E. Tropical rain forest

14. Parent material is best defined as:

    A. Loose and partly decayed organic material
    B. Bedrock material
    C. A light-colored zone of leaching
    D. An accumulation of clay and rock
    E. Mineral matter mixed with humus

15. Grasslands found in the United States are commonly referred to as:

    A. Llanos
    B. Pampas
    C. Prairie
    D. Steppes
    E. Veld

16. Which of the following is the greatest overall threat to the survival of terrestrial species?

    A. Habitat loss
    B. Resource extraction
    C. Introduction of nonnative species
    D. Overgrazing
    E. Pollution

17. Which of the following is the greatest overall threat to the survival of aquatic species?

    A. Acidification of the water
    B. Global climate change
    C. Habitat loss
    D. Overharvesting
    E. Pollution

18. Every ten years, the United States conducts a census that is the actual count of the population at the given date. All the following are reasons for conducting the census EXCEPT:

    A. To allocate federal funds
    B. To distribute subsides given to agriculture, mining, forestry, and other businesses
    C. To redistribute the federal House of Representatives
    D. To abide by the U.S. Constitution
    E. To redistrict in states for local, state, and federal elections for elected government officials

19. Which of the following is an argument against genetically modified foods?

    I. Unknown long-term effects on human health
    II. Built-in resistance to pests
    III. Destruction of native food sources

    A. I only
    B. II only
    C. III only
    D. I and II only
    E. I and III only

20. Which method of tree harvesting causes the most damage to an ecosystem?

    A. Strip cutting
    B. Shelter wood harvesting
    C. Selective harvesting
    D. Seed tree harvesting
    E. Clear cutting

Questions 21–23 refer to the following answer choices.

    A. Love Canal
    B. Union Carbide Chemical Co., Bhopal
    C. Cuyahoga River
    D. Lake Erie
    E. *Exxon Valdez*

21. In upstate New York, chemicals were buried underground. Eventually the land was sold to a school and houses were built in the area.

22. High concentrations of phosphates, nitrates, and other chemicals from heavy industry led to eutrophication and large fish die-offs.

23. Heavy oil, trash, debris, and other floating chemicals caught fire in 1969. This incident was covered in *Time* magazine.

24. Which of the following best explains why CAFE standards were created?

    A. To establish minimum standards for car mileage per gallon of fuel for all manufactured vehicles
    B. To establish minimum standards for the percentage of a population using public transportation (such as buses and light rail)
    C. To establish minimum standards for car mileage per gallon of fuel only
    D. To establish minimum standards for average fuel usage per weight of cargo for the transportation of goods via large trucks and trains
    E. To establish minimum standards for fuel usage per passenger in air travel

25. Which of the following is considered mainly an indoor air pollutant?

    A. Carbon dioxide
    B. Carbon monoxide
    C. Formaldehyde
    D. Nitrous oxide
    E. Sulfur dioxide

26. *Genetic pollution* is a relatively new term and refers to which of the following?

    A. The cross-contamination of plant genes into animals
    B. Research involving genetically modified organisms in which genes from an animal are crossed with that of an unrelated animal species
    C. The cross of genetically modified organisms with other species in a research facility
    D. The unintended spread of genes from genetically modified organisms to natural organisms
    E. Research involving genetically modified organisms in which genes from a plant are crossed with that of an unrelated plant species

27. Which of the following set of reactions shows the depletion of ozone by chlorofluorocarbons (CFCs)?

    A. $O_2 + UVC \rightarrow O + O$
        $O + O_2 \rightarrow O_3$
    B. $CFC + UV \text{ radiation} \rightarrow CFC + Cl$
        $Cl + O_3 \rightarrow ClO + O_2$
        $ClO + O_3 \rightarrow Cl + 2 O_2$
    C. $CO_2 + H_2O + energy \rightarrow C_6H_{12}O_6 + O_2$
    D. $C_6H_{12}O_6 + O_2 \rightarrow CO_2 + H_2O + energy$
    E. $NH_3 + H_2O \rightarrow NO_3^- + H^+$
        $NO_3^- + H^+ \rightarrow N_2O + N_2$

28. In a food chain where krill consumes phytoplankton, penguins and squid consume krill, and orcas consume penguins, which of these organisms is considered the producer?

    A. Krill
    B. Orca
    C. Phytoplankton
    D. Squid
    E. Penguin

29. Which of the following sets of species includes only K-selected species?

    A. Humans, red ants, and elephants
    B. Blue whales, giraffes, and mosquitoes
    C. California gray whales, banana slugs, and redwoods
    D. Giant sequoias, California condors, and humans
    E. Bumble bees, lions, and white rhinoceroses

30. Which of the following best describes how coal is formed?

    A. Tiny aquatic plants and animals die and sink to the ocean floor, where they are covered in mud and silt. In an anaerobic reaction over time, pressure compresses out the liquid and leaves behind carbon to form short carbon chains.
    B. The remains of plants from crops are pressed to remove the liquid and are then heated at high temperatures until coal is formed.
    C. Vegetation dies and is covered in mud in an anaerobic environment. Over time, the pressure compresses out the liquid, leaving the carbon matter behind to form complex chains of carbon compounds.
    D. Tiny aquatic plants and animals die and sink to the ocean floor, where they are covered in mud and silt. In an anaerobic reaction over time, pressure compresses out the liquid and leaves behind carbon to form long carbon chains.
    E. Charcoal forms when wood is heated to high temperatures, causing thermal decomposition. A mixture of gases and water vapors escape, leaving the solid residue called charcoal.

31. All the following are consequences of global climate change EXCEPT:

    A. Melting of glaciers and polar ice caps
    B. Rising sea levels
    C. Alteration of worldwide precipitation patterns
    D. Little or no impact on the human food supply
    E. Increased global temperatures

32. Which of the following terms is used to describe a species that reflects the health of an ecosystem, such as lichen or amphibians?

    A. Keystone species
    B. Indicator species
    C. Foundation species
    D. Specialist species
    E. Generalist species

33. One of the biggest threats to rangeland is overgrazing of vegetation by livestock. All the following are consequences of overgrazing EXCEPT:

    A. Soil erosion
    B. Soil compaction
    C. Desertification
    D. The proliferation of invasive species
    E. An increase in native biodiversity

Question 34 refers to the following table.

Changes in Concentration of Greenhouse Gases		
Greenhouse Gas	**Preindustrial Levels (ppm)**	**Current Level (ppm)**
Carbon dioxide	280	388
Methane	700	1,745
Nitric oxide	270	314
CFCs	0	533

34. The table shows dramatic increases in greenhouse-gas levels. Combustion of fossil fuels accounts for changes in CO_2 and NO levels. The increasing populations of cattle and other animals for human consumption accounts for the increase in CH_4. What accounts for the change in CFCs?

    A. CFCs were not used prior to the Industrial Revolution.
    B. CFCs were discovered and manufactured starting in the 1930s.
    C. CFCs are a secondary air pollutant, and levels were not significant until concentrations of primary air pollutants were high.
    D. CFCs were in the atmosphere prior to the Industrial Revolution, but humans did not have the means to measure the gases until instruments were developed.
    E. CFCs are released in the processing of uranium for use as a fuel in nuclear reactors and, therefore, were not produced until the 1950s, when reactors were first developed.

Questions 35–38 refer to the following answer choices.

    A. Ammonification
    B. Denitrification
    C. Nitrification
    D. Nitrogen fixation
    E. Assimilation

35. NO_3 is converted to N_2.

36. NH_4^+ is converted into NO_2^- and then into NO_3^-.

37. Plants take up NH_3 and NH_4^+.

38. N_2 is combined with H_2 to form NH_3.

39. In the 1960s, several events occurred as a result of increasing water pollution levels, including the burning of the Cuyahoga River, fish die-offs in Lake Erie, and a crude oil spill off the coast of Santa Barbara, California. Which of the laws below is NOT related to aquatic environments or water quality?

    A. Safe Drinking Water Act
    B. Federal Water Pollution Control Act
    C. Ocean Dumping Act
    D. Waste Water Reduction Act
    E. Clean Water Act

Question 40 refers to the following table.

Power Production in the Top Five Nuclear-Power-Producing Countries	
Country	**Megawatt Capacity**
United States	100,000
France	63,000
Japan	46,000
Russia	22,000
Germany	20,000
World	**370,000**

40. Approximately what percent of the world's total nuclear power is produced by the top five nuclear power-producing nations?

    A. 25
    B. 37
    C. 55
    D. 68
    E. 75

41. Managing federal lands is very complex due to the vast ecosystems found in the United States, the physical size of the country, the historical usages of many land areas, the need for recreation, and the use of materials for the production of goods. Which of the following government organizations operates Yellowstone National Park, Gettysburg Battlefield, the Washington Monument, and the Appalachian Trail?

    A. National Forest Service
    B. National Park Service
    C. National Resource Lands
    D. National Wilderness Preservation System
    E. Bureau of Land Management

42. Which of the following best defines *sustainability?*

    A. The development of methods that use resources wisely
    B. The ability to find alternative energy sources for most to the world's energy needs
    C. The efforts to find methods to reduce poverty and the effects of poverty on the environment
    D. The ability to maintain our current lifestyle and reduce our ecological footprint
    E. The ability to meet the needs of the present human population without compromising the ability of future generations to meet their needs

43. Which of the following statements best describes carbon monoxide?

    A. Carbon monoxide is made up of small particles approximately 10 mm or less in size that can irritate the lungs.
    B. At low concentrations, carbon monoxide can cause nausea, impaired vision, confusion, and fatigue.
    C. When combined with water in the air, carbon monoxide produces an acid that will fall to the Earth as acid deposition.
    D. At ground level, carbon monoxide is a pollutant; in the stratosphere, carbon monoxide blocks UV radiation.
    E. Carbon monoxide was a major air pollutant until gasoline was reformulated.

44. Of the following forms of alternative energy, which currently contributes LEAST to the global energy supply?

    A. Biomass
    B. Geothermal
    C. Solar energy
    D. Wave energy
    E. Wind power

45. Which of the following forms of toxins targets the nervous system, affecting motor control and brain function?

    A. Allergen
    B. Carcinogen
    C. Mutagen
    D. Neurotoxin
    E. Teratogen

46. In many developing countries, chronic hunger is an ongoing problem, whereas in developed countries, most of the population has access to food. Which of the following is a major health concern facing the population of the United States?

    A. Smoking
    B. Obesity
    C. Lower life expectancy
    D. Gang violence
    E. High infant mortality

Questions 47–50 refer to the following answer choices.

    A. Dose
    B. Dose-response
    C. Persistence
    D. Response
    E. Toxin

47. The effect of a toxin or drug on an organism.

48. The concentration or amount of a substance experienced by an organism.

49. When a pollutant remains in the environment for a long period of time.

50. A substance that is poisonous to an organism.

51. In which stage of demographic transition do birth rates start to decline?

    A. Pre-industrial stage
    B. Transitional stage
    C. Industrial stage
    D. Post-industrial stage
    E. Urbanization

52. Where did the most severe nuclear accident occur in the United States?

    A. Chernobyl
    B. Yucca Mountain
    C. Shoreham
    D. Three Mile Island
    E. Love Canal

53. Which of the following energy sources produce the least emissions?

    A. Wind, biomass, and solar
    B. Solar, hydroelectric, and wind
    C. Wind, biomass, and nuclear
    D. Nuclear, solar, and biomass
    E. Solar, hydroelectric, and biomass

54. The United States consumes approximately what percentage of the world's oil?

    A. 10
    B. 25
    C. 50
    D. 80
    E. 95

55. Species that can survive in a variety of habitats with a range of resources are considered

    A. Generalists
    B. K-selected
    C. Specialists
    D. r-selected
    E. Survivors

56. Which of the following soil types is most effective at retaining water and nutrients at a neutral pH?

    A. Silt
    B. Loam
    C. Sand
    D. Clay
    E. Sandy clay

57. Many ocean fisheries are declining in numbers, but often fishing boats are still filling their hulls. How is this possible?

    A. Fishing in shallower depths

    B. Returning to harvesting using traditional methods without the use of technology

    C. Fishing over a longer period of time

    D. Using drift-netting more often

    E. Restocking the oceans with farm-raised fish

58. Which of the following biomes has the most fertile soil?

    A. Tropical rain forest

    B. Tundra

    C. Temperate deciduous forest

    D. Desert

    E. Savanna

Questions 59–60 refer to the following diagram.

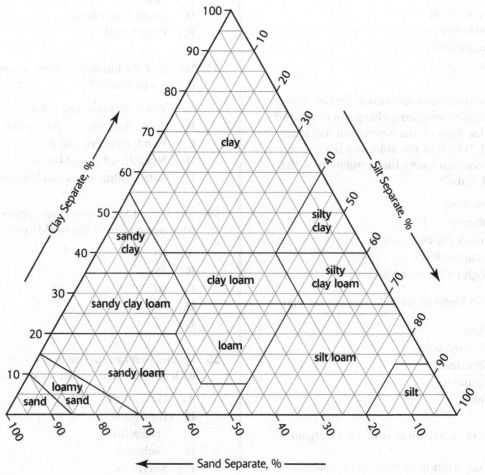

Source: U.S. Department of Agriculture

59. Which of the following soil types best describes the soil if it has 30 percent clay and 70 percent sand?

   A. Sandy loam
   B. Silty loam
   C. Silty clay
   D. Sandy clay
   E. Sandy clay loam

60. Which of the following describes why sandy soils would not be the best soil type for plant growth?

   A. They would hold water and cause water-logging of the soil.
   B. They would not retain water well.
   C. They have excessive nutrient content.
   D. They are excessively basic on the pH scale.
   E. They are hard to work.

61. Which of the following are the most effective methods for long-term disposal of hazardous waste?

   A. Hazardous waste landfills
   B. Injection wells
   C. Surface impoundments
   D. General landfills
   E. Incineration

62. A savannah is characterized by:

   A. Minimal rainfall throughout the year
   B. Large amounts of grasses and tall trees
   C. Distinct rainy seasons, creating dramatic variations in annual rainfall
   D. Consistent rainfall throughout the year
   E. Dry soils

63. Which of the following is a result of overgrazing?

   A. A positive feedback loop where the soil becomes eroded but quickly recovers
   B. A negative feedback loop where the soil becomes eroded and continues to deteriorate
   C. A negative feedback loop where the soil becomes eroded but quickly recovers
   D. A positive feedback loop that turns into a negative feedback loop
   E. A positive feedback loop where the soil becomes eroded and continues to deteriorate

64. Why is the amount of deforestation higher in tropical rain forests compared to other forest types?

   A. The forests have more secondary growth trees.
   B. Often, governments in the primarily developing countries that hold tropical rain forests sell the rights to their natural resources as a way of bringing additional money to the country.
   C. The trees are mainly hardwood trees.
   D. The forests are made up mainly of fast-growing trees.
   E. It is more economical to harvest from tropical rain forests than from other types of forest.

65. How can water vapor become a problem in the Earth's atmosphere?

   A. Increasing water vapor in the atmosphere creates a positive feedback loop, intensifying the greenhouse affect.
   B. Excess water vapor creates more intense storms.
   C. Decreasing water vapor in the atmosphere creates a positive feedback loop, intensifying the greenhouse effect.
   D. Increased water vapor can lead to an increase in other greenhouse gases.
   E. Less water vapor increases cloud production.

66. Which element powers nuclear power plants?

   A. Radon
   B. Thorium
   C. Plutonium
   D. Uranium
   E. Radium

67. In the oceans, downwellings bring

   A. Oxygen-deprived water to deep waters
   B. Nutrients to the benthic environment
   C. Areas of high primary productivity
   D. Nutrients to the surface
   E. Oxygen for life in deep waters

68. Biomes are classified based on:

    A. Climate
    B. Plant type and vegetation pattern
    C. Temperature and precipitation
    D. Location
    E. Latitude

69. If the planet continues in the direction of accelerating climate change and warming, which of the following is a feasible consequence?

    A. Oceans freeze over.
    B. Atmospheric circulation stops.
    C. All vegetation dies.
    D. There is a shift in the location of biomes.
    E. The Earth's magnetic poles flip.

70. A family lives in a small house with the water heater close to the bedrooms. The heater has a leak. Which of the following might the family be exposed to, potentially leading to sickness or death?

    A. Carbon dioxide
    B. Methane
    C. Sulfur dioxide
    D. Carbon monoxide
    E. Nitrogen dioxide

Questions 71–72 refer to the following table.

U.S. Methane Emissions by Source (TgCO$_2$ Equivalents)							
Source Category	1990	1995	2000	2005	2006	2007	2008
Enteric fermentation	132.4	143.7	136.8	136.7	139.0	141.2	140.8
Landfills	149.3	144.1	120.7	125.6	127.1	126.5	126.3
Natural gas systems	129.5	132.6	130.7	103.6	103.1	99.5	96.4
Coal mining	84.1	67.1	60.4	56.9	58.3	58.1	67.6
Manure management	29.3	33.9	38.6	42.2	42.3	45.9	45.0
Forest land remaining forest land	3.2	4.3	14.3	9.8	21.6	20.0	11.9
Petroleum systems	33.9	32.0	30.2	28.2	28.2	28.8	29.1
Wastewater treatment	23.5	24.8	25.2	24.3	24.5	24.4	24.3
Stationary combustion	7.4	7.1	6.6	6.6	6.2	6.5	6.7
Rice cultivation	7.1	7.6	7.5	6.8	5.9	6.2	7.2
Abandoned underground coal mines	6.0	8.2	7.4	5.6	5.5	5.7	5.9
Mobile combustion	4.7	4.3	3.4	2.5	2.4	2.2	2.0
Composting	0.3	0.7	1.3	1.6	1.6	1.7	1.7
Petrochemical production	0.9	1.1	1.2	1.1	1.0	1.0	0.9
Field burning of agricultural residue	0.8	0.7	0.9	0.9	0.9	1.0	1.0
Iron and steel production and metallurgical coke production	1.0	1.0	0.9	0.7	0.7	0.7	0.6
Ferroalloy production	+	+	+	+	+	+	+
Silicon carbide production and consumption	+	+	+	+	+	+	+
International bunker fuels	+	+	+	+	+	+	+
Total for U.S.	**613.4**	**613.2**	**586.0**	**553.2**	**568.2**	**569.2**	**567.6**

Source: Environmental Protection Agency

71. What is the percent change in methane emissions from enteric fermentation (digestive processes in organisms) from 1990 to 2008?

   A. Methane emissions increased by 6.3 percent.
   B. Methane emissions decreased by 6.3 percent.
   C. Methane emissions increased by 8.4 percent.
   D. Methane emissions decreased by 8.4 percent.
   E. Methane emissions increased by 6 percent.

72. What is the most likely reason for the decrease in emissions from landfills between 1990 and 2008?

   A. Decreased disposal of waste in landfills
   B. Less decomposition occurring in landfills
   C. Fewer methane-producing items disposed of in landfills
   D. Increased capture and reuse of the methane produced by landfills
   E. Lack of accurate data

73. Which of the following is the main component of acid drainage from mining activities?

   A. Sulfuric acid
   B. Hydrochloric acid
   C. Nitrogen dioxide
   D. Methane
   E. Nitric acid

74. Sand has

   A. High porosity and low permeability
   B. Low porosity and low permeability
   C. High porosity and high permeability
   D. Equal porosity and permeability
   E. Low porosity and high permeability

75. Which of the following explains how a species can become invasive when introduced to an ecosystem?

   I.   Ability to outcompete native species
   II.   Ability to reproduce quickly
   III. Lack of limiting factors

   A. I only
   B. II only
   C. III only
   D. I and III only
   E. I, II, and III

76. All the following are benefits of a kelp forest EXCEPT:

   A. It provides shelter for fish.
   B. It serves as a food supply for many invertebrates.
   C. It can provide components of cosmetic products.
   D. It reduces the effects of eutrophication.
   E. It protects the coastline.

77. Ocean currents transport energy as they move throughout the Earth, with water temperature being a major driver of this circulation. Which of the following statements most accurately describes this phenomenon?

   A. Surface waters are cooler, less dense, and less saline than deeper waters are.
   B. Surface waters are warmer, less dense, more saline than deeper waters are.
   C. Surface waters are warmer, less dense, and less saline waters than deeper waters are.
   D. Surface and deeper waters are both warm, less dense, and less saline in the equatorial regions and colder, denser, and more saline in the polar regions.
   E. Surface waters are warmer, more dense, and more saline waters than deeper waters are.

78. When hosts and parasites develop adaptations in response to each other, it is considered:

   A. Cooperation
   B. Mutualism
   C. Co-evolution
   D. Symbiosis
   E. Dependent evolution

79. The giant panda is one of the most visible endangered species in need of protection. Why is conservation awareness focused on a single flagship species?

   A. It helps to draw attention to an ecosystem in need of protection by using a species that can capture the public's eye.
   B. It helps to protect the species most in need of protection.
   C. There is not enough money available to protect all organisms, so efforts are put towards conserving keystone species.
   D. Flagship species are the main species contributing to biodiversity of an ecosystem.
   E. There is not enough money available to protect all organisms, forcing efforts to focus on conserving the large animals.

80. How is modern population growth different from growth during the Agricultural Revolution?

   A. Modern growth has high birth and death rates, while during the Agricultural Revolution birth and death rates were both low.
   B. Modern growth has a low birth rate and a high death rate, while during the Agricultural Revolution birth and death rates were both high.
   C. Modern growth has low birth and death rates, while during the Agricultural Revolution birth and death rates were both high.
   D. Modern growth has low birth and death rates, while during the Agricultural Revolution birth rates were low and death rates were high.
   E. Modern growth has high birth and death rates, while during the Agricultural Revolution birth rates were high and death rates were low.

81. Which of the following could feasibly explain why hurricanes and tropical storms have increased in intensity in recent decades?

   A. Increase in tropical sea surface temperatures
   B. Rising sea levels
   C. Decrease in sea surface temperatures
   D. Increasing levels of greenhouse gases in the atmosphere
   E. Alteration of ocean circulation patterns

Questions 82–84 refer to the following answer choices.

   A. Open-pit mining
   B. Subsurface mining
   C. Bore mining
   D. Surface mining
   E. Placer mining

82. Which form of mining uses running water to separate heavier minerals from lighter minerals?

83. With this form of mining, quarries are created with terraced sides for access into the mine.

84. Due to the confined nature of this type of mine, particulate matter can accumulate in the air and become a health hazard for miners.

85. Critics point to all the following as potential negative consequences of producing genetically modified foods EXCEPT:

   A. The increasing need for more powerful pesticides and herbicides due to growing resistance in pests and weeds
   B. The destruction of native crops
   C. The ability for foods to stay fresh longer, giving them the ability to be transported farther and have a longer shelf-life
   D. The possibility of exacerbating allergies in people
   E. The potential to create new disease, because bacteria and viruses are sometimes used to create genetically modified foods

86. An evolutionary adaptation in which different species divide a limited resource by specializing in different ways is considered

   A. Co-evolution
   B. Resource partitioning
   C. Allotropic speciation
   D. Sympatric speciation
   E. Natural selection

87. Which of the following statements correctly describes the relationship between altitude and atmospheric pressure?

    A. With decreasing altitude, atmospheric pressure decreases.
    B. With increasing altitude, atmospheric pressure increases.
    C. With increasing altitude, atmospheric pressure decreases.
    D. With decreasing altitude, atmospheric pressure increases.
    E. When altitude increases, atmospheric pressure stabilizes.

88. Which of the following could cause birth rates to increase back to a rate similar to that seen during the pre-industrial stage of demographic transition?

    A. Increase in disease and death among the young
    B. Decrease in disease and death among the young
    C. Increase in the elderly population
    D. War
    E. Female empowerment

89. Who is responsible for the creation of the National Wildlife Refuge System?

    A. Rachel Carson
    B. Gifford Pinchot
    C. President Herbert Hoover
    D. President Theodore Roosevelt
    E. Aldo Leopold

90. Why are wetlands considered an especially valuable ecosystem?

    A. Wetlands store pollutants so that they do not flow into the oceans.
    B. Wetlands help to stop waterlogging and saltwater intrusion.
    C. Wetlands help to increase the flow of water into oceans and lakes.
    D. Wetlands provide many ecosystem services, such as filtering pollutants.
    E. Wetlands provide many raw materials for industry.

91. One benefit of organic agriculture is the:

    A. Increase in crop yields
    B. Use of transgenic seeds
    C. Increase in monocultures
    D. Use of synthetic chemicals
    E. Use of natural as opposed to synthetic inputs

92. Which of the following organizations has created a global tree-planting campaign to encourage the planting of indigenous trees?

    A. United Nations Environmental Program
    B. World Bank
    C. European Union
    D. World Trade Organization
    E. Federal Reserve

93. Which of the following forms of energy do developing nations use the most?

    A. Coal and natural gas
    B. Natural gas and oil
    C. Oil and biomass
    D. Solar and wind
    E. Oil and wind

Questions 94–96 refer to the following answer choices.

    A. Lead
    B. PBDEs
    C. POPs
    D. VOCs
    E. Bisphenol-A

94. Commonly used as a fire-retardant in many products but can act as an endocrine disruptor.

95. A group of chemicals that bioaccumulate, persist, and travel long distances.

96. A heavy metal that can have negative effects on the nervous system.

97. Genetic pollution is a result of:

    A. The unintended spread of altered genetic information from genetically engineered organisms to natural organisms
    B. Inbreeding
    C. Loss of biodiversity
    D. Loss of genetic diversity
    E. A decrease in the use of genetically engineered organisms.

98. What is the main reason for the reduction in water volume of the Aral Sea?

    A. A trench opening due to tectonic plate shift
    B. A dryer climate resulting in excessive evaporation
    C. Excessive water withdrawal for use in irrigation
    D. The building of a dam on a river feeding it
    E. Seepage of the water into underground aquifers

99. If soil and groundwater become contaminated due to a leaking underground tank, what process would need to be conducted in order to clean up the site?

    A. Desalinization
    B. Deep-well injection
    C. Drainage of the groundwater
    D. Composting
    E. Remediation

100. Why is kudzu considered an invasive species?

    A. It is a specialist.
    B. It is fast growing, hard to kill, and smothers other types of vegetation.
    C. It is slow growing but hard to kill.
    D. It co-evolves with bird species.
    E. It develops a symbiotic relationship with other organisms.

IF YOU FINISH BEFORE TIME IS CALLED, CHECK YOUR WORK ON THIS SECTION ONLY. DO NOT WORK ON ANY OTHER SECTION IN THE TEST.

Section II: Free-Response Questions

Time: 90 minutes

4 questions

Directions: Each question is equally weighted. Plan to budget your time and allow yourself approximately 20 minutes per question. Write clearly to show any calculations when computations are necessary. Calculators are not allowed. Where an explanation or discussion is required, support your answers with relevant information, facts, and/or specific examples.

Question 1 refers to the following article from the Cornell Chronicle Online.

Rattlesnakes Sound Warning on Biodiversity and Habitat Fragmentation

Like the canary in the coal mine, the timber rattlesnake may be telling us something about the environment we share.

Cornell University researchers—using cutting-edge tools including fine-scale molecular genetics and microsatellite markers—tracked the rattlesnakes to understand how wildlife habitats are affected by even modest human encroachment.

"We used this species as a model to investigate general processes underlying population-level responses to habitat fragmentation," said the authors, led by Cornell post-doctoral researcher Rulon Clark, in the paper "Roads, Interrupted Dispersal and Genetic Diversity in Timber Rattlesnakes," currently available online and to be published in the journal *Conservation Biology*.

Researchers discovered that fragmentation of natural habitats . . . has had a significant effect over the past 80 years on genetic structure of timber rattlesnakes in four separate regions of upstate New York.

1. As human population increases, so, too, does habitat fragmentation, negatively impacting many organisms and global biodiversity.

   A. Discuss how habitat fragmentation can impact the genetic diversity of a species.
   B. Cite and explain two human activities that have led to habitat fragmentation.
   C. Explain how the fragmentation of habitats can lead to the loss of biodiversity.
   D. Discuss two solutions to reduce habitat fragmentation as our global human population continues to grow.
   E. Explain what is meant by the reference to the "canary in a coal mine." Relate this idea to this article's description of the rattlesnake.

2. There are plans to build a new coal-fired power plant near a city in the Midwest. This plant is controversial in the local area and has brought many concerns about potential negative environmental effects on local ecosystems. Efforts are being made, though, by local leaders to show the amount of energy the plant will bring to the area and also ways individuals can lower their own energy usage.

   A. A large, coal-fired power plant produces 64 million kWh of electricity each day. Assume the following: 10,000 BTUs are required to produce 1 kWh of electricity, 1 pound of coal produces 5,000 BTUs of heat, each coal car can hold 100 tons, and 1 ton is 2,000 pounds.
   i. How much heat in BTUs is needed to produce the power each day?
   ii. How many coal cars will be needed to operate the power plant for the day?
   iii. How many trains will be needed to power the plant for a day if the train pulls 80 coal cars?
   B. Coal mines in the west tend to be strip mines. Describe how a strip mine is mined to obtain the coal. Explain one impact on aquatic ecosystems from strip mining.
   C. Discuss one environmental impact related to attaining energy from a coal-fired power plant, aside from the effects of the mining and combustion of the coal.
   D. Describe two methods to reduce home energy usage.

3. The carbon cycle is one of the major biogeochemical cycles. Biogeochemical cycles are natural processes that recycle nutrients in various chemical forms from the nonliving environment to living organisms and then back to the nonliving environment. These global cycles recycle nutrients through the Earth's air, land, water, and living organisms, connecting past, present, and future life.

    A. Explain how the carbon balance on Earth is shifting from the lithosphere or biosphere to the atmosphere.

    B. Explain how the carbon cycle contributes to the regulation of the Earth's temperature.

    C. Describe two natural processes that occur in the carbon cycle.

    D. Describe two ways in which humans affect the carbon cycle.

    E. Describe two ways humans impact other biogeochemical cycles.

4. Hydrogen is an emerging alternative energy source, but as with many other energy sources, it is not without drawbacks.

    A. Explain how hydrogen is attained for use as an energy source.

    B. Discuss two positive aspects of hydrogen as an energy source.

    C. Discuss three reasons why opponents to hydrogen energy do not see it as a viable alternative to fossil fuels.

    D. In what ways has hydrogen fuel already been made available to consumers?

    E. Discuss two reasons why alternative energy is currently an essential component of the world's energy supply and may become more so in the future.

IF YOU FINISH BEFORE TIME IS CALLED, CHECK YOUR WORK ON THIS SECTION ONLY. DO NOT WORK ON ANY OTHER SECTION IN THE TEST.

Answer Key

Section I: Multiple-Choice Questions

1. D	26. D	51. C	76. D
2. E	27. B	52. D	77. C
3. A	28. C	53. B	78. C
4. E	29. D	54. B	79. A
5. E	30. C	55. A	80. C
6. D	31. D	56. B	81. A
7. A	32. B	57. C	82. E
8. B	33. E	58. C	83. A
9. D	34. B	59. E	84. B
10. D	35. B	60. B	85. C
11. D	36. C	61. A	86. B
12. C	37. E	62. C	87. C
13. C	38. A	63. E	88. A
14. B	39. D	64. B	89. D
15. C	40. D	65. A	90. D
16. A	41. B	66. D	91. E
17. D	42. E	67. E	92. A
18. B	43. B	68. B	93. C
19. E	44. D	69. D	94. B
20. E	45. D	70. D	95. C
21. A	46. B	71. A	96. A
22. D	47. B	72. D	97. A
23. C	48. A	73. A	98. C
24. A	49. C	74. C	99. E
25. C	50. E	75. E	100. B

Answer Explanations

Section I: Multiple-Choice Questions

1. **D** An extinct volcano is a volcano that is not erupting and most likely will not erupt at any point again.

2. **E** A shield volcano is a slowly erupting volcano with a broad base, gradual slopes, and usually craters at the top.

3. **A** An active volcano is a volcano that is presently erupting or has a large amount of seismic and thermal activity and will eventfully erupt.

4. **E** Traditional agriculture uses manual labor, animal labor, and simple tools to grow crops.

5. **E** The Green Revolution of the 20th century was characterized by the development of high-yield crops, the wide use of pesticides, and the augmentation of irrigation infrastructure.

6. **D** Beneficial ozone acts as a protective layer, filtering ultraviolet radiation in the stratosphere including all UVC, 95 percent of UVB, and most all UVA. The majority of UV rays that reach the Earth's surface are UVA.

7. **A** 25 watts × 10,000 hours = 250,000 Wh. Then, 250,000 Wh × (1 k ÷ 1,000) = 250 kWh. And 250kWh × $0.10/kWh = $25.

8. **B** 100 watts × 1,000 hours = 100,000 Wh. Then, 100,000 Wh × (1 k ÷ 1,000) = 100 kWh. And 100kWh × $0.10/kWh = $10.

9. **D** 1 CFL averages 10,000 hours, while an incandescent bulb average 1,000 hours. Therefore, you will need 10 incandescent bulbs to have 10,000 hours (10,000 ÷ 1,000 = 10). The total cost of the energy for the incandescent bulbs is $10 × 10 bulbs = $100, so the savings is $100 – $25 = $75.

10. **D** If located a great distance from a municipal treatment center, a house is most likely using a septic system to collect and treat sewage.

11. **D** A telephone ringing is not considered noise pollution because the decibel level from the telephone is below the level considered harmful.

12. **C** The mid-Atlantic ridge is a divergent plate boundary, meaning the plates are moving away from each other.

13. **C** The grassland has a thick O (organic) horizon. Deserts, semi-desert, and chaparral have relatively thin O horizons. The same is true in a tropical rain forest, in which dead plants and animals decay relatively quickly and live plants soon absorb the nutrients, leaving a thin O horizon.

14. **B** The parent material is the lowest level of the soil horizon and is comprised of the bedrock material.

15. **C** The grasslands of the United States are called prairies. The pampas are the grasslands of temperate South America, llanos are the grasslands of tropical South America, steppes are the grasslands of Europe, and veld are the grasslands in Africa.

16. **A** The greatest threat to the survival of terrestrial species is the loss of habitats. The destruction of habitat occurs when land is cleared and altered for homes, businesses, and food production. Notice that each of this question's incorrect answers can *lead* to habitat loss, but habitat loss itself is the most common threat.

17. **D** The greatest threat to aquatic species is overharvesting, which is the overfishing of organisms as a food source for humans or as a food source for other species that are grown for human consumption. Cod, salmon, sole, and tuna are just some of the species that have been overharvested. Notice that this question's incorrect answers are themselves also dire threats.

18. **B** Subsidies are based on the location of agriculture, mining, forestry, and other businesses, not on the location of current population centers.

19. **E** Built-in resistance is an advantage of genetically modified crops. Crops have now been created that contain resistance to disease and pests, reducing or eliminating the need for pesticides. Unknown long-term effects on human health and the destruction of native food sources are arguments against the use of genetically modified crops.

20. **E** Clear-cutting cuts down all the trees in the area, leaving soil bare and subject to erosion. It also reduces habitat and shelter for animals and leaves a minimal basis for the forest to reseed itself and, thus, grow back.

21. **A** Love Canal was a former canal in upstate New York where a large number of steel drums containing toxic chemicals were buried. Eventually the land was covered and sold to a local community for a school and housing. The drums rusted and the chemicals leaked, seeping through the soil and asphalt and contaminating the soil and groundwater. This led to birth defects, cancers, and other human health issues.

22. **D** Lake Erie was one of the most polluted lakes in the United States as a result of polluted rivers such as the Cuyahoga River flowing into the lake, as well as heavy industry along the lake that ultimately lead to a large fish die-off in 1969.

23. **C** Oils, trash, debris, and other flammable chemicals were floating on the surface of the Cuyahoga River when it caught fire in 1969. This was not the first river fire, but it brought awareness to the issue because *Time* magazine published an article about the event.

24. **A** CAFE is an acronym for *corporate average fuel economy,* which is a regulation that established the average miles-per-gallon of a manufacturer's fleet of cars. It was also expanded to include light trucks.

25. **C** Formaldehyde is found almost entirely as an indoor air pollutant, coming from pressed woods, carpets, and furniture. Both carbon dioxide and carbon monoxide are found indoors, but they are also found in large quantities outdoors. Nitrous oxide and sulfur dioxide are found mostly outdoors.

26. **D** One concern with GMOs is that the genes from these engineered plants and animals will unintentionally spread to the naturally occurring plants and animals via dispersion and/or interbreeding.

27. **B** Ozone is destroyed by chlorofluorocarbons (CFCs) when CFCs react with UV radiation from the sun to produce more CFCs while releasing a chlorine atom. (Note that the acronym *CFC* is shorthand and not a proper representation of the chemical's atoms, so chemical equations containing "CFC" need not appear balanced.) The chlorine atom then reacts with ozone to form chlorine monoxide and oxygen. The ClO reacts with ozone to form more chlorine molecules and oxygen. This is an ongoing cycle because more chlorine atoms are created in the process.

28. **C** Phytoplankton are the producers in this food web, turning the sun's energy into energy that is usable by the rest of the ocean food chain.

29. **D** Giant sequoias, California condors, and humans are K-selected species. They take a long time to reach maturity and generally produce only a few offspring at a time.

30. **C** Coal is formed when vegetation dies and is covered in mud, creating an anaerobic environment. Over millions of years pressure squeezes out the liquid, leaving the carbon matter behind to form complex chains of carbon compounds. These carbon compounds make up coal.

31. **D** Global climate change will have an effect on the human food supply. Crops grown along coastal areas may be flooded by rising seas and, thus, have to be relocated. Changes in precipitation patterns may lead to a need for an increase in crop irrigation or the need to move fields to areas that receive more rainfall. Higher temperatures also may lower crop yields or require a change in selecting where certain crops are grown.

32. **B** An indicator species reflects the quality of the water, soil, or air in a given area. If pollutants are present or the ecosystem is altered, these indicator species that are more sensitive to change will be affected first, likely dying, becoming ill, or moving from one location to another.

33. **E** Overgrazing leads to a reduction in native biodiversity because many native grasses struggle to cultivate and grow after being overgrazed. This could be due to reduced soil quality, soil compaction, or an intrusion of invasive species.

34. **B** CFCs were not developed until the 1930s, when they were manufactured in large quantities for use as refrigerants.

35. **B** Denitrification is the process by which bacteria convert nitrates (NO_3^-) into gaseous nitrogen (N_2), which is released into the atmosphere.

36. **C** Nitrification is the process of converting ammonium (NH_4^+) into both nitrite ions (NO_2^-) and nitrate ions (NO_3^-), both of which can be used by plants.

37. **E** Assimilation is the process of plants taking in the ammonia (NH_3) and ammonium (NH_4^+).

38. **A** Ammonification is the process of combining nitrogen gas (N_2) with hydrogen gas (H_2) to form ammonia (NH_3).

39. **D** The Safe Drinking Water Act sets standards for drinking-water quality in water sources both above and below ground. The Ocean Dumping Act prohibits the dumping of anything into U.S. waters without a permit. The Clean Water Act, also called the Federal Water Pollution Control Act, regulates the discharge of pollutants into waterways and sets quality standards for surface waters, including wastewater standards for industries. Waste Water Reduction Act is a fictitious name.

40. **D** Add the total of the five countries shown: $100,000 + 63,000 + 46,000 + 22,000 + 20,000 = 251,000$. Now divide this total by the world total and multiple by 100 to get the percentage: $(251,000 \text{ MW} \div 370,000 \text{ MW}) \times 100 = 67.8$ percent, which can be rounded to 68 percent.

41. **B** The National Park Service operates national parks, national recreation areas, and areas of historic significance.

42. **E** To live sustainably, we need to meet the needs of the present human population without compromising the ability of future generations to meet their needs. Considerations include sustainable use of land, water, and resources.

43. **B** Exposure to carbon monoxide can cause nausea, impaired vision, confusion, and fatigue at low concentrations. In the bloodstream, CO binds with hemoglobin, displacing oxygen and inhibiting oxygen from binding with the hemoglobin. This can result in suffocation, because oxygen is not circulating in the blood.

44. **D** Wind and solar energy are widely used in many nations and their use continues to grow. Geothermal energy is being used in several countries including the United States and Iceland. Biomass is the oldest form of power and is still used in many areas around the world. Harnessing wave motion is a potential way to capture the ocean's energy. Wave technology is currently under development, but it is mainly experimental in its design and implementation.

45. **D** Neurotoxins affect the nervous system. An allergen stimulates a response in the immune system. A carcinogen is a cancer-causing toxin. A mutagen can cause mutations in the DNA of an organism. A teratogen can affect embryo development.

46. **B** Excess weight and obesity are becoming some of the biggest health issues in the United States, with over 66 percent of the population overweight or obese.

47. **B** A dose-response is the effect of an amount of toxin or drug on an organism or population.

48. **A** A dose is the amount or concentration of a substance experienced by an organism.

49. **C** Persistence refers to a substance remaining in the environment for an extended period of time.

50. **E** A toxin is a substance that is poisonous to an organism.

51. **C** The industrial stage of demographic transition is the point at which birth rates begin to decline due to the decreased need for children to work on farms or as laborers, and an increase in the availability of contraception.

52. **D** Three Mile Island was the site of the most severe nuclear accident in U.S. history. The accident was caused by a loss of reactor coolant. The failure was mechanical in nature in the beginning, followed by

human failure to recognize the problem, and the result was a partial meltdown. In the end, the reactor was brought under control and a total meltdown was avoided.

53. **B** Solar, hydroelectric, and wind energy produce the least amount of direct emissions compared to other sources. Assessment of emissions in this situation does not includes emissions from mining, manufacturing, transportation, construction, and disposal aspects of the energy generation processes.

54. **B** The United States consumes close to 25 percent of the world's oil, yet produces about 8 percent of the world's supply. The large population, combined with the economic ability to consume, feeds this consumption. Oil is used in large quantities for transportation, industry, and agriculture.

55. **A** Generalists fulfill a broad niche and can survive in a variety of habitats with a range of resources. This gives them a better chance of survival in times of environmental change.

56. **B** Loam is the most effective soil type at retaining water and nutrients at a neutral pH. Loam is a relatively even combination of sand, silt, and clay, giving it a mixture of pore sizes and even soil porosity and permeability.

57. **C** Even though ocean fisheries are declining in numbers, boats can still come into dock with full hulls because fishermen are spending more time fishing. They are also going farther and fishing in deeper waters. Therefore, fishermen are spending more time and effort to bring in the same numbers of catch as they did in previous years.

58. **C** Temperate deciduous forests have fertile soil due to the organic matter that accumulates on the top of the soil. As leaves are shed from the deciduous trees, they fall to the ground and decompose. The decomposition of leaves and other dead organic matter such as animal waste, grasses, and tree branches, returns nutrients to the soil, making it fertile.

59. **E** Sandy clay loam would describe soil that is 30 percent clay and 70 percent sand. In the soil texture diagram, the percent clay is on the left side and the percent sand is on the bottom. Follow 30 percent from the clay and 70 percent from the sand. The resulting soil is sandy clay loam.

60. **B** Sandy soils are made up of larger particles and have larger pore spaces, so water can flow through sandy soils easily.

61. **A** A hazardous waste landfill is widely considered the most effective choice for long-term disposal of hazardous waste because it is specially designed with a leachate removal system and impermeable liner. However, this type of landfill acts as a storage option as opposed to a place for the hazardous waste to break down. Surface impoundments have a tendency to leak waste, and some waste may be blown away or evaporated. Injection wells can leak into soil and groundwater due to corroded pipes.

62. **C** A savannah has distinct rainy seasons, creating dramatic variations in annual rainfall. This uneven distribution of precipitation throughout the year has given savannahs their unique vegetation pattern of grasses interspersed with patches of trees. In the Northern Hemisphere, most savannah rainfall occurs from November through March.

63. **E** Overgrazing can lead to a positive feedback loop where the soil becomes eroded and continues to deteriorate. In a positive feedback loop, once a system starts moving in a direction, it continues in that direction unless there is an intervention to stop the progression. This ultimately drives a system to an extreme, and in this case the extreme is degraded, unusable land.

64. **B** Deforestation is often higher in tropical rain forests because of the potential economic gain for the country in which the forest is located. Often, governments sell the rights to their natural resources to international buyers as a way to generate additional revenue.

65. **A** Increasing water vapor in the atmosphere creates a positive feedback loop, intensifying the greenhouse effect. As global temperature increases, more water evaporates from the oceans, seas, lakes, and rivers. This puts an increasing amount of water into the atmosphere, which, in turn, continues to warm the climate because water vapor is a greenhouse, heat-trapping gas.

66. **D** Uranium is a radioactive element mined from within the Earth and its isotopes are listed in nuclear power plants. U-235 is used directly and U-238 is converted into a plutonium isotope, Pu-239, to use as an energy source.

67. **E** Downwellings carry oxygen and other gases from surface waters to deeper ocean waters.

68. **B** Biomes are classified based on plant type and vegetation. Each region classified as a specific biome has vegetation similar to other areas also classified as that biome. Note that similarities in vegetation are due to the climate, amount of rainfall, temperatures, and amount of solar radiation.

69. **D** If the climate change continues to accelerate, there could be a shift in the location of biomes. As climate, rainfall, temperatures, and amounts of solar radiation shift due to climate alteration, the locations of biomes will shift as well.

70. **D** Carbon monoxide is produced as part of the incomplete combustion of fossil fuels. If a home appliance such as a hot water heater or clothes dryer has a leak, CO can escape and build up in the home. CO is a colorless and odorless gas that can lead to asphyxiation. If the presence of CO goes undetected, it can lead to illness or death.

71. **A** To calculate percent change, use the following formula:

$$\text{Percent Change} = \frac{V_2 - V_1}{V_1} \cdot 100$$

$$= \frac{140.8 - 132.4}{132.4} \cdot 100$$

$$= \frac{8.4}{132.4} \cdot 100$$

$$= 0.063 \cdot 100$$

$$= 6.3\%$$

72. **D** The decrease in emissions from landfills between 1990 and 2008 is most likely due to the increased capture and reuse of the methane produced by landfills. New technology, along with awareness of the negative results of methane in the atmosphere, have led to more landfills capturing and reusing the methane produced as a result of the decomposition of the waste.

73. **A** Sulfuric acid is the main component of acid drainage from mining activities. When sulfur contained in rocks is exposed during mining, it reacts with air and water to form sulfuric acid.

74. **C** Sand has high porosity and high permeability. This means that water can flow through easily and the pore spaces between sand particles do not hold water easily.

75. **E** The ability to outcompete native species, the ability to reproduce quickly, and the lack of limiting factors all help to explain how a species can become invasive when introduced to an ecosystem. The ability of an introduced species to thrive when introduced into an environment is dependent upon the ability of a species to survive in that environment.

76. **D** A kelp forest provides shelter for fish, serves as a food supply for many invertebrates, can provide components of cosmetic products, and protects the coastline. Kelp forests do not help to reduce the effects of eutrophication, though, which is caused by an influx of nutrients into an aquatic environment.

77. **C** Ocean currents transport energy as they move, with water temperature being a major driver of this circulation. Surface waters are warm, less dense, and less saline than deeper waters are. Surface waters are warmed by solar radiation in equatorial regions. As the warm waters move away from the equator, they cool and sink. As cold water moves toward warmer regions, the water warms and some of it rises. This constant rising and sinking of ocean water helps to move the water and circulate nutrients and gases.

78. **C** Co-evolution occurs when hosts and parasites develop adaptations in response to one another. As one organism develops an adaptation through the process of natural selection, the other organism may adapt in response to the other organism's adaptation.

79. **A** Focusing conservation on one charismatic species raises awareness of the need to protect an entire ecosystem. Because some species are more appealing to the public, they can be used to help conservation efforts not only for the species itself, but also for other species and the ecosystem as a whole.

80. **C** Modern growth has low birth and death rates. Low death rates are due to efficient medical care and low infant mortality, while low birth rates are due to factors such as increased use of contraception, females joining the workforce, and family planning. During the Agricultural Revolution, birth and death rates were both high because of high infant mortality, poor sanitation and healthcare, and the need for children to help with farming.

81. **A** Tropical storms and hurricanes are believed to be increasing in intensity in recent decades due to warming tropical sea surface temperatures. It is possible that the warming water temperatures are due to global warming, but this point is still being studied and debated.

82. **E** Placer mining uses running water to separate out the heavier minerals from the lighter ones.

83. **A** In open pit mining, quarries are created with terraced sides to allow access into the mine.

84. **B** Subsurface mines often are used in coal mining. Particles are disrupted in this process and become airborne. If not managed properly and without the proper protective gear, this environment can become a health issue affecting the respiratory system.

85. **C** Critics propose that the negative consequences of producing genetically modified foods include the following: the increasing need for more powerful pesticides and herbicides because of the growing resistance of pests and weeds, the destruction of native crops because of genetic contamination from wind-blown and water-carried genetically modified seeds, the possibility of exacerbating allergies in people, and the potential to create new disease because bacteria and viruses are sometimes used to create genetically modified foods. The ability for foods to stay fresh longer, giving them the ability to be transported farther and have a longer shelf life, is considered a benefit of genetically modified crops.

86. **B** An evolutionary adaptation in which different species divide a limited resource by specializing in different ways is considered resource partitioning. This allows similar species to survive within the same habitat by focusing survival efforts in unique ways. Note that this division of habitat occurs over generations through the process of natural selection.

87. **C** With increasing altitude, atmospheric pressure decreases. This is because, at high altitudes, fewer air particles are pushing down from above.

88. **A** The increasing spread of disease and death among the young could cause birth rates to increase and return to a rate similar to that seen in the pre-industrial stage of demographic transition. Historically, if death rates for the young start increasing, parents will start having more children to compensate for the loss.

89. **D** President Theodore Roosevelt was responsible for the creation of the National Wildlife Refuge System in 1903, which aims to preserve wildlife, populations, habitat, and land.

90. **D** Wetlands are valuable ecosystems because they provide many ecosystem services such as filtering pollutants, recharging aquifers, and flood reduction.

91. **E** One benefit of organic agriculture is its use of natural as opposed to synthetic inputs. Natural inputs have less impact on the environment, allowing native ecosystems to continue thriving in the absence of man-made chemicals.

92. **A** The United Nations Environmental Program aims to protect biodiversity and conserve natural resources on a global level, including an initiative to encourage the planting of indigenous trees. The organization helps nations find ways to address and solve environmental issues.

93. **C** Oil and biomass are the most widely-used forms of energy in developing nations. Biomass is widely used because it is relatively easy and inexpensive to attain. Often, people use biomass in the form of crop residue and animal manure from their own property. Oil is becoming more commonly used in developing countries as they become industrialized and not only need but can acquire oil.

94. **B** PBDEs are commonly used as fire retardants in many products. Unfortunately, they can act as endocrine disruptors in humans and other organisms.

95. **C** POPs are a group of chemicals that bioaccumulate, persist, and travel long distances.

96. **A** Lead is a heavy metal, and heavy metals can have negative effects on the nervous system.

97. **A** Genetic pollution is the unintended spread of altered genes from genetically modified organisms to natural organisms. Genetic pollution is becoming more common as the use of GMOs is becoming more common.

98. **C** The main reason for the reduction in water volume of the Aral Sea is excessive water withdrawal for use in irrigation. The region is also hot, dry, and prone to drought, making the replenishment of withdrawn water difficult.

99. **E** The process of remediation would be used to clean up soil and groundwater contaminated by a leaking underground tank. Possible remediation techniques include excavation, extraction, bioremediation, aeration, phytoremediation, and thermal remediation.

100. **B** Kudzu is an invasive species because it is fast growing, hard to kill, and smothers other types of vegetation. It is not originally native to North America as it is indigenous to Asia.

Section II: Free-Response Questions

1. This question is worth a maximum of 10 points, as follows:

A. Discuss how habitat fragmentation can impact the genetic diversity of a species. (2 points maximum)
   - 1 point: It limits gene interchange through a population.
   - 1 point: It can lead to inbreeding depression.
   - 1 point: There is increased susceptibility to disease.

B. Cite and explain two human activities that have led to habitat fragmentation. (2 points maximum)
   - 1 point: Development of roads, highways, canals, and irrigation ditches through ecosystems.
   - 1 point: Alteration of the path of a river.
   - 1 point: Development of buildings and communities.
   - 1 point: Creation of parks and other man-made ecosystems.
   - 1 point: Land converted for agricultural purposes.
   - 1 point: Deforestation.
   - 1 point: Timber harvesting.

C. Explain how the fragmentation of habitats can lead to the loss of biodiversity. (3 points maximum)
   - 1 point: Reduction of population immigration and emigration reduces gene flow.
   - 1 point: A decrease in the number of available mates reduces reproduction rates of a species, ultimately decreasing the numbers of a population.
   - 1 point: Species may be cut off from needed resources in other parts of the historic habitat.
   - 1 point: There is a decrease in the range for animals that require a large range.
   - 1 point: Barriers to migration are created for migratory species.
   - 1 point: There is an increase in disease and parasites at the edges of the habitats.

D. Discuss two solutions to reduce habitat fragmentation as our global human population continues to grow. (2 points maximum)
   - 1 point: Conversion of unused agricultural land back to natural habitat.
   - 1 point: Protection of large pieces of land through minimal-use guidelines.
   - 1 point: Protection of large pieces of land through establishment of parks and reserves.
   - 1 point: Use of land trusts to protect pieces of land in their natural state.
   - 1 point: Creation of biosphere reserves, incorporating areas of complete biodiversity preservation with sustainable and limited land use.
   - 1 point: The use of corridors for migrating species.

E. Explain what is meant by the reference to the "canary in a coal mine." Relate this to rattlesnakes and habitat fragmentation. (1 point maximum)

■ 1 point: Historically, mine workers carried canaries with them into subsurface coalmines. If the canary died, it meant there was a problem with air quality, signaling the workers to leave the mine. In examining the genetic diversity of rattlesnakes due to habitat fragmentation, if their diversity is being reduced, then it is likely that the genetic diversity of other organisms may be reduced due to the fragmentation as well.

2. This question is worth a maximum of 10 points, as follows:

A. Calculations

i. How much heat in BTUs is needed to produce the power each day? (2 points maximum—1 point for setting up the problem, 1 point for arriving at the correct answer)

Set up the problem:

$$\frac{64 \text{ million kWh}}{\text{day}} \left| \frac{10,000 \text{ BTU}}{1 \text{ kWh}} \right. =$$

Cancel the units:

$$\frac{64 \text{ million } \cancel{\text{kWh}}}{\text{day}} \left| \frac{10,000 \text{ BTU}}{1 \cancel{\text{kWh}}} \right. =$$

Solve the math:

$$\frac{64 \text{ million}}{\text{day}} \left| \frac{10,000 \text{ BTU}}{1} \right. = \frac{640,000 \text{ million BTU}}{\text{day}}$$

ii. How many coal cars will be needed to operate the power plant for the day? (2 points maximum—1 point for setting up the problem, 1 point for arriving at the correct answer)

$$\frac{640,000 \text{ million BTUs}}{\text{day}} \text{ or simplified } \frac{640 \text{ billion BTUs}}{\text{day}}$$

Set up the problem, cancel the units, and simplify the units:

$$\frac{640,\cancel{000} \text{ million } \cancel{\text{BTU}}}{\text{day}} \left| \frac{1 \cancel{\text{lb coal}}}{5,000 \cancel{\text{BTU}}} \right| \frac{1 \cancel{\text{ton}}}{2,000 \cancel{\text{lb coal}}} \left| \frac{1 \text{ coal car}}{\cancel{100} \text{ tons}} \right. =$$

Solve the math:

$$\frac{6,400}{\text{day}} \left| \frac{1}{5} \right| \frac{1}{2} \left| \frac{1 \text{ coal car}}{1} \right. = \frac{6,400 \text{ coal cars}}{10 \text{ days}} = \frac{640 \text{ coal cars}}{\text{day}}$$

Final answer:

$$\frac{640 \text{ coal cars}}{\text{day}}$$

iii. How many trains will be needed to power the plant for a day if the train pulls 80 coal cars? (1 point maximum)

$$\frac{640 \cancel{\text{coal cars}}}{\text{day}} \times \frac{\text{trains}}{80 \cancel{\text{coal cars}}} = \frac{8 \text{ trains}}{\text{day}}$$

B. Coal mines in the west tend to be strip mines. Describe how a strip mine is mined to obtain the coal. Explain one impact on aquatic ecosystems from strip mining. (2 points maximum)

- ■ 1 point: Strip mining, one form of surface mining, is the removal of soil and rock that are above the coal. Large "earthmover" equipment is needed to remove the soil and rock. Then additional machines (excavators) remove the coal.
- ■ 1 point: When it rains, the water may wash soil and small rocks down into the stream, increasing turbidity, which can then decrease photosynthesis and alter the entire ecosystem.
- ■ 1 point: Acid drainage can occur. During mining, when rock is exposed, naturally occurring sulfide minerals also are exposed. When it reacts with oxygen and water, the sulfide turns into sulfuric acid. This can run off into waterways and become toxic to organisms.

C. Discuss one environmental impact related to attaining energy from a coal-fired power plant, aside from the effects of the mining and combustion of the coal. (1 point maximum)

- ■ 1 point: The transport of the coal from the location of the mine to the power plant requires the use of fossil fuels to operate trains, as do the machinery and vehicles necessary to mine the coal. The combustion of fossil fuels emits carbon dioxide and other greenhouse gases that are contributing to climate change.
- ■ 1 point: The infrastructure necessary to build and operate the plant has an environmental impact. The building of the power plant as well as roadways and railways all require land. This alters and destroys ecosystems and fragments habitats.
- ■ 1 point: Infrastructure is necessary to carry the electricity from the plant to homes and businesses. This requires the establishment of underground lines as well as aboveground lines. Ecosystem alteration and habitat fragmentation can result from this.

D. Describe two methods to reduce home energy usage. (2 points maximum)

- ■ 1 point: Insulation helps prevent warm air from escaping from a building during winter months and keeps cool air inside in the summer months. This makes a building more energy efficient.
- ■ 1 point: The addition of weather stripping around doorways to the outside reduces drafts coming in at the doorframe.
- ■ 1 point: Lowering the thermostat in the winter and raising it in the summer uses less energy.
- ■ 1 point: Replacing single-pane windows with double- or triple-pane windows filled with noble gases cuts down the exchange of hot and cold air on opposite sides of the glass.
- ■ 1 point: Replace older appliances and equipment with more energy-efficient models. This may include water heaters, washers, dryers, dishwashers, heaters, air conditioners, stoves, and refrigerators.
- ■ 1 point: Cut down on phantom energy loss by unplugging electrical equipment when it is not in use.
- ■ 1 point: The addition of ceiling fans can redistribute warm air during the winter months and cool air during the summer months.
- ■ 1 point: Install electronic switches to turn the heater and air conditioner on and off.
- ■ 1 point: Install dimmer switches to regulate lighting.

3. This question is worth a maximum of 10 points, as follows:

A. Explain how the carbon balance on Earth is shifting from the lithosphere or biosphere to the atmosphere. (3 points maximum)

- ■ 1 point: Fossil fuels, which come from the decomposition of dead organic matter, contain carbon and have been sequestered in the lithosphere for millions of years.
- ■ 1 point: Humans use fossil fuels for energy through combustion processes. This is releasing the carbon into the atmosphere.
- ■ 1 point: Combustion of biomass releases carbon into the atmosphere.
- ■ 1 point: Deforestation increases the concentration of carbon in the atmosphere because photosynthesis is not occurring and using carbon from the atmosphere.
- ■ 1 point: Trees are considered carbon sinks because they store large amounts of carbon. Deforestation releases the stored carbon into the atmosphere.

B. Describe how the carbon cycle contributes to the regulation of the Earth's temperature. (1 point maximum)
- 1 point: CO_2 is a greenhouse gas that helps trap heat in the atmosphere. An increase in the concentration of CO_2 will lead to an increase in the Earth's temperature over time, and a decrease in the concentration will result in lower temperatures over time.

C. Describe two natural processes that occur in the carbon cycle. (2 points maximum)
- 1 point: In photosynthesis, energy is used to combine CO_2 with H_2O to form glucose ($C_6H_{12}O_6$) and oxygen.
- 1 point: In cellular respiration, glucose ($C_6H_{12}O_6$) in the presence of oxygen is burned to release CO_2 and H_2O and energy.
- 1 point: During the decomposition of dead organisms, CO_2 is released.
- 1 point: CO_2 exists in equilibrium between the water and atmosphere. Increasing CO_2 in the atmosphere increases CO_2 in aquatic systems.

D. Describe two ways in which humans affect the carbon cycle. (2 points maximum)
- 1 point: As humans burn fossil fuels and biomass for energy, CO_2 is being released at an increasing rate. This increases the amount of CO_2 in the atmosphere, which causes the concentration of CO_2 in the oceans to increase. Carbon dioxide in the oceans forms carbonic acid, so with an increasing amount of CO_2 in the oceans, more carbonic acid is formed, lowering the pH of the oceans.
- 1 point: The increase in CO_2 in the atmosphere may be leading to an increase in photosynthesis, increasing plant life and, therefore, the concentration of oxygen in the atmosphere.
- 1 point: Burning of fossil fuels increases the amount of CO_2 concentrations in the atmosphere. CO_2 is considered a greenhouse gas, and greenhouse gases contribute to climate change.
- 1 point: Deforestation is causing an increase in CO_2 concentrations in the atmosphere because trees and vegetation hold large amounts of CO_2. As forests are cleared, CO_2 is released into the atmosphere. CO_2 is considered a greenhouse gas, and greenhouse gases contribute to climate change.

E. Describe two ways humans impact other biogeochemical cycles. (2 points maximum)
- 1 point: In the phosphorus cycle, an increase in phosphorus into an aquatic system may result in an increase in plant growth. This may lead to algae blooms, eutrophication, and potentially hypoxia.
- 1 point: Phosphorus can be introduced into an ecosystem through runoff containing detergents, raw sewage, and fertilizers.
- 1 point: In the oxygen cycle, chlorine-containing compounds may cleave an oxygen molecule from ozone, ultimately depleting the ozone layer. This can increase the amount of UV radiation reaching Earth's surface, harming humans, animals, and plants.
- 1 point: Humans have altered the nitrogen cycle by artificially fixing nitrogen through the use of fertilizers. This process, called the Haber-Bosch process, has almost doubled the amount of nitrogen fixation that occurs.
- 1 point: The sulfur cycle has been altered in large part by the burning of coal, which emits SO_2 and H_2SO_4. When they chemically react with components in the atmosphere, acid rain, pollution, and smog can form.

4. This question is worth a maximum of 10 points, as follows:

A. Explain how hydrogen is attained for use as an energy source. (2 points maximum)
- 1 point: Hydrogen gas needs to be isolated, as it does not exist on its own naturally.
- 1 point for one of the following methods:
  Water is split into oxygen and hydrogen using electricity in a process called electrolysis.
  Hydrogen can be extracted from hydrocarbons (mainly from natural gas) with extreme heat and pressure.

B. Discuss two positive aspects of hydrogen as an energy source. (2 points maximum)
- 1 point: Hydrogen can be produced domestically, reducing dependence on foreign energy supplies.
- 1 point: The only emissions from hydrogen combustion are water and heat.
- 1 point: Hydrogen has three times the energy per mass of natural gas.
- 1 point: Hydrogen is the most abundant element in the universe, so it will not be depleted.

- 1 point: Unlike batteries, fuel cells do not need to be recharged by the addition of energy from another source.
- 1 point: When compressed, hydrogen is not more dangerous than gasoline.

C. Discuss three reasons why opponents to hydrogen energy do not see it as a viable alternative to fossil fuels. (3 points maximum)

- 1 point: Hydrogen needs to be isolated prior to use.
- 1 point: Currently, most hydrogen is produced from hydrocarbons in natural gas, a fossil fuel. This does not help to reduce dependency on fossil fuels, and the process also releases carbon dioxide into the atmosphere. This means that the hydrogen economy is dependent upon the price and availability of natural gas.
- 1 point: Because it has low density, the storage of hydrogen is a challenge. It needs to be compressed into a denser form for storage and transport.
- 1 point: Hydrogen can make metals brittle, weakening their structure. This creates challenges for storage, transport, and use.
- 1 point: The process of isolating hydrogen for use may require large energy inputs, which could necessitate greenhouse gas emissions.
- 1 point: Currently, little infrastructure exists for the transport, storage, and retrieval of hydrogen.

D. In what ways has hydrogen fuel already been made available to consumers? (1 point maximum)

- 1 point: Currently, vehicles powered by hydrogen fuel cells—including cars, buses, and boats—are available for purchase.

E. Discuss two reasons why alternative energy is currently an essential component of the world's energy supply and may become more so in the future. (2 points maximum)

- 1 point: It reduces dependency on foreign energy supplies.
- 1 point: It provides a sustainable and renewable energy supply that will exist indefinitely.
- 1 point: It reduces harmful greenhouse gas emissions that contribute to climate change.
- 1 point: It reduces the environmental impact of drilling, mining, and other destructive processes associated with the extraction and refinement of fossil fuels.
- 1 point: It reduces or eliminates emissions harmful to human health, wildlife, and ecosystems.

PART III

RESOURCES

RESOURCES

Glossary

acid deposition Commonly used when referring to acid rain; primary pollutants, sulfates, and nitrates combine with water in the atmosphere to form sulfuric acid (H_2SO_4) and nitric acid vapor (HNO_3).

active volcano A volcano that is presently erupting, or a volcano that has a large amount of seismic and thermal activity.

acute exposure Intense exposure to pollutants, toxins or radioactive materials occurring over a brief period of time.

adaptations The developed traits that make an organism especially suited to its environment; also called adaptive traits.

aerosols Solid particles and droplets suspended in the atmosphere.

age structure The number of organisms in each age range within a population.

age structure diagrams Used to show the distribution of ages throughout a population and can help to forecast what might happen to a population over time. Also called age pyramids.

Agricultural Revolution Began about 10,000 years ago when humans first started to grow crops and raise livestock.

agriculture The growth of crops and the raising of livestock.

air pollution Any chemical or particulate matter found in the atmosphere at high enough concentrations to harm humans, other animal life, vegetation, rocks, soils, and other building materials.

allergens Substances that overactivate the immune system, stimulating an unwanted or unnecessary response.

allopatric speciation The process of a new species being created over time due to a physical separation of a population and resultant divergent evolution.

altitude The distance above the Earth's sea level.

amensalism A species interaction in which one organism harms another while remaining unaffected itself.

ammonification A step in the nitrogen cycle in which nitrogen is combined with hydrogen to form ammonia (NH_3) during the process of nitrogen being fixed for use by plants.

anthropogenic Describes events that result from human activities.

aphelion The point, in July, at which the Earth is farthest from the sun.

artificial selection The process of humans selecting for desired traits during the breeding of organisms.

asbestos A naturally occurring, fibrous mineral previously used as insulation for pipes, soundproofing, roof tiles, and fire retardant. It is considered a carcinogen.

asthenosphere Found below the lithosphere but above the lower mantle, a plastic-like layer within the Earth that tends to flow.

autotrophs Another term for producers in the environment.

autumnal equinox The date with equal day and night that marks the beginning of fall in the Northern Hemisphere and spring in the Southern Hemisphere, occurring on or about September 23.

background extinction rate The natural rate of extinction, as opposed to the accelerated rate due to human activity.

bioaccumulation The process of a toxin concentrating in muscle tissues of organisms.

biodiversity The total number of types of species in a given area at a specific time.

biogeochemical cycles The natural movement of nutrients and other products through ecosystems (for example, the water or nitrogen cycles).

biological weathering The process of rock material being changed chemically or physically by the activities of living organisms, most commonly splitting due to tree roots but also including reactions with the acids contained in lichens, plants, and/or animals.

biomagnifications The buildup of toxins within an organism through the consumption of other organisms containing toxins (for example, mercury accumulation in tuna).

biomass The total dry weight of all the living organisms that can be supported at each trophic level in a food chain or food web; the dry weight of all the organic material in an ecosystem; plant material and animal waste used as a fuel for energy production.

biome A large ecological area primarily defined by a dominant plant type (for example, a coniferous forest).

biophilia The instinctive connection of humans to nature and other life.

biosphere reserves Protected areas designated with the intention of preserving biodiversity while balancing it with sustainable land use, education, and scientific research.

biotic potential An organism's potential number of offspring.

Black Death The deadliest pandemic in history, it was an outbreak of bubonic plague, peaking in Europe between 1348 and 1350. It is estimated to have killed between 30 percent and 60 percent of Europe's population. It took approximately 150 years for Europe's population to recover.

boreal Another name for the taiga, a forest biome that consists primarily of coniferous trees (pines), located south of the Arctic tundra in North America, Europe, and Asia.

bottom-trawling A method of fishing in which a large net is dragged along the ocean bottom to capture benthic organisms.

Bt-corn Genetically modified corn that contains insecticide, eliminating the need for chemical spraying.

Bt-cotton Genetically modified cotton that contains insecticide, eliminating the need for chemical spraying.

by-catch Fish and other organisms caught unintentionally.

carbon monoxide (CO) A colorless, odorless gas that results when fossil fuels are not fully combusted.

carbonic acid (H_2CO_3) Formed when water reacts with carbon dioxide; used to carbonate soft drinks.

carcinogen A cancer-causing substance.

carnivore An animal that feeds on other animals.

carrying capacity (K) The maximum number of individuals in a population of a species that an environment can support.

cellular respiration The process of converting glucose and oxygen into carbon dioxide and water.

chemical energy The energy stored in the bonds of atoms and molecules.

chemical weathering The process by which rocks are degraded due to chemical reactions borne of interactions with water and atmospheric gases.

chemosynthesis The formation of organic compounds using chemical reactions instead of sunlight.

chlorofluorocarbons (CFCs) Carbon-based compounds that contain chlorine and fluorine, the primary human-made compounds involved in the depletion of ozone. They were commonly used as refrigerants in air conditioners, refrigerators, and aerosol propellants.

chloroplasts The organelles in plant cells involved in photosynthesis that capture the energy in light and convert carbon dioxide and water into glucose and oxygen.

chronic exposure Repeated exposure to toxins or radioactivity over a long period of time, in small doses.

cinder cone volcanoes Violently eruptive volcanoes made of viscous, quartz-rich, extrusive deposits that plug the volcanic neck. When they erupt, cinders are blown into the air; then they settle around the opening of the volcano, forming a small, steep-sided mountain.

clear-cutting The process of removing all trees from an area in a forest. The process of clear-cutting leaves nothing standing.

climate The prevailing weather patterns (temperature, precipitation, and so on) of a region averaged over an extended period of time (usually for at least 30 years).

climate change Any change in the state of the climate (such as temperature) that persists steadily for many years (decades or longer).

clumped distribution Organisms organized in groups, usually gathering around a necessary resource.

coal A solid combustible fossil fuel, used primarily for the production of electricity.

co-evolution The simultaneous evolution of two organisms interacting with one another.

command-and-control strategy A form of pollution control in which legal limits are set and strictly enforced by the government.

commensalism A species interaction in which one organism benefits and the other is unaffected.

community Multiple populations of different species in a given area.

competition A species interaction in which organisms vie for the same resources, resulting in one outperforming the other.

composite volcanoes Tall, symmetrical, steep volcanoes built by alternating layers of ash, cinders, and lava; also called stratovolcanoes.

compressed natural gas (CNG) Natural gas that is compressed to less than 1 percent of the volume it occupies at standard atmospheric pressure; used primarily in cars, trucks, and buses as an alternate, cleaner-burning fuel than gasoline or diesel.

condensation The change in the phase of water from gas to liquid, usually in the form of droplets.

conifers Cone-bearing trees (such as firs, pines, and spruces) that have needle-shaped or scaled leaves; also known as coniferous trees.

consumer Any organism that cannot produce its own food and gets its energy and nutrients by feeding on other organisms.

continental drift The shifting of the continents due to the movement of the tectonic plates upon the asthenosphere.

contour farming Plowing rows into the side of a hill, perpendicular to the slope, following the shape of the land in order to create flat terraces; used to reduce erosion and disperse water evenly throughout crops.

controlled burns See prescribed burns.

convection currents Result from fluids or gases being heated, becoming less dense as they expand, rising, cooling, becoming denser, and sinking. Examples include the rising and sinking currents of magma below the Earth's crust, water in the ocean, and air.

conventional agriculture Large-scale farming and livestock production in which crops are grown for many people with the use of a variety of inputs, such as fertilizer, pesticides, irrigation, seeds, fossil fuels, monoculture, and human power; also called industrial agriculture.

conventional tillage A form of farming in which soil is ploughed and turned, which ultimately can lead to soil erosion and soil compaction in the deeper layers.

convergent plate boundary A zone where tectonic plates move toward each other, sometimes making contact.

core The dense center of the Earth. It is subdivided into the solid inner and liquid outer cores.

Coriolis effect The apparent deflection of a moving object (planetary winds, ocean currents, projectiles) due to rotation of the Earth. These objects are deflected to the right in the Northern Hemisphere and to the left in the Southern Hemisphere.

Corporate Average Fuel Economy (CAFE) Regulations enacted in 1975 that establish fuel economy standards across auto manufacturers' fleet of cars and trucks.

cost-benefit analysis (CBA) Used to assess the costs and benefits of a decision, helping to determine whether a particular action should be taken.

criteria pollutants Six common air pollutants monitored by the Environmental Protection Agency and used as a way to gauge air quality.

crop rotation The alternation of the types of crops grown on a piece of land from year to year or season to season.

crude oil A liquid combustible fossil fuel that is refined into several fuels used in transportation (gasoline, diesel, aviation), heating oils, asphalt, and other chemicals. Many crude oil by-products are used in manufacturing plastics, pharmaceuticals, fertilizers, and other materials.

crust The outermost layer of the Earth and the surface on which we live (or the surface covered by ocean).

cultural eutrophication Ecosystem eutrophication due to excess nutrients added by human activity.

dead zone An aquatic environment devoid of any life.

deciduous Trees that shed their leaves in cold winters or in dry seasons (for example, oaks and maples).

decomposers Bacteria or fungi that absorb nutrients from nonliving organic matter such as plant material, the waste of living organisms, and dead organisms.

deforestation The clearing of forests for other uses, such as agriculture and development.

demographic transition The transition from high birth and death rates to low birth and death rates that accompanies a country's industrialization.

denitrification The process in the nitrogen cycle whereby bacteria convert nitrates into gaseous N_2, which returns to the atmosphere.

denitrifying bacteria Bacteria that conduct the process of denitrification.

density-dependent factors Factors that limit a population's density, such as disease, availability of mates, and predation.

density-independent factors Limiting factors that do not depend on population density, including natural disasters, extreme temperature fluctuations, or lack of sunlight.

desertification The loss of soil productivity due to erosion, overgrazing, drought, soil compaction, and any other factors that deplete the soil.

detritivores Organisms that derive their energy from consuming nonliving organic matter such as dead plants and animals.

developed country A highly industrialized country with a high per-capita income. There are 38 developed countries, including the United States, Japan, and most of Western Europe.

developing country A country with low to moderate industrialization and low to moderate per-capita income. Most developing countries are in Latin America, Asia, and Africa.

directional selection Natural selection that drives evolution toward an extreme (for example, a population in which successive generations have increasingly long necks).

disruptive selection Natural selection that favors individuals with adaptations at one or the other extreme (for example, a population in which either long or short necks, but not average necks, are adaptive).

divergent plate boundary A zone where tectonic plates move away from one another.

dormant volcano An inactive volcano that could erupt again.

dose The amount or concentration of a substance experienced by an organism.

dose-response relationship The effect of an amount or concentration of a toxin on an organism or population.

doubling time The amount of time it takes for a population to double. Doubling time is commonly calculated by using the Rule of 70, in which 70 is divided by the population's annual percentage growth rate.

drift netting The practice of dragging large nets through the water to catch fish.

Dust Bowl A period in the 1930s in the Midwestern United States during which drought and overuse of the land led to dust storms and desertification.

earthquakes Vibrations in the Earth's crust due to plate movements created by the sudden release of pressure built up at plate boundaries. Localized earthquakes also can be due to magma intrusions in volcanic areas.

ecological pyramids Diagrams that are used to show relative biomass or productivity (and, thus, energy loss) at each trophic level in an ecosystem; also called energy pyramids.

ecological succession The process by which a community of plants and animals replaces a less complex community of plants and animals or develops in an uninhabited area.

economics The production, distribution, regulation, and consumption of goods and services.

ecosystem The interconnected interactions of all living and nonliving things in a specific area at the same time.

ecosystem services Services provided by our ecosystems that help to support life on Earth.

ED$_{50}$ The dose of a substance at which 50 percent of a test population is affected.

El Niño The warming phase of ENSO in the eastern Pacific Ocean, accompanied by higher air surface pressure in the western Pacific Ocean.

El Niño/La Niña-Southern Oscillation cycle (ENSO) A periodic climate pattern in the tropical Pacific Ocean with an approximately five-year cycle (varying from three to seven years), characterized by variations in the surface temperature of the tropical eastern Pacific Ocean and the air pressure in the tropical western Pacific Ocean.

electric cars Cars that run solely on electricity stored in batteries.

electrical energy Energy produced by the movement of electrons, typically moving through a wire. Usable electrical energy is produced by a generator in which relative motion of coiled copper wire and a magnetic field results in a flow of electrons.

electromagnetic energy Nonmechanical energy that travels in waves, including the entire electromagnetic spectrum, from low-energy radio waves, through microwaves, ultraviolet waves, through the visible light spectrum (ROYGBIV), through the ultraviolet waves, X-rays, and highest-energy gamma rays.

emissions Common term for the gases discharged into the atmosphere from burning of fossil fuels. The primary sources include coal and natural gas electric power plants and emissions from transportation (cars, trucks, buses, trains, and planes).

endemic Localized, or occurring only in one location on the planet; commonly used to describe species that live in only one place.

endocrine disruptor A substance that alters the hormone (endocrine) system by binding to substances that would normally bind specific hormones, thus blocking the hormone and impeding normal reactions.

environmental resistance All limiting factors acting on a population, restricting an organism's biological potential.

epicenter The point directly above the focus of an earthquake.

equinox The time when the sun crosses the ecliptic plane of Earth's equator, making day and night equal length. It occurs twice a year, on or about March 21 and September 23.

erosion The process of soil and sediment being transported from a location via wind or water.

eutrophication The process of excess nitrogen or phosphorous entering an aquatic system, leading to an excessive growth of phytoplankton, algae, and other plants, which commonly consume the system's available oxygen.

evaporation Phase change of liquid to gas, from the surface of water.

even-aged Term used to describe trees that are planted and then harvested at the same time, so they are all the same age.

evolution The change of a population's genetic makeup through generations.

exponential growth Growth at a constant rate. If population increases by a fixed percentage per unit time, the gross rate of population growth increases.

extinct volcano A volcano that is not erupting and most likely will not erupt at any point again.

extirpation The destruction or disappearance of a population from a particular area while populations remain elsewhere.

Ferrel air circulation cell The air circulation cell that causes the temperate convection current (between the tropical convection current and polar convection current).

focus The location from which an earthquake originates within the Earth.

food chain A simple path of energy flow from the producer to the various consumers.

food web Multiple intertwined food chains in which energy from multiple producers flows though many levels of consumers and finally through the decomposers.

forestry The practice of balancing humans' use of wood products with the importance of forests as ecosystems.

fossil fuel Energy sources formed by the decomposition of plants and animals that have been compressed and heated in the Earth's crust for millions of years; they include coal, crude oil, and natural gas.

Freon The DuPont trade name for chlorofluorocarbons (CFCs)

freshwater Naturally occurring water on the Earth's surface that is low in concentrations of dissolved salts and other dissolved particles. Freshwater is primarily found in glaciers, ice sheets, and ice caps, with a relatively small amount found in groundwater, ponds, lakes, rivers, and streams.

generalists Organisms that have a broad tolerance and can adjust to different situations.

genetic engineering The creation of new organisms by changing segments of DNA; also called genetic modification.

genetic pollution The unintended spread of altered genetic information from genetically engineered organisms to natural organisms.

genetically modified organisms (GMOs) Organisms that have altered DNA as a result of genetic engineering.

geologic time scale The 4.54 billion years of Earth's history.

geothermal energy The energy of hot underground rock formations, molten rock, and hot subterranean water; used to turn a water source into steam, which, in turn, drives turbines, creating electricity.

global warming The current steady increase in the average temperature of the Earth's surface that may be caused by man-made greenhouse emissions.

golden rice Genetically modified rice that contains vitamin A, a missing nutrient in many developing counties.

Green Revolution The advent of industrialized agriculture in the mid- and late 20th century, when more effective farming techniques were combined with new methods of increasing crop production to create greater and more efficient output.

green tax A tax placed on any activity considered to be harmful to the environment.

greenhouse effect A naturally occurring atmospheric effect trapping heat that would otherwise reflect into space, which helps warm the Earth's surface temperature. Without the natural greenhouse effect, the Earth's average temperature would be close to –15°C (5°F) instead of 15°C (59°F). In addition to this natural greenhouse effect, an anthropogenic greenhouse effect adds greenhouse gases to this reflective layer in the atmosphere, trapping additional heat energy and resulting in a further increase in temperature.

greenhouse gases Gases in the Earth's troposphere that cause the greenhouse effect. Greenhouse gases include water vapor, carbon dioxide, methane, ozone, chlorofluorocarbons, nitrous oxide, carbon tetrachloride, halons, and others.

ground-level ozone A secondary air pollutant found in the troposphere, usually near the Earth's surface; considered a pollutant and a human health hazard.

groundwater Water that is located beneath the ground's surface, located in the pores of soils and the fractures in rock formations.

growth rate A population's net change in size per 1,000 individuals. The formula used to calculate growth rate is

Growth Rate = (Birth Rate + Immigration) – (Death Rate + Emigration)

habitat The environment in which an organism lives, including soil, vegetation, water supply, and many other factors.

habitat destruction The process of making a natural area uninhabitable for plants and animals, primarily as a result of human activities, usually for harvesting the habitat's natural resources (mining, deforestation), agriculture, or urbanization.

habitat fragmentation The division of a habitat into smaller areas between which migration is impossible, usually as a result of human activities.

Hadley air circulation cell The air circulation cell that causes the tropical convection current near the equator, which extends to the temperate convection current.

half-life The time it takes for half of a sample of radioactive material to decay.

halogens Elements of the periodic table in group 17—namely, fluorine (F), chlorine (Cl), bromine (Br), iodine (I), and astatine (At).

halons A group of chemical compounds that include a halogen.

hazardous waste Waste that is flammable, corrosive, toxic, or reactive.

herbivores Plant-eating organisms.

herbivory A species interaction in which plants are consumed by animals.

HIPPCO The acronym used by biologists to summarize the important causes of the premature extinction of organisms. Initially the acronym was HIPPO, but it was recently changed to HIPPCO. *H* stands for habitat destruction and fragmentation, *I* stands for invasive species, *P* stands for population growth, *P* stands for pollution, *C* stands for climate change, and *O* stands for overharvesting.

host An organism being invaded by a parasite.

hot spots Locations where magma emerges from the Earth, usually at the inner part of a tectonic plate.

hybrid electric vehicles Vehicles with electric motors, which are supplemented as needed by small gasoline engines.

hydrochlorofluorocarbons (HCFCs) A group of manmade compounds that contain hydrogen, chlorine, fluorine and carbon and have the potential to react with stratospheric ozone. Because they have shorter atmospheric lifetimes than chlorofluorocarbons, they tend to break down in the troposphere before delivering reactive chlorine to the stratosphere.

hydroelectric power Power that is produced by dammed water that is allowed to flow over turbines in a controlled fashion, turning the turbines to produce electricity.

hydrofluorocarbons (HFCs) A group of manmade compounds containing carbon, hydrogen, and fluorine. HFCs contain no chlorine and do not directly affect stratospheric ozone. Viewed as an acceptable long-term alternative to CFCs and HCFCs, HFCs may still contribute to global warming.

hydrogen fuel cells Cells that use hydrogen and oxygen in a chemical reaction to produce energy and water.

hypoxic Describes an aquatic environment lacking in oxygen.

ice age A geological period of long-term reduction in the Earth's surface and atmospheric temperature, resulting in the presence or expansion of ice sheets and glaciers.

ice core A sample of ice that is typically drilled and removed from an ice sheet, usually the polar ice caps of Antarctica or Greenland. Layers of the ice core are analyzed for trapped gas and deposits, which give an accurate representation of historical climate and can be used to develop a climate record over a long period of time.

ice sheet A mass of ice that covers an area greater than 50,000 square kilometers (20,000 square miles). Ice sheets also may be referred to as continental glaciers and are now found only in Greenland and Antarctica.

ice-minus strawberries Genetically modified, frost-resistant strawberries.

igneous rock Rock formed from cooling magma or other volcanic action.

Industrial Revolution The period of urbanization starting in the 1700s during which sanitation and medical care improved, and manufacturing started to supplant agriculture as the primary human livelihood.

industrial smog Formed when anthropogenic sulfur dioxide (SO_2) absorbs ultraviolet radiation in the atmosphere.

industrial waste Waste created during industrial processes such as agriculture, mining, consumer goods production, and the extraction and refining of petroleum products.

infiltration The process by which water on the Earth's surface enters the soil.

inner core The solid part of the Earth's core that is mainly made up of nickel and iron.

innocent until proven guilty When addressing a substance's toxicity, the approach that assumes a product to be harmless until proven otherwise.

integrated pest management (IPM) A form of pest control that uses knowledge about the pest's life cycle and environmental interactions in conjunction with other control methods such as biological control, crop rotation, and chemicals when necessary. The goal of IPM is to reduce pest impact while also reducing pesticide use.

intercropping The planting of alternating crops throughout a field (as opposed to monoculture).

International Union for Conservation of Nature (IUCN) An international organization dedicated to the conservation of natural resources. The goal of IUCN is to help find solutions to the most important environmental issues. The organization publishes an influential "Red List" showing the world's most endangered species.

interspecific competition The process by which two different species compete.

intraspecific competition The process by which members of the same species compete.

IPAT model A model proposing that environmental impact (I) is the product of population (P), affluence (A), and technology (T), represented by the formula $I = P \cdot A \cdot T$. Sometimes S is added to represent the sensitivity of an ecosystem.

irrigation The practice of supplying water for agricultural purposes.

kinetic energy The energy possessed by a moving object; a form of mechanical energy.

K-selected species Species that have relatively few offspring and devote a large amount of time, energy, and resources toward nurturing and raising their young.

La Niña The cooling phase of ENSO in the eastern Pacific Ocean, accompanied by lower air surface pressure in the western Pacific Ocean.

land pollution See *soil pollution*.

latitude A measurement of distance from the equator, measured in angular degrees by lines that are parallel to each other. The equator is 0°, the North Pole is 90° N, and the South Pole is 90° S.

latitudinal gradient The increase in biodiversity closer to the equator.

laws of thermodynamics The transport of heat and work in the thermodynamic processes. The first law of thermodynamics states that energy is neither created nor destroyed but can change forms. The second law of thermodynamics states that in any conversion of heat energy into useful work some of the initial energy is lost.

LD$_{50}$ The dose of a substance that is lethal for 50 percent of the test population.

leaching The process by which water, filtering down through the soil, dissolves and transports materials, including naturally occurring minerals and nutrients and man-made toxic substances.

lichen Organisms made up of the symbiotic relationship between a fungus and a photosynthetic organism (usually a green alga) or a cyanobacterium. Lichen are able to colonize nutrient-poor environments and are commonly seen on leaves, tree branches, bare rock, and exposed soil.

light pollution A result of the excessive use of artificial light, which can cause glare, over-illumination, sky glow, and decreased night visibility, while also using excessive amounts of energy.

limiting factors The factors that control a population's growth. These include availability of food, shelter, water, mates, or anything else an organism depends upon for survival.

lithosphere The rigid outer layer of the Earth. It is comprised of the crust and upper mantle.

lithospheric plates See *tectonic plates*.

logistic growth curve Represents a population that grows exponentially and then levels off as it reaches environmental carrying capacity (K).

longitude The east/west location on Earth in relationship to the Prime Meridian, which runs from the poles through Greenwich, England, usually measured in degrees from 0° to 180°. The longitude lines, which are farthest apart at the equator and meet at the poles, are often referred to as meridian lines.

long-lasting tomatoes Genetically modified tomatoes that remain fresh longer.

long-lining The practice of dragging a long fishing line behind a boat or attaching it to an anchor with baited hooks along the length of the line.

malnutrition A condition afflicting people who do not receive enough daily nutrients.

manganese nodules Ball-like structures that form on the ocean floor and contain manganese, along with many other minerals in smaller amounts, such as copper, zinc, and nickel.

mantle The layer of the Earth found below the crust; contains the upper mantle and lower mantle.

marginal benefit An economic term describing the change in additional benefit associated with a change in output level.

marginal costs Costs associated with an increase or decrease in output.

market effect Results that are measurable in dollar amounts.

mass extinction event An extinction that occurs quickly and on a large scale, affecting many species.

mesopause The boundary between the mesosphere and the thermosphere. The lowest temperatures on Earth exist in the mesopause.

mesosphere The third layer of the Earth's atmosphere.

metamorphic rock A rock type formed under extreme heat and pressure, usually deep underground.

mechanical energy Energy possessed by moving objects (kinetic) or energy stored in objects by tension or position (potential).

methane A naturally occurring gas with the chemical formula CH_4; one of the major fossil fuels. Methane in the atmosphere is considered a greenhouse gas.

methane hydrates Recently discovered sources of methane (natural gas) that are locked in ice formed at low temperatures and high pressures, found in the tundra beneath the permafrost or deep in the oceans.

mid-ocean ridge An opening in the Earth's crust beneath an ocean where magma emerges and creates new, elevated sea floor. A mid-ocean ridge appears as a scar along the crust of an ocean bottom.

mobile source pollution Pollution emitted from a moving source such as a car, truck, train, boat, or plane.

monoculture The planting of only one crop over a farmed area.

mountaintop removal A form of mining in which the tops of mountains are blasted off in order to access natural resources.

municipal waste Waste from homes, businesses, schools, hospitals, and other institutions.

mutagen A toxin that causes mutations in the DNA of organisms.

mutualism A species interaction in which all engaged species benefit.

natural gas A gaseous combustible fossil fuel used in the production of electricity and home uses (heating, water heaters, and cooking).

natural selection The process by which genetic traits that strengthen an organism's chance of survival and reproduction are passed on from generation to generation, eventually dominating less successful genetic traits.

neurotoxin A toxin that affects the nervous system, including motor control and brain function.

niche An organism's specific ecosystem position, described by its resources, role in the community, habitat use, food consumption, interactions with other species, shelter, and other factors.

nitrification The stage of the nitrogen cycle during which NH_4^+ is converted into nitrite ions (NO_2^-), and then into nitrate ions (NO_3^-).

nitrifying bacteria Bacteria that conduct nitrification as part of the nitrogen cycle.

nitrogen dioxide (NO_2) A reddish-brown gas with a strong odor created from combustion processes at high temperatures, most commonly in vehicles and electric utilities.

nitrogen-fixing bacteria A type of bacteria that "fixes" atmospheric nitrogen to a form that can be absorbed by plants. Nitrogen-fixing bacteria live in the soil and in nodules on the roots of legumes.

nitrous oxide (NO_x) Gases containing nitrogen and oxygen that play a role in photochemical smog; they include nitrogen oxide (NO) and nitrogen dioxide (NO_2).

noise pollution Any unwanted, disturbing, or harmful sound that causes irritation or harm to humans.

nonmarket effect A result for which a fixed dollar amount cannot be attached.

nonnative species A species that migrates into an ecosystem or is deliberately or accidentally introduced into an ecosystem by humans.

non-point-source pollution Pollution for which it is difficult to identify the main source and that may come from a multitude of smaller sources.

nonrenewable resource A resource with a finite supply that has the potential to be renewed only over hundreds of millions to billions of years. Nonrenewable resources include fossil fuels and metals.

normal fault A fault caused by tectonic plates or rock strata pulling apart.

no-till farming A farming method in which soil is minimally disturbed while it is being prepared for crops.

nuclear energy The energy stored in the nuclei of atoms. It is released by the splitting (fission) or the joining (fusion) of atoms.

nuclear fission The process of an atom splitting into two smaller elements, releasing neutrons and heat energy. In nuclear power generation, fission is caused by bombarding unstable elements with neutrons.

nuclear fusion The process in which the atomic nuclei of two elements are forced together under high pressure, releasing large amounts of energy under conditions present in stars, such as the sun.

oil A liquid fossil fuel derived from crude oil.

oil sands See tar sands.

oil shale Sedimentary rock that is rich in kerogen, an organic compound from which liquid hydrocarbons can be extracted when heated.

old growth A forest prior to its trees ever being harvested.

omnivore An animal that eats both plants and other animals as a source of energy and nutrients.

open pit mining Mining that involves digging up the land in order to reach the desired resource.

ore Rock containing desired mineral elements or molecular compounds.

organic farming Farming or livestock raising that uses no chemicals, including pesticides, hormones, fertilizers, or antibiotics.

outer core The liquid part of the Earth's core; comprised mainly of molten iron and nickel.

overnutrition A condition resulting from people receiving too many calories on a daily basis, leading to obesity and many other health issues.

ozone (O_3) A colorless gas found in both the stratosphere and troposphere. "Good" ozone is located naturally in the stratosphere and protects the Earth from the sun's harmful ultraviolet radiation. "Bad" ozone is located close to the ground in the troposphere, is the main component of smog, and is considered a greenhouse gas.

ozone depletion The loss of ozone in the stratosphere (for example, as a result of CFCs).

ozone hole An area of depletion in the ozone layer that forms over Antarctica and the Arctic and moves toward the equator.

ozone layer The concentration of ozone in the stratosphere that helps protect the Earth from harmful UV radiation.

parasite Any organism that uses another organism for food and nutrients at a cost to the host.

parasitism A species interaction in which one organism uses another organism for food and nutrients, harming the host.

parent material The main component of soil, created from eroded and weathered existing geologic material in a given area.

particulate matter Solid or liquid particles suspended in the atmosphere or in water.

percolation The movement of water through porous soil and rock.

perihelion The orbital point in January when the Earth is closest to the sun.

permit trading The practice in which governments issue certain levels of permits to polluters, who can then trade or sell their permits to other polluters as needed. This promotes more sustainable environmental actions through economic policy.

peroxyacetyl nitrate (PAN) Produced by the reaction of some volatile organic hydrocarbons with oxygen and nitrogen dioxide, partially responsible for some negative effects of smog.

persistence The ability of a substance to remain in the environment for an extended period of time.

petroleum See *crude oil.*

pH Measures hydrogen ion concentrations on a scale of 1 to 14, with 7 being neutral; acidic substances range from 1 to 6.9, and alkaline (or basic) substances range from 7.1 to 14.

photochemical smog Smog formed when nitrogen dioxide (NO_2) reacts with the heat of UV radiation from the sun.

photosynthesis The natural process in which plant chlorophyll converts carbon dioxide (CO_2) and water (H_2O) into glucose ($C_6H_{12}O_6$) and oxygen (O_2) in the presence of sunlight.

physical weathering Occurs when rock material is broken down without any chemical change taking place, usually through gravitation, wind, running water, or ice expansion; also called mechanical weathering.

pioneer species The first species to colonize an area that has not previously been colonized. A pioneer species begins the first steps of ecological succession.

placer mining A mineral mining technique that uses water to separate out the heavier minerals from lighter mud and debris.

point-source pollution Pollution emitted from a specific place, such as wastewater from an industrial plant, acid drainage from a mine, noise from a jet plane, or oil from a tank.

polar air circulation cell The air circulation cell that causes the polar convection current, extending north and south from the temperate convection current.

polybrominated diphenyl ethers (PBDEs) Chemicals that are used as flame retardants in household items such as televisions, furniture, fabrics, wire insulation, drapes, small appliances, and other electronics.

population A group of individuals of the same species living in the same area at the same time.

population density The number of individuals in a population per unit area.

population dispersion See population distribution.

population distribution The spatial arrangement of organisms in an area, with types including random, uniform, or clumped distribution. Also called population dispersion.

population size The number of individuals in a population at a given time.

potential energy The energy stored in an object or system; usually a form of mechanical energy, but may originate from atomic or chemical energy.

precautionary principle The principle that a substance is assumed to be harmful until proven otherwise.

precipitation Condensation of atmospheric water vapor that is pulled to the Earth's surface by gravity, usually in the form of rain, snow, sleet, or hail.

predation A species interaction in which one species hunts, captures, kills, and consumes another species.

prescribed burns The burning of forests under controlled conditions, usually to decrease the likelihood of later, larger fires; also called controlled burns.

primary treatment The process by which a sewage treatment system physically removes suspended solids in settling tanks.

producers Organisms that use solar energy (green plants) or chemical energy (cyanobacteria) to manufacture organic compounds needed for their energy and nutrition.

pyramid of biomass A graphical representation showing the biomass at each trophic level in an ecosystem.

radon An extremely toxic, naturally occurring radioactive gas that is produced from the decay of radium, which is, in turn, produced from the decay of uranium.

random distribution Distribution of organisms arbitrarily, with no organization or intention.

rangelands Large expanses of undeveloped land that mainly contain low vegetation such as grasses and shrubs and are suitable for grazing of livestock.

reclamation The restoration of the land after disturbance from mining.

relative abundance The number of each species in an area in relation to other species.

remediation The cleanup of contaminated soil or water.

renewable resource A resource that can be replenished within a human lifetime, including trees, grasses, animals, and water.

reservoir An artificial lake that is used to store water behind a dam; commonly constructed to supply a constant source of water or to prevent downstream flooding; may be combined with a generator to produce hydroelectric power.

resource partitioning The process by which species evolve to divide an area's resources, allowing decreased competition for any one resource.

response The reaction of a plant or animal to a substance.

reverse faults Faults caused from compression of tectonic plates or rock strata.

r-selected species Small organisms that have short gestation times and produce thousands of offspring at one time, therefore having high biotic potential.

Rule of 70 The mathematical method used to determine a population's doubling time. The formula is Doubling Time $= \frac{70}{r}$, where r is the growth rate of the population in percent. Doubling time is commonly expressed in years.

runoff Water that flows along the Earth's surface without entering the soil; also called surface runoff.

salinization Occurs where salts accumulate on the soil's surface. Evaporation pulls water and its dissolved salts toward the surface from deeper within the soil horizon; when the water evaporates, the salts are left behind on the soil surface.

seafloor spreading The process that keeps the tectonic plates in motion. As magma rises through the midocean ridge, the magma hardens and creates new land. Convection currents in the asthenosphere are pushing apart the plates that create the seafloor.

season A division of the year that is marked by changes in weather, ecology, and sunlight intensity, resulting from the yearly revolution of the Earth around the sun and the tilt of the Earth on its axis. Temperate and polar regions usually experience four seasons (fall, winter, spring, and summer), while tropical and subtropical regions more commonly having only a wet and a dry season or sometimes hot, rainy, and cool seasons.

secondary growth New growth that emerges in a forest after the original, virgin forest has been cut down.

secondary treatment The stage in a sewage treatment system in which oxygen enters the water from continual mixing and movement, encouraging aerobic decomposition.

sedimentary rock Rock formed when sediment from erosion and weathering, biogenic decomposition, or chemical deposition is compressed and/or cemented together, or "lithified."

seed bank A place for housing and preserving many seed types as a way to protect seed diversity and safeguard the food supply in the event of disaster.

seed tree The forestry practice of leaving mature and seed-producing trees standing, providing the seeds necessary for the regrowth of forest trees after harvesting.

selection system A partial harvest method in which only a few trees are harvested from an area at a time.

sex ratio The ratio of number of males to number of females in a population.

shelterbelt A protective border created when tall plants or trees are planted along the edges of fields or farms in order to reduce erosion from wind.

shelterwood system The forestry practice of leaving a few full-grown trees in order to create shelter for emergent seedlings. Cutting is done on a regular basis with select trees taken each time.

shield volcano A slowly erupting volcano with a broad side, gradual slopes, and usually a crater at the top; the least explosive volcano type, with slow-moving liquid lava due to its low silica content.

sink A natural or artificial reservoir that stores an element, such as carbon, for an indefinite period. Natural sinks tend to be much larger than man-made sinks. Natural sinks include water, biomass, fossil fuels, rocks and soil. Artificial sinks include proposed carbon capturing and storage in a process called carbon sequestration.

soil permeability The ability of a liquid to flow through the soil.

soil pollution The contamination of soil by anthropogenic chemicals, commonly including fertilizers, pesticides, oil and fuel spills, leaching of waste from landfills, and the movement of contaminated surface water to subsurface areas; also called land pollution.

soil porosity The amount of open space between soil particles; the ratio of void space to total volume.

soil profile A soil cross-section showing the depths of the layers including (from the surface down) the O Horizon, A Horizon, E Horizon, B Horizon, C Horizon, and R Horizon.

solar Energy coming from the sun.

solstice The date at which the sun is most north or south of the celestial equator. The summer solstice is June 21 and the winter solstice is December 21.

specialists Organisms that are adapted to only one specific environment, making them more vulnerable to any type of ecosystem change.

speciation The process through which new species are created.

species A group of organisms that share particular characteristics and can breed and reproduce to create fertile offspring.

species richness The number of species in an area, related to biodiversity.

stabilizing selection Natural selection in which extreme traits are selected against, creating a population with relatively homogenous traits and low genetic variation.

stratopause The boundary between the stratosphere and the mesosphere.

stratosphere The second layer of the Earth's atmosphere. The ozone layer that protects the Earth from harmful UV radiation is located within the stratosphere.

stratospheric ozone The ozone layer that protects the Earth.

strike slip fault A fault caused by tectonic plates sliding past one another horizontally.

subduction A plate boundary phenomenon resulting from tectonic plate movement, in which a denser oceanic plate is pushed below a lighter continental plate, creating a subduction zone.

subsidy Financial assistance given by the government to a business, person, or economic sector in an effort to support an activity that is thought to be beneficial to the public.

subsistence agriculture A method of crop production resulting in the production of enough food for one family but not for others or for commerce.

subsurface mining A form of mining that uses deep underground shafts to access and extract resources from pockets or seams.

sulfur dioxide (SO_2) Formed when sulfur combusts (usually when burning coal and oil) and the released sulfur reacts with oxygen in the atmosphere.

sulfur oxide (SO_x) The gases containing sulfur and oxygen that play a role in industrial smog. They include sulfur dioxide (SO_2) and sulfur trioxide (SO_3).

Superfund sites Polluted sites that are specified to be part of the federal government's program to clean up hazardous waste.

surface mining A type of mining that removes the soil and rock surface over a large amount of land.

surface water Water that collects on the Earth's surface, usually in the form of streams, rivers, lakes, and oceans.

survivorship curve A graph that represents the number of individuals surviving at each age for a given species. The y-axis shows the number of individuals and the x-axis reflects time or age. There are Type I, Type II, and Type III survivorship curves.

sustainability The nondepletion of resources, usually referring to human use that allows resources to regenerate at a pace commensurate with use.

sympatric speciation A type of speciation that occurs when a population of organisms evolves to use a location's resources in different ways, eventually becoming so distinct that they lose the ability to interbreed.

synfuel Synthetic, liquefied fuel obtained from nonpetroleum sources such as coal, natural gas, oil shale, and biomass; synthetic fuel derived from waste, such as plastic or rubber.

taiga A forest biome composed primarily of coniferous trees (pines), located south of the Arctic tundra in North America, Europe, and Asia; also called the boreal.

tar sands A combination of sand, clay, water, and bituminous sands; also known as oil sands.

tectonic plates The seven major plates and many smaller plates, all in constant motion, that make up the crust of the Earth; also called lithospheric plates.

teratogen A substance that affects embryo development or harms or kills the fetus.

terracing A farming technique used on steep slopes of a mountainous terrain. Often looking like steps, terracing is used to minimize erosion and retain water in areas otherwise unable to be used for crops.

thermal energy Heat energy from the vibration and movement of atoms and molecules within substances.

thermopause The boundary between the thermosphere and the exosphere.

thermosphere The fourth and deepest layer of the Earth's atmosphere, above the mesosphere and below the exosphere.

threshold dose The minimum amount or concentration of a substance that affects an organism or population.

timber plantations Typically, monocultures of fast growth species of trees planted by timber companies in order to maximize an area's economic benefit.

toxin Poisonous or toxic substance.

traditional agriculture Agriculture that uses human power, animal power, and simple tools.

transform plate boundaries Areas where tectonic plates slide past one another.

transgenic A term used to describe an organism that has genetic material artificially transferred from another organism.

transpiration The loss of water vapor from plants, especially in the leaves, but also through stems, flowers, and roots.

trophic level The position an organism occupies on the food chain, defined as the number of energy levels an organism is from the original source of energy. For example, all producers belong to the first trophic level and all herbivores belong to the second trophic level in a food chain or web.

tropopause The boundary between the troposphere and the stratosphere.

troposphere The first layer of the Earth's atmosphere. It contains 75 percent of the Earth's atmospheric mass but is the shallowest atmospheric level.

tsunami A giant wave generated from undersea earthquakes or volcanic eruptions. *Tsunami* is Japanese for "seismic seawave."

tundra A cold biome of restricted tree growth, further divided into arctic and alpine regions. The arctic tundra is located between the ice caps of the North Pole and the boreal forest and is characterized by permafrost. The alpine tundra is located in the higher elevations of the mountains around the world, above the tree line and below the permanent snow line.

ultraviolet radiation (UV) Radiant energy with wavelengths shorter than the minimum that the human eye is able to see.

undernourished A term used to describe people who do not receive enough calories on a daily basis.

uniform distribution Even spacing of organisms.

urbanization The movement of human populations from rural to urban lifestyles.

vernal equinox The date with night and day of equal length that signifies the start of spring in the Northern Hemisphere and start of fall in the Southern Hemisphere, occurring on or about March 21.

volatile organic compounds (VOCs) Unstable substances that can be released as gases from a wide variety of products, including carpeting, paints, aerosol sprays, cleaning products, building supplies, pesticides, printers, glues, wood preservatives, moth balls, and air fresheners.

waste-to-energy A term used to describe waste incineration plants where heat that is generated during waste combustion is captured and used to generate electricity.

wastewater Water that is flushed, goes down the drain, or runs into sewers from streets.

water pollution Any physical or chemical change to the water (surface or groundwater) that can be harmful to living organisms or make it unfit for other uses.

water vapor Gaseous water.

waterlogged A term used to describe soil that has become saturated or oversaturated with water due to over-irrigation and a rising water table, which can ultimately suffocate plant roots, compact soil, and lead to salinization.

weather The short-term description of temperature, wind, and precipitation in a given geographical area.

weathering The process whereby parent material is broken down or eroded by water, wind, sunlight, temperature fluctuations, and living organisms.

wetlands Terrestrial areas with large amounts of water saturating the soils, including marshes, swamps, and bogs.

wind farm A collection of wind turbines used to produce electrical power.

wind power The conversion of wind energy into a useful form of energy, most commonly the turning of wind turbines to produce electricity.

Case Studies

Reviewing case studies is an important part of your preparation for the AP Environmental Science exam and an important part of your knowledge about global environmental issues. Case studies can help you learn about environmental concerns by providing you with perspectives on real-world concepts such as laws and treaties. On the multiple-choice section of the exam, you may be given a set of events and then asked to match the event with a provided case study. On the free-response section of the exam, you will be asked to write about a particular case and then asked to provide additional, related examples.

This section of the book describes several case studies that are common in the AP Environmental Science course.

Species

Loss of Amphibians

Although the loss of any species or group of species impacts its ecosystem, the loss of amphibians is an especially important warning sign of the decline of ecosystem health as a whole. Because of their sensitivity to environmental change and pollution, amphibians (frogs, toads, and salamanders) are considered to be indicator species, which means declining population indicates likely environmental damage. The numbers of amphibians are declining globally, and up to 200 species have gone extinct within the past 20 years. In addition to indicating ecosystem health, amphibians carry out important roles, including controlling insect populations, acting as a food source for many other species, and providing products for pharmaceuticals such as antibiotics and painkillers.

Spending portions of their lives in both aquatic and terrestrial ecosystems, amphibians are exposed to a multitude of environmental risks. Major threats come from the loss of habitat due to fragmentation of land, filling in of wetlands, development of land, and deforestation. Pollution also has a harmful impact on amphibians, as does disease, overhunting, and the introduction of predators and competitors. Global climate change alters the temperatures of regions, which can lead to drought and the drying up of standing water pools. Since amphibians depend on this water to lay eggs and for early stages of life, the loss of these watering pools affects the survival of a population and, ultimately, a species. Amphibians also require wet skin. Any weakening of the organisms from events such as long-term drought or increased pollution can devastate a population, making the organisms more susceptible to fungi, bacteria, parasites, and viruses.

There is no definitive answer to the cause of the global decline in amphibian species, but it is likely due to some combination of the listed factors working in unison. For example, climate change is warming some environments, which increases the growth of some fungi, especially the chytrid. This fungus can be lethal for amphibians and tends to proliferate in warm temperatures. With the increase in temperatures in many regions and the expanding reach of the warmer climate, the chytrid fungus has grown exponentially in many areas, killing many amphibians, and has potentially contributed to the demise of the golden toad in Costa Rica.

No matter the specific reason for decline, the increasing loss of amphibians on a global scale is a warning to humans that ecosystems are being altered and the environment is changing quickly.

Zebra Mussels: Invasive Species

With the increase in trade between nations, there has been an increase in the number of nonnative species introduced throughout the world. The impact from the introduced species can cause major economic issues, physical damage, and ecosystem alteration. For example, the zebra mussel is an invasive species that has caused major damage in the United States. Zebra mussels first arrived in North America attached to the hulls and in the ballast water of ships from Europe, populating Lake Clair in Canada in 1988, and then spreading to the Great Lakes and their connected rivers, tributaries, and lakes. The ability of their larvae to drift far in flowing water, and for adults to attach to many structures and then be transported, allowed their quick spread. And since zebra mussels were nonnative to both the United States and Canada, they had no natural predators, competitors, or diseases in the region, allowing them to proliferate without check.

Impacts from the spread of the mussels were far-reaching. Due to their small size, the zebra mussels not only damage boats, fishing gear, and docks, but also can damage and/or clog engines and pipes. Ecosystems can be altered because mussels consume large amounts of phytoplankton and zooplankton, reducing energy available to other species, and native mollusks can be suffocated when the mussels attach to their shells. Because of the large amount of food consumed by the zebra mussels, they deposit high quantities of nutrients on the bottom, which feeds the benthic population. Too much of this, though, can lead to eutrophication of the water. Because of invasive zebra mussels, large expanses of the Great Lakes that once teemed with life are nearly barren. Zebra mussels have caused extensive physical damage, and there are high costs associated with repair of this damage and with the eradication of this invasive species.

Extinction of the Passenger Pigeon

At one time, passenger pigeons were the most abundant birds in North America, nesting in huge colonies and flying in enormous flocks, sometimes numbering over a billion individuals. Unbelievably though, the passenger pigeon is now extinct, mainly due to deforestation, leading to loss of habitat and food sources, and from over-hunting. Pigeons were edible, and people also used them for other purposes, including using feathers for pillows and bones for fertilizer.

Because of the vast number of large flocks, commercial hunters could kill many birds easily, sometimes over a thousand in one hunting session. Pigeons were seen as disposable—killed freely, easily, and indiscriminately. During a 70-year period, pigeon populations declined from their historic billions to only a few thousand. Because of the breeding habits of the birds, the regeneration of the species was slow. A female laid one egg per nest per year.

The last passenger pigeon died in 1914 in the Cincinnati Zoo. This is a prime example of how humans can single-handedly bring a species to extinction within a brief period of time.

DDT

Diphenyl-trichloroethane (DDT) is a pesticide that was widely used from 1939 until 1973, when it was found to be toxic to humans, wildlife, and ecosystems. In 1973, it was banned in the United States and eventually became illegal in many other nations as well. The author Rachel Carson raised awareness of the dangers of DDT and other poisonous pesticides with her book *Silent Spring,* published in 1962. DDT effectively kills insects including malaria-carrying mosquitoes, but the risks of its use outweigh the benefits in most situations.

Nations at extreme risk of malaria still use DDT. Despite a treaty to reduce and phase out DDT, its use will likely continue until a safer, effective, inexpensive alternative is developed. Much of the DDT used internationally is, in fact, manufactured in the United States. Unfortunately, there is a chance that when we *import* goods from these countries that use DDT, the products we import may contain trace amounts of the chemical.

The results of historic DDT use in the United States include the decline and near extinction of birds of prey such as hawks, ospreys, brown pelicans, peregrine falcons, and bald eagles. The existence of DDT in water sources led to its proliferation throughout food webs where it began to bioaccumulate in organisms and biomagnify throughout food webs. In birds of prey, the pesticide weakens egg shells; ultimately, eggs break before hatching. This led to the decline in the birds' populations, and in the case of many, helped to endanger the species.

Although DDT was banned in 1973, it has persisted in the environment and is still found in some groundwater and aquifers in the United States.

Kudzu Invasion

Kudzu is an invasive plant that was intentionally introduced in the United States from Asia in 1876 for decorative purposes and also was used as soil cover to help control erosion in much of the Southeastern United States.

Although it has helped reduce erosion problems, kudzu is a fast-growing, hard-to-kill vine and can quickly smother other plants and trees by depriving them of carbon dioxide, water, and sunlight. Kudzu photosynthesizes quickly, has the ability to fix atmospheric nitrogen, absorbs large amounts of water through its roots, and can take root in almost any soil, allowing it to frequently out-compete native species. Biodiversity can decrease and entire ecosystems can be altered due to the kudzu invasion.

Grazing has been successful in reducing and controlling kudzu populations when done regularly during growing seasons. This weakens their tissues over time, and ultimately reduces their growth. Other methods of removal include the use of herbicides and removal of the plant and its roots. Of course, all of this requires time and money. The control and removal of kudzu costs companies, the U.S. government, and individuals millions of dollars every year. The repair of damage from kudzu also contributes to the cost of the invasive species. Because of its ability to grow almost anywhere quickly, it can grow on buildings, railroad tracks, and other vegetation. The weight and the roots can damage and deteriorate these structures. Many efforts are in place to eliminate kudzu, but it is a continual and never-ending battle. In the United States, kudzu is now listed as a federal noxious weed.

Reintroduction of Gray Wolves to Yellowstone National Park

The gray wolf is native to North America and once roamed the United States in large numbers. The colonization of the country, though, brought a dramatic decline in the population of gray wolves throughout the United States. To protect livestock and large game animals, humans killed over 1 million wolves, leaving a meager population throughout the northern United States (excluding Alaska). In 1974, the gray wolf was designated an endangered species.

We now have a better understanding of the species and its importance. The gray wolf acts as a keystone species, helping to keep the ecosystem in balance by controlling the populations of prey species and by providing food for other animals such as scavengers. With the dramatic decrease in their population, herbivores such as elk and deer became more prevalent and consumed more vegetation, drastically decreasing vegetation in areas including Yellowstone National Park. Vegetation loss led to soil erosion, loss of ecosystem niches, and less food for herbivores.

Noticing this ecosystem decline, officials decided to reintroduce gray wolves to Yellowstone National Park. In 1995, gray wolves were relocated to the park from Canada and the reintroduction began. Populations increased over time, and the ecosystem of the park started to rebalance back to its previous state. Having fewer large herbivores increased vegetation along streams, leading to an increase in beaver populations. More kills by the wolves meant more food for scavengers. And more wolves also meant more coyotes killed by the larger wolf, leading to an increase in smaller animal populations such as foxes and rodents.

Because of the success of the reintroduction, gray wolves were downgraded to threatened status in 2003.

California Condor

California condor numbers declined dramatically in the 20th century as result of habitat destruction, lead poisoning from consuming lead shot while scavenging hunting remains, poaching, and the inability of the birds to adapt to the changing environment caused by humans. In 1987, there were 22 remaining wild condors—7 in the wild and 15 in captive breeding programs. The last remaining condors in the wild were captured to expand the breeding programs at the San Diego and Los Angeles zoos. The San Diego Zoo's population was moved to the San Diego Wild Animal Park. The birds' DNA was tested so that the most unrelated birds could be mated to avoid over-similarity in the gene pool.

As the population in the two zoos grew, additional breeding programs were established, including in the Oregon Zoo and at the World Center for Birds of Prey in Boise, Idaho. Beginning in 1991, condors were released in California; in 1996, they were released in Arizona. Currently, wild condors can be seen in three sites in California; at Zion National Park in Utah; in the Grand Canyon area in Arizona; and in Baja California, Mexico. As of August 2010, there are 384 birds, including 188 in the wild. However, the birds continue to struggle to reproduce in the wild.

The California Condor recovery project is the most expensive species conservation project in U.S. history, costing over $35 million including $20 million in federal and state funding. Several milestones have been reached in the wild. In early 2007, a condor laid an egg in Mexico for the first time since the 1930s, with a second egg being laid in 2009.

Special note: Several sources suggest that DDT has played a role in the decline of the California condor. On the 2003 APES, the use of DDT as an explanation for the decline of the California condor *was not allowed.*

Water

Lake Erie Waste Dumping

By 1969, Lake Erie was generally regarded as dead due to a low amount of dissolved oxygen, high pollution concentrations, and large amounts of algae. The lake is surrounded by a large number of major cities, each contributing sewage and industrial wastes. Detroit was the capital of the automotive industry, Cleveland had petrochemical and steel industries, Toledo had steel works, Erie had paper mills, and chemical manufacturing took place in Buffalo. By the 1960s, the area was home to 9 million people on the U.S. side of Lake Erie. Partially treated waste was commonly discharged into the lake, and another 2 million people had septic-tank waste systems with waste that also frequently reached the Lake. By the 1960s, fish die-outs in the lake were common.

Changes were made in local and federal laws that reduced the waste dumped into Lake Erie. High-phosphate detergents were banned in several surrounding states, industrial waste dumping was put under strict controls, and municipal sewage was extensively treated before being discharged into the lake. As a result, it is making a comeback. The dissolved oxygen levels are improving, the algae are decreasing, and some game fish have been reintroduced. Beaches that had been closed for decades have reopened. The improvement is great but not complete.

St. James Bay Hydroelectric Dams

The St. James Project is a series of hydroelectric dams built in Quebec, Canada, since 1974. The eleven hydroelectric power stations are built on four rivers.

The four rivers affected directly by dams, and several rivers' waters were diverted into the major rivers to increase their flow. For example, the La Grande River's flow was substantially increased while the downstream flow of diverted rivers was decreased by as much as 90 percent, drastically affecting ecosystems. Major portions of the local boreal forest have been submerged behind the dams along the rivers. The waters in the affected areas fluctuate, filling shorelines with dead trees; shoreline plants are destroyed as well. The area is subject to earth tremors caused by the weight of the artificial rivers and reservoirs behind the dams, resulting in a shifting of rocks. There is the potential for great harm to the local population and the surrounding environment as fault lines are now present in the valley.

Other changes to the ecosystem include the decline of salmon spawning in the area as dams built in some areas block fish migrations, and other rivers' flow rates have been reduced, doing away with spawning sites altogether. Beaver habitats have been dislodged as the rivers and streams that fill the rivers have been altered. Migrating herds of caribou and flocks of Canadian geese and other migrating birds have been affected as the shores of the James and Hudson bays have been altered.

Gulf of Mexico's Dead Zone

Both the Mississippi and Atchafalaya rivers empty into the Gulf of Mexico, carrying with them the pollutants and nutrients they pick up along their courses. These pollutants include fertilizer, untreated sewage, deposition from fossil-fuel combustion, runoff from streets, and discharge from industries.

Every spring, the wealth of nutrients introduced into the Gulf of Mexico creates a great bloom in algae and plankton populations. However, with the increase in life is also an increase in death and decomposition, during which bacteria use oxygen. Over time, this depletes an aquatic ecosystem of dissolved oxygen and the area becomes hypoxic. Lack of oxygen affects all other organisms in the area. So, the organisms die or leave the area. Ultimately, this creates a dead zone, where there is no life.

Although one of the largest in the world, the Gulf of Mexico dead zone is not the only one. In fact, there are now over 400 dead zones found throughout the world. This number has doubled since 2000. Since such an area becomes devoid of life, the ecosystem ceases to function and must start over again when the oxygen levels return to normal levels. Economically, dead zones cost fishermen income and also can affect tourism dollars.

Aral Sea

In the middle of central Asia in both Uzbekistan and Kazakhstan (once part of the former Soviet Union), the Aral Sea was once the fourth largest inland body of water in the world. Although it has always been a saline lake, it has progressively become more saline and has also been dramatically depleted due to diversion of water from the two rivers that empty into the lake, for use in irrigation in this hot, dry, drought-ridden region. The lake's volume has decreased by 75 percent, and its salinity has increased dramatically. Instead of being one large lake, the Aral Sea has been separated into three smaller lakes due to the extremely low water levels.

The ecosystem now cannot support the same amount of life and biodiversity it once could. Much of the wetlands have been lost, which in turn decreased the habitats for birds and small mammals, as well as native fish in the lake. In fact, all fish species once found in the Aral Sea have gone extinct or have been extirpated due to the extreme salinity levels, and plants and animals living on the surrounding land have vanished from the area or become extinct as well. The economic impact also has been extreme. The fishing industry that once depended on the sea is now nonexistent.

The extensive size of the Aral Sea once regulated the region's climate, helping to keep summer heat and winter cold to moderate temperatures. With the loss of such a high portion of the water from the lake, though, the regional climate is not moderated, leading to hotter and drier summers and colder winters. This has shortened the growing season and reduced crop yields.

One surprising consequence of the dropping water level in the Aral Sea is increased pace of snow melt in the Himalayas, in part because of the salty dust that blows from the dried-up Aral Sea and gets deposited on the mountains. The salty dust affects crops, vegetation, and wildlife. There is also an increased use of chemicals such as fertilizers and pesticides to help the growth of crops on the deteriorating soils. These chemicals, as well as contamination from the increasing population in the area, percolate down to the groundwater, the sum of which impacts human health.

Efforts are being made to improve the health of the ecosystems and of people through increasing flow back into the Aral Sea, implementing more efficient ways to irrigate the lands, purifying groundwater for consumption, using crops that are less water-dependent, and creating wetlands to reinvigorate life at the water's edge. Promises of a renewed Aral Sea are starting to be seen, including a return of fish to the lake. Although some parts of the past Aral Sea are forever damaged, there is hope that most of it will eventually return to a productive and thriving ecosystem.

Three Gorges Dam

The building of the Three Gorges Dam, the world's largest, was controversial and problematic. Completed in 2009 on the Yangtze River in China, the dam is being used to provide hydroelectric power throughout the country. Unfortunately, its construction displaced at least 1.2 million people, as their towns and cities were flooded when the reservoir was filled, and it flooded priceless archeological sites. The potential for water pollution in the reservoir also exists, since many industrial and agricultural areas, mines, and waste sites were also flooded. These pollutants can affect not only water, but also bottom sediment and surrounding lands. Because of the dam, there is less downstream flow of water, which reduces the natural recycling and cleaning processes that remove chemicals and contaminants. Also, from the slowed water flow of a reservoir, more sediment is deposited on the bottom, which can build up over time and slow shipping and block flood control gates.

Ecologically, the Three Gorges Dam presents another set of issues and threats. Upstream, in the flooded areas, cropland and forests have been lost. Downstream of the dam, there is less nutrient-rich sediment being deposited in the benthic environment, altering the nutrient availability for organisms. The dam also has disrupted the spawning and migration patterns of some fish below the dam. At the mouth of the Yangtze River, where it runs into the East China Sea, there has been increased saltwater intrusion into the drinking water due to the decreased water flow of the river pushing outward. With less freshwater being held in the groundwater, the saltwater from the ocean seeps in, taking its place. When the reservoir started filling, there were numerous landslides on its banks, with the slippage of large amounts of earth into the water creating huge waves.

However, the ecological impact of the Three Gorges Dam project is not all bad. For example, it has the ability to generate cleaner energy for at least 10 percent of China's population, from the largest hydrostation in the world. It is reducing air pollution and carbon dioxide emissions from fossil fuel combustion (mainly coal) and will also diminish China's reliance on imported energy. Commerce ships and commercial fishing boats can travel a considerable distance along the river. Seasonal flooding downstream has been lessened as well, while water available for irrigation for land below the dam has increased.

The controversy over the building of the Three Gorges Dam will continue well into the future, as there are no definitive answers and the pros and cons are both valid.

California Water Project

With the growth of Southern California, especially including Los Angeles and San Diego, the demand for freshwater in the region has increased dramatically. Since Southern California is in an arid and semiarid climate without a large natural freshwater source, a water diversion project was constructed, diverting water from other parts of California to meet the needs for Los Angeles and the rest of the Southland. A huge network of aqueducts, pipelines, pumps, and dams was built to transfer water from northern and eastern California and Arizona to Southern California. Starting in 1916, water was diverted from the Owens River Valley and then from the Colorado River. Then in 1941, due to a continually expanding population, a new aqueduct was added to the Owens Aqueduct, bringing water from Mono Basin north of the Owens Valley. In the 1950s, the aqueduct was expanded once again to access water from Northern California.

The massive diversion and consumption of water from these regions has had a devastating impact on the local ecosystems, including the drying of Owens Lake and subsequent desertification of much of the Owens Valley. Lack of water traditionally used for agriculture sparked anger and violence from local farmers, and resulted in the farmers sabotaging part of the aqueduct in 1924. Los Angeles was taking their water and destroying their lives and their livelihood. Farmers' concerns failed to stop water diversion; in fact, even more was taken, as groundwater was eventually also pumped to feed the aqueduct.

The Mono Basin experienced a similar fate. Water from the creeks that fed Mono Lake was diverted to the aqueduct, thus reducing water flow into the lake. The water level dropped and became more saline and alkaline (basic). This change in the water led to dramatic ecosystem alteration in and around Mono Lake. For example, brine shrimp populations declined and migratory bird populations left the area. Because of the drop in water level, a land bridge was exposed, making the eggs of some nesting birds easy food for some predators, impacting the birth rate of species such as the gull.

In 1994, pointing to the devastation of the Mono Basin, the Audubon Society and the Mono Lake Committee (among other concerned groups), were able to gain protection for Mono Lake and its streams. The water level has since risen and the potential for drought and desertification were avoided.

However, the Owens Valley and Owens Lake were slower to gain protection. After extensive court battles and litigation between the city of Los Angeles and the Owens Valley, in 2006 courts ordered that some water be returned to the Valley. The river is now flowing and the aquatic ecosystem and the land along its banks is returning to life, slowly.

Human

China: One-Child Policy

In 1979, China was experiencing food shortages and famine, so it instituted a "one-child" policy to reduce stress on the food supply. This policy required that people of the ethnic Han majority in China have only one child. This law does not apply to minority groups or many rural areas. Among other penalties, the consequences of having more than one child without a permit is a heavy fine. There have been reports that people have lost jobs, land, livestock, healthcare, and other privileges. Forced abortions and sterilizations are also said to have occurred, and extensive measures have been taken to collect unpaid fines. Couples who delay childbearing or who have only one child are rewarded in various ways, including longer maternity leave, higher salaries, better healthcare, and priority in school enrollment.

Because of social and cultural pressures, many Chinese families prefer a male child. This combined with the opportunity to have only one child, leads to prenatal sex discrimination, in which a high number of female children are aborted. In an attempt to alleviate this issue, it is now illegal to determine the sex of a baby prior to birth, although some places still offer this practice illegally. Male preference has altered China's sex ratio, which is now 120 males for every 100 females, leaving many males without partners.

While low or declining population growth has many benefits, there are negative consequences as well. Because there are fewer working-age individuals and more elderly, there is more pressure on younger people to take care of their aging parents. There is also a smaller labor market and fewer people to enter the military. The aging population also takes an economic toll, as more money is required to care for the retired and elderly.

The "one-child" policy has seen great success in reducing the population and growth rate in China. It has also reduced pressures on food supplies. Economic stability is prevalent as people have been able to spend and invest money rather than spending it on child rearing. Because of its success, the "one-child" policy has been reinstated for at least the next ten years.

Easter Island: Tragedy of the Commons

The civilization of Easter Island ended due to destruction of the local environment. Off the coast of South America in the Pacific Ocean, Easter Island was once covered with dense forest and, until 2,500 years ago, was home to a thriving society. Unfortunately, the people who lived on Easter Island overused their resources—namely, the timber—and started to deplete their supplies.

The trees provided shelter, fuel, tools, boats, and nets, and were used for many other functions, providing the basis of the civilization's survival. As timber became scarce, people were unable to make canoes and rope, which affected their ability to fish and travel away from the island. When resources were depleted even further, food sources declined. With a lack of vegetation and trees, freshwater levels declined, erosion became prevalent, and crop yields declined. Famine spread, fueling both the death of the islanders and fighting over the remaining food and resources. Eventually, clashes and theft became commonplace. When the remaining people were found on Easter Island in 1722, they were living in caves, hungry, on treeless land.

The decline of the civilization on Easter Island is an example of a "tragedy of the commons," in which an unregulated resource is overexploited and used unsustainably, ultimately depleting the resource beyond recovery. Because it is in every individual's best interest to exploit rather than conserve, over time resources are lost and all suffer. There are many modern examples of tragedies of the commons.

Biosphere 2

To help further study the interconnectedness of agents within ecosystems, and the ecosystems themselves, a man-made closed, self-contained network of ecosystems was created with the intention of having eight people live there for two years. This facility, called Biosphere 2, was started outside Tucson, Arizona, in 1991. Designers imagined that the ecosystems would naturally recycle air, nutrients, and water necessary for survival for all living organisms found in Biosphere 2. It included more than 4,000 organisms making up a savanna, tropical rain forest, desert, freshwater and saltwater wetlands, an ocean with a coral reef, and lakes and streams.

Unfortunately, the extensive planning failed to correctly predict the complicated interactions, and carbon dioxide levels quickly rose to toxic levels, as oxygen was consumed quickly by bacteria in the soil. Nitrogen oxide also rose to toxic levels. Both the carbon cycling and nitrogen cycling were failing. Due to unpredicted levels of cloudiness in Arizona, photosynthesis levels dropped. Also, excess nutrients ended up in the water supply as nutrients were leached from the soil. Species extinctions also occurred rapidly and in large numbers. Insects were killed off by local ants that entered the facility from the outside ecosystem; most pollinators eventually died off and 19 small animal species went extinct, as did some bird species. Other species became pests, proliferating in the environment. These included cockroaches and vines. Although there were many roadblocks and difficulty in growing crops, the inhabitants were still able to produce 80 percent of their food supply.

The human occupants were able to survive in the closed environment for the entire two-year plan for the project, despite the setbacks, and without the desired complete closure to outside influences. A leading-edge experiment, Biosphere 2 served as a basis for many unique studies and research. The experiment also demonstrates the massive complexity and non-replicable structures of Earth's natural ecosystems.

Events

Bhopal Chemical Disaster

Union Carbide Chemical Co., Bhopal, India, created what is often referred to as the Bhopal disaster or Bhopal gas tragedy. The Bhopal disaster is history's worst chemical industrial catastrophe. A leak of methyl isocyanate (MIC) gas and other chemicals developed on the night of December 2, 1984, exposing several thousand people to the toxic fumes and chemicals. The official immediate death toll related to the release of the gases was 2,259 and the confirmed death toll was 3,787. Other agencies estimated the death toll at 15,000. In 2006, the government confirmed that the leak, in fact, caused 558,125 fatalities.

Chernobyl Nuclear Disaster

The Chernobyl disaster is the worst nuclear reactor disaster in history. Although the city of Chernobyl was part of the Union of Soviet Socialist Republics (USSR) until 1991 when the USSR dissolved and Chernobyl became part of the Ukraine. The disaster occurred on April 26, 1986, when reactor number four suffered a power output surge during an unauthorized system test. When an attempt was made to perform an emergency system shutdown, a more extreme power output spike occurred, which ruptured the reactor vessel and caused a series of explosions. The graphite moderator was exposed to the air and ignited. The resulting fire sent a plume of radioactive fallout into the atmosphere, covering an extensive area. Over 350,000 people were eventually evacuated from the worst contaminated areas. Twenty-eight emergency responders died in 1986 from Acute Radiation Syndrome and 19 more died later as a result of exposure. It is estimated that 4,000 deaths will ultimately be attributed to the accident due to increased cancers.

Cuyahoga River Fire

The Cuyahoga River is located in northeast Ohio and is most famous for being "the river that caught fire." In fact, there have been 13 reported fires on the river—one of the country's most polluted—the first being in 1868. The largest fire occurred in 1952, causing over $1 million in damages. On June 22, 1969, the river caught fire again, this time making national news when *Time* magazine described it as the river that "oozes rather than flows." The river was filled with chemicals from the many manufacturers along its banks. The 1969 Cuyahoga River fire helped spur water control legislation that resulted in the Clean Water Act, the Great Lakes Water Quality Agreement, and the creation of the federal Environmental Protection Agency.

Deepwater Horizon Oil Spill

The *Deepwater Horizon* oil spill (also referred to as the BP oil spill or the Gulf of Mexico oil spill) was a major oil spill in the Gulf of Mexico that flowed for approximately three months in 2010. The broken well was capped, but the impact of the spill continued. It is the largest accidental marine oil spill in the history of the petroleum industry. The spill originated on April 20, 2010, when the *Deepwater Horizon* drilling rig exploded. The well was capped on July 15, 2010, but not before an estimated 5 million barrels of crude oil had been released. The spill caused extensive damage to the marine life in the Gulf of Mexico and the habitats along the coast.

The spill created a threat to the environment due to the toxicity of the petroleum, depletion of dissolved oxygen, and the use of the oil dispersant, Corexit. Eight U.S. National Parks in the area are threatened. More than 400 species live in the islands and coastline of the mainland, and 8,332 species live in the Gulf spill area, including four species of sea turtles, 1,200 fish, 200 birds, 1,400 mollusks, 1,500 crustaceans, and 29 marine mammals. As of August 13, 2010, 4,678 dead animals had been collected. The oil spill has also had a harsh impact on the local fishing industry, tourism industry, and other businesses dependent on the Gulf.

Exxon Valdez Oil Spill

The *Exxon Valdez* tanker struck a reef in Prince William Sound on March 24, 1989. The oil tanker was bound for Long Beach, California, when it ran aground and spilled 260,000 to 750,000 barrels of crude oil. It is considered to be one of the worst environmental disasters caused by humans. It was the largest oil spill in U.S. waters until the *Deepwater Horizon* oil spill in the Gulf of Mexico in 2010, although the spill ranks low on the list of worldwide spills.

The *Exxon Valdez* oil spill occurred in a very remote location with limited access. The area was accessible only by boat, plane, or helicopter, which made it difficult to respond to the spill. Clean-up efforts also were hampered by the amount of coastline, rocky coves and inlets, and cold temperatures. The spill covered 1,300 miles of coastline and 11,000 square miles of ocean. The region is a major habitat for salmon, sea otters, seals, and seabirds. The immediate effects included the estimated deaths of 100,000 to 250,000 seabirds, at least 2,800 sea otters, approximately 12 river otters, 300 harbor seals, 247 bald eagles, 22 killer whales, and billions of salmon and herring eggs.

In response to the oil spill, the U.S. Congress passed the Oil Pollution Act in 1990. The law included a gradual phase-in of double-hull ships that provide an additional layer between the oil tanks and the ocean. The law includes a provision that prohibits any ship that has caused an oil spill of more than one million gallons in any marine area from operating in Prince William Sound.

Fukushimi Daiichi Nuclear Disaster

The most recent global nuclear event occurred at the Fukushimi Daiichi plant in Japan as a consequence of an offshore earthquake and resulting tsunami. The plant was damaged after the earthquake, aftershocks, and a tsunami impacted the costal facility, rendering it nonfunctioning. Multiple hydrogen explosions occurred as well, weakening the structure even further.

At the time of the writing of this book, the nuclear disaster is still not under control. Due to the damaged instruments and the danger of entering the reactors, it is not yet known what is actually happening inside and if nuclear fuel is leaking out of the core. Radiation levels are being monitored throughout the entire country and globally to ensure radiation is not increasing to harmful levels in both the atmosphere and ocean. Residents have been evacuated within a 12-mile radius of the nuclear plant. Because there is still so much unknown about this disaster and the seismic activity in the region near Japan continues, the short-term and long-term consequences and impacts on ecosystems, human health, and the economy are still unknown.

Hurricane Katrina

Hurricane Katrina was one of the deadliest hurricanes in U.S. history, and one of the costliest. At least 1,836 people died in the hurricane and the resulting floods, and total property damage is estimated at $81 billion. The Category 3 storm made landfall on the morning of August 29, 2005, in southeast Louisiana, causing damage from central Florida to Texas. The worst-hit area was between New Orleans, Louisiana, and Biloxi, Mississippi. Most life was lost in New Orleans, which flooded as the levee system failed and waters from Lake Pontchartrain combined with the waters from the storm, flooding 80 percent of the city and most of the local parishes.

Hurricane Katrina also had a profound effect on the environment. The storm surge caused substantial beach erosion, and several barrier islands were moved closer to the coastline. The Chandeleur Islands region was damaged the year before by Hurricane Ivan and was completely eliminated by Hurricane Katrina and Hurricane Rita. The lands that were lost were breeding grounds for marine mammals, birds, turtles, and fish. Over 20 percent of local marshlands were permanently covered with water from the storm. Breton National Wildlife Refuge lost half its area in the storm. This was vital habitat for several sea turtle species, the Mississippi sand hill crane, red-cockaded woodpecker, and the Alabama beach mouse.

The marshlands along much of the Gulf coast had been filled in for use as farmland and for the construction of towns and cities. Previously, the natural marshlands helped provide a natural protection for the coastline by absorbing much of the energy from hurricanes. But with the marshlands filled in, hurricanes can travel further inland where they can create more damage.

Kissimmee River Dredging

The Kissimmee River originally stretched 103 miles between Lake Kissimmee and Lake Okeechobee. The river is a major drainage system for the Florida Everglades ecosystem. During the 1947 hurricane season, two major hurricanes produced heavy rain and flooding in most of central and southern Florida. Florida requested assistance in controlling future floods and, in 1954, the U.S. Congress authorized the canalization of the river. From 1962 to 1970, the U.S. Army Corps of Engineers dredged a straight canal down the length of the twisting Kissimmee Valley, shortening the 103-mile distance between the two lakes to 56 miles.

The project damaged the river and surrounding lands, including parts of the Everglades. The fast-moving water sped the process of draining the surrounding land, which dried faster than rains replaced the water. As a result, 40,000 acres of floodplain below Lake Kissimmee dried out, reducing waterfowl habitats by 90 percent, and reducing the number of herons, egrets, and wood storks by two-thirds. Largemouth bass populations also declined. Prior to the channelization, the Kissimmee was not a major source of pollution to Lake Okeechobee. But without the winding distance and slow flow, surrounding lands were not able to effectively filter river water. In the 1970s, the straightened river contributed 25 percent of the nitrogen and 20 percent of the phosphate of the lake's pollutants.

As scientists began to realize the environmental damage of the straightened river, efforts were proposed to return the oxbows that slowed the water flow. In 1992, Congress approved efforts to restore the Kissimmee River to its original flow and modifications began in 1997, with the goal of completing the project by 2011, with 43 miles to be restored. Wildlife has returned to much of the restored sections of the river. Sandbars have returned, dormant plants have reestablished themselves, increased levels of dissolved oxygen in the water have increased populations of insects, mollusks, and crayfish, which, in turn, have increased the populations of fish, birds, and alligators. The entire food chain has benefited from the restoration. The Kissimmee River restoration is considered to be one of the world's rare successes of ecosystem restoration.

London Fog Air Pollution

The London Fog, also referred to as the Great Smoke of 52 or the "Big Smoke," was a severe air pollution event that occurred from December 5 to December 9, 1952. The event occurred as a result of increased coal burning during periods of cold weather, combined with windless conditions that allowed airborne pollutants to collect.

At the time, it was not thought to have been a significant event—London had experienced other smog events in the past. But in the following weeks, medical reports estimated that 4,000 had died and 100,000 became ill due to the effects of the smog on the respiratory system. Recent research suggests that the actual number of fatalities was probably closer to 12,000. The event led to several changes, including the U.K. Clean Air Act of 1956.

Love Canal Waste Dumping

William Love envisioned a canal connecting the two levels of the Niagara River that were separated by the Niagara Falls. He believed that such a canal would provide much needed hydroelectric power to the area, and later he envisioned a shipping lane that would bypass the falls and reach Lake Ontario. Love dug a canal approximately 1 mile long, 50 feet wide, and 10 to 40 feet deep before he stopped. The canal filled with water and became a swimming hole in the summer and a skating pond in the winter.

In the 1920s, the canal became the dumping site for the municipality of Niagara Falls. In 1942, Hooker Chemical Company was granted permission by the Niagara Power and Development Company to dump waste in Love Canal. The canal was drained and lined with thick clay. Hooker placed 55-gallon metal barrels full of hazardous chemicals in it, which were buried 20 to 25 feet deep. In 1947, Hooker purchased the canal and a 70 foot-wide bank on either side of the canal. The dumpsite was closed in 1953. During the time the canal was open, 21,000 tons of chemicals were added to the canal dumpsite. The canal was covered with a clay cap and then a layer of topsoil. Vegetation began to grow atop the dumpsite.

The local school board purchased the site shortly after it was closed due to an increase in the population of Niagara Falls. The Hooker Chemical Company initially tried to tell the school district of the chemicals below the surface but the district refused to believe the company and nevertheless proceeded to purchase the land. In the agreement, Hooker included a section that explained the site's potential dangers. In so doing, Hooker believed they were releasing themselves from all liability. Despite the disclaimer, the board began construction of a new school in 1954 on part of the site. The city of Niagara Falls constructed sewers for a home development, also on a part of the site. While building the sewer system, construction crews broke through the clay cap and breached the canal walls. Additionally, dirt was moved from atop the cap for fill in other locations, and holes were punched to build water lines and a highway. This allowed toxic wastes to escape into the surrounding areas when rainwater flowed through the toxic dump.

In the summer of 1978, an informal door-to-door survey showed a higher than normal number of birth defects and other anomalies near the dump. The New York State Health Department followed up with the initial findings to discover a high number of miscarriages. The dumpsite was declared an emergency on August 2, 1978, and limited evacuations were ordered. Further testing revealed the size of the dumpsite to be larger than originally thought and the evacuation zone was enlarged. Of the children born between 1974 and 1978, 56 percent of them showed some signs of birth defects. Of the 900 families in the area, over 800 were forced to move or chose to move out of the area.

Santa Barbara Oil Spill

The Santa Barbara oil spill occurred in January and February of 1969 in the Santa Barbara Channel. It was the largest oil spill in U.S. waters until the *Exxon Valdez* in 1989. The source of the oil spill was a blowout on January 28, 1969, on Union Oil's Platform A. The well was capped within minutes but rupture of the ocean floor allowed an estimated 80,000 to 100,000 barrels of crude oil to spill into the channel and eventually drift onto beaches from Goleta to Ventura and the northern shores of four Channel Islands. The spill had an impact on marine life in the channel, killing thousands of sea birds, and marine mammals such as dolphins, elephant seals, and sea lions. The coverage by the media ultimately resulted in numerous environmental legislations over the next several years, forming the framework of the modern environmental movement in the United States. The oil spill, along with other events, helped create legislation that led to the formation of the Environmental Protection Agency, as well as policies including the National Environmental Policy Act and the Clean Water Act. In California, the California Coastal Commission was formed and the California Environmental Quality Act (CEQA) was passed in response to the Santa Barbara oil spill.

Three-Mile Island Nuclear Disaster

Caused by a loss of reactor coolant, the Three-Mile Island accident was a partial core meltdown in a pressurized water reactor on March 28, 1979. It is the worst nuclear accident in U.S. history. The accident released 13 million curies of radioactive gases but less than 20 curies of the dangerous I-131 (iodine-131) isotope. The initial mechanical failure was followed by human failure to quickly recognize and correct the problem. In the end, the reactor was brought under control and a total meltdown was avoided. Studies concluded that the amount of released radioactive material was small. Studies also predicted an undetectable increase in cancer cases.

Public reaction to the event was probably influenced by the release of the movie *The China Syndrome* 12 days before the accident. The movie depicted an accident at a nuclear power plant. The accident at Three-Mile Island crystallized the anti-nuclear movement in the United States and was a contributing factor in the decline of new reactor construction.

Common Labs

In this section are some of the common labs used on the AP Environmental Science exam. Keep in mind that there are no specific labs for the exam and that labs may vary from year to year. Review the labs and consider the basic principles behind each lab. The labs will help to strengthen your knowledge and understanding of the AP Environmental Science curriculum.

Acid Deposition

Acid deposition, also known as acid rain, is commonly caused by sulfur and nitrogen compounds emitted by burning fossil fuels. Sulfur dioxide and nitrogen dioxide each react with water to form their corresponding acid, reducing soil and groundwater pH. The basic setup for this lab uses a combustion chamber to collect the gases from burning fossil fuel and to test the pH of the gas. The net result is a lower pH.

Air Quality

The following tests are commonly used in lab settings to evaluate air quality:

- **Particulates:** There are several ways to collect particulates from the air, including attaching a white sock to the tailpipe of an older car or diesel vehicle. Another method of trapping particulates in the air is to hang a sticky paper outside and collect it after a few days. In both cases, observe the inside of the sock or the sticky paper with a magnifying glass or microscope to view the particulate material. The particulate may include pollen, dust, soot, or other large particles.
- **Ozone:** In this lab, you can use a commercial ozone detector, an ecobadge, or a homemade potassium iodine gel to collect data on ground-level ozone (troposphere ozone). The ecobadge or KI gel will become more intensely colored as the concentration of ozone increases.
- **Carbon dioxide:** A commercial sampler is needed to test car exhaust, burning charcoal or other biomass, or another potential source of carbon dioxide.

Biodiesel from Vegetable Oil

In this lab, students learn to convert vegetable oil into biodiesel that can be used as an alternative fuel in cars and generators. Used or new oil can be used, with the procedure varying only slightly. At the end of the procedure, the students will have created diesel fuel, called "biodiesel" because the source is vegetable—from biomass.

Biodiversity of Invertebrates (Shannon-Wiener Diversity Index)

This lab determines the biodiversity of insects in a given area. A trap is set up and insects are captured. The insects are counted and the species are identified; calculations are made based on the total number of species and the total of each species. The Shannon-Wiener Index is then calculated most commonly by the equation: $H = -\text{sum} (pi \cdot ln\, pi)$. H represents the Shannon-Weiner Index, pi is the ratio of the number of organisms of a particular species to the total number of organisms, and $ln\, pi$ is the natural log of pi. Traps may include fall traps, sticky paper, or bait traps like tuna or sugar.

Composting with Worms

Students can complete this lab at home or in the classroom. Students monitor the results of their composting on a weekly basis, keeping track of how much biomass they add by weight (wet weight) and the type of biomass. Students then collect the compost, analyze it for nutrient content, and develop a procedure to test it using growing plants.

Coriolis Effect

This simple activity requires a lazy Susan, three pieces of paper cut into the shape of the lazy Susan's circle, and markers. Mark the center of each paper. Set the first sheet of paper on the lazy Susan and draw a line from the center to the edge. Rotate the paper one-third turn and draw another line from the center to the edge. Rotate one-third turn and draw a final line from the center to the edge. Because the lazy Susan is not moving, there will be three straight lines (as shown in Figure C-1). Label the paper "No Earth rotation."

Figure C-1: No Earth rotation.

Now, place a second piece of paper on the lazy Susan and, this time, rotate the platter counter-clockwise. Draw three lines from the center while the platter is moving. The lines will come out curved as you draw the lines on the paper (see Figure C-2). Label this paper "Earth rotation Northern Hemisphere." Repeat this procedure, except rotate the lazy Susan clockwise (see Figure C-3). Label this paper "Earth rotation Southern Hemisphere."

Figure C-2: Earth rotation Northern Hemisphere.

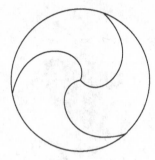

Figure C-3: Earth rotation Southern Hemisphere.

Eco-Columns

Eco-columns (like the one shown in Figure C-4) are mini ecosystems made up of three chambers. The bottom section is an aquatic chamber containing a fish and plant to replicate photosynthesis and cellular respiration. This chamber has a small slit to allow the students access to test the water for changes. The middle section is usually a decomposition section, but it can be reversed with the top, terrestrial section. The decomposition section contains worms and organic matter that, when broken down, move to the aquatic section. The terrestrial section usually has a small plant and sometimes a small animal. The top has a small cap with holes to allow watering if needed. Usually, after a few weeks, the system seldom needs water. The water cycle is very visible in the column. Other biogeochemical cycles are also found, and students learn to identify which cycles are in the column. This activity also teaches observation skills.

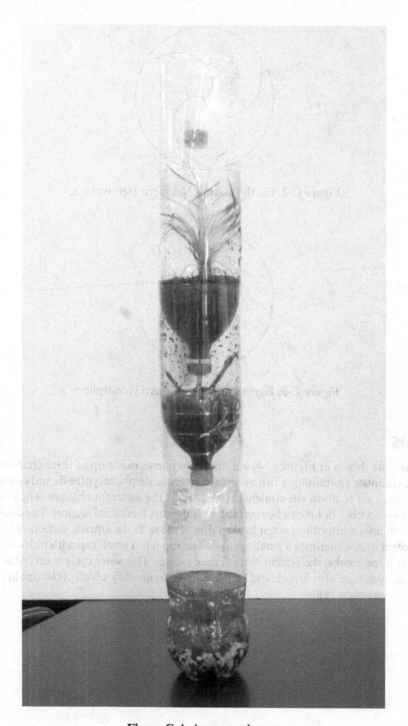

Figure C-4: An eco-column.

Ecological Footprint

Students take an online survey answering questions about their lifestyles and then, based on their answers, see their calculated impact on the Earth—often referred as their footprint. Students can take the survey multiple times to see how hypothetical changes in their lifestyles may affect their footprints.

Ecosystem Ecology

This field experiment examines the biotic and abiotic components of a local ecosystem and gives students the opportunity to learn how to use common environmental measurement instruments such as barometers, hygrometers, and thermometers. Students observe and note plants, consumers, decomposers, elements, and compounds. Depending on design, data is recorded over a period of time, possibly two to four different times. The flow of energy throughout the ecosystem, species interactions, and human impacts on the ecosystem are noted.

Energy Audits

Students examine energy usage at home or school and determine ways to make changes to save energy. This may include looking at the home energy bill to determine how much energy is used in kWh. Surveys may be conducted to see the number of light bulbs in the house, wattages of bulbs already in use, dimmer switches used, how many are compact fluorescent lights (CFLs), or how many incandescent bulbs can be converted to CFLs or replaced by lesser-wattage incandessent bulbs. Students may watch a meter to compare energy use when an appliance is turned on to energy use when the same appliance is turned off. From the results, the students develop a plan to use less energy.

Field Studies

Field studies study natural areas and might include determining the types of plants and animals in the areas, and the role of the water, weather, terrain, and human influences. Additional studies may include determining water quality, air quality, soil studies, and transects. (See "Ecosystem Ecology," earlier, as an example of a field-study lab.)

Food Webs

There are several activities showing food webs in action. Students identify producers, primary consumers, secondary consumers, tertiary consumers, and decomposers. Students set up the various links between species, show energy flow from the lower to the higher trophic level, and to decomposers. Finally, exploring webs can help students discuss the ramifications if one species is removed.

Mining

Students construct a model of a mine, illustrating different layers of the Earth and the location of the desired ore. Then students trade models with a partner and try to mine the partner's model. The goal is to maximize the ore collected and minimize the damage done to the mine. This activity can also be done using chocolate chip cookies.

LD$_{50}$: Bioassay

Although this lab is often referred to as lethal dose (LD), most labs for AP Environmental Science are actually lethal concentration (LC) labs, in which test organisms are placed in a known concentration of the test medium. LD is the lethal dose that the organisms receive. The 50 refers to the number of the test organisms that die, in this case 50 percent. The number can be changed for different criteria. Often, copper sulfate is used with brine shrimp. The brine shrimp are placed in a range of copper sulfate solutions. After 24 hours, a count of live and dead brine shrimp is made and the number of dead shrimp is plotted on a graph. From the graph, you can determine the threshold and the lethal concentration that causes 50 percent of the test organisms to die.

Oil Spill Cleanup

This activity involves cleaning up a simulated oil spill in water. Vegetable oil is poured into a pie tray containing water. A straw blows the oil around to simulate waves and wind in the oceans. Then students try a variety of methods to remove the oil and leave the water behind. String and small straws can be used as booms to surround the water. Cotton balls and pads, cloth, newspaper, and a variety of other material can be used to absorb the oil. At the end, the water is dumped out and students can feel how much oil remains on the pie tray.

Predator-Prey Simulation

This lab demonstrates the relationship between population sizes of predators and prey, usually mice and coyotes. When predator numbers decline, prey numbers increase, and when predator numbers rise, prey numbers decrease. Similarly, more prey leads to more predators, and fewer prey leads to fewer predators. This lab is conducted with pieces of paper representing mice and coyotes. Data is recorded after each round, representing generations, and a cyclical pattern of population numbers should emerge.

Productivity

In this lab, grass captures energy from the sun through the process of photosynthesis, resulting in a measured increase in the biomass of grass (the net primary productivity). The gross primary productivity is the amount of biomass produced by photosynthesis per unit of area over time. The net primary productivity is the production of glucose during photosynthesis minus the energy from glucose used to complete cellular respiration in the plant during photosynthesis.

Population Growth in *Lemna minor*

Lemna minor, also known as duckweed, is commonly used as an aquatic test plant for new pesticides and removes nitrates and phosphates in wastewater. It also can be harvested, dried, and used as feed for animals, especially chickens. In AP Environmental Science, this lab involves measuring the growth of duckweed in waters containing varying concentrations of nitrates, phosphates, pesticides, or salts.

Porosity

In this lab, different soil samples are collected in tubes capped on the bottom end. Samples usually include gravel, sand, and fine sand. Water is then poured into the sample and the length of time it takes for water to reach the bottom is recorded. The activity illustrates the fact that porosity and permeability increase with larger particle size. Soil that has tighter pore spaces and smaller particles has a greater chance of runoff and flooding because water cannot permeate easily.

To calculate percent porosity, use the following formula:

$$\text{Percent Porosity} = \text{Volume of Voids} \div \text{Total Holding Volume} \times 100$$

Salinization

The buildup of salts in soil is an increasing problem in areas where there is heavy crop irrigation, as in the Central Valley of California. In this lab, students germinate seeds in increasing concentrations of salt to determine the point at which the seeds cease sprouting. Any seeds can be used, but fast-germinating seeds such as Mung beans are commonly used because you can see results in about five days. Salt concentrations begin at 0 percent (as the control) and are increased up to about 4 percent, usually in 0.5 percent increments. The data can be graphed to show results.

Soil Analysis Labs

During this series of labs, students conduct both chemical and physical tests on soil samples. The results help determine the suitability of the soil to grow crops. The lab directs students to construct an assortment of buildings, bury septic systems, and conduct additional activities.

Chemical properties:

- **pH:** measures the concentration of H⁺ and OH⁻ ions. The pH scale ranges from 1 to 14, with 7 being neutral. Values below 7 are acidic, and values above 7 are basic. Some soil types require additives to help neutralize the soil. In low-pH soils, some nutrients will not be available to be used by plants.
- **Nitrogen:** Common plant nutrient; major component of most commercial fertilizers.
- **Phosphorus:** Common plant nutrient; major component of most commercial fertilizers.
- **Potassium:** Common plant nutrient; major component of most commercial fertilizers. Also called potash.

Physical properties:

- **Color:** Moist soils are darker than dry soils and commonly contain many nutrients from decaying organic material. Other soil colors may indicate the presence of iron and/or other minerals.
- **Friability:** This is the ability of the soil to crumble into smaller pieces with little pressure. This is important for the roots of plants to grow. The greater the friability, the easier it is for plant roots to grow.
- **Percent humus:** This test determines the soluble organic component of the soil. The higher the percent, the better the water-holding capacity.
- **Permeability:** This is the measure of how much fluid can flow through soil. This can be determined by investigating pore size and the connection between soil particles.
- **Ribbon test:** Roll a sample of moist soil beneath your fingers; the longer the roll of soil, the greater the percentage of clay.
- **Soil type (particle size distribution):** Determines the percentage of clay, silt, and sand by placing a mixture of soil in a cylinder, allowing the soil sample to settle, and then determining the percentage of each. Sand, being heaviest, settles first; then silt; and finally clay. The percentages of each are then used to determine the soil type, according to the soil texture triangle shown in Figure C-5.
- **Water-holding capacity:** How much water is held by the soil. Sand has the least, while clay has the greatest.

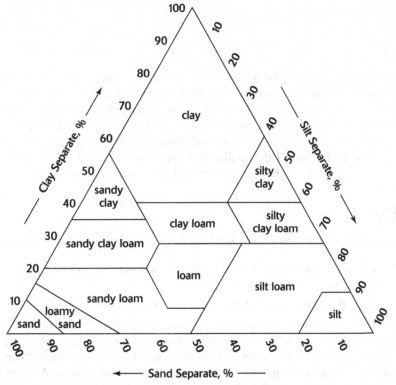

Source: U.S. Department of Agriculture

Figure C-5: Soil texture triangle.

Solar Cooker/Solar House

This activity allows for creativity and innovation while designing a solar house or solar cooker that uses the sun's rays to magnify and/or trap heat. Lab objectives include defining the difference between active and passive solar energy, learning how both can be utilized, and discovering how to identify the important components of each. Active solar power uses the sun's radiation as energy to power electrical or mechanical equipment (equipment that moves). Passive solar power does not use another energy source or active mechanical systems. Active systems use fans, pumps, and other technology, while passive systems are simple and have minimal moving parts.

Specific Heat: Solar Absorption

With the increasing use of solar energy, it is important to understand how this energy is best captured. All substances absorb heat, and their capacity to do so is called their "specific heat." Specific heat is the amount of heat needed to raise the temperature of 1 gram of a substance by 1°C. Different materials have different specific heats, which affects the amount of solar radiation needed to heat a particular substance. In this lab, the heat-holding capacity of various substances is tested.

The principle of specific heat also applies to the atmosphere and climate. This particular lab compares the specific heat of soil to that of water and then relates the results to effects on climate.

Tragedy of the Commons

The *commons* is any resource that is shared by a group. This includes the air we breathe, water we drink, and fish taken from the oceans. It also refers to city parks and many other things that are shared by a group or are used by the public.

In this activity, students "fish" from a common ocean of fish (goldfish crackers, M&M's, or other similar products may be used) and usually all the "fish" are taken on the first round. In subsequent games, students learn to cooperate to avoid depleting the ocean.

Transects

Frequently, instead of studying entire areas, scientists sample small sections and then extrapolate the data to represent likely conditions in the area as a whole. One method of sampling is to run a 100m tape transect line. At every 10m interval, a 1-square-meter area is placed, first on the left side of the tape and then on the right side, alternating sides every 10m. In each square-meter area, the percentage of ground cover is estimated. Then the plant species are identified and the percentage of each is determined. Next, any animal present in the square or evidence of animals in the square is recorded. Finally, the information is tallied and compared to other transects in the study area. This is an excellent activity to repeat on a regular basis to examine seasonal variation.

Water Quality

A variety of tests can be conducted to test water quality. A brief description of each is noted below:

- **pH:** Measures the concentration of either free H^+ or OH^- ions. Normal pH for freshwater is between 6.5 and 8. The pH of saltwater is 8.2.
- **Temperature:** Measures the heat content of the water usually in °C (sometimes °F).
- **Dissolved oxygen (DO):** A measure of the amount of oxygen dissolved in the water. The concentration of DO is temperature-influenced, with higher temperatures able to hold less DO. Other factors that can influence the concentration of DO in water include the amount of organic waste, the plant and animal communities present, the water depth, and the flow rate of rivers and streams. Average needed DO concentration is 4 ppm for freshwater fish, 5 ppm for saltwater fish.

- **Percent saturation:** Measures the amount of oxygen dissolved in the sample water compared to the maximum that could be present at that temperature. One hundred percent saturation is the maximum amount of DO that the water can hold at that temperature. DO percent saturations between 80 percent and 120 percent are considered excellent.

- **Turbidity:** Measures the clarity of the water. The test can be conducted using a Secchi disk, usually divided into quarters with opposite black and white quadrants. A colored disk also can be used in areas where the water is very clear, usually in the open ocean water. A turbidity test is a measurement of the dissolved solids in the water. High turbidity means much suspended solid material in the water, which results in the water being less clear. This reduces the penetration of sunlight and reduces photosynthesis in the water, which, in turn, can affect the food chain.

- **Phosphate:** Phosphate is an important nutrient for plant growth, usually found in fertilizers and runoff from agricultural lands. Excessively high phosphate levels can lead to excessive growth and ultimately eutrophication. Phosphate levels should be 0.05 mg/L in flowing water, 0.025 mg/L in still waters.

- **Nitrates:** Nitrates are important for plant growth, usually found in fertilizers and runoff from agricultural lands. Excessively high nitrogen levels can lead to excessive growth and ultimately eutrophication. A concentration greater than 0.1 mg/L is considered high and the Environmental Protection Agency (EPA) limit is 10 mg/L.

- **Alkalinity:** Measures compounds that can change the pH toward the alkaline (basic). The normal range is between 100 ppm and 250 ppm. The EPA has no standards for alkalinity.

- **Biological oxygen demand (BOD):** Required for aerobic organisms in a body of water. Unpolluted waters have a concentration less than 5 mg/L. High nutrient levels are associated with high BOD.

- **Fecal coliform:** Bacteria that ferments lactose and produces gas when grown in a lactose broth. New tests have been developed that produce a color change in addition to gas.

- **Total solids:** Weight of the suspended solids and dissolved solids. All water contains some solids, but problems can arise from suspended sewage, industrial waste, soil erosion, and excess amounts of algae.

- **Total dissolved solids:** Occur naturally in water but may be objectionable in drinking water due to taste. At high levels of dissolved solids, water may be unsuitable for irrigation, because salts may leave residue and can accumulate over time. The EPA standard is 500 mg of dissolved solids per liter of water, but the range is 20 mg/L to 2,000 mg/L.

- **Chlorine:** The EPA standard caps chlorine concentration at 250 mg/L. NaCl is applied to roads in the winter to make driving on snowy and icy roads easier and safer. These salts can run off into the streams, increasing local chlorine concentrations. Other sources of chlorine include animal waste, potash fertilizers, and septic-tank effluent. Chlorine also may leach out of limestone formations.

- **Hardness:** Measures dissolved salts that include calcium, magnesium, or iron. Hard water is 121 ppm, and soft water is less than 20 ppm.

- **Iron:** Normal range is 0.1 ppm to 0.5 ppm.

Weathering

There are two types of weathering labs:

- **Chemical weathering:** This lab tests the effects of acid rain on different types of rock. Rock such as limestone, granite, and marble is exposed to dilute hydrochloric acid (HCl) and observations are made to see the effect of the acid on the rock. Additionally, the mass of the rock can be measured before and after exposure to dilute acid. This activity can be repeated to see the long-term effects on rock of the exposure to dilute acid. Chemical weathering may include hydrolysis, oxidation, or dissolving reactions.

- **Mechanical weathering:** In this lab, shaking rock samples in a container of water simulates mechanical weathering. Rock is weighed, placed in a container with water, and shaken; then the water is drained. The rock is rinsed and dried and then weighed a second time, and the difference in mass is calculated. Mechanical weathering may include wind, water (erosion), ice, plant growth, and human-related actions.

Analysis of Past Exams

Analyzing past exams can help you prepare for the AP Environmental Science exam. In this section, we provide information is provided on the labs used in free-response questions and experimental-design questions in the past. Review these sections to get a sense of how labs have been used on the exam in years past.

Free-Response Questions

Information from labs is frequently used in the free-response questions. Here is a brief description of the labs or parts of labs that have been used in past free-response questions:

- In 1998, students were asked to determine the pH range for a fish species, explain how to determine that a lake's pH has changed, and explain how to remediate the acidification.
- In 1999, students were asked to list three water quality tests and explain what information each water quality test provides.
- In 2001, students were asked to draw a small food web from given information. In addition, points were awarded for correct connections and energy flow between the species.
- Also in 2001, an information table was provided for four water quality tests and students were asked to interpret the data. In addition, they had to provide two more water tests and the expected outcomes.
- In 2002, data from an LD_{50} test on brine shrimp was provided, and students had to graph the data and determine the threshold concentration and the concentration where 50 percent of the test species died.
- In 2003, students were asked to describe what changes might occur if worms ate all the leaf litter. Some of the changes would involve soil quality.
- In 2004, students were asked to describe one physical soil test and one chemical soil test.
- In 2005, students were asked about surface mining, especially regarding the replacement of the removed soil.
- In 2007, students were asked about primary and secondary sewage treatment and disinfection.

Experimental-Design Questions

Labs are also used in experimental-design questions. Review the labs and develop a detailed approach to answering this type of question. You will also find it helpful to review the introduction of this book for more information regarding experimental-design questions.

Here is a brief description of the labs or parts of labs that have been used in past experimental-design questions:

- In 1999, students were given a study and asked to describe the hypothesis, identify the variable being manipulated, outline a procedure including what data they would collect, discuss the results, and relate the results to the distribution of an insect population.
- In 2001, students were asked to define a hypothesis and design a controlled experiment testing the production of acorns and the gypsy moth population.
- In 2003, students were asked to design a controlled experiment that demonstrates cause and effect in a forest ecosystem. The experiment had to include the environmental factor that would be tested, the hypothesis that would be tested, and the data that would be collected.

Laws and Treaties

On recent AP Environmental Science examinations, students were asked to:

- Identify two federal laws that might be used to save a bird or its habitat.
- Identify a U.S., federal, or international treaty to prevent the extinction of animals.
- State two specific provisions of the Clean Water Act.
- Propose two incentives to switch to electric cars.
- Discuss the law that requires monitoring of treated sewage discharged into a river.

This appendix provides basic information on key environmental laws and treaties that protect ecosystems, wildlife, and human health. There are many other laws and treaties, both in the United States and worldwide, but this list describes the most common—those most likely to appear on the AP Environmental Science exam.

Laws are formal rules of conduct that people, businesses, or even government agencies must follow; they are enforced by designated authorities. Laws are created and enforced at the local, state, or federal level. Federal laws are passed by Congress and administered and enforced by specific government agencies. Laws may be periodically amended.

Regulations are the detailed rules and procedures necessary to enforce a law, commonly established by the agency designated to administer the law. Most federal environmental laws are administered and enforced by the Environmental Protection Agency (EPA), with some being administered by other U.S. government agencies. The laws included in this section that are not regulated through the EPA are noted.

Treaties are formal agreements between international participants. They are also known as protocols, conventions, agreements, and covenants.

United States Federal Laws

Alaska National Interest Lands Conservation Act (1980): Provided for the creation or revision of 15 National Park properties and set aside other public lands for the U.S. Forest Service and the U.S. Fish and Wildlife Service. This act is administered by the Department of the Interior.

Clean Air Act (CAA) (1970): Regulates emissions from both mobile and stationary sources, as well as hazardous emissions; establishes National Ambient Air Quality Standards (NAAQS) to protect human health.

Clean Water Act (CWA) (1972): Regulates the discharge of pollutants into waterways and establishes quality standards for surface waters, including industry wastewater standards.

Coastal Zone Management Act (1972): Allows for the protection of United States coastal zones from environmentally harmful overdevelopment. Federal monies are given to participating coastal states to be used to conserve coastal areas.

Comprehensive Response Compensation and Liability Act (CERCLA) (1980): Provides for federal money to be used for the cleanup of hazardous waste sites, including accidents and spills. If a responsible party can be identified, the EPA has the power to hold the party responsible for remediation. If a responsible party cannot be identified or if the responsibility party is unable to pay for cleanup, "Superfund" monies will pay for the remediation of the hazardous waste site. This act is commonly known as **"Superfund."**

Emergency Planning and Community Right-to-Know Act (EPCRA) (1986): Protects communities from the harmful effects of hazardous chemicals. It requires companies to disclose information about toxic substances that they are emitting into water, air, and land sources. This act also mandates that each state establish a State Emergency Response Commission (SERC).

Endangered Species Act (ESA) (1973): Protects threatened and endangered species and their habitats. The U.S. Fish and Wildlife Service (FWS) and the U.S. National Oceanic and Atmospheric Administration (NOAA) are the organizations responsible for enforcing the ESA, with the FWS in charge of maintaining a global endangered species list.

Energy Policy Act (EPA) (2005): Creates standards governing energy production in the United States, including energy efficiency, electricity, energy tax incentives, climate change technology, renewable energy, oil, coal, gas, nuclear energy, hydrogen power, hydropower, geothermal energy, and vehicles and motor fuels.

Farm Bill: See Federal Agricultural Improvement and Reform Act.

Federal Agricultural Improvement and Reform Act (Freedom to Farm Act) (1996): Addresses farm conservation and wetland protection; makes loans available in some situations for particular crops; improves the production of milk, peanuts, and sugar; and created a commission to review past and current agricultural production practices. This law is administered by the U.S. Department of Agriculture.

Federal Insecticide, Fungicide, and Rodenticide Act (FIFRA) (1996): Regulates pesticide sale, distribution, and use. Pesticides must be reviewed and registered prior to use in the United States. If at any time a pesticide is found to cause harm, the registration can be canceled, thereby banning the use of the pesticide.

Federal Land Policy and Management Act (1976): Protects, manages, develops, and enhances public lands. It governs the use of public lands by protecting historic, scenic, scientific, and ecologically important areas. This law is administered by the Bureau of Land Management.

Fish and Wildlife Act (1956): Establishes a comprehensive fish, shellfish, and wildlife resource policy with an emphasis on the commercial fishing industry. This is administered by the Department of the Interior.

Fisheries Conservation and Management Act (1976): Allows for the management and control of U.S. marine fishery populations, with the goals of maintaining and restoring population levels to healthy numbers and avoiding overharvesting. This law is also known as the **Magnuson-Stevens Act.**

Food Quality Protection Act (1996): Aids protection of public health by setting and maintaining strict food safety standards. It safeguards infants and children from pesticide exposure in food, water, and indoor sources. This law overhauled the Federal Food, Drug, and Cosmetic Act and the Federal Insecticide, Fungicide, and Rodenticide Act.

Food Securities Act–Swampbuster Provision (1985): Discourages the alteration of wetlands for the use of agriculture. Farmers who fill in or alter a wetland are not eligible for farm program benefits. This is administered through the Department of Agriculture.

Fur Seal Act (1966): Prohibits the taking of fur seals on U.S. lands except by indigenous peoples who live in the Pacific Northwest. It is administered by the Department of the Interior.

General Mining Act (1872): Gives people the right to prospect and mine on federal lands, with the exception of those protected from human impact (for example, National Parks). Originally it was used as a way to promote the settling of unused land. This law is administered by the Bureau of Land Management.

Homestead Act (1862): Provided for the transfer of up to 160 acres of undeveloped federal land to an individual who lived on the parcel of land for five years or more and cultivated the land throughout this time. Homesteading was ended with the Federal Land Policy and Management Act of 1976.

Lacey Act (1900): First passed to protect game species and wild birds and has since been expanded to include all plants and animals. The act prohibits the trade in wildlife, fish, and plants that have been illegally taken, possessed, transported, or sold. It is administered through the Departments of the Interior, Commerce, and Agriculture.

Marine Mammal Protection Act (1972): Seeks to protect whales, dolphins, sea lions, seals, manatees, and other species of marine mammals, many of which remain threatened or endangered. The law requires wildlife agencies to review any activity—for example, the use of underwater explosives or high-intensity active sonar—that has the potential to "harass" or kill these animals in the wild. The law is our nation's leading instrument for the conservation of these species and is an international model for such laws.

Marine Protection, Research, and Sanctuaries Act (MPRSA) (1988): Also known as the **Ocean Dumping Act,** prohibits the dumping of anything into the oceans, either transported from the United States or transported into U.S. waters, without a permit. A permit is issued only when it has been determined that the permitted activity will not overly degrade or endanger the marine community.

Migratory Bird Treaty Act (1918): Makes it unlawful to pursue, hunt, take, capture, kill, or sell birds that are listed as migratory. This includes live and dead birds as well as bird parts including feathers, eggs, and nests. Over 800 species are currently on the list. This act is administered by the Department of the Interior.

Multiple Use–Sustained Yield Act (1960): Governs the administration of renewable resources including timber, range, water, recreation, and wildlife on National Forest lands, taking into account the needs of multiple user groups. This act is administered by the Department of Agriculture.

National Environmental Policy Act (NEPA) (1969): Broadly covers environmental protection by requiring that proper consideration be given to the environment when federal actions are undertaken. Included in this requirement is the creation of environmental impact statements (EISs) and environmental assessments (EAs) prior to any government project that may have environmental implications.

National Forest Management Act (1976): Directs every national forest to have a resource management plan, which must be based on sustainable yields and multiple-use guidelines. This law is administered by the U.S. Department of Agriculture.

National Park Service Organic Act (1916): Also called the **National Park Service Act,** it was created to manage the parks that existed at that time. The National Park Service Department is under the direction of the Department of the Interior. Today, the number of national parks has grown to 58. In addition, the National Park Service manages other units including historical monuments, national seashores, historical buildings, and national recreation areas.

National Wildlife Refuge System Act (1966): Governs the administration and management of all the areas in the wildlife refuge system, including the protection and conservation of fish and wildlife that are threatened with extinction. This law has been amended by the National Wildlife Refuge System Improvement Act of 1997 and is administered by the Department of the Interior.

National Wildlife Refuge System Improvement Act (1997): An addition to the 1966 act, it ensures that the national Wildlife Refuge System is managed as a national system of lands and waters and is in the interest of the protection and conservation of the nation's wildlife resources.

Noise Control Act (1972): Works toward reducing and eliminating noise pollution that poses a threat to human health and welfare.

Nonindigenous Aquatic Nuisance Prevention and Control Act (1990): Establishes rules and regulations to prevent the introduction and spread of introduced aquatic nuisance species, as well as the brown tree snake. This is administered by the Department of Agriculture.

Ocean Dumping Act: See the Marine Protection, Research, and Sanctuaries Act (MPRSA).

Oil Pollution Act (OPA) (1990): Addresses the prevention of and response to catastrophic oil spills, including a tax on oil used to clean up spills when the responsible party is incapable or unwilling to do so. It also requires that oil companies submit plans to the government outlining how oil storage facilities and vessels will respond to an accident if one should occur, and establishes regulations for aboveground storage facilities and oil tankers. The development of an Area Contingency Plan is also required. This plan explains the preparation and planning for oil spill response on a regional scale.

Oil Pollution Prevention Act (OPP) (1990): Mandates that facilities with oil or fuel storage capacity greater than 1,320 gallons create spill prevention, control, and countermeasures (SPCC) plans.

Pollution Prevention Act (PPA) (1990): Examines the efficient reduction of pollution through changes in production, operation, and the use of raw materials. The goal is to address pollution issues at the source prior to production, as opposed to monitoring waste or pollution emitted from the source after production.

Public Rangelands Improvement Act (1978): Balances the management of public rangelands for sustainable use and productivity. It also sets a fair and equitable fee for the use of this land and protects populations of wild burros and horses. This law is administered by the Bureau of Land Management and the U.S. Forest Service.

Resource Conservation and Recovery Act (RCRA) (1976): Controls hazardous waste throughout its entire life cycle, including generation, transportation, treatment, storage, and disposal. RCRA also manages nonhazardous solid waste.

Rivers and Harbors Act (1899): Requires Congressional approval before building a dam, bridge, pier, wharf, jetty, or dike in or over a waterway. It also specifies that a waterway cannot be filled, excavated, or altered without federal approval. This act is administered by the U.S. Army Corps of Engineers.

Safe Drinking Water Act (SDWA) (1974): Serves to protect drinking water sources, both above and below ground. Minimum standards are set for drinking water quality.

Soil Conservation Act (1935): Established the Soil Conservation Service (SCS) to address soil erosion issues and preserve natural resources. This law is administered by the U.S. Department of Agriculture.

Superfund Amendments and Reauthorization Act (SARA) (1986): Reauthorized cleanup activities of hazardous waste sites through the Comprehensive Response Compensation and Liability Act (CERCLA). This includes amendments, clarification of definitions, and technical requirements to CERCLA and also authorized the Emergency Planning and Community Right-to-Know Act (EPCRA).

Surface Mine Control and Reclamation Act (SMCRA) (1977): Regulates coal-mining activities to protect both humans and environments. It also governs the restoration of abandoned mining locations.

Taylor Grazing Act (1934): Established to protect public lands from overgrazing. This was later replaced by the Federal Land Policy and Management Act.

Toxic Substances Control Act (TSCA) (1976): Establishes requirements for the reporting, recording, and testing of chemical substances, as well as restrictions on these substances. This includes the production, importation, use, and disposal of specific harmful chemical substances such as radon, lead-based products, asbestos, and PCBs (polychlorinated biphenyls). Some substances are not included under the TSCA, including pesticides, food, drugs, and cosmetics, as they are regulated under specific laws.

Wilderness Act (1964): Established the National Wilderness Preservation System with the goal of preserving federally owned land for present and future use. This law is administered by the Bureau of Land Management and the U.S. Forest Service.

International Treaties

Agenda 21 (1992): A program run by the United Nations (UN) to help promote sustainable development by offering action recommendations to be taken globally, nationally, and locally by UN organizations, governments, and major groups that impact the environment.

Agreement on Port State Measures to Prevent, Deter, and Eliminate Illegal, Unreported, and Unregulated Fishing (2009): Attempts to prevent illegally caught fish from entering international markets. Permission to dock is required for foreign vessels, regular inspections are conducted by participating countries, and a network has been created for the sharing of information.

Antarctic Treaty System (ATS) (1961): Established to encourage cooperative research and exploration of the Antarctic while also banning any military activity there. The sharing of research information is encouraged as well as protecting the environment and marine organisms.

Basel Convention on the Control of Transboundary Movements of Hazardous Wastes and Their Disposal (1992): Controls the transport of hazardous waste between nations, and particularly the transfer of waste from developed to less developed countries. It also focuses on management practices and the reduction of toxicity of waste through monitoring of storage, transfer, reuse, recycling, and disposal of hazardous waste.

Convention for the Conservation of Antarctic Marine Living Resources (CCAMLR) (1982): Established to conserve marine life and ecosystems in and close to Antarctica. It does not ban fishing in the included waters, but supports sustainable harvesting. It is part of the Antarctic Treaty System.

Convention on Biological Diversity (CBD) (1993): Created to protect and maintain biodiversity, including the sustainable use of resources and the sharing of newly developed genetic resources.

Convention on International Trade in Endangered Species of Wild Fauna and Flora (CITES) (1963 and 1973): Bans the international transportation of animal products taken from endangered species. The treaty ensures that the international trade in wild animals and plants does not threaten their survival. It currently provides protection to more than 33,000 species.

Convention on Long-Range Transboundary Air Pollution (CLRTAP) (1979): Aims to limit and reduce air pollution with the long-term goal of eliminating it completely. It also includes transboundary pollution that travels extended distances. Strategies are developed to reduce air pollution through collaboration and the sharing of information.

Convention on the Conservation of Migratory Species of Wild Animals (CMS or Bonn Convention) (1979): Aims to regulate and conserve migratory species, including avian, marine, and terrestrial organisms that cross national boundaries, protecting them throughout their migratory paths.

Copenhagen Protocol (2009): Addresses climate change by stressing the urgent need for emission-reducing technology. The protocol encourages countries to conduct research and development for new technologies while also preserving forests and evaluating sustainability. This is to serve as a follow-up to the Kyoto Protocol, which expires in 2012.

International Atomic Energy Agency Convention on Nuclear Safety (1994): Provides safety standards for land-based nuclear power plants in regard to the design, construction, and operation. It also makes financial and human resources available for assessment and verification of safety, quality assurance, and emergency preparedness.

International Convention on Oil Pollution Preparedness, Response, and Cooperation (1995): Requires participants to create procedures for handling oil pollution incidents. This includes reporting the incident, having equipment ready to handle a spill, running practice drills for handling an accident, and responding to help others in the event of a spill.

International Whaling Commission (IWC) (1946): Established by the International Convention for the Regulation of Whaling with the goal of setting annual quotas for whaling to prevent overharvesting. It did not work, so in 1970 the United States ceased all commercial whaling and banned all imports of whale products. In 1986, the IWC imposed a ban on all commercial whaling.

Kyoto Protocol (1997): A protocol to the United Nations Framework Convention on Climate Change, focusing on combating global warming through the stabilization of the concentrations of greenhouse gases in the atmosphere. Thirty-nine industrialized countries and the European Union are committed to the reduction of four greenhouse gases (carbon dioxide, methane, nitrous oxide, and sulfur hexafluoride) along with two groups of gases (hydrofluorocarbons and perfluorocarbons). They agreed to a reduction of their greenhouse gas emissions by 5.2 percent from 1990 levels. The United States has not signed the Kyoto Protocol.

Montreal Protocol (1987): A protocol detailing the Vienna Convention for the Protection of the Ozone Layer and aims at limiting the production of substances harmful to the stratospheric ozone layer by reducing and phasing out the production of ozone-destroying compounds. The treaty has been modified seven times and still highlights the importance of completely phasing out CFCs. Since the protocol came into effect, the atmospheric concentrations of CFCs and related hydrocarbons have either leveled off or decreased. The Montreal Protocol is one of the most successful international environmental agreements in history.

Northwest Atlantic Fisheries Treaty (1950): Aims to protect and conserve fisheries of the northwest Atlantic Ocean in order to maintain a maximum sustained catch from those fisheries.

Polar Bear Treaty (1973): An agreement between Canada, Denmark, Norway, Russia, and the United States to protect polar bears through conservation efforts, including limiting the hunting, killing, and capturing of bears. It also protects the ecosystems of polar bears.

Protection of the Arctic Marine Environment (PAME) (1991): Mandates sustainable use of both land and sea Arctic marine environments.

Ramsar Convention on Wetlands of International Importance (Ramsar) (1971): Works to preserve wetlands and use their resources sustainably. Under this convention, wetlands include swamps, marshes, lakes, rivers, wet grasslands, peatlands, oases, estuaries, deltas, tidal flats, near-shore marine areas, mangroves, coral reefs, and human-made sites such as fish ponds, rice paddies, reservoirs, and salt pans. This is the only international environmental treaty that addresses one type of ecosystem.

Rio Declaration on Environment and Development of the United Nations Conference on Environment and Development (UNCED) (1992): Reaffirms the Declaration of the United Nations Conference on the Human Environment (1972). It created 27 principles to guide sustainable development.

Rotterdam Convention on the Prior Informed Consent Procedure for Certain Hazardous Chemicals and Pesticides in International Trade (PIC) (1998): Aims to protect human and ecosystem health through proper use of potentially harmful pesticides and industrial chemicals. It also promotes sharing of information and responsibility.

Stockholm Convention on Persistent Organic Pollutants (POPs) (2004): Established to ban or phase out 12 of the worst persistent organic pollutants (POPs), including DDT, eight other pesticides, PCBs, dioxins, and furans. These were called the "dirty dozen."

UN Convention to Combat Desertification (CCD) (1994): Hopes to reduce desertification and the effects of drought through international cooperation on issues of conservation, rehabilitation, and sustainable development. It focuses especially on areas with large drought issues, including Africa.

UN Convention on the Law of the Sea (UNCLOS) (1982): Establishes rules for the many uses of the ocean and its resources and addresses multiple issues in the world's oceans including piracy, navigational rights, economic rights, pollution, scientific research, and preserving marine organisms. It is one of the longest treaties in history.

UNECE Convention on Access to Information, Public Participation in Decision-Making, and Access to Justice in Environmental Matters (Aarhus Convention) (1998): Creates public access to environmental information, public involvement in environmental decision-making, and public access to impartial review processes.

UN Fish Stocks Agreement (UNFSA) (1995): Focuses on the long-term conservation and sustainable use of migratory ocean fisheries, aiming to improve the management of these fisheries. It stresses the precautionary principle and the interconnectedness of ecosystems as well as the obligation of nations to monitor fishing activities, pollution, and waste in international waters. This agreement addresses issues that were omitted or not sufficiently covered by the UN Convention on the Law of the Sea.

UN Framework Convention on Climate Change (UNFCCC) (1992): Established to address climate change and stresses international cooperation and collaboration to stabilize greenhouse gas concentrations in the atmosphere. The updated version of this convention is the Kyoto Protocol.